Phaidon Press Limited
Regent's Wharf
All Saints Street
London N1 9PA

Phaidon Press Inc.
180 Varick Street
New York, NY 10014

www.phaidon.com

First published 2006
© 2006 Phaidon Press Limited

ISBN 0 7148 4399 7 (3-volume set)

A CIP catalogue record of this book is available from
the British Library.

Art Direction by Alan Fletcher
Design by Hoop Design

Printed in China

ACKNOWLEDGEMENTS
The publishers wish to thank the designers,
manufacturers, archives and museums that kindly
supplied the wide range of material included in this
book. Thanks are also due to the academics, critics,
historians, curators, journalists, designers and architects
who assisted in the selection of the 999 objects.

picture credits

John Gardner: **569**

© Garrods of Barking Ltd: **010** (lh)

Gebrüder Thonet Vienna: **023** (1 rh); **029**; **064** (lh); **081**

General Electric Archives, Schenectady Museum: **038** (1 rh, 2)

General Motors: **327** (lh b)

Sergio Gnesin - Murano Glass Gallery: **367**

Georg Jensen: **086**; **119**; **160**; **495**

George Nakashima Woodworker: **556** (photos by Sally Hunter)

Getty images: **571** (photo by David Cairns)

Peter Ghyczy: **691**

Gibson: **413**

Gillette Company: **741**

Stefano Giovannoni: **926** (lh b, rh photos by Domenico D'Erasmo - Santi Caleca, Stefan Kirchner); **950** (photos by Studio Cordenons Loris)

GlaxoSmithKline: **055**

GM Motors US: **280**; **611**

Mark Greenberg: **851**

Greyhound Lines, Inc: **327** (lh t)

Grob-Werke GmbH & Company KG: **820**

GUBI: **199**

Ken Guenther: **823**

Guus Gugelot: **388** (1)

Guzzini: **450**

## H

© Habitat: **065** (rh); **116**

Hackman: **954**

Hangzhou Zhang Xiaoquan Group: 001 (photo by Hua Qianlin)

Ulf Hanses: **838**

Harley Davidson: **256**; **510**; **701** (2); **985**

Hasbro: **829** (rh)

Head: **772** (lh)

Heller Designs: **629** (photos by Mario Carrieri)

Helmut Lang: **553** (rh photo by Stephen Wong)

Henkel: **700**

Herman Miller: **307** (photos by Phil Schaafsma); **311** (photos by Bill Sharpe, Charles Eames); **321** (photos by Phil Schaafsma, Ezra Stoller); **322** (photos by Charles Eames); **324**; **350**; **352** (photos by Earl Woods, Rooks Photography, Charles Eames); **372** (photos by Charles Eames); **381** (rh photo by Rooks Photography); **399** (photos by Charles Eames, Rooks Photography); **467** (rh photo by Earl Woods); **487**; **489** (photos by Earl Woods); **503**; **526** (1 rh, 2 photos by Earl Wood); **551** (photos by Nick Merrick, Hedrich Blessing, art director: Michael Barile); **585** (photos by Nick Merrick, Hedrich Blessing, art director: Michael Barile); **620** (photos by James Bayne Company); **624** (photos by Phil Schaafsma, Earl Woods); **921** (rh photo by Nick Merrick, Hedrick-Blessing)

Hermann Kuhn AG: **291** (2 lh)

HfG-Archiv Ulm: **386** (lh); **536** (photos by Wolfgang Siol, HFG-Ulm, Klaus Wille)

H.J. Heinz Company: **050**

Hobie Cat Europe: **674** (photos by Sean Douglas)

Charles Hollis Jones: **686**

Homer Laughlin China Company: **245**

Honda: **533**; **705**; **747**

Honey Association: **066** (rh)

Honeywell: **294**

Hoover: **249**

Isao Hosoe: **718**

House Industries: **299** (photos by Carlos Alejandro)

Howe: **631**

Hugh Moore Dixie Cup Collection, Skillman Library, Lafayette College: **088**

Hungarian Post Museum: **776** (lh)

## I

IBM: **544**

Iittala: **207**; **258**; **330**; **346**; **420**; **483**; **563**; **875**; **961**; **974**

IKEA: **800** (2); **916** (lh tr, rh)

Illinois State Museum: **194** (lh)

Image Courtesy of the Advertising Archives: **053** (2 lh)

Indecasa: **806**

International Dragon Association: **190** (photo by Heinrich Hecht, Jacques Vapillon)

Alan Irvine: **020** (lh)

James Irvine: **928**

Isokon: **285**

Iwachu: **002**

## J

Jacob Jansen Design: **752**; **918**

Jaguar: **591**; **576**

Jasper Morrison: **857** (lh); **876**; **897** (lh photo by Santi Caleca); **925** (photo by Miro Zagnoli); **962** (photos by Rmak Fazel); **968** (photos by Walter Gumiero, Ramak Fazel); **997** (photos by Christoph Kicherer)

Jeager-Le Coultre: **203**

JM Originals: **337**

Jo Klatt Design + Design Verlag: **537**

JongeriusLab: **922**

The following abbreviations have been used to locate the position of images in this book:

# A

# B

## picture credits

Ben Hughes 030, 107, 178, 221, 249, 261, 417, 456, 465, 511, 523, 544, 557, 581, 610, 710, 741, 814, 910, 917

Iva Janakova 192

Meaghan Kombol 052, 059, 073, 127, 135, 165, 300, 337, 396, 419, 474, 478, 528, 613, 642, 650, 776, 784, 980

Kieran Long 027, 041, 053, 091, 104, 136, 346

Donna Loveday 007, 119, 250, 317, 338, 450, 473, 517, 744, 794, 826, 855, 877, 928

Hansjerg Maier-Aichen 177, 663, 727, 836, 835, 897, 907, 942, 973, 976

Sara Manuelli 126, 155, 176, 230, 287, 324, 357, 376, 380, 394, 403, 437, 538, 560, 562, 590, 622, 639, 624, 654, 678, 681, 695, 714, 806, 870, 876, 915, 936

Michael Marriott 020, 043, 045, 277, 293, 580, 607, 668, 769, 782, 804, 846, 968, 996

Catherine McDermott 507, 643, 684

Justin McGuirk 187, 202, 240, 245, 255, 370, 728

Charles Mellersh 002, 005, 006, 031, 033, 128, 149, 153, 163, 174, 180, 196, 210, 222, 232, 238, 265, 318, 343, 349, 373, 395, 414, 433, 443, 452, 462, 476, 484, 486, 512, 514, 522, 530, 543, 545, 600, 625, 641, 652, 656, 661, 676, 682, 686, 700, 828, 854, 856, 893

Alex Milton 017, 079, 082, 152, 167, 193, 264, 268, 276, 291, 345, 366, 427, 482, 554, 627, 638, 696, 752, 757, 831, 839, 918, 921, 947, 948

Christopher Mount 075, 227, 297, 424, 464, 680, 719, 768

Tim Parsons 026, 034, 036, 100, 106, 116, 350, 721, 819, 963

Jane Pavitt 038, 132, 139, 172, 406, 425, 564, 583, 584, 595, 649, 662, 665, 702, 703, 742, 748, 754, 815, 848

James Peto 166, 214, 218, 229, 257, 322, 334, 435, 467, 487

Phaidon Editors 144, 170, 294, 635, 751, 774, 789, 797, 829, 843, 885, 901, 923, 934, 944, 946, 966, 970, 978, 979, 982

Michael Pritchard 068, 101, 146, 182, 233, 242, 252, 259, 348, 356, 540, 601, 605, 634, 683, 749, 862, 896, 938

Mark Rappolt 049, 050, 094, 179, 212, 266, 290, 295, 317, 326, 397, 472, 578, 644, 657, 672, 691, 692, 731, 733, 759, 764, 813, 823, 852, 899, 930

Hani Rashid 588, 598

Louise Schouwenberg 900, 903, 905, 922, 941, 965

Daljit Singh 320, 489, 628, 801, 832

Rosanne Somerson 004, 024, 195, 299, 309, 391, 416, 441

Penny Sparke 248, 271, 283, 328, 332, 460, 461, 470, 480, 496, 503, 576, 606, 778

Thimo te Duits 055, 064, 081, 157, 173, 191, 367, 444, 455, 550, 6770, 712, 762, 810, 879, 914, 972, 987, 992

Anthony Whitfield 032, 066, 120, 145, 262, 263, 269, 329, 333, 369, 384, 415, 485, 619, 655, 690, 760, 792, 822, 837, 840, 925, 950

William Wiles 018, 021, 057, 102, 118, 148, 241, 344, 393, 529, 592, 706, 720, 725, 766, 781, 787

Gareth Williams 070, 083, 183, 308, 374, 448, 477, 497, 551, 719, 818, 861, 865, 890, 902, 909, 956, 964, 977

Megumi Yamashita 123, 134, 138, 161, 181, 313, 365, 421, 549, 558, 566, 603, 621, 699, 785, 894, 927

Yolanda Zappaterra 009, 037, 042, 062, 098, 200, 197, 209, 226, 339, 359, 362, 392, 871

Texts were written by the following (the numbers refer to the relevant product entries):

**Simon Alderson** 051, 056, 084, 109, 115, 121, 147, 175, 184, 185, 186, 198, 216 223, 399, 494, 515, 559, 587, 602, 604, 651, 708, 729, 807, 811, 858, 874, 876, 945

**Ralph Ball** 023, 157, 307, 311, 372, 408, 526, 509, 546, 608, 631, 844

**Edward Barber** 001, 025, 302, 342, 355, 398, 572

**Lis Bogdan** 289, 321, 352, 386, 572, 574, 710, 732, 746, 796

**Annabelle Campbell** 044, 065, 110, 122, 151, 159, 160, 201, 246, 273, 306, 319, 323, 382, 385, 390, 404, 463, 492, 495, 531, 536, 567, 589, 629, 646, 647, 656, 664, 671, 673, 687, 765, 777, 779, 790, 798, 805, 833, 849, 850, 884, 888, 892, 911, 924, 925, 949, 974, 984, 988, 991

**Claire Catterall** 454, 704, 722, 726, 736, 740, 750, 755, 773, 793, 799, 809, 821, 827, 830, 842, 857, 860, 866, 913, 920, 926, 959, 971

**Daniel Charny / Roberto Feo** 103, 108, 224, 247, 422, 559, 593, 599, 812, 864

**Andrea Codrington** 014, 015, 029, 069, 071, 088, 131, 217, 244, 247, 267, 285, 286, 288, 314, 341, 358, 402, 413, 481, 488, 506, 521, 553, 609, 658, 707, 723, 905

**Louise-Anne Comeau / Geoffrey Monge** 130, 235, 251, 347, 400, 586, 679, 689, 791, 827, 834, 887, 929, 962, 940, 951, 957, 975, 986, 989, 994, 997

**Alberto Cossu** 105, 190, 234, 281, 340, 407, 447, 669, 674, 739, 803, 931

**Ilse Crawford** 009, 048, 150, 154, 275, 375, 457, 469, 504, 563, 745, 895

**Kevin Davies** 061, 111, 198, 205, 206, 207, 208, 211, 243, 250, 282, 330, 331, 364, 378, 383, 420, 423, 438, 460, 483, 498, 500, 513, 519, 552, 561, 579, 612, 645, 694, 737, 743, 774, 786, 916

**Jan Dekker** 008, 046, 050, 076, 078, 080, 099, 141, 143, 168, 270, 284, 292, 353, 361, 377, 388, 426, 429, 432, 499, 518, 520, 524, 542, 575, 615, 713, 763, 886, 912, 955, 993

**John Dunnigan** 035, 254, 262, 274, 371, 418, 505, 534, 597, 881

**Caroline Ednie** 039, 040, 077, 086, 090, 112, 253, 272, 296, 363, 434, 449, 458, 459, 527, 548, 570, 573, 582, 594, 636, 659, 660, 666, 698, 715, 717, 758, 767, 771, 772, 783, 800, 802, 824, 825, 838, 845, 867, 872, 882, 891, 906, 935, 937, 953, 960, 983, 995

**Aline Ferrari** 010, 013, 019, 089, 169, 256, 335, 387, 442, 490, 868, 939, 998

**Max Fraser** 022, 072, 085, 142, 188, 204, 381, 405, 428, 444, 508, 555, 596, 626, 675, 709, 711, 738, 770, 788, 808, 847, 853, 863, 919, 958, 981

**Richard Garnier** 114, 162, 203, 213

**Charles Gates** 215, 351, 431, 516, 532, 535, 537, 640, 718, 795

**Laura Giacalone** 003, 446, 648

**Grant Gibson** 016, 047, 054, 060, 067, 117, 125, 129, 194, 236, 288, 304, 325, 354, 445, 594, 614, 618, 697, 730, 735, 756, 859, 873, 875, 883, 990, 933, 999

**Anna Goodall** 012, 028, 056, 095, 097, 158, 303, 412, 501, 502, 623, 630, 753, 820, 904

**Katy Djunn** 063, 140, 164, 189, 219, 220, 239, 312, 327, 585, 688, 841

**Ultan Guilfoyle** 092, 113, 133, 137, 231, 279, 298, 310, 316, 360, 410, 510, 493, 533, 547, 571, 569, 577, 591, 653, 677, 685, 701, 705, 761, 851, 880, 908, 932, 951, 985

**Roo Gunzi** 087, 237, 336, 368, 379, 389, 468, 889, 943

**Bruce Hannah** 011, 074, 278, 301, 411, 436, 451, 616, 780

**Sam Hecht** 479, 632, 637, 734, 969

**Albert Hill** 124, 305, 401, 409, 440, 453, 471, 475, 491, 525, 541, 556, 568, 617, 620, 633, 693, 869, 961

**authors**

Kappa Knives, Dr Karl-Peter Born **927**
JI1 Sofa Bed, James Irvine **928**

**1995**
Mono Tables, Konstantin Grcic **929**
X-Shaped Rubber Bands, Läufer Design Team **930**
Genie of the Lamp, Wally with Germán Frers **931**
Aprilia Moto 6.5, Philippe Starck **932**

**1996**
Meda Chair, Alberto Meda **933**
Washing-Up Bowl, Ole Jensen **934**
Ginevra, Ettore Sottsass **935**
Nokia 5100, Frank Nuovo, Nokia Design Team **936**
TGV Duplex, Roger Tallon **937**
Canon Ixus, Yasushi Shiotani **938**
Aquatinta, Michele De Lucchi, Alberto Nason **939**
Loop Coffee Table, Barber Osgerby **940**
Jack Light, Tom Dixon **941**
Polypropylene Stand File Box, MUJI Design Team **942**
U-Line, Maarten van Severen **943**
Motorola StarTAC Wearable Cellular Phone, Motorola
    Design Team **944**
Knotted Chair, Marcel Wanders, Droog Design **945**
The Block Lamp, Harri Koskinen **946**

**1997**
Fantastic Plastic Elastic, Ron Arad **947**
Cable Turtle, Jan Hoekstra, FLEX/the INNOVATIONLAB
    **948**
Dish Doctor, Marc Newson **949**
Bombo Stool, Stefano Giovannoni **950**
MV Agusta F4 Serie Oro, Massimo Tamburini **951**
Yamaha Silent Cello Model N. SVC100K,
    Yamaha Design Team **952**
Silver/Felt Bracelet, Pia Wallén **953**
Bowls and Salad Cutlery, Carina Seth Andersson **954**
Apollo Torch, Marc Newson **955**
Tom Vac, Ron Arad **956**
Garbino, Karim Rashid **957**
Wait, Matthew Hilton **958**

**1998**
Dahlström 98, Björn Dahlström **959**
Fortebraccio, Alberto Meda, Paolo Rizzatto **960**
Citterio 98, Antonio Citterio, Glen Oliver Löw **961**
Glo-Ball, Jasper Morrison **962**
Optic Glass, Arnout Visser **963**
Ypsilon, Mario Bellini **964**
May Day Lamp, Konstantin Grcic **965**

**1999**
Aibo Robot, Hajime Sorayama, Sony Design Team **966**
Soundwave, Teppo Asikainen **967**
Air-Chair, Jasper Morrison **968**
Wall-Mounted CD Player, Naoto Fukasawa **969**
Random Light, Bertjan Pot **970**
Low Pad, Jasper Morrison **971**
Relations Glasses, Konstantin Grcic **972**
930 Soft, Werner Aisslinger **973**

**2000**
Citterio Collective Tools 2000, Antonio Citterio,
    Glen Oliver Löw **974**
LEM, Shin Azumi **975**
Strap, NL Architects **976**
Spring Chair, Ronan Bouroullec, Erwan Bouroullec **977**

**2001**
PowerBook G4, Jonathan Ive, Apple Design Team **978**
iPod, Jonathan Ive, Apple Design Team **979**
Wednesday Garland, Tord Boontje **980**
PET Bottle, Ross Lovegrove **981**
Segway Human Transporter, Segway Design Team **982**
Oil Lamp, Erik Magnussen **983**
One-Two, James Irvine **984**
V-Rod, Willie G Davidson **985**
Aquos C1, Toshiyuki Kita **986**
Joyn Office System, Ronan Bouroullec,
    Erwan Bouroullec **987**

**2002**
Outdoor Cooking Tools, Harri Koskinen **988**
MVS Chaise, Maarten van Severen **989**
BeoVision 5, David Lewis **990**
Kyocera KYOTOP Series, Kyocera Corporation Design
    Team **991**
Pipe Sospensione, Herzog & de Meuron **992**
PAL Henry Kloss, Tom DeVesto **993**

**2003**
Time & Weather, Philippe Starck **994**
Beolab 5, David Lewis **995**
Chair_One, Konstantin Grcic **996**
Brunch Set, Jasper Morrison **997**

**2004**
iMac G5, Apple Design Team **998**
Lunar, Barber Osgerby **999**

Corkscrew, Peter Holmblad **774**

4875 Chair, Carlo Bartoli **775**

Rubik's Cube®, Ernö Rubik **776**

Banco Catalano, Óscar Tusquets Blanca, Lluís Clotet **777**

VW Golf A1, Giorgetto Giugiaro **778**

Chambord Coffee Maker, Carsten Jørgensen **779**

Vertebra Chair, Emilio Ambasz, Giancarlo Piretti **780**

**1975**

Kickstool, Wedo Design Team **781**

Brompton Folding Bicycle, Andrew Ritchie **782**

Papillona Lamp, Afra Scarpa, Tobia Scarpa **783**

Tratto Pen, Design Group Italia **784**

**1976**

Uni-Tray, Riki Watanabe **785**

Suomi Table Service, Timo Sarpaneva **786**

Kryptonite K4, Michael Zane, Peter Zane **787**

Ashtray, Anna Castelli Ferrieri **788**

Sonora, Vico Magistretti **789**

Glass Chair and Collection, Shiro Kuramata **790**

**1977**

Nuvola Rossa, Vico Magistretti **791**

Cricket Maxi Lighter, Cricket Design Team **792**

Vacuum Jug, Erik Magnussen **793**

Atollo 233/D, Vico Magistretti **794**

Telephone Model F78, Henning Andreasen **795**

Cab, Mario Bellini **796**

Atari Joystick CX40, Atari Design Team **797**

9090 Espresso Coffee Maker, Richard Sapper **798**

**1978**

Proust Chair, Alessandro Mendini **799**

Billy Shelf, IKEA of Sweden **800**

ET 44 Pocket Calculator, Dieter Rams, Dietrich Lubs **801**

A'dammer, Aldo van den Nieuwelaar **802**

Mattia Esse, Enrico Contreas **803**

Frisbi, Achille Castiglioni **804**

5070 Condiment Set, Ettore Sottsass **805**

Gacela (part of Clásica collection),
   Joan Casas y Ortínez **806**

**1979**

Maglite, Anthony Maglica **807**

Boston Shaker, Ettore Sottsass **808**

Balans Variable Stool, Peter Opsvik **809**

Absolut Vodka, Carlsson & Broman **810**

Headphone Stereo Walkman, TPS-L2 Sony
   Design Team **811**

**1980**

Post-it ® Notes, Spencer Silver, Art Fry **812**

Dúplex, Javier Mariscal **813**

Praxis 35, Mario Bellini **814**

Parola, Gae Aulenti **815**

Wink, Toshiyuki Kita **816**

Panda, Giorgetto Giugiaro **817**

Tavolo con ruote, Gae Aulenti **818**

Acetoliere, Achille Castiglioni **819**

Grob 102 Standard Astir III, Grob-Werke
   Design Team **820**

La Conica Coffee Maker, Aldo Rossi **821**

**1981**

Callimaco Lamp, Ettore Sottsass **822**

Commodore C64, Commodore Design Team **823**

Sinclair ZX81, Sir Clive Sinclair **824**

**1982**

Durabeam Torch, Nick Butler, BIB Consultants
   for Duracell **825**

18-8 Stainless Steel Flatware, Sori Yanagi **826**

Chair, Donald Judd **827**

MR30 Stabmixer, Ludwig Littmann **828**

Voltes V Transformer, Kouzin Ohno **829**

Costes Chair, Philippe Starck **830**

Renault Espace I, Matra Design Team, Renault
   Design Team **831**

LOMO-Compact-Automate, Mikhail Holomyansky **832**

Global Knife, Komin Yamada **833**

Philips Compact Disc, Philips/Sony Design Team **834**

Croma & Piuma, Makio Hasuike **835**

First Chair, Michele De Lucchi **836**

**1983**

PST (Pocket Survival Tool), Timothy S Leatherman **837**

Streamliner, Ulf Hanses **838**

Lightning TRS, Rollerblade Design Team **839**

Swatch 1st Collection, Swatch Lab **840**

9091 Kettle, Richard Sapper **841**

**1984**

Can Family, Hansjerg Maier-Aichen **842**

Apple Macintosh, Hartmut Esslinger, frogdesign **843**

Sheraton Chair, 664 Robert Venturi **844**

Gespanntes Regal, Wolfgang Laubersheimer **845**

Ya Ya Ho, Ingo Maurer & Team **846**

**1985**

Pasta Set, Massimo Morozzi **847**

**1663**
Household Scissors, Zhang Xiaoquan **001**

**1700s**
Arare Teapot, Designer Unknown **002**

**1730**
Sheep Shears, Designer Unknown **003**

**1760s**
Sack-Back Windsor Chair, Designer Unknown **004**

**1766**
Jigsaw Puzzle, John Spilsbury **005**

**1783**
Hot Air Balloon, Joseph de Montgolfier, Etienne de
  Montgolfier **006**

**1796**
Traditional White China, Josiah Wedgwood & Sons **007**

**1825**
Garden Chair and Bench for Potsdam, Karl Friedrich
  Schinkel **008**

**c.1825**
Le Parfait Jars, Designer Unknown **009**

**c.1830**
Galvanized Metal Dustbin, Designer Unknown **010**

**1837**
Gifts, Friedrich Froebel **011**

**1840**
Hurricane Lantern, Designer Unknown **012**

**1842**
Pocket Measuring Tape, James Chesterman **013**

**1849**
Safety Pin, Walter Hunt **014**

**1850s**
Jacks, Designer Unknown **015**
Clothes Peg, Designer Unknown **016**
Moleskine Notebook, Designer Unknown **017**
Textile Garden Folding Chair, Designer Unknown **018**
Scissors, Designer Unknown **019**

**c.1855**
Tripolina, Joseph Beverly Fenby **020**

**1855**
Colman's Mustard Tin, Colman's of Norwich **021**

**1856**
Lobmeyr Crystal Drinking Set, Ludwig Lobmeyr **022**

**1859**
Chair No. 14, Michael Thonet **023**

**1860s**
Shaker Slat Back Chair, Brother Robert Wagan **024**
Folding Ruler, Designer Unknown **025**
English Park Bench, Designer Unknown **026**

**1861**
Yale Cylinder Lock, Linus Yale Jr **027**

**1866**
Key-Opening Can, J Osterhoudt **028**
Damenstock, Michael Thonet **029**

**1868**
Remington No. 1, Christopher Latham Sholes,
  Carlos Glidden **030**
Tabasco Bottle, Edmund McIlhenny **031**

**1869**
ABC Blocks, John Wesley Hyatt **032**

**1870s**
Waribashi Chopsticks, Designer Unknown **033**

**c.1873**
Sugar Bowl, Christopher Dresser **034**

**1874**
Peugeot Pepper Mill, Jean-Frédéric Peugeot,
  Jean-Pierre Peugeot **035**

**1878**
Toast Rack, Christopher Dresser **036**

**1879**
National Standard Pillar Box, Post Office
  Engineering Department **037**
Type Edison Lamp, Thomas Alva Edison **038**

chronology

Yamaha Silent Cello **952**

designers

designers

**designers**

**666**

Lamy 2000 Fountain Pen (1966)
Gerd Alfred Müller (1932–1991)
Lamy 1966 to present

**When it was introduced** in 1966, the Lamy 2000 marked a defining moment in the evolution of the fountain pen. Its precision technology and sleek, Bauhaus-inspired modern design would set it apart from its competitors and place it in the same league as the elegant, technologically advanced products that were emerging at the time from visionary manufacturers such as Olivetti and Lamy's German counterpart, Braun. The Lamy 2000 Fountain Pen was designed by Gerd Alfred Müller, who had made a name for himself with the Sixtant (1962), a breakthrough contemporary electric shaver design for Braun. With the Lamy 2000, as with his Braun products, Müller approached the design in the no-fuss tradition of the German modernist. Yet the Lamy fountain pen is much more than a minimalist piece of precision engineering; it is also a gem-like luxury item. The Makralon and stainless-steel brush-finished instrument boasts a platinum coat and 14 ct gold nib. The Lamy 2000 model also involves innovative design solutions in terms of its spring-mounted clip. Previously, pens depended on the material they were made from to provide their springiness; the Lamy 2000 clip is made from solid stainless steel, with the spring coming from an internal mechanism. This solution also has a practical advantage in that the clip holds the pen in place. Müller's fountain pen set a benchmark in terms of its technical invention, clean lines and modern monochromatic palette. It also attempted to go further than any of its predecessors in terms of its advanced ergonomics, and improved reliability and durability. In many ways, by the mid-1960s the fountain pen had been forced into a small corner of the market due to the popularity of the disposable Bic pens. But the Lamy 2000 model helped turn around the fountain pen's fortunes, as well as marking a turning point in the Lamy company. Until the success of the Lamy 2000 the company had been a modestly sized firm, but with the success of the fountain pen the company repositioned itself into one of the foremost design-led manufacturers of writing instruments in the world.

**Bulb** is the ultimate Pop Art lighting product, a bulb within a bulb, the casing an exaggerated replica of an everyday product. The inner bulb is chromed to reflect and diffuse the light, and is set within a crystal glass casing with a chromium-plated neck. Bulb is the first of a series of bulb-featured objects produced by Ingo Maurer throughout his career as a lighting designer. 'The bulb is my inspiration,' he has said. 'I have always been fascinated by the light bulb because it is the perfect meeting of industry and poetry.' In 1966 he created three bulb products: Bulb, Bulb Clear and Giant Bulb. He made a number of early versions that were sold through word of mouth, but it swiftly grew into a viable business. The Bulb lamp began Maurer's career in lighting. Trained as a graphic designer, he worked as a commercial artist in the 1960s before producing the Bulb lamp as an experiment in translating Pop Art ideas into product design. Maurer was inspired by Pop's fascination with mundane objects and its practice of creating exaggerated, over-sized or cartoon-like replicas of everyday things. In 1958, the American artist Jasper Johns had made *Lightbulb II*, a replica of an Edison light bulb cast in bronze. Maurer's bulbs, however, are always practical lighting products. He founded his studio, Design M, now known as Ingo Maurer, in Munich in 1963, but demand for his lighting products was such that by the end of the 1960s he began to concentrate solely on this field. By the 1980s Maurer had moved into high-tech experimentation, and his company had grown from design studio to full-scale manufacturer. Maurer's work consistently engages with conceptual ideas, and is rooted in the crossover practice between art and design he established in the 1960s. Ingo Maurer still produces the Bulb lamp alongside a number of bulb-related products that represent an imaginary dialogue between Maurer and his inspiration, Thomas Edison. In 1997 Maurer perfected a holographic image of a light bulb captured inside a shade and entitled 'Wo Bist Du, Edison?' ('Where are you, Edison?')

**665**

Bulb (1966)
Ingo Maurer (1932–)
Ingo Maurer 1966 to present

**66-4**

Chicken Brick (1966)
Designer Unknown
Habitat, Weston Mill Pottery 1966 to present

**The terracotta Chicken Brick** oven is a clear example of good design at its most unpretentious and sincere. Instantly recognizable for its distinctive and somewhat quirky, comical, bulbous form, the Chicken Brick is simple and honest, with no excess features or ornament. It is easy to use, and is made of material perfect for its function. Cooking in wet terracotta clay pots is an ancient tradition that dates back to the Etruscans and this type of oven existed in continental Europe for centuries before Terence Conran put it into his Habitat shops in 1966. However, it was because of its sales through Habitat that the Chicken Brick became so popular and in the United Kingdom. The Chicken Brick creates an enclosed environment for baking in any oven and follows in the long tradition of baking food by wrapping it in a suitable material and placing it directly into a fire. The terracotta heats evenly and allows for uniform cooking of the food, while the sealed environment maximizes the flavours without any drying out. The terracotta brick itself imparts a flavour that is unique to ovens of this type and because of the moist heat characteristic of clay-pot cooking, little salt or fat is needed to achieve satisfying results. The pot is easy to use and once the pot is put into the oven, the cook can go about other tasks and leave the dish unattended. In the 1960s the Chicken Brick's appeal was both practical and exotic. Its popularity reflected the emerging influence of travel on the middle classes and the shift towards home entertaining. Today, it still appeals to our health-conscious generation as no basting or fat is required. Although at first glance this rotund little object may seem slightly absurd, it is a practical, functional and successful item, that is loved by all who have used it.

HABITAT CHICKEN BRICK

**In the 1970s,** Italian furniture companies experimented with laminate polyester combined with glass fibre, a technique traditionally used in ship production. The first furniture designs to use this technique, such as the various chair designs by Joe Colombo, caused a stir in the design world. The technique allowed designers to think about soft shapes, and to create uniquely sculptured three-dimensional products, avoiding any mechanical constructions traditionally used in wooden and steel furniture production. The Dedalo Umbrella Stand is part of an office line that was first produced in 1966, and was the largest item in the line and at that time was an ideal product for this technique. The financial investment for the steel mould necessary to produce the piece was enormous and could be recouped only by producing large quantities, which implied a distribution system on a large scale. The creation of a perfect mould, however, was the key to manufacturing a product with a superior finish and sufficient thickness, and paid off the initial investment. The resulting product was unmistakable compared with existing umbrella stands of the time. The stand's softly shaped spherical body, with seven integrated holes, created a sculptural effect perfectly suited to the use of injection-moulded technology. The stand's shiny surface was perfectly in keeping with contemporary consumers' tastes, and the introduction of different colours responded to seasonal fashion, meaning the product could match other interior features such as carpets or upholstery.

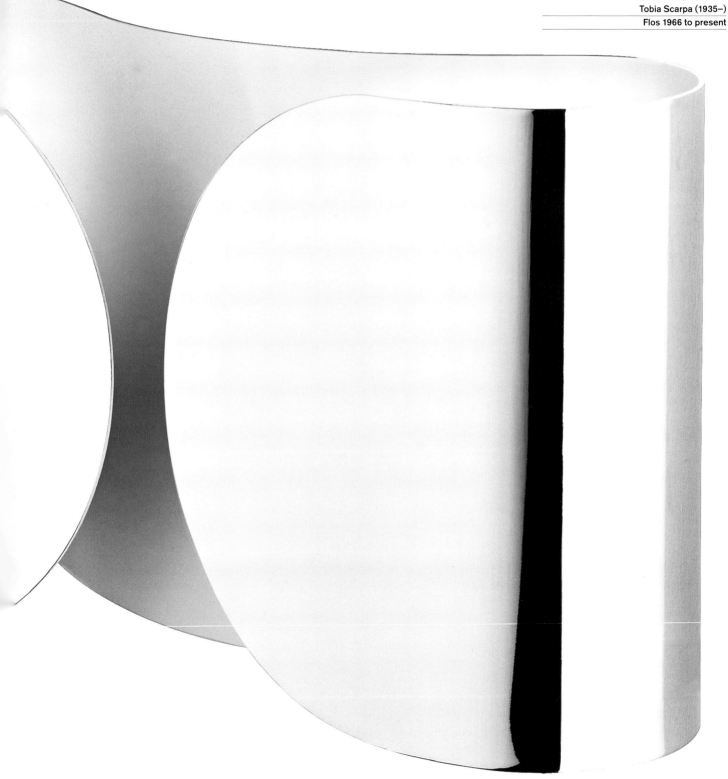

**The Foglio Lamp** is a simple and elegant modern version of a wall sconce, formed like a curl of paper or parchment. It is made from a single sheet of chrome with a white enamelled interior, which is folded at either end to enclose the bulb and acts to diffuse the light down the wall. Although unadorned, the lamp suggests the capital from a column or a furled folio. Tobia Scarpa's work, like that of his father, the architect Carlo Scarpa, reveals a desire to combine the old with the new and to unite traditional craftsmanship with modern needs. Scarpa and his wife and collaborator, Afra, graduated in architecture from the University of Venice in the late 1950s. Tobia's first work as a designer was for Venini, a leading glassworks in Murano, Venice. Since 1957 Tobia has worked in partnership with his wife in the field of architecture as well as product design. A significant proportion of their work has been the sensitive restoration of historical buildings. They are also known for their use of sumptuous materials such as leather and marble, and for their restrained approach to design tailored to a luxury market. Foglio was one of a number of lighting products designed by Scarpa for Flos, which had been founded in 1962 as a specialist lighting company to harness the talents of Italian designers. Scarpa, along with Pier Giacomo Castiglioni, was invited to design the company's first products.

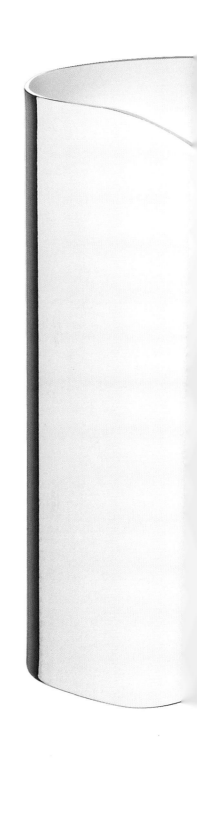

**Close on the heels** of the earthy tone and mood of the 1950s, the 1960s bore witness to an era of rapid social change marked by an increased permissiveness at all levels of society, especially in design. Youth culture was proving ever more influential, and the somewhat stricter domestic dictum of the 1950s generation gave way to an exploration of informality and convenience in the home. Within this context, the Cassina 780/783 Stacking Tables, created in 1966 by Gianfranco Frattini, can be put forward as an archetypal example of design from this period. These low tables come in two sizes (42 cm/16.5 in and 60 cm/23.6 in in diameter) and each set consists of four tables with an ever-decreasing height. When stacked, the table legs interlock to form a solid, drum-like shape that possesses an attractive sculptural quality. When separated, the tables provide an elegant yet casual, low-slung surface. The tables are manufactured from a beech frame, and with a plastic laminate top in natural, white or black lacquer, or stained walnut, with a reversible monochrome design. The tops of the tables pop out and reverse to show a different colour. They are reflective of the period because they update the idea of a traditional nest of tables into a much more modern proposition; they were aimed at a more youthful audience. The effect is modern, yet timeless in character and no doubt one of the reasons for the continued production of the tables today. Frattini was a committed exponent of the 1960s ideal; he produced a noteworthy body of work during this period, much of which was in association with Cassina, the Italian manufacturer with a similarly progressive outlook. Whereas the traditional nesting table was the embodiment of middle-class respectability, somewhat formal and staid, Frattini's reinterpretation embraced a 1960s trademark black-and-white colour scheme and a degree of spontaneity that attracted a younger generation of furniture buyers. 780/783 is a neat summation of design of the 1960s, a period marked by optimism and experimentation.

**Cronotime (1966)**
**Pio Manzù (1939–69)**
**Ritz-Italora 1968 to 1970s**
**Alessi 1988 to 2002**

**The taut tenets** of rationalist principles combine with wit and warmth in Pio Manzù's Cronotime table clock to create a wonderfully idiosyncratic design, Manzù's personal homage to the dynamics of the motor car. The battery clock, encased in a single piece of moulded ABS and standing 9 cm (3 in) high with a diameter of 7 cm (2 in), was originally designed for Fiat as a gift item. And there is a certain novelty character to the clock, which looks like a car engine component shifted and shaped into something completely different. The influence of Manzù's father, Giacomo Manzù, who was a sculptor, is evident in the tactile, sculptural quality of the piece. The flexibility of the components allows for easy repositioning; by rotating the two sections of curved cylinder, the clock face – seen as a 'section' of its casing – can be reorientated and revolved, giving it a practical as well as a playful twist. In fact, the design approach has much in common with the formal ingenuity and humour embodied in the designs of Achille Castiglioni, with whom he designed the Parentesi lamp in 1971. Beneath the quirky humour beats the heart of a precision timepiece. Manzù had previously studied at the Hochschule für Gestaltung in Ulm, standard bearer of the rationalist approach to industrial design from the mid-1950s to the late 1960s, with a curriculum that emphasized maths, sociology and ergonomics, as well as design. Here Manzù discovered a passion for motor-car design, developing prototype models of medium and small powered cars, and he joined the Centro Stile Fiat as a consultant. It was during this stint that he designed the Cronotime clock, which was one of Manzù's final designs before his untimely death in a road accident in 1969.

Warren Platner

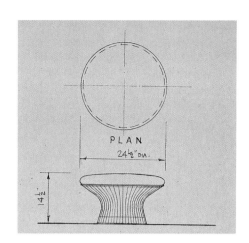

PLAN

24½" DIA.

14½"

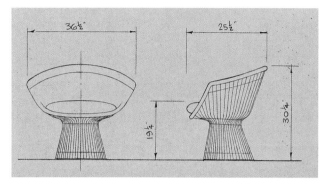

36½"

25½"

30¼"

19¼"

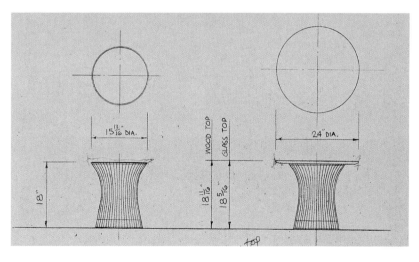

15 13/16" DIA.

24" DIA.

WOOD TOP

GLASS TOP

18"

18 11/16"

18 5/16"

top

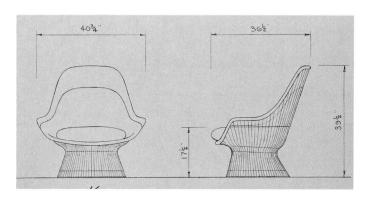

40¾"

36½"

39½"

17½"

Warren Platner

**Warren Platner's Chair and Ottoman,** designed as part of a nine-piece collection for Knoll, were a technical tour de force not only in their innovative steel-wire construction, but also in the optical conundrum that their structure created, effectively making these pieces the furniture equivalent of the colourful, kinetic Op Art paintings that were emerging during the mid-1960s. Platner arrived at the Chair and Ottoman's design by welding a series of curved, vertical steel rods to a circular frame, creating a 'moiré' effect, much in the same way as Bridget Riley did when she laid a transparent pattern over a second pattern to create a flickering, pulsating illusion in her canvases of the period. For three years prior to approaching Knoll, Platner had researched the manufacturing technology involved in producing steel-wire structures, visiting factories specializing in fan casing and shopping carts, as well as experimenting himself. The modern mantra of combining elegant design with technological innovation was central to Platner's approach and one which he had honed as a result of working with legendary designers Raymond Loewy, Eero Saarinen and I M Pei. Steel-wire construction had previously been explored in the 1950s by designers such as Charles and Ray Eames and Platner's Knoll predecessor Harry Bertoia. But whereas Bertoia's iconic Diamond Chair was more a transparent sculptural study in space, form and metal, Platner's Easy Chair and Ottoman were rooted in functionality, luxurious functionality at that, with their shiny nickel finish and colourful, moulded-latex seat red cushions on rubber platforms. Indeed, Platner liked to refer to the decorative period style of Louis XV when asked to describe the inspiration for his collection for Knoll. The nine-piece Platner collection, which in addition to the Easy Chair and Ottoman included a Side Chair and a Lounge Chair with complementary stool, received the American Institute of Architects International Award in 1966. It continues to be a popular draw in the Knoll catalogue, as much for its comfort quota and graceful forms as for its dazzling Op Art effects.

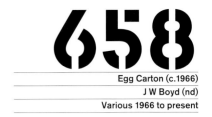

**658**

Egg Carton (c.1966)
J W Boyd (nd)
Various 1966 to present

**If the 1920s** were a busy time for practitioners of modernist design and architecture, it seems to have been an even busier time for inventors set on puzzling through the best way to carry eggs home from the market without breaking them. Although it is difficult to pinpoint the exact date and designer of the Egg Carton, the paper container that exists to this day in supermarkets the world over, there are a few key people whose names pop up in patent searches. The UK Patent Office alone turns up 620 designs that have directly to do with egg cartons, and the US Patent and Trademark Office offers an endless array, proving that nature's perfect design demands nothing but the finest in human ingenuity for its protection. There was L A Degginger's double tubular structure of folded cardboard from 1915, which looks like some strange woodwind instrument, and Morris Koppelman's 1925 'container for eggs or the like' that cleverly holds the fragile object in place with folded cardboard indentions from top and bottom. But it was an inventor named Francis H Sherman of Palmer, Massachusetts, who seems to have applied the latest pulp-sucking and fibre-felting processes of the day toward the creation of 'cellular packages formed of cellulosic material' that cradled eggs safely and enabled housewives with newfangled refrigerators to stock up on supplies for the week rather than go to market every day. Sherman's 1925 honeycomb-reminiscent cartons certainly set the initial breed standard, although his design arranged the dozen eggs in a three-by-four pattern rather than what later became the two-rows-of-six convention. The outwardly angled walls of each cell enabled the round ends of the eggs to be held above the surface on which the container rests, ensuring extra shock absorption; the mouldable paper pulp both protected notoriously porous eggshells from absorbing smells from other icebox inmates, and isolated the occasional rotten egg from stinking up the house. One of the most successful and familiar versions of the Egg Carton is J W Boyd's 1966 patent for a carton construction. Although new designs continue to populate patent offices the world over, and now include plastic and Styrofoam versions, the moulded-fibre model and its variations win enduring kudos for structural engineering and reasonably ecological materials.

**Nutrition**

| Typical Composition | 100g (3½oz) provide |
|---|---|
| **Energy** | 627kJ |
| | 151kcal |
| **Protein** | 12.5g |
| **Carbohydrate** | trace |
| of which sugars | 11.2g |
| **Fat** | 3.4g |
| of which saturates | 4.4g |
| mono-unsaturates | 1.7g |
| polyunsaturates | 0g |
| | 0.1g |
| | (24% RDA) |
| | (% RDA) |

**Free range**

These Tesco Free Range eggs have been laid by hens that have constant access to range outdoors during daylight hours.

They have been produced to high environmental and welfare standards, and the hens enjoy a cereal based vegetarian diet.

The Lion Quality Mark guarantees that these eggs have been laid in the UK and have a 'best before' date 21 days from pack to ensure maximum freshness and quality.

*Visit Tesco on-line at www.tesco.com*

UNDERSTANDING EGG CODES

1UK12345

**Although best remembered** as the car that starred alongside Dustin Hoffman in *The Graduate* (1967), the Alfa Romeo Duetto has more properly earned a place in the cultural history of the twentieth century for its beautiful design. Launched at the 1966 Geneva Motor Show, the car remained in production for the next twenty-six years, with worldwide sales of almost 120,000 units. The last car to be personally designed by Battista Pininfarina, the most celebrated of Italian car designers and founder of the styling house that bears his name, the Duetto is for many the definitive model in Alfa Romeo's 'Spider' range of cars. The name 'Duetto' was Giudobaldo Trionfi's winning entry, out of 140,501, to a competition organized by Alfa Romeo to find a name for what was essentially the Spider 1600. The prize was the car itself. The name, however, which was supposed to encapsulate the car's twin-cam engine and two-seater configuration, disappeared three years after the Duetto was launched, when the manufacturer brought out the Spider 1750. In essence, Pininfarina's design aimed at producing a shape that was as clean and aerodynamically efficient as possible. His design is enduring because it looks as though beauty and elegance were his only concerns. This was also important because the Duetto was relatively expensive and had to compete in the marketplace against the likes of the Jaguar E-Type . Nevertheless, the distinctive shape of the Duetto's plunging, low-set bonnet helps contribute to negative lift, while the design of a soft-top hood that folds almost completely away, and the tapered 'cuttlefish-bone' (sometimes also called the 'boat shape') form of the rounded nose and tail made the car one of the most aerodynamic cars of its day. Many of the other key styling features, such as the scalloped side panels and the central, low-slung radiator grille, have established the classic Alfa Romeo look and can still be found in the manufacturer's cars today.

# 656

Grillo Telephone (1966)
Marco Zanuso (1916–2001)
Richard Sapper (1932–)
Telecomunicazioni AUSO Siemens
1966 to c.1973

**The design of the** Grillo Telephone by Marco Zanuso and Richard Sapper for Siemens in 1966 marked a turning-point in how handsets would come to look in the future. It did so by challenging the 1950s idea of the telephone with a wholly modern alternative. Born of a compact, streamlined and technically creative brief, it became a landmark in telephone design, it was the point at which the telephone became a status symbol. Stylistically speaking, Grillo held little in common with its ancestors, but was similar to Henry Dreyfuss' Trimline telephone, 1965. It was conspiciously smaller than any other telephone of the time and so, in order to accommodate all the necessary features within its diminutive form, it was forced to adopt a wholly new shape. When sitting face-down on a surface, the phone takes on the appearance of a clam-shell, with the smooth surface and compact, one-piece unit disclosing little indication of its true identity. All becomes clear once you pick the phone up and the design reveals its major innovation: a spring-loaded mouthpiece that flips away from the main body, activating the receiver as it does so. At the same time, the tight circular keypad and earpiece are exposed. A wire leads from the handset to a moulded plastic plug, which also houses the bell, giving the ring tone a peculiar sound, hence the name 'Grillo' (cricket). This plug matches the colour of the handset: a further measure of style befitting a marketplace becoming increasingly aware of designer statements. Marco Zanuso was an architect and industrial designer known for an elegant, functionalist style, with a keen eye for new materials and a bold use of colour. He was a leading exponent of the potential of plastic in furniture design, a material previously confined to the production of mass-market low-cost goods. However, the Grillo design, one of the most famous product designs Zanuso created with Sapper, leveraged this versatile material into bold new effects and pioneering design heights. Grillo would prove to be not just one of the first plastic telephones, but would lead the innovation by putting the dial and the earpiece in the same unit, reducing the size of the phone; it won a Compasso d'Oro Prize in 1967. Not only did the Grillo go on to inform generation of static telephones, its influence lives on in the design of mobile phones.

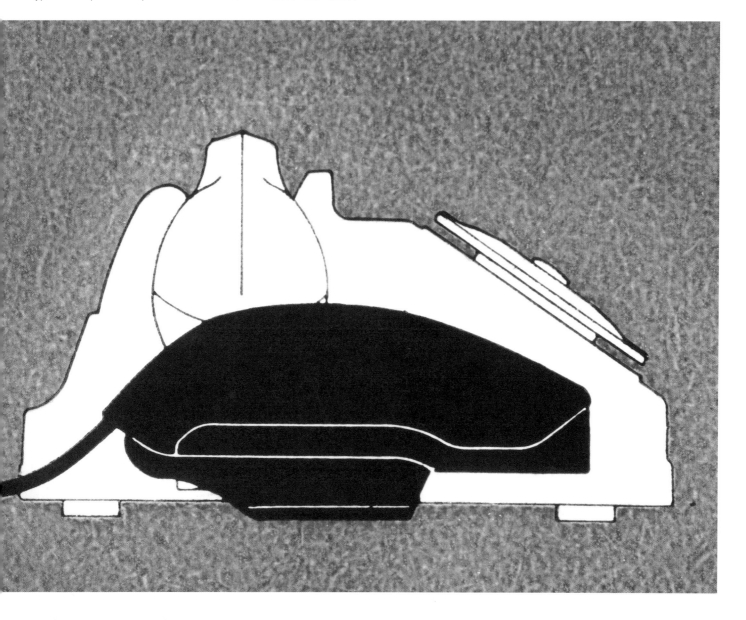

Certain typologies of furniture fail to achieve huge numbers in their production; the nature of their utility is so specific that demand for them is limited. Chaises longues, valet, conversation or rocking chairs often fall into this category. Nevertheless, their position in the catalogue of design can be secured by their uniqueness, innovation or beauty. The Dondolo Rocking Chair is one of these pieces. Unlike many rocking chairs it deviates greatly from the form of an average four-legged or wire-framed chair. The Dondolo is as much about the gesture it makes in a room as it is about the experience of the sitter. It requires considerable space to function and be seen to its greatest advantage. The sweep of the single line that describes the chair in profile is at once serpentine and calligraphic. Beginning with the cantilever of its seat, that line continues into a dramatic loop that returns below the seat as the chair's rocker. An extrusion of that line defines the Dondolo as a three-dimensional form. Its structural integrity is established by a series of ribs that repeat the chair's outline. They act as perpendicular reinforcements, supporting a floating seat and a rocking motion that is achieved by the sitter shifting weight onto a footrest. Because the chair has no arms that might assist in the rocking motion, displacement of the sitter's weight onto the footrest is the critical factor in the Dondolo's action. According to Cesare Leonardi's daughter, the Dondolo was originally designed by Leonardi and Franca Stagi one night in 1965. The unusual chair was reworked between 1966 and 1967 and the prototype was financed by Bernini in 1967 and 1968. Finally produced in three colours of fibreglass-reinforced polyester resin, it was introduced at the Milan Furniture Fair in 1969. Bernini went out of business in 1970 and the production of the Dondolo Rocking Chair was continued by the Fiarm brand division of Bellato until 1975, but only fifteen to twenty pieces have ever been made. Nevertheless, the Dondolo Rocking Chair stands as a unique example of structurally manipulated fibreglass capturing the spirit of the mid-1960s in which engagement with one's environment was being actively questioned along with every other aspect of Western culture.

# 655

Dondolo Rocking Chair (1965–7)
Cesare Leonardi (1935–)
Franca Stagi (1937–)
Bernini 1967 to 1970
Bellato 1970 to c.1975

**A ubiquitous design,** still found extensively in institutional environments and offices in Europe, Gino Colombini's 1965 Umbrella Stand combines functionality with technical innovation. The stand is made out of ABS plastic and available in striking colours such as cobalt blue, yellow, red, smoke grey and silver, and sometimes sold with a mounted ashtray. Originally the stand was intended for everyday domestic use. Highly practical, it is among the first designs to exploit the potential of injection-moulded plastics as materials for high-volume mass production. The stand combines low-cost manufacturing with principles of structural, material and unity of design. A disciple of Franco Albini, whose studio he joined in 1945, until 1953, Colombini made his name designing plastic items. He was the head of Kartell's technical department from 1953 to 1960 and produced diverse ranges of small, plastic household goods. Another of his best-sellers was a complete series of baskets for the home and office, characterized by the use of elementary geometric forms. As well as performing beside the work desk or in the bathroom, the baskets provided a decorative element. Colombini's enduring reputation in design was ensured by his timely use of plastics in a period in which they were gaining favourable acceptance by large audiences, allowing Italian and Northern European companies to promote and develop research projects involving important designers. Visually, Colombini's work belongs to a second 'phase' of Italian design, one in which designers projected their optimistic visions of a new society towards smaller, everyday objects and accessories, sometimes leaving utility behind in favour of a revision of past models and furnishing needs. Colombini's designs were given the recognition they deserved, and he received the prestigious Italian Compasso d'Oro award four times between 1955 and 1960.

1st BULTACO SHERPA
BUILT AND DEVELOPED BY
SAMMY MILLER
WINNER OF SCOTTISH SIX DAYS
BRITISH CHAMPIONSHIPS
BRITISH EXPERTS, Etc, Etc.

669 NHO

# Características

## MOTOR
Número de cilindros . . . . . 1
Ciclo . . . . . . . . . 2 tiempos
Diámetro/carrera . . . . 72 x 60 mm.
Cilindrada. . . . . . . . . 244,29 c. c.
Relación de compresión . . . 9 : 1
Potencia máxima . . . . . 19,8 cv. a 5500 r. p. m.

## CARBURADOR. . . . . . AMAL 627/6-D

## EQUIPO ELECTRICO. Magneto alternador a volante FEMSA

## TRANSMISIONES . Por cadenas con tensores
Transmisión total . 8,79 vueltas del motor por 1 de la rueda

## CAMBIO . . . 5 velocidades en toma constante
Relación. . . . I. 0,263
II. 0,342
III. 0,442
IV. 0,723
V. 1

## EMBRAGUE . . Discos múltiples en baño de aceite

## SUSPENSION DELANTERA
Tipo . . . . . Telescópica con amortiguadores hidráulicos interiores
Recorrido . . . 165 mm.

## SUSPENSION TRASERA
Tipo . . . . . Horquilla oscilante con amortiguadores hidráulicos graduables (3 posiciones)
Recorrido . . . 100 mm.

## NEUMATICOS
Delantero . . . { 2.75 x 21" Trial
3.00 x 21" Cross
Trasero . . . . 4.00 x 18" Trial/Cross

## FRENOS
Tipo . . . . . . . Expansión interna
Area de frenado delantero 7.650 mm²
Area de frenado trasero . 11.360 mm²

## CARACTERISTICAS GENERALES
Capacidad del depósito . . . . . 4,5 ls.
Distancia entre ejes . . . . . . 1330 mm.
Alto del manillar . . . . . . 1040 mm.
Ancho del manillar . . . . . . 810 mm.
Largo total . . . . . . . . 2020 mm.
Altura sillín sobre el suelo . . . . 750 mm.
Altura libre sobre el suelo . . . . 280 mm.
Altura estribos sobre el suelo . . . 350 mm.
Altura filtro aire sobre el suelo . . . 620 mm.
Peso en vacío . . . . . . . 92 kgs.

RESERVADO EL DERECHO A INTRODUCIR CUALQUIER MODIFICACION

# Specifications

## ENGINE
Number of cylinders. . . . . . . 1
Cycle . . . . . . . . . . . . 2 Stroke
Bore and Stroke . . . . . . . . 72 x 60 mm.
Displacement . . . 244.29 c. c.
Compression ratio. . . . . 9 : 1
Brake horsepower. 19.8 at 5500 rpm

## CARBURETOR . AMAL 627/6-D

## IGNITION. . . . Flywheel magneto FEMSA

## TRANSMISSIONS
Chains with tensioners
Overall ratio. 8.79 revs. of the crankshaft for each rev. of the rear wheel

## GEARBOX . . . . . 5 speed
Ratios . . . I. 0.263 - II. 0.342
III. 0.442 - IV. 0.723 - V. 1

## CLUTCH . . . . Multiple plates in oil bath

## FRONT SUSPENSION
Type. . . . . . . . . Telescopic with hydraulic damping
Travel . . . . . . 6 1/2" (165 mm.)

## REAR SUSPENSION
Type. . . . . . . . . Swinging arm
Type shock absorbers. . . 3-Way adjustable telescopic with hydraulic damping
Travel . . . . . . . . 3 15/16" (100 mm.)

## BRAKES
Type. . . . . . . . . . Internal expanding
Front brake diameter and width . . . 7 650 mm.²
Rear brake diameter and width . . 11 360 mm.²

## TYRES
Front tyre. . . . . . . . { 2.75 x 21" Trial
3.00 x 21" Knobby
Rear tyre. . . . . . . . 4.00 x 18" Trial or Knobby

## GENERAL DETAILS
Gas-Tank capacity. . . . . . . . 1 imperial gallon (4.5 litres)
Wheelbase . . . . . . . . 52.3" (1330 mm.)
Overall lenght . . . . . . . . 79.3" (2020 mm.)
Handlebar, height & width . . . . . . 41" x 32" (1040 x 810 mm.)
Saddle height above ground. . . . . . 30" (750 mm.)
Ground clearance. . . . . . 11" (280 mm.)
Footrest height above ground . . . . 13.8" (350 mm.)
Air-cleaner height above ground . . . 24.4" (620 mm.)
Empty weight . . . . . . . . 203 lbs. (92 kgs.)

CONSTANT IMPROVEMENTS WILL SUBJECT SPECIFICATIONS TO CHANGE WITHOUT NOTICE

**COMPAÑIA ESPAÑOLA DE MOTORES, S. A.**
San Adrián de Besós - Barcelona - SPAIN

Art.º 80.34-001/N

# 653

Bultaco Sherpa T 244cc (1965)
Sammy Miller (1933–)
Francisco Xavier Bultó (1912–98)
Bultaco 1965 to 1981

**Created by Irish trials** rider Sammy Miller and Spanish motorcycle maker Bultaco, the Sherpa T 244cc took the sport of bike trials by storm when Miller rode it to victory in its first event in 1965. It went on to dominate the bike trials market for the next fifteen years. In the rather eccentric sport of motorcycle trials, competitors have to negotiate obstacles around a course without putting their feet down or stopping. Speed is not usually a factor. In the 1950s and early 1960s, trials were an essentially British sport and Sammy Miller was king. In 1963 the Spanish firm Bultaco was producing some 12,000 road and race motorcycles a year, largely for the Spanish market. Francisco Xavier Bultó, the firm's founder, was keen to expand his market, and wanted to introduce a light two-stroke motorcycle to the sport of trials, where heavy single-cylinder four-stroke bikes, the British models AJS and Ariel particularly, were preferred. Bultó approached Miller to design and develop a new model and in the summer of 1964, they worked together with Bultaco engineers at the Barcelona factory. The key design decision was the introduction of Bultaco's lightweight two-stroke engine. Unlike a four-stroke engine, which has a heavy valve mechanism and complicated engineering, a the lighter engine uses suction to get its petrol mixture into the cylinder for firing. The result is a high revving engine, quite powerful for its size. When Miller chose to abandon his famous British Ariel in 1965 and ride an unproven Spanish two-stroke that frankly did not look tough enough, he sent shock waves through the sport. But Miller won his first event on the Sherpa T and went on winning, and the entire sport was soon converted to this light alternative. Forty years later it is recognized as the most successful trials bike of the modern era.

**During the fourteen-year span** of its availability until when it was taken off in the market in 1979, (the camera was only in production for just five years), the Polaroid Swinger Model 20 became one of the most widely adopted cameras in history. The highly simplistic design was a boon to a generation of amateur photographers looking to capture the increasingly fast-paced life of the late 1960s. Made from high-impact moulded plastic, the camera's monochrome black and white design is punctuated only by a small logo and the exposure button, picked out in red. A large viewfinder adorns the top of the camera in the centre, otherwise the designers left the model free from excessive detail. The camera exemplified Polaroid's brand values of photographic innovation and convenience by opening up the field of affordable point-and-press cameras to an eager public. Crisply focused photography was made possible by the camera's biggest innovation, the 'Yes' shutter design. The photographer had simply to twist the red trigger knob to compare two different apertures that, when matched, the 'Yes' signal would appear in the viewfinder. The camera relied on high-speed type 20 film, the first roll film to develop outside the camera and one that minimized the effects of motion. The promise of sharply focused, wallet-sized black and white photographs proved to be a golden ticket for the marketing men at Polaroid. The camera was priced at a very accessible $19.95 and promoted on the back of the now legendary TV advertising campaign that launched the career of the fledgling actress Ali MacGraw. When the advertisement aired in Canada on a Friday evening it caused a stampede to the shops the next day. Eighty per cent of the original allotment was sold by that Monday evening and the rest was gone by the end of the week. The Swinger Model 20 remains collectable today, having set the standard in high quality, instant photography.

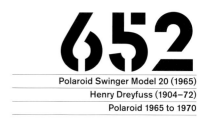

**652**

Polaroid Swinger Model 20 (1965)
Henry Dreyfuss (1904–72)
Polaroid 1965 to 1970

TAGESLICHTAUFNAHMEN

ROT:     DEN ROTEN KNOPF SEITLICH ZUSAMMEN-
         DRÜCKEN UND DREHEN BIS DAS "YES" AM
         KLARSTEN ERSCHEINT. KNOPF LOSLASSEN—DAS
         "YES" VERSCHWINDET.

WEISS:   DURCH HERUNTERDRÜCKEN DES WEISSEN
         KNOPFES AUSLÖSEN.

BLAU:    BLAUE TASTE MIT RECHTEM DAUMEN EIN
         DRÜCKEN UND FILMSTREIFEN VORZIEHEN BIS ER
         AN DER GESTRICHELTEN LINIE AUTOMATISCH
         ANGEHALTEN WIRD. 15 SEKUNDEN WARTEN. BILD-
         EINHEIT ZUR BLAUEN TASTE HIN ABREISSEN. BILD
         VOM NEGATIV TRENNEN. INNERHALB ZWEI STUNDEN
         MIT LACKSCHWÄMMCHEN ÜBERSTREICHEN.

BLITZAUFNAHMEN—(AG-1 ODER AG-1B BLITZBIRNEN
              VERWENDEN)

ROT:     ENTFERNUNG ZUM AUFNAHMEOBJEKT DURCH
         DREHEN DES ROTEN KNOPFES AN DER BLITZ-
         SKALA EINSTELLEN.

WEISS UND BLAU: WIE BEI TAGESLICHTAUFNAHMEN.

         MADE IN THE UNITED KINGDOM

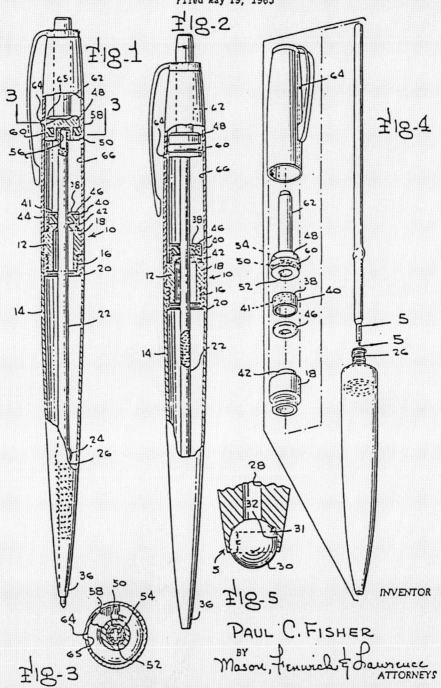

· Nov. 15, 1966　　　　P. C. FISHER　　　　3,285,228

ANTI-GRAVITY PEN

Filed May 19, 1965

*Fig-1*

*Fig-2*

*Fig-4*

*Fig-3*

*Fig-5*

INVENTOR

PAUL C. FISHER

BY

Mason, Fenwick & Lawrence

ATTORNEYS

The Anti-Gravity Pen was first developed for NASA
for use in zero gravity. It had a pump that temporarily
pressurized the ink cartridge, so the pen would write upside
down or without the aid of gravity for a limited time of about 30 minutes.
It led Fisher to the permanently pressurized Space Pen.

Ultra-hard
tungsten carbide ball

Sliding float separates
ink from pressurized
nitrogen gas

Gas plug

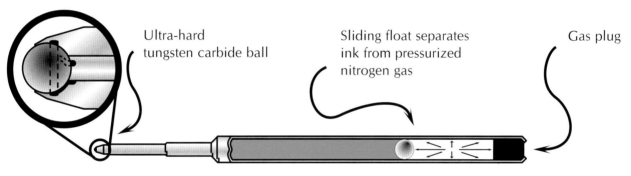

Stainless steel, preceision-
machined socket prevents
leaks and oozing, yet
delivers instant uniform
ink flow

Thixotropic ink in a
hermetically sealed and
pressurized reservoir
writes three times longer

Ink will not dry out for
over one hundred years!
Writes at any angle at
temperatures of -30$^0$F to
+250$^0$F

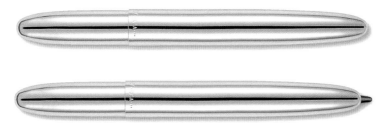

**In 1965** Paul Fisher was successful in his application to patent his original AG-7 Space Pen. The design allowed for the pen to write in any position and in virtually any environment. The cartridge was pressurized with nitrogen, negating the need for gravity to assist ink flow. Further, Fisher used thixotropic ink, a semi-solid ink that liquefied against the shearing action of the rolling ball only when the ball was in motion. The result was ink flow only when needed. The control of the supply of ink was something of a revolution within its market area, as all other ballpoints either 'bled' or dried up. The durable AG-7 not only had an infinite shelf-life, but was dependable in diverse environmental conditions from freezing cold to dry heat. It could write under water and upside down. Aesthetically, its finely tapered shaft with a circular milled grip was not dissimilar to other pens on the market, but it provided a shape that combined with its technology to create a futuristic vision. Fisher's company went on to exploit the pen's visual possibilities with a host of casing designs, many with commemorative insignia. Paul Fisher's design came at an opportune time and a marketing coup raised the international profile of the Space Pen. Astronauts on the Mercury and Gemini missions had been using pencils to make notes in space. Fisher's design was clearly a more practical option. He supplied NASA with the AG-7 Space Pen and in October 1968 the Apollo 7 mission began using it. The topicality of space travel raised the profile of the Space Pen, while the extreme conditions in space provided ready proof of the pen's improved performance. It was readily accepted in the consumer marketplace. The Space Pen's outer casing is less significant than the technical workings within. It relies on an enormous range of body designs to suit the subjective and ever-changing tastes of consumers, but its true strength is in its revolutionary cartridge.

**NATIONAL AERONAUTICS AND SPACE ADMINISTRATION**
MANNED SPACECRAFT CENTER
HOUSTON, TEXAS 77058

IN REPLY REFER TO: CB

**MAY** 2 6 1969

Mr. Paul C. Fisher
President
Fisher Pen Company of California
5900 North Burnet Avenue
Van Nuys, California 91401

Dear Mr. Fisher:

Thank you very much for your test models of the improved
#AG7 space pen for our evaluation.  It is encouraging to
find out that American interprise is complete capable of
developing new and quality products without using government subsidies as a crutch.

The statistics you quote on the pen are quite impressive
and I certainly hope that we will find your improvement to
be a benefit to our efforts.  You might be interested to
know that the original #AG7 which I received several years
ago is still going strong.

Best wishes to you and the Fisher Pen Company.

Sincerely,

Neil A. Armstrong
NASA Astronaut

Sherman Poppen

**On Christmas Day 1965,** when Sherman Poppen bound a pair of skis together so that his daughter could ride along the snow like a surfer, he set the ball rolling for what would eventually become a worldwide craze and an Olympic sport. This extra-wide ski was designed to be ridden standing up, and a rope, tied to the nose of the board, allowed the rider some control over steering. Poppen's wife suggested the name Snurfer, a combination of snow and surf, and after witnessing the excited reaction from other kids in the neighbourhood, Poppen knew he was on to something. Poppen, an engineer specializing in chemical gases, had an eye for innovation and had previously invented an aerosol product for cleaning welding guns. Recognizing the potential of the Snurfer, he licensed the idea to be manufactured as a children's toy. Launched in 1966, it was an immediate hit and the Brunswick Toy Company, calling itself 'the only name in Snurfing', sold around 400,000 Snurfers before sales eventually began to tail off. Poppen further guaranteed the popularity of snurfing by organizing competitions, many of which attracted Snurfers who would go on to take the sport to even greater heights. Perhaps the most important of these competitors was Jake Burton Carpenter, who, having taken part in Snurfer competitions, went on to design his own boards. He called his design the Snurfboard and it was only after realizing that the name Snurf was owned as a trademark by Poppen that he renamed it a snowboard. As competitions became more regular and snowboarding gained notoriety as a sport, it was not long before ski slopes began accommodating snowboarders. With films and magazines celebrating the art of snowboarding, and new designs allowing for greater dexterity, it was only a matter of time before snowboarding became a successful industry. In the 1980s snowboarding competitions began to attract corporate sponsorship and has become a popular event at the Winter Olympics since first appearing in 1998.

Snurfer (1965)
Sherman Poppen (1930–)
Brunswick 1966 to 1984

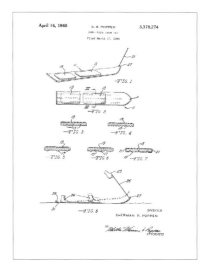

# SNURFING!

## the greatest word in downhill fun since YAHOOOooooooooooo!

### the thrills of SKIING!
### the skills of SURFING!

Snurfing is winter's newest snowtime thrill. Makes tobogganning tame, puts sleds in the kiddie class. You don't just *ride* the Snurfer, you *guide* it! From the top of the hill to the bottom, Snurfing is one long "YAHOOOoooo!"

OFFICIAL
## Snurfer
BY BRUNSWICK

Available in standard model . . . or the Super Snurfer racing model (below)...both are priced under **$10.00**.

Look for the official Snurfer in this display at your dealer.

**Brunswick**

*The Only Name in Snurfing*

69 West Washington Street  Chicago, Illinois 60602

**The Eclisse** ('eclipse') is a bedside lamp made of an enamelled metal casing that houses two overlapping, half-spherical shells held on a pivot so they can be turned to regulate the light. Vico Magistretti experimented with spherical and organic forms in both lighting and furniture, turning to new developments in the creation of plastics to help him achieve the forms he wished. In 1964 he sketched designs for a pod-like lamp attached to a bed head; this grew into the idea for the Eclisse the following year. In 1968 he revised the idea of the Eclisse lamp to create the Telegono lamp, which uses the same principle of the spherical shells, but is made of plastic. The Eclisse lamp exemplifies Magistretti's technical and visual preoccupations in the 1960s. His design method was pragmatic and systematic and he worked closely with manufacturers to progress an initial idea. He would make a study of use and submit sketches rather than technical drawings to manufacturers. Technicians would then be

expected to use his sketches to develop the technical means by which his idea could be realized. Magistretti claimed that, in the case of the Eclisse, the nature of the mechanism was not important as long as it facilitated the basic idea of the light, i.e. that it be adjustable from a small blade of light to a full beam. The Eclisse lamp won the Compasso d'Oro in 1967 and is featured in many museums, including The Museum of Modern Art in New York. In awarding the 1967 prize, the judges commented that 'the object embodies the double quality of high design value and good commercial potential. Moreover, the technical solution adopted is innovative, in that the flow of light can be regulated by simply moving the rotating shade.' The lamp has remained as a bestseller for Artemide since it was first produced.

DSC Series (1965)
Giancarlo Piretti (1940–)
Castelli/Haworth 1965 to present

**'Once an artist finds his own language,** he is freed from the fatigue of the avant-garde.' Determined to experiment with new and untried materials, Piretti was just twenty-five when he joined Castelli as a designer. Since 1963 Piretti had been thinking about a chair suitable for both domestic and public spaces that would infringe upon the materials and technologies of the established canon. This is why Piretti opted to use press-moulded aluminium, a material that had not yet raised any interest among furniture designers. He began focusing his attention on pressure die-casting, which was then mostly used in the production of motors. Although Piretti's pioneering ideas did not fit in with Castelli's main production of quality wooden furniture for offices, the owner of the company, Cesare Castelli, let him experiment and allowed him free access to the company at any hour of the day or night. The result was the 106 chair, with its seat and backrest as shells of pre-shaped plywood held together by two press-moulded aluminium clamps, fixed using only four screws. Presented in 1965, at the Salone del Mobile, the unconventional 106 was an immediate success and soon became established as the archetype of a whole new family of chairs: the DSC Series. Thus the 106 generated the Axis 3000 and Axis 4000 collective seating ranges: all stackable, interconnecting, fitted with different types of armrest and flip-up writing tops, document holders, seat or row markers, and even supplied with their own transport trolley. In the development of the system, the peculiarities of Piretti's design are very noticeable, especially the extreme flexibility and ease with which the parts are assembled in both its single and multiple configurations. Today the whole system of chairs is widely used in offices and public spaces, such as conference rooms, waiting areas and theatres – a tribute to the versatility of the DSC series. A great achievement for its ambitious creator, determined since his youth 'to be a designer … not a furniture designer', it established his trademark synthesis between technological experimentation, practicality and elegance.

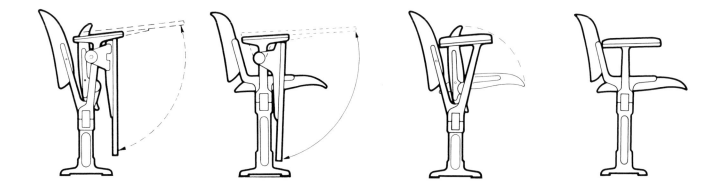

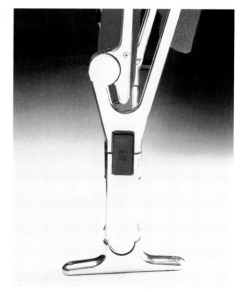

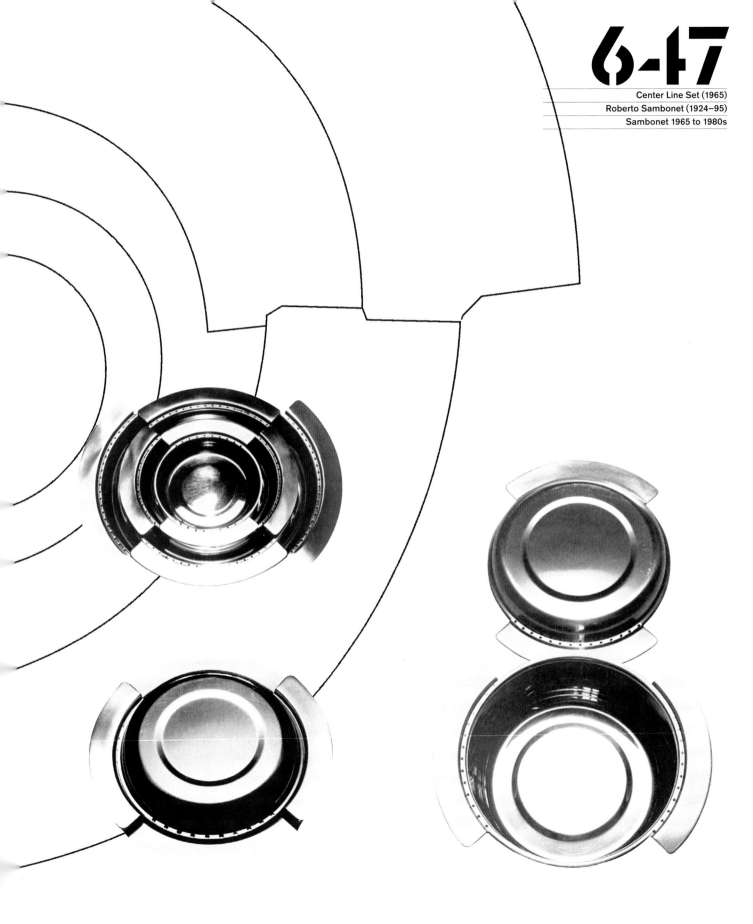

**The interlocking** logic of the Center Line Set cookware helped win Roberto Sambonet the Compasso d'Oro award for metal cookware in 1970, the awarding panel commenting that his pieces: 'reveal technical ability, sensitivity of design and a capacity to see objects as a series … They demonstrate a rational utilization of space and an appropriate use of material employed.' The range, however, had already been in production since 1964 as part of a series of stainless-steel cookware and tableware designed by Sambonet for his family's company of the same name. With this cookware Sambonet demonstrated beautifully his underlying interest in aesthetic formalist principles and their application to domestic and industrial design products. The precision and dedication of form is exactly what one would expect from a designer who trained as an architect and was also a successful painter. The Center Line design clearly illustrates Sambonet's personally developed design idiom, which is implicit in the consistency of his creative output and his preoccupation with organizing objects in systems. The Center Line cookware is composed of four deep pots and four shallow pots with corresponding diameters. These can then be used as either lids for the deeper pot, or as pans in their own right. This truly utilitarian cookware was made in graduating stainless steel, allowing the set to be used in the oven and on the stove top as well as for storage and as serving dishes on the table top. With no traditional pan handles, the dishes can nest and take up no more space than the profile of the largest and deepest dish in the set. Each dish has a flared flange forming opposite quarters of the rim, which can be used to lift and move the pot. The perfectly matched shallow dish, when used as a lid, then exactly completes the circle of the rim with the precisely interlocking flange. This system of stacking and interlocking makes the Center Line Set an outstanding example of formalist complexity within a logical and functionalist design solution.

Thrift (1965)/Café (1982)
David Mellor (1930–)
Walker and Hall 1966 to c.1970
David Mellor 1982 to present

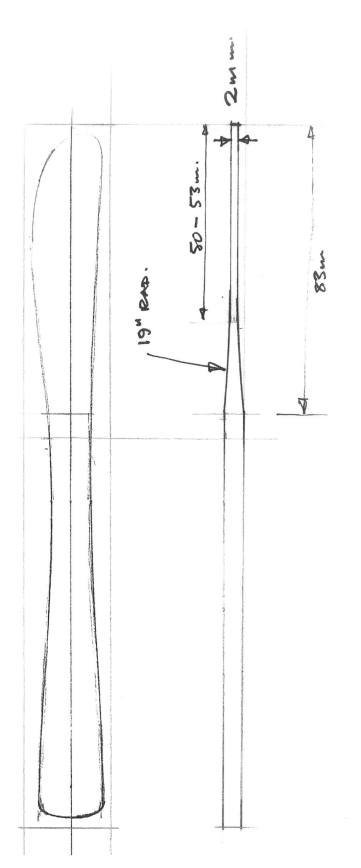

2 mm

50 - 53 mm.

83 mm

19" RAD.

**David Mellor** is a designer whose name is synonymous with British cutlery design. Mellor upholds an old-fashioned ideal of industrial design: that it can be ubiquitous, yet essentially anonymous. The cutlery service of 1965 was developed by Mellor as the Thrift service (now re-issued as Café). Following his earlier 1963 commission to design a completely new range of silver for use in British embassies, the government was led two years later to employ Mellor's design skills to produce new tableware for use in government canteens, hospitals and prisons, and by British Rail. For many traditionalists the radical element in the design of Thrift was that Mellor cut down the traditional eleven-piece setting to a basic five-piece set. In replacing the Civil Service standard-issue 'Old English' cutlery, Thrift dealt a blow to class tradition, and it horrified conservative cutlers by omitting the fish knife. Contemporary British and Scandinavian design deeply influenced Mellor's work, and he had a strong understanding of how the modern age could express itself through modern products. The successful juxtaposition of manufacture and design was to become an inherent feature of Mellor's work, perhaps most importantly through his preoccupation with the making and shaping of the knife, fork and spoon. Despite the mass production and mass use of Thrift there is no compromise in style, material or finish. The monolithic knife from the Thrift range is a flash of startling modernity. The round bowls of the spoons, the short four-pronged fork and the smooth form of the handles all contribute to Thrift's success as a modern standard worthy of national use and distribution. Encouraged by the spirit of the age, Mellor was more than a traditional craft silversmith, but was concerned with the possibilities of design for production in stainless steel, a material that was durable and allowed for mass production of one-piece designs such as Thrift.

controlled rigour of the curve and the subtle suggestion of steady balance with the base are what give the PK24 its presence, but they also exemplify the unsparing attention to detail for which Kjærholm was renowned. Unlike his Danish contemporaries, who were proponents of using the tradition of wood, Kjærholm was interested in using steel for the frame, as his work in general was focussed more towards industrial manufacture, and mass production. Using steel as the frame, the U-shaped base is cleverly attached by means of a moveable strap, which can be adjusted to each individual who reclines on it. The PK24's perfection lifts it beyond the role of the chair into the realm of sculpture, crowned with an upholstered headrest, which gently hangs over the back of the chaise. Of course, it still functions as seating, but the irregularities of the human form might destroy such an immaculate vision.

PK24 Chaise Longue (1965)
Poul Kjærholm (1929–80)
Ejvind Kold Christensen 1965 to 1981
Fritz Hansen 1981 to present

**Poul Kjærholm's output,** despite his long career as a furniture designer, was relatively small. In part this is because he struggled to find a manufacturer capable of meeting his exacting standards. Eventually, on the recommendation of Hans Wegner, he teamed up with the firm of Ejvind Kold Christensen. The result of that collaboration was a small collection of sleek furniture in the International Style, with the PK24 Chaise Longue as its centrepiece. Most of Kjærholm's seat furniture, belying his training as a cabinet-maker, is made from thin strips of chrome-plated steel upholstered with visually and texturally contrasting materials like leather or, as in the case of the PK24, woven cane. Kjærholm divided the object into a separate, very stable base, supporting a long reclining seat that can be tipped on its runners in adjustment. The most dramatic element of the PK24 lies in the mathematical precision of the unfolding sweep of the seat. The

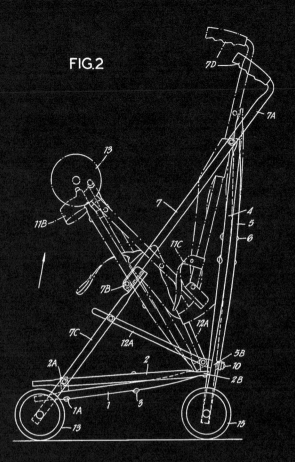

FIG.2

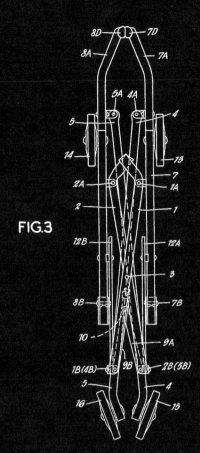

FIG.3

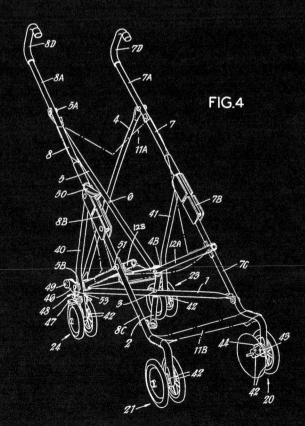

FIG.4

Baby Buggy (1965)
Owen Finlay Maclaren (1907–78)
Maclaren 1967 to 1976

**At first glance,** the Maclaren Baby Buggy appears to be little more than a stripy canvas deckchair on wheels. But it is a design that revolutionized the world of baby carriages by a retired aeronautical engineer who had worked in the aviation industry. The buggy's British inventor, Owen Finlay Maclaren, after struggling to carry his granddaughter's unwieldy stroller through an airport, decided to use what he had learned from aviation to bring baby buggies into the jet age. This is most visibly evident in the Maclaren's double wheels, which allow for better steering than a single wheel and were inspired by the landing gear of jet planes. More importantly, Maclaren applied the aeronautical industry's principles of lightweight construction to his new design. Consequently, the buggy is built around a tubular aluminium frame that weighs only 3 kg (6.5 lb). And, thanks to its two X-shaped hinge mechanisms (one at the back and one underneath), the buggy folds away as neatly as any landing gear, to a size much smaller than any buggy that came before. Where previous strollers had simply folded in half, Maclaren's folded in half and in on itself (like an umbrella) as well. Indeed, so innovative was Maclaren's transfer of technology, that the original he created still looks remarkably modern and the company he founded remains one of the market leaders today. When the buggies first went on sale in 1967 Maclaren produced 1,000 in a stable he had converted into a workshop. By the time of his death in 1978 more than 280,000 had been exported.

# It's so simple...

MACLAREN

**Baby Buggy**

*The manufacturers reserve the right to alter details and specifications without notice.*

**ANDREWS MACLAREN LTD**
Station Works, Long Buckby, Northampton NN6 7PF
Tel: Long Buckby (0327) 842662. Telex: 31432

Printed in England.

# 6-43

Sedia Universale (1965)
Joe Colombo (1930–71)
Kartell 1967 to present

**As an artist turned designer,** Joe Colombo's work has become inextricably linked with the political and social context of Italy in the 1960s and 1970s, its optimism about the future of production and its emerging Pop culture. Colombo's work can be characterized by its innovative use of new materials, and a modular, flexible approach to furniture. After giving up painting in the late 1950s, Colombo began working as an interior designer, which encouraged to him design furniture for his schemes. His early training as a painter, however, continued to resonate in his work as a designer and throughout his career he drew heavily on the organic forms and fluidity of postwar Expressionism. His furniture designs attracted the interest of Giulio Castelli of furniture manufacturer Kartell, who invested and supported his ideas. The 1965 Sedia Universale (Universal Chair) was the first chair design to be moulded entirely from one material. Colombo originally designed it to be manufactured in aluminium, but his interest in experimenting with new materials led to a prototype moulded in thermoplastic. After many unsuccessful attempts with prototypes that had moulding defects, the design was a success. Colombo designed the chair with interchangeable legs to adapt to a range of environments. It could function as a standard dining chair, with the option of shorter legs for more casual use or for use as a child's chair, or alternatively, a longer base element could be added to raise the height of the chair for use as a high chair or bar stool. These early designs for Kartell represented the first successful use of new materials in Italian design. Colombo's furniture offered a fresh new appearance, colourful and flexible, which perfectly suited the spirit of the 1960s.

Spirograph (1965)
Denys Fisher (1918–2002)
Kenner 1965 to 1991
Hasbro 1991 to present

**For nearly forty years** the Spirograph has filled houses with endless patterns and creations by applying a new use to the common purpose of the wheel. With the aid of the most simple materials – plastic gear circles and shapes, paper and a pen – one was able to spend hours creating mesmerizing ellipses, symmetrical patterns and mirroring curves. The concept behind the Spirograph is based on creating curved patterns by using two geared shapes (or circles), with one fixed and the other moving around it. Galileo studied such a curve for nearly forty years before finally calling it the cycloid in 1599. In fact, many famous scientists and distinguished mathematicians have studied the properties of such curves, but it was not until mechanics were applied to the traditional cycloid in the 1600s, by placing gear teeth on the curves, that the necessary functions were developed to create such objects as the pendulum clock. These same mechanics were applied to the Spirograph. Invented by the British engineer, Denys Fisher, the Spirograph both entertained and illustrated mathematical concepts to all ages by simply creating spiral designs with the supplied tools of geared shapes, paper and a pen. In 1965 Fisher debuted his creation at the Nuremburg International Toy Fair, where it was picked up by Kenner Products. Within two years millions of Spirographs were sold in the US alone, and in 1967 the Spirograph received the British Toy of the Year award. You did not need to be a scientist to understand the Spirograph's mathematical complexity; it was made for children from five and up and was a wonderful unisex toy for all ages. Depending on the user's skill, anything could be made, from the most basic spiral to complicated, labyrinthine patterns. Parents beamed as children spent hours unknowingly applying mathematical concepts to create exciting designs. Today Spirograph toys can be purchased with an array of patterns, from a rocket ship, to crab claws or an alien. These patterns, together with instructions on how to create more elaborate drawings, continue to add the Spirograph to children's wish lists. In an age where computer programs and battery-activated games have taken over, it is reassuring to see that the Spirograph's wheels are still turning.

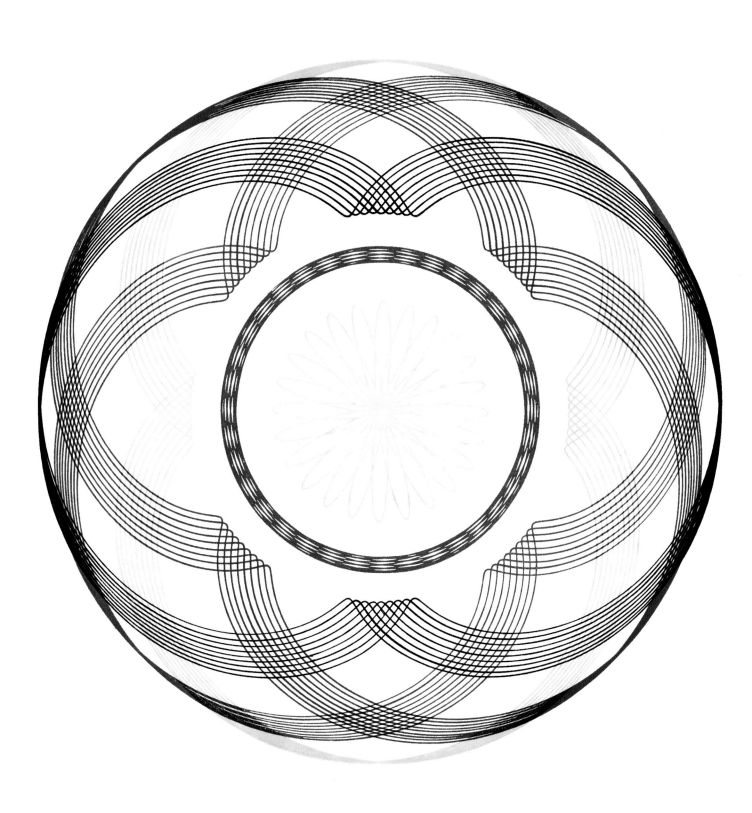

**Of all the careers** affiliated with the pioneering 1960s, Joe Colombo's

body of work puts forward one of the most memorable representations, of which

the Spider Lamp is considered a landmark. Colombo's design philosophy was

unflinchingly modern and, as showcased here, he embraced new materials and

technologies. The rectangular light fixture is designed to incorporate a new

lighting innovation of the time, the distinctive onion-shaped Cornalux bulb by

Philips. Silver coating was applied to the underside of the unit, and a neat

rectangular cut-out in the casing exposed the bulb to view. Made from a stamped-

plate design, painted in a range of colour options that includes white, black,

orange and brown, the light box clamps to a tubular chrome stand by means of an

adjustable melamine joint. In turn, the lamp can travel the full length of the stand

from the top where the flex joins, down to the circular metal base that provides an

anchor for the slim stand. The overall effect is of an architecturally influenced

design that is industrial, if not institutional, in feel. Colombo designed the lamp as

part of the Spider Group series, which featured table, floor, wall and ceiling

models. This naturally extended the commercial potential for O luce, the lamp's

manufacturer, as well as adding weight to Colombo's own vision of an interior

comprising systems as opposed to single elements. Joe Colombo's death in 1971,

aged only forty-one, cut short a career full of promise. In this context, his

contribution appears ever more potent and recognition of this was given in 1967

when the lamp won the prestigious Compasso d'Oro prize.

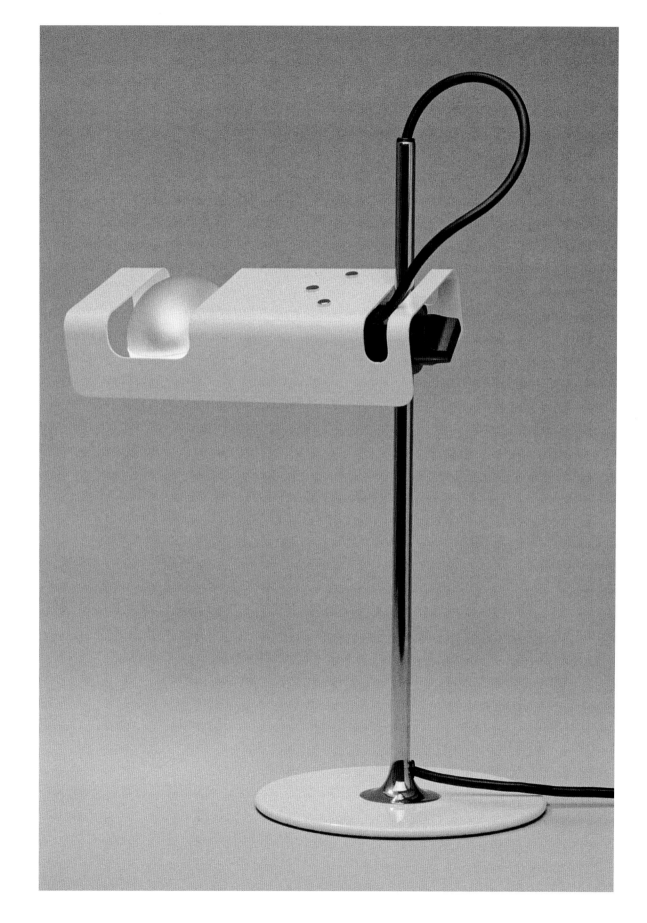

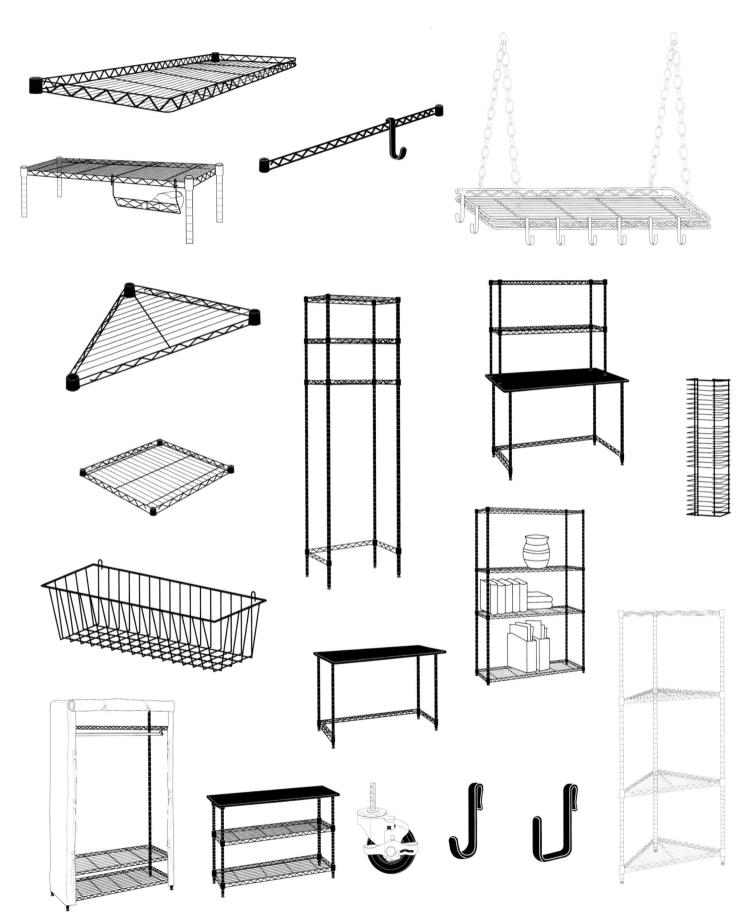

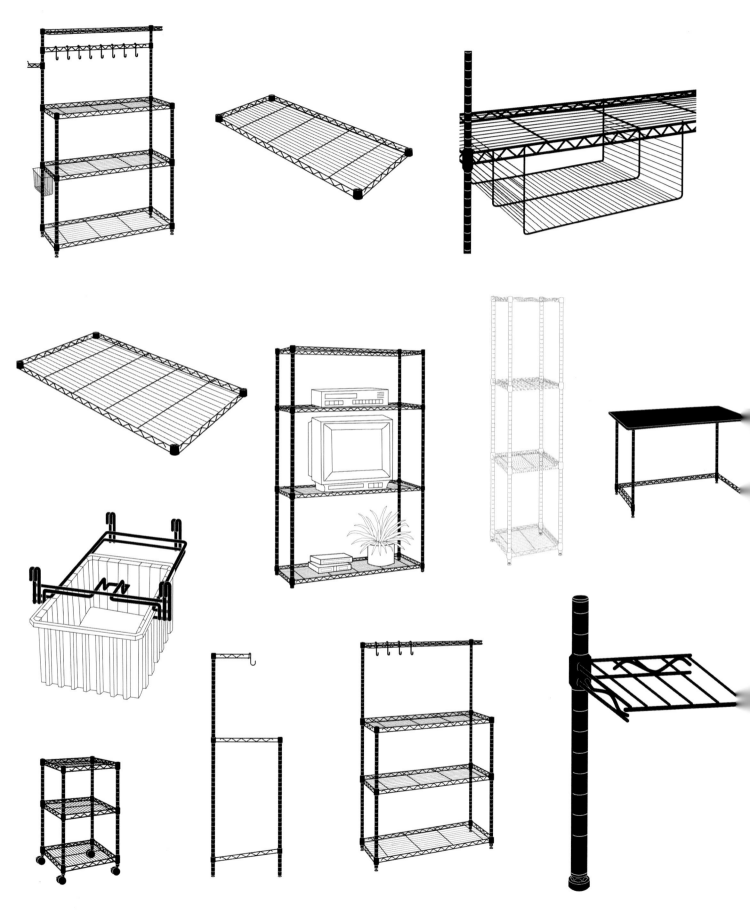

**The Super Erecta Shelving System,** developed in 1965 by Slingsby, in Bradford, Great Britain, and the Metro Corporation of the United States, is simple, requires no tools to put together and is endlessly flexible. The modular system means consumers can purchase a starter pack of four posts and as many shelves as required and can then buy more materials as needed. A simple four-shelf unit can be extended by buying four more shelves and two more posts. The new shelves are then connected to the existing unit with an ingenious S-hook. This clever extension system can be continued almost indefinitely and the simple click-together method for attaching makes it easy for companies to expand or reduce their storage capacity. The simplicity of the system is the secret to its enduring commercial life and also why it inspired product designers looking to produce cheap, self-assembly furniture for the new house owners of the property boom in the 1980s. This boom forced designers to look for ways to make furniture more flexible and compact and Slingsby Metro's ingenious commercial and industrial shelving system began to influence consumer product design in the 1980s and 1990s, even though the shelves had been used purely for industrial purposes up until this time. As developers began to adapt former industrial spaces into apartments during the 1980s and 1990s the industrial language of products like the Super Erecta Shelving began to filter into domestic design. The new apartments were often small, so the furniture had to be adaptable and compact. The idea of self-assembly, established by the Super Erecta thirty years earlier, has been picked up by a number of manufacturers, and applied to their furniture designs. The importance of the legacy of the Super Erecta System was acknowledged by its inclusion in an exhibition at the Victoria and Albert Museum, London, in 1997, entitled 'Flexible Furniture', further marking its move from a highly successful commercial product to an acknowledged ingenious design.

Achille Castiglioni

**639**

Allunaggio (1965)
Achille Castiglioni (1918–2002)
Pier Giacomo Castiglioni (1913–68)
A/P 1965
Zanotta 1965 to 1971, 1981 to present

**Originally launched in** Milan
at an exhibition of the work of the Castiglioni
brothers, this enamelled tubular-steel frame
with aluminium seat was designed for both
indoor and outdoor use. The stool's structure
is minimal, but its oversized support frame
turns it into another member of the 'zoomorphic'
family of designs devised by the Castiglioni
brothers. At the same time, it is a very light
piece, which fits within the 1960s futuristic
concept of the space age and notions of
buildings of the future. Allunaggio is part of
the 'ready-made' series of seats designed by
the Castiglioni brothers, and proof of how to
turn inexpensive, mass-produced materials
into novel designs. Although the pieces in the
series bear the weight of previous utilitarian
associations (in this case a tractor seat), they
have been adapted to contemporary needs
and new furnishing uses. The chair was called
'Allunaggio' as a homage to the moon landing,
which is also reflected in the design of the
wide legs. However, the excessive, ironic
emphasis on the formal rather than the
functional aspect of the design delayed its
production. It was only after a long consultation
between Castiglioni and Zanotta that a
commercial model was agreed upon and
manufactured. For Zanotta the 'ready-made'
series marked an interesting departure from
more commercially orientated products. It
allowed the manufacturer to become a
commissioner of pieces that reflected socio-
cultural changes and, as such, to fly the flag
for the modified habits of contemporary
domestic living. In 1981 Allunaggio was
nominated for the prestigious Italian
Compasso d'Oro award and became part of
the Kunstgwerbe Zurich Museum collection.

**The Brionvega TS 502** Radio's distinctive plastic clamshell, symbolized the synthetic pop aesthetic of the 1960s. Designed by the partnership of Marco Zanuso and Richard Sapper, it took advantage of the advent of battery-powered transistors by creating a lightweight, portable FM radio that appealed to a younger market than competitors' products, because of its playful form and striking use of materials. The use of ABS plastic emphasized the cultural chasm opening up in society as the Brionvega, modernity incarnate, dramatically differed from its traditional wooden-veneered competitors such as the Roberts Radio beloved of an earlier generation. The bold graphical exterior form was saturated in strong vibrant colours such as bright red and orange, highly redolent of the period, as well as minimalist white and black. Like a James Bond gadget, the technology was hidden away, only becoming apparent when the user wished to impress his friends with a blast of sixties pop culture and opened up the sleek plastic form. The cube hinged open to reveal the analogue dials and controls on one side and the integral speaker on the other. The interface was a masterpiece of Functionalism, with clear geometric dials and speaker grille, creating a radio that fused design with technical innovation and visual simplicity. Architecturally trained Italian, Marco Zanuso, and German designer Richard Sapper collaborated for fifteen years. During their association they created transformable designs such as the Grillo telephone for Siemens, which was the first one-piece telephone to feature a flip-down mouthpiece, pre-empting today's mobile phones, together with a succession of iconic televisions and radios for Brionvega. The company emerged during Italy's postwar boom and established themselves at the forefront of consumer electronic design by employing leading designers to create their radical product range. Because of its form, characteristic of Italian design in the 1960s, the TS 502 has become a cult object, gaining international recognition, awards and permanent display in The Museum of Modern Art in New York. Recently reissued with up-to-date technology and a return to its original interface panel, the Brionvega TS 502 continues to appeal to today's retro-influenced consumers.

**638**

TS 502 Radio (1965)
Marco Zanuso (1916–2001)
Richard Sapper (1932–)
Brionvega 1965 to present

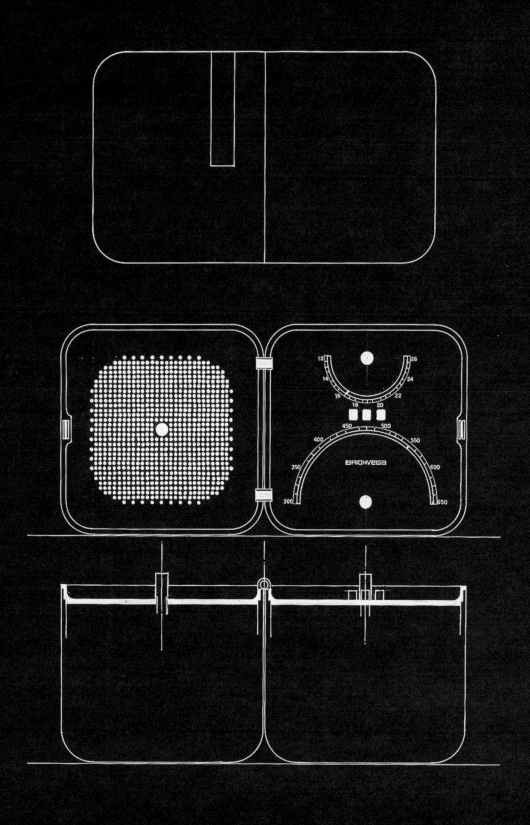

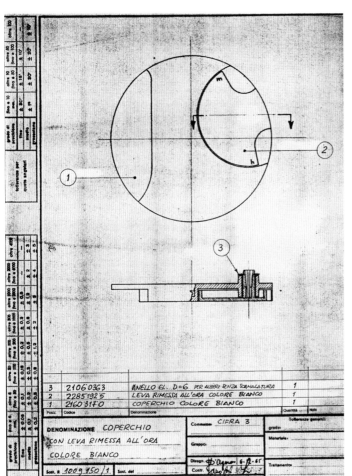

| 3 | 2106 0363 | ANELLO EL. D=6 PER ALBERI SENZA SCANALATURA | 1 | |
|---|-----------|---------------------------------------------|---|---|
| 2 | 2285 1925 | LEVA RIMESSA ALL'ORA COLORE BIANCO | 1 | |
| 1 | 2160 3170 | COPERCHIO COLORE BIANCO | 1 | |
| Posiz. | Codice | Denominazione | Quantità | Note |

DENOMINAZIONE COPERCHIO
CON LEVA RIMESSA ALL'ORA
COLORE BIANCO

Commessa: CIFRA 3
Gruppo:
Disegn. D'Agno 6-12-65
Contr.

Tolleranze generali
grado:
Materiale:
Trattamento:

Sost. il 1009 450/1  Sost. del

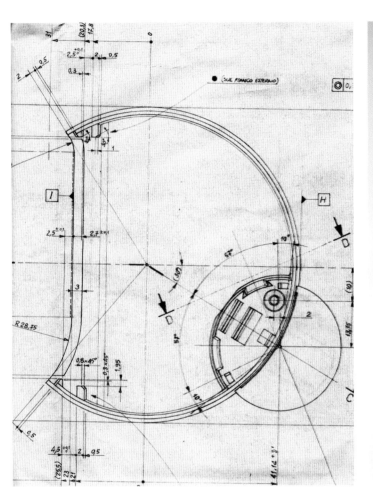

# 637

**Cifra 3 (1965)**
**Gino Valle (1923–)**
**Solari di Udine 1966 to present**

**Solari was a** successful manufacturer of
measuring devices and information systems when
it asked Gino Valle to design a table clock. The
company's technology was a precursor of digital
displays that used revolving, silk-screened flap
numerals and text for automated transport terminal
displays. Information could be changed instantly,
easily comprehended and seen from any angle.
Valle was an interesting choice for such a project
as most of his career had centred on architecture.
He had done only a few small product designs
beginning in 1956 with Zanussi Rex. He built the
Industrial Design Unit team, responsible for
producing a collection of appliances absent of
style and formal qualities but unified by size and
appearance. The original Cifra 3 clock was mains-
powered and consisted of a simple round tube of
coloured plastic, with the opaque half containing the
mechanism and the transparent half displaying the
time. Most clocks are some form of tube, usually a
shallow slice of one, so there seems an immediate
familiarity and correctness in Valle's choice of form.
The tube configuration also reflects the motion of
the mechanism, similar to the revolutions of a
Rolodex. But the most striking element of the
design is the system for setting time. On the left
side of the tube, a disc is clicked up or down to
change the minutes and hours, with simple
depressions for fingers. Valle could have used the
more conventional approach of buttons, but the joy
and satisfaction of rotating the disc control with only
one hand contributes a lot to the design. The later
battery version added a second tube to the back,
but its controlled proportions did nothing to spoil it,
and its liberating factor of portability appealed to a
new generation. Valle said that he did not enjoy
designing products – his interest had waned
considerably by the mid-1970s – and it is a pity. It is
clear his contribution to the dialogue of product
design had significant potential.

SUPER BALL
OFFICIAL
BOUNCE
TOURNAMENT
SCALE

| 100% |
| 90% |
| 80% |
| 70% |
| 60% |
| 50% |
| 40% |
| 30% |
| 20% |
| 10% |
| 0 |

636
Super Ball (1965)
Norman H Stingley (nd)
Wham-O 1965 to c.1969, 2001 to present

**When the Super Ball was** introduced in the mid-1960s by Wham-O Manufacturing Company it immediately became a craze that swept America, reaching sales of around 20 million before its appeal waned at the end of the decade. The Super Ball was a tightly compacted high-friction ball constructed of Zectron, a newly coined name with a wonderfully intergalactic-sounding ring that seemed to be entirely in tune with America's obsession with outer space at the time. Zectron was composed primarily of polybutadiene with smaller amounts of sulphur to reinforce the material and serve as a vulcanizing agent. According to the patent, issued in March 1966, the ball had a resilience factor in excess of 90 per cent. This factor, combined with the high-friction coefficient it contained, caused the ball to react in an unpredictable manner. In other words, it bounced uncontrollably and powerfully, which was great fun for the most part, but the ball was also famed for picking up so much reverse spin that black eyes and bruises with the circumference of a Super Ball were fairly common among its users. Norman Stingley, a chemical engineer working for the Bettis Rubber Company of Whittier, California, came up with the prototype Super Ball when experimenting with synthetic rubber under pressure. Due to the fact that the material used in the early ball tended to disintegrate easily, Stingley's employer knocked back the chance to develop the product. Stingley then approached Wham-O, a California-based company that pioneered the concept of creating marketing crazes around ideas taken off the street; most notably it had enjoyed phenomenal success with the Frisbee disc and the Hula Hoop. Wham-O agreed to take on and develop the product, as well as market this latest fad as the Super Ball. Like all fads the Super Ball craze fizzled out. By the late 1960s a host of imitators had flooded the market, so the decision was taken to discontinue production. That is until December 2001, when Wham-O reintroduced the ball, and in doing so not only tapped into the current retro-loving, nostalgia-driven consumer trends, but also succeeded in introducing a simple, inclusive and lively toy to a new generation much more accustomed to relatively complex, virtual and recumbent modes of play via digital media.

included it in his epoch-making film *2001: A Space Odyssey* (1968), in which an arrangement of red Djinns stood out against the ultra-slick white surroundings of the rotating space capsule. The Djinn chaise longue, with its blend of functionality and futuristic imagery, thus became a definitive symbol of the style of the 1960s, representing its desire for freedom, versatility and unconventionality. Selected for MoMA's design collection in New York as well as for the Centre Georges Pompidou in Paris, Djinn has gained its status due to its highly influential and unusual form.

**635**

Djinn Series (1965)
Olivier Mourgue (1939–)
Airbourne International 1965 to c.1986

Olivier Mourgue

*2001: A Space Odyssey* (1968), directed by Stanley Kubrick

**The Djinn chaise longue** was the one of the first piece of furniture to be designed with a tubular-steel frame padded with Polyurethane foam. This innovative structure allowed the chaise longue to be shaped with its characteristic gentle curves. Djinn, which was available as either a single or double unit, was wrapped in a removable jersey wool cover in an array of different colours. Its design made it light yet strong, which meant that it was readily portable, being easily carried around under the arm. Djinn was therefore perfectly in tune with contemporary lifestyle trends that advocated the creation of user-friendly objects which were made for dynamic and stylish living. The chaise longue was conceived by the multi-talented French designer Olivier Mourgue, who is also known for his paintings and *jardins imaginaires*. Djinn's identity is derived from Muslim mythology, with its name stemming from the mysterious and powerful beings that are more popularly known as genies, and are best characterized through stories such as that of Aladdin and his genie of the lamp. The chaise-longue's organic shape and colourful appearance attracted the attention of the director Stanley Kubrick, who famously

**The Asahi Optical Company** (AOC), later known as Pentax, was the first to create the Japanese 35 mm single lens reflex camera, the Asahiflex I of 1952. It has been responsible for a number of important innovations in camera design, most notably the first camera with a pentaprism and reflex mirror system, the Pentax Camera of 1957. The design was quickly adopted as the standard SLR design. Founded by Kumao Kajiwara as Asahi Kogaku Goshi Kaisha, the company originally started producing spectacle lenses. In 1923 it began the manufacture of cine projectors and by 1932 and 1933 it was making lenses for Minolta and Konishiroku respectively. The company renamed itself the Asahi Optical Company in 1938 and began work on government contracts producing optical instruments. With peacetime the company returned to producing optics for camera manufacturers and its president Suburo Matsumoto began to explore the possibilities of producing its own range of cameras. Research and development work began in 1950, and in late 1951 a prototype 35 mm SLR camera based on the East German Praktiflex Camera was produced and refined into the Asahiflex, which was launched on to the Japanese market in 1952. The Asahiflex IIB of 1953 introduced a mirror that instantly returned to the viewing position once the shutter had fired. The next significant development took place in 1960 when Asahi Optical Company showed a prototype camera at the international trade fair Photokina. The new camera was called the Spotmatic and took exposure measurements directly through the camera lens; a revolutionary technical achievement. The camera underwent further development and testing and was finally launched in early 1964 as the Spotmatic. The camera had an average reading through-the-lens (TTL) exposure meter that gave more consistent results than that of the prototype. Although Asahi had invented the TTL metering system, the manufacturer, Tokyo Kogaku, beat it to commercial production when its Topcon RE Super was introduced in April 1963. Between 1967 and 1969 Asahi Optical produced two million SRL cameras, much of which was directly attributable to the Spotmatic range. By 1971 the company reached the three million mark. The Spotmatic range of cameras was further refined and the original was joined by several other models, including the ES in 1971, the world's first camera with aperture priority exposure, along with variant body finishes in black paint and chrome. In 1966 the Pentax Spotmatic Motor Drive won the German Good Design of the Year award, the first time the award had been given to a non-German product, and in the same year the Spotmatic Camera was awarded the Good Design prize accolade from the Japanese Ministry of International Trade and Industry. The Spotmatic range was discontinued in 1975 when Pentax introduced a new wider lens mount called the K-mount, although the new cameras were initially based on the Spotmatic models.

**633**

Segmented Table (1964)
Charles Eames (1907–78)
Ray Eames (1912–88)
Herman Miller 1964 to present
Vitra 1974 to present

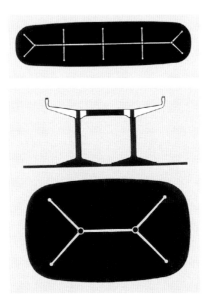

**When Charles and Ray Eames** set out to create a versatile table, able to suit the most diverse needs, they avoided anything complex and created the satisfyingly simple Segmented Table range. Standing almost alert, on aluminium legs, the Segmented Table has become something of a favourite in boardrooms across the world since its introduction in 1964. The primary reason for its popularity is the sheer range of shapes and sizes in which the table is available. The base can be easily dismantled, and the table extended or contracted by adding or removing parts. Whether a boardroom meeting is an intimate talk between two people or a group discussion among twenty, the table can be adapted accordingly. The core components of the table – aluminium legs, black steel pedestals and black steel stretchers – can be matched with a wide variety of tops, whether circular, square or even oval. Herman Miller, which has continually produced the table since it was first designed by the Eames office, offers finishes in white oak, walnut, teak and rosewood, to name but a few. Perhaps the most impressive (and pricey) tabletop available, though, is in white Italian marble. A distinctive aluminium spider base on top of the steel pedestal connects the table's lower half to its top, giving it a reassuring solidity. It is this sort of detail in which the Eameses excelled and, like everything else designed by the husband-and-wife team, the Segmented Table range is a direct consequence of their gift for clear and concise thinking. The tables might not be the most poetic pieces of furniture the Eameses ever designed, but they are certainly among the most practical.

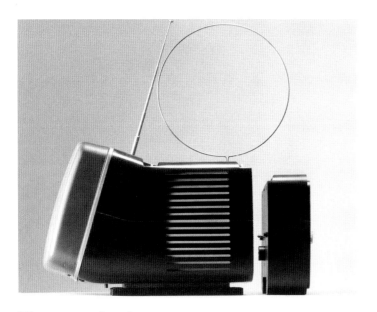

**The recent reissue** of the Algol portable television – now digitally enhanced – substantiates the belief of many experts that twenty-first century television design remains far behind the possibilities of modern technology. This product represents a call for manufacturers and designers to better understand the relationship between designer and producer. Marco Zanuso and Richard Sapper were designers who believed not only in the power of their product's outward appearance but also in the need to shape its internal components to achieve the best possible design. The Algol, which was the first truly portable television (the original model could be powered by battery), was designed keeping its materials, production, and, above all, its user very much in mind. This approach was unique at the time because there was no formal industrial-design education – Zanuso had studied architecture and Sapper philosophy, economics, and graphic art. Sapper and Zanuso gave industrial design a new sense of freedom and responsibility that was different from that of other rationalists of the time. The Algol, a descendent of Brionvega's Doney 14 television (1962), which had also been designed by the pair, is filled with character and intimacy; Zanuso compared the model to a small dog that watched in on its landlady, an effect created by the upward tilting of its screen. The designers placed the controls and antenna at the junction of the tilted curve and the main body of the set, which gives the television a simple organic unity and allows the controls to be found easily in the dark. The plastic of the casing was carefully considered to make cleaning easy, and its metal handle, which sits flush when not in use, feels reassuringly sturdy when the television is carried. The internal components are also arranged rationally to allow for easy maintenance and compactness – design ideas that heralded the onslaught of component miniturization.

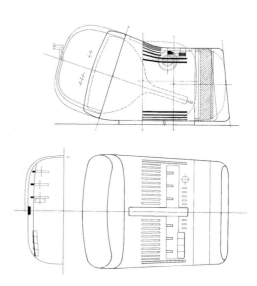

# 631

Model 40/4 (1964)
David Rowland (1924–)
General Fireproofing Company 1964 to present
Howe 1976 to present

David Rowland

**This chair** is one of the most elegant and efficient stacking chairs ever produced – a triumph of structural engineering and visual refinement. In appearance it consists simply of two side frames made from 10 mm (0.39 in) round steel rods. The separate seat and back are made of contoured panels in pressed steel and span between the two side frames. This basic description, however, does not convey the sophisticated realization of the structural detailing and the ingenuity with which Rowland puts these parts together. The exceptionally thin structural profile together with carefully devised nesting geometry means that these chairs will stack together with no gaps between them. Every point on the bottom parts of one chair touches the same adjacent points on the top sections of the chair below. The consequence of this is that the chairs can be stacked very densely and efficiently. Forty stacked chairs take up only 4 feet in vertical height, giving rise to the chair's pragmatic name 40/4. The inventive economy does not end here. To achieve such a thin profile and maintain the required structural rigidity, additional bracing was needed within the steel rod frame. Rowland ingeniously added flat flanges to the back leg elements, which not only provided the necessary rigidity but also enabled the chairs to be locked together in rows. A plastic foot detail is also used to connect the chairs together in line. Using back and base plane to lock chairs in line turns a linked group into a lattice beam. Four link-locked chairs can be picked up together and stacked in groups of four if needed. Locked lines of chairs are therefore evenly spaced – ideal for dense auditoria and conference environments. Unsurprisingly, the chair's space economy and versatility has been much copied, but none of the copies has yet outranked the original – and definitive – model.

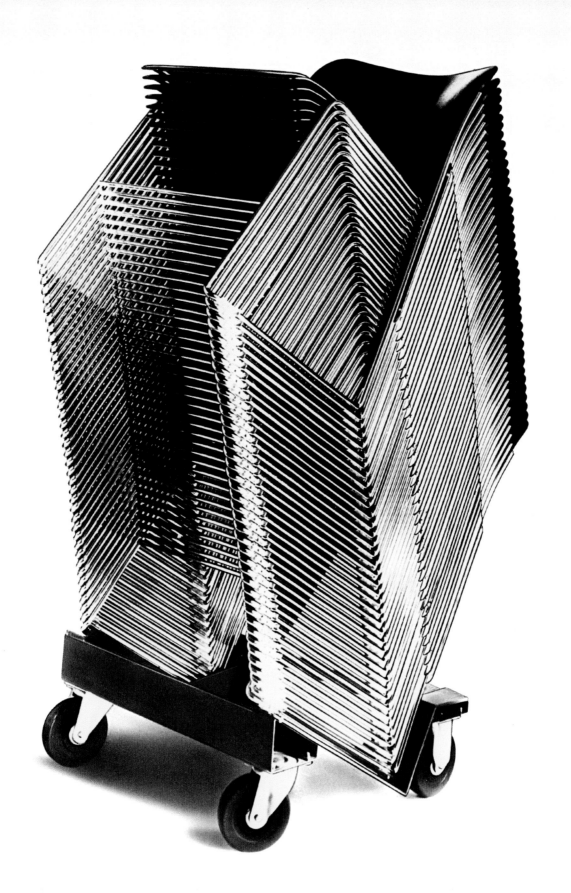

**Viewed from the front** the Lockheed SR-71 'Blackbird' is a breathtakingly sinister and dramatic sight. This 33 m (107 ft) strategic reconnaissance aircraft is an extraordinary technical achievement; it was one of the most significant breakthroughs in supersonic travel and also marked the beginnings of stealth technology. The design challenge for Clarence L Kelley Johnson and his legendary Skunk Works team was daunting. The demands of supersonic travel at three times the speed of sound, or Mach 3, meant that virtually every facet of the craft had to be specially adapted so that it could withstand the environmental challenges of supersonic waves and extremes of heat caused by flying at a maximum speed of over 3,200 kph (2,000 mph), at maximum altitudes of over 25,900 m (85,000 ft). The idea was that the 'Blackbird' would travel so fast that it could neither be shot down nor properly detected on radar equipment as it collected classified global intelligence for the US government. Work began in the late 1950s and the Blackbird's earliest manifestation, the A-12, first flew in April 1962. Just two years later, the slightly larger SR-71 took to the skies and was ready for operational service in January 1966. In order to facilitate the supersonic needs of the craft, it was built almost entirely of titanium alloy, with a heat-resistant glass cockpit, both of which ensured that the plane could withstand high temperatures. The two pilots also had to wear pressure suits in case of sudden pressure loss during flight. The unofficial name 'Blackbird' derives from the special jet-black paint used to coat the craft, adding further to its portentous and intimidating air. The paint assisted the aerodynamically designed bodywork by absorbing the maximum amount of radar signals to prevent detection behind enemy lines; it also radiated away some of the incredible heat that the craft produced in flight. Unsurprisingly, the 'Blackbird' is the holder of numerous records. One example that makes commercial transatlantic flights seem sluggish is its flight on 1 September 1974, covering the distance from New York to London in a staggering 1 hour, 54 minutes and 56 seconds. Although the fleet was officially retired in 1990, NASA has since used SR-71s for research and scientific flights and in 1995 the Skunk Works team refurbished two 'Blackbirds' for the US Air Force.

THE NEW YORK TIMES, SATURDAY, JULY 10, 1971
*Dishes That Have Been in Museums*

Max 1 tableware was first designed by Massimo Vignelli and received the coveted Compasso d'Oro at the Milan Triennale, the same year of its design. The modular service is successful in its design solution to stacking and function, and as a simple clean form. The design was originally produced for a brief period in melamine by the Italian company Giovenzana before being picked up several years later and mass-produced using the original moulds by the newly formed American company Heller. Originally marketed as Max 1 dinnerware, in 1972 further items such as mugs were added to the service marketed under the title of Max 2. The Max 1 set consisted of a rectangular base tray, which was square at one end and rounded at the other; six sets of large plates, small plates and small bowls; two more small bowls with lids; and a large bowl with lid. The service was expanded from 1970 with the addition of a sugar bowl, creamer and the cup and saucer, which were designed in that year. The cup was discontinued after a short production run and replaced a mug, called the Maxmug, designed in 1972, which became a bestseller. The final pieces added to the line included a series of square and rectangular trays, which were the only flat designs with right angles, other than the base tray and the pitcher, designed in 1978. Vignelli's dinnerware has been in continuous production by Heller since 1971. The current production range consists of the dinner plate, salad plate, soup/cereal bowl and mug, all in white, making the earlier brightly coloured pieces highly collectable. The stacking system owes its immediate popularity to the interest in both systems furniture and products that stacked and interlocked, and the use of plastics such as melamine, ABS and polythene. Such system design had the function of being space saving, but the design also showed the potential for plastics to look good in the home and be used for an integrated alphabet of shapes. As Vignelli declared, 'The size of the plates, their edge-wall concept, their stackability, and the brilliant rainbow colours quickly captured consumers' attention, and the product became a symbol of contemporary houseware.'

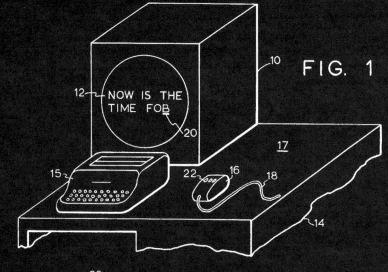

FIG. 1

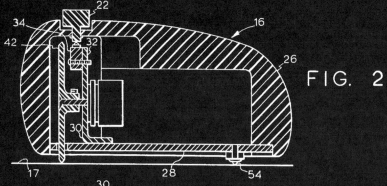

FIG. 2

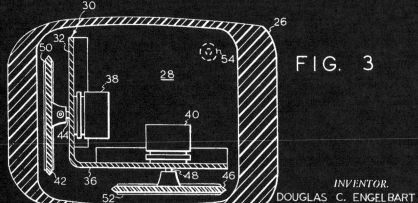

FIG. 3

INVENTOR.
DOUGLAS C. ENGELBART
BY
Lindenberg & Freilich
ATTORNEYS

# 628

Computer Mouse (1964–8)
Douglas Engelbart (1925–)
Apple 1984 to present
Various 1984 to present

**Four years in the making,** the first common pointing device was bulky, had a single button and used two gear wheels perpendicular to each other; the rotation of each wheel was translated into motion along one axis in the plane. It was developed by Douglas Engelbart, graduate of electrical engineering at Oregon State University. It has been nearly forty years since the unveiling of the mouse to a thousand computer professionals at the Stanford Research Institute, California in 1968. It is widely believed that alongside the use of the graphical user interface, the mouse is probably the most important factor leading to the success of the household personal computer. The mouse evolved further at the Xerox Palo Alto Research Center, notably with the introduction of a rolling-ball mechanism replacing the wheels, making it more commercially attractive. The mouse appeared before the public in 1981 in the Xerox Star Workstation and then, in 1984, Apple Macintosh popularized the mouse even more, selling it alongside the first home computer. Despite the mouse's ability to induce the debilitating Carpal-Tunnel, Synovitis and Rotatorcuff syndromes, its invention alone has been imminently influential. Engelbart's mouse has led to many kinder interpretations in the form of graphic tablets, trackballs, pointing sticks and the touchpads now integrated into laptop computers. However, studies have consistently shown that the mouse outperforms these devices for its pointing ability. Since its creation, the shape of the mouse has been reinvented in numerous forms and has developed from a box-like form into the more ergonomic shapes in use today. The mouse is one of the most commonly used devices of our time, and is constantly being developed to evolve and improve the ease and performance of our interaction with computers. Contemporary versions are now cordless and generally deploy more sophisticated infrared and Bluetooth technologies. Douglas Engelbart was also responsible for a number of interactive information systems taken for granted today: windows, shared screen teleconferencing, hypermedia and groupware.

Douglas Engelbart

**627**

Tokaido Shinkansen (Bullet Train) (1964)
Hideo Shima (1901–98)
Japanese National Railways 1964 to 1987
Central Japan Railway Company
1987 to present

**The Tokaido Shinkansen** or Bullet Train, the world's first intercity, high-speed railway system, began operations on its route of over 500 km (311 miles) between Tokyo and Osaka in 1964, in time for the opening of the Olympic Games in Tokyo. Symbolizing Japan's remarkable recovery from the devastation of World War II, the design made a major contribution as the country's principal transportation artery. It was immediately hailed as a triumph as it shortened the journey time between Tokyo and Osaka from six and a half hours to about three hours, with the trains running at a maximum speed of over 210 kph (130 mph), contributing to economic growth. The nose profile was reportedly based on that of the DC-8 aeroplane, which represented state-of-the-art international air travel in the 1960s. The Shinkansen standard track gauge of 1,435 mm (56.5 in) enabled 25 m (82 ft) long bodies to be built wider than previous trains running on the standard Japanese 1,067 mm (42 in) gauge. The interiors became more spacious, and the seats could be rotated to face the direction of travel, or form bays of four or six seats. Initially formed as twelve-car units, all cars were powered by an overhead supply. Power was provided by traction motors driving each axle, rather than the European model of using a single locomotive unit to pull a train. The electric multiple-unit system was chosen for various reasons: the axle load has even weight distribution, which does not put as much pressure on the structure of the track. Moreover, the brakes could be applied to all the axles at once and a failure of a car did not affect the whole operation of the train. The Shinkansen trains have run for an aggregate distance of 1 billion km (621 million miles), transporting over 3 billion passengers since their initial service in 1964. They have never suffered a derailment or collision accident, and are renowned for their legendary punctuality, creating the highest level of efficiency, safety and reliability of any train system in the world. The success of Japan's Shinkansen is such that it has been adopted as the template for high speed railways, such as the TGV in France.

mm.

135 · 390 · 475 · 475 · 390 · 135

110 · 390 · 390 · 110

posizione fori

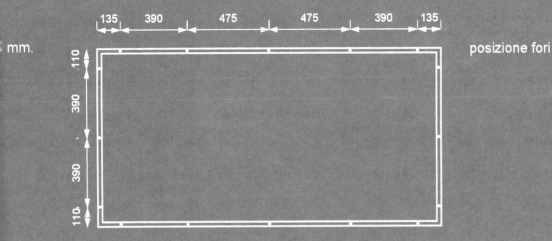

pianta

Ø 8 foro svasato

Ø 4

scala 1:5

12,5

22

R 3

foro per gommino          pianta base

sezione tubo

Ø8  foro svasato

Ø 4

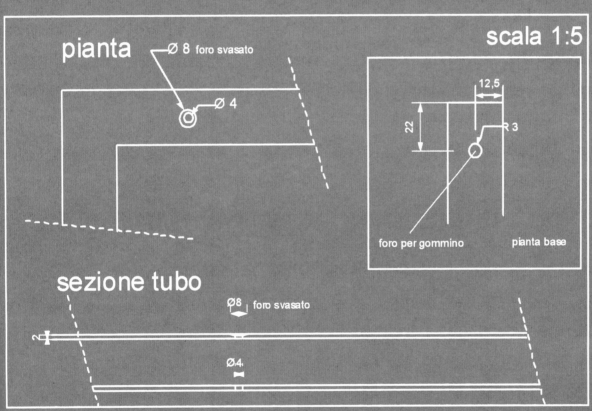

cappellini

**Prodotto** FRONZONI Tavolo FR/27

**Materiale** base metallo verniciato, top truciolare          **Data** 05-06-2001

**Descrizione**                                    **Rev.**     **Scala** 1:25    **Unità** mm

**Progettista** Fronzoni          **Responsabile** Massimo Marelli

**Autore** Michela Catalano          **Cod. progetto**          **Cod. disegno**

Via Marconi 35 - 22060 Arosio (co) Italy - Tel. +39-31-759111 - Fax +39-31-763322 - e-mail: cappellini@cappellini.it - web: http://www.cappellini.it

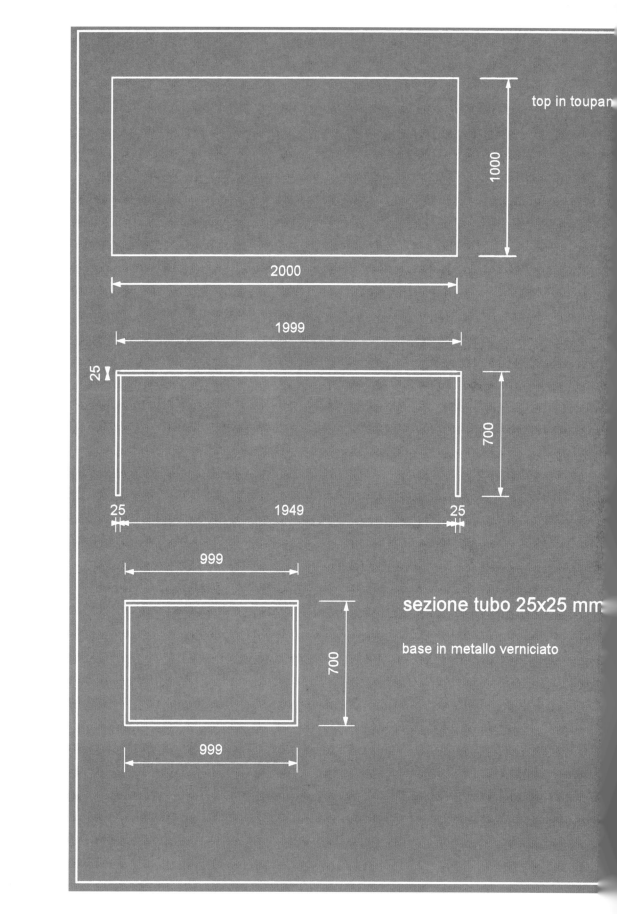

top in toupan

1000

2000

1999

25

700

25    1949    25

999

sezione tubo 25x25 mm

700

base in metallo verniciato

999

Tavolo 64 (1964)
A G Fronzoni (1923–2002)
Pedano 1972 to 1974
Galli 1975 to 1978
Cappellini 1997 to present

**Minimalism has become** a fashionable word, used rather loosely to describe objects that have been pared down to the bare essentials through a combination of simple forms, materials and colour (or lack of it). A G Fronzoni's table of 1964 encapsulates the true meaning of the word, as the designer's reductionist approach gave rise to an object that consists only of the essential elements needed to function. The designer has created a table of universal acceptance that avoids any references to a particular culture, country, company, individual or era. Developing the concept mathematically, Fronzoni captured the necessary dimensions for efficiency using a square tubular-steel base with a wooden top of the same thickness. The geometric design is produced in black or white, as any other colours would surely imply subjective decision-making by Fronzoni. The result should be devoid of any 'designer' personality. Fronzoni believed that the pure, graphic and unobtrusive form, derived from his dislike of waste and excessive decoration, would place more emphasis on the objects and environment surrounding it. That said, cluttered surroundings might have the effect of making the table stand out even more. A bed, chair, armchair and shelving unit also accompanied Fronzoni's table design of 1964. For the designer it was important that this brutally honest collection should communicate its objectives in isolation, without contextualizing additions. Designs of such striking simplicity were a gutsy statement as, indeed, such creations could perhaps be considered too easy, obvious, simple or plain. The collection must act as a reminder to subsequent designers of the overriding importance of remembering practicality before becoming too concerned with technical and material innovations, ergonomic subtleties and emotionally driven styling touches.

**625**

Cesta (1964)
Miguel Milá (1931–)
DAE 1980s to 1995
Santa & Cole 1996 to present

**Designed by** the Barcelona-born architect turned industrial and interior designer Miguel Milá, the Cesta lantern is a landmark piece in modern Spanish design. And although the lantern is instantly recognizable to the generation of 1970s households that grew up with it, the uninitiated would be forgiven for questioning exactly which continent the design hails from. This is because the Cesta is a collection of contradictory design influences. For instance, the delicate cherry wood frame, incorporating a tall, domed handle, is reminiscent of the portable torches that originated in China, or the lanterns that appeared in Japanese palaces of the Edo period. But the effect of the delicate wooden structure set against the ambient glow of the oval glass dome is warm, and possibly Mediterranean, in feel. Milá's inspiration came, in fact, from the traditional lanterns that were hung outside coastal homes, as a signal to returning fishermen. And while the designer enjoyed the rustic nostalgia of the historical context, his architectural leanings and meticulous eye for detail created a lamp that ultimately would feel more at home on the contemporary terraces, salons and balconies of Spain's more discerning residences. By housing the glass globe within a frame, the lantern becomes as much a piece of furniture as a mere decorative lighting flourish: the structure of the frame is a piece of architectural ingenuity in itself. Both the design of the frame and the attached sweeping handle, use heat-curved cherry wood to elegant effect. In addition, all mechanical components used in the frame, including the screws, are made from wood and carefully concealed from view. In 1996, the design was upgraded from the original by replacing the Manila cane frame with cherry wood, upgrading the plastic shade to an opal crystal globe and by adding a dimmer to moderate light intensity. The lantern remains in production today by Spanish lighting and furniture specialists, Santa & Cole, who produce various vintage designs.

**George Nelson's** Sling Sofa is made of six loose black leather cushions supported by a fabric-reinforced webbing hung from a tubular chrome frame. Nelson's inspiration for the sofa allegedly came from the seat design of his car, the Citroën 2CV. Intrigued by the composition of the latex-supported seat, Nelson developed his design, which led, after three years, to the production of the Sling Sofa. Although the use of bent tubular metal could be seen as a reference to the earlier work of Marcel Breuer, who in 1925 had designed the first bent tubular metal chair, Nelson's final design is an example of excellence in advanced technique, and a departure from both previous tubular metal furniture and upholstered furniture designs. Seating design always appealed to Nelson. In his 1953 book, *Chairs*, Nelson noted that every culture seems to focus its decorative efforts on particular symbolic items and that post-World War II, designers focused on chairs. During this time built-in storage systems, recessed lighting and a modernist approach to clutter meant that the design spotlight could focus on seating. Over a period of twenty-five years Nelson's collaboration with Herman Miller allowed him to create some of the most pioneering designs of the modern era. When commenting on his chief designer, Herman Miller famously wrote that he 'is not playing follow the leader'. The Sling Sofa was one of Nelson's last major seating designs for Herman Miller. After that his attention turned largely to the design of office environments.

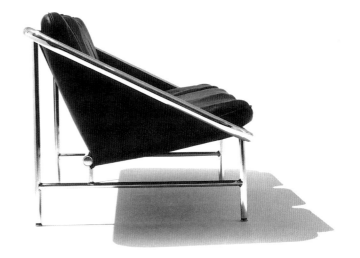

Mikoyan MiG-23 Flogger (1964)
Mikoyan-Gurevich Design Bureau
Russian Aircraft Corporation MiG
1969 to 1980s

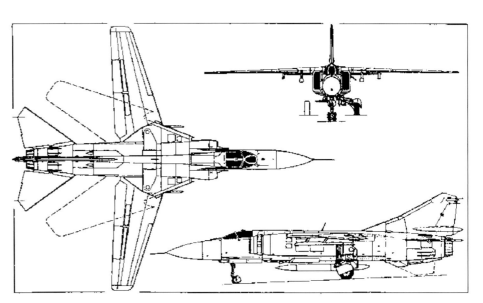

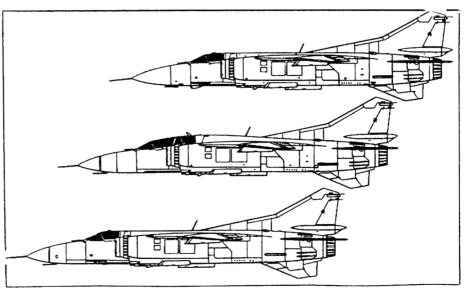

## Designed and built in the Soviet Union by

the Mikoyan-Gurevich Design Bureau, the first prototype of the MiG-23 Flogger (a reporting name given to it by NATO), was displayed in June 1967 at an air show fly-past at Moscow's Domodvedovo airport. It was an important moment. A lot was invested in this new fighting machine, which it was hoped would become a hard-hitting rival to its US contemporary, the powerful Phantom F-4. Designed by Arton Mikoyan (1905–1970) and Mikhail Gurevich (1896–1976), it has garnered mixed reviews since the MiG's entry into military service in 1979. Its lack of agility, the subsequent high demands on the pilot and some notably poor performances in combat have not made it a favourite in the annals of aviation history. However, this doggedly tough fighter cannot be so easily written off, and for good reason: it has seen service in over twenty countries including the former Czechoslovakia, Poland and Iraq, and the Flogger was only officially retired from the Soviet Air Force in the late 1990s. It is certainly not the most attractive of craft, with its large, flat wings attached to a thick, tubular fuselage and a small cockpit, which gave pilots very limited visibility. But the Flogger's daunting strengths lie in its considerable weaponry capacity and a powerful engine that enables this heavy

fighter to travel at supersonic speeds of over 2,400 kph (1,500 mph) at Mach 2.35. It was primarily designed to be a fighter-interceptor but could also second as a ground-attack aircraft, with its near relation the MiG-27 specifically designed to be a ground bomber. More significantly, optimum versatility came from the MiG-23 being one of the first fully operational variable-geometry aircraft. Using swing-wing technology the plane was able to adjust its wing's position to 16, 45 or 72 degrees, thus giving the MiG-23 incredible adaptability in the uncertain and often treacherous conditions of war. Prior to the MiG-23, all Russian fighter jets required a prepared and long runway for take-off. By moving its wings to the forward position (so that the wings offered greater wind resistance) the Flogger could take off from semi-prepared strips even when carrying its maximum load of weaponry, and for the same reason could land safely and gradually on rough surfaces. However, when the wings were set back, the drastically reduced resistance enabled the craft to go at supersonic speeds that even today rate the MiG-23 as among the fastest fighter planes of all time.

# 622

Perch Stool (1964)
George Nelson (1908–86)
Bob Propst (1922–2000)
Herman Miller 1964 to present
Vitra 1998 to present

**This tall, narrow stool** was a part of the 1964 Action Office that George Nelson designed with Bob Propst. The framework of Action Office 1, created for Herman Miller, was an innovative office furniture system made of several freestanding units whose diverse configurations could be adapted to suit the changing needs of the office. The Perch Stool was so called because the designers wanted workers to have a place to perch while doing stand-up work. In keeping with the ergonomic belief that movement is healthy, the Perch's design encourages the user to change work positions regularly throughout the day. The Perch has a small, foam-padded, height-adjustable seat. A separate padded backrest may also be used as an armrest. The ring-shaped tubular steel footrest helps the sitter stay 'perched' in a comfortable position. The Nelson-Propst collaboration was instrumental in the creation of new office furniture that could cater for changes in office planning. In particular, Nelson is often credited as the founder of the modern open-plan office, helping to create the style for many corporate environments in 1950s America. As the design director of Herman Miller, Nelson developed the first L-shaped desk, a precursor of today's workstation, and the table lounge unit sofa, a flexible-use seating system that has a slab space between the cushions that can function as a table. Whilst still in production by Herman Miller, Vitra also started producing the Perch in 1998 due to the increasing demand for furniture suitable for flexible working environments. Touch-down points, conference call rooms and multi-purpose workstations are all scenarios that are increasingly being adopted by employers in a bid to cater for a mobile workforce. The Perch Stool, which provides both standing and sitting positions, and which can also be employed by those standing in informal and dynamic conference scenarios, continues to respond to the evolving needs of the workplace.

**It is difficult to imagine** that this long lamp comes in such a small box. Once unpacked and hung from the ceiling, the Falkland lamp extends to its full 165 cm (66 in) length. Designed by the Italian artist and designer Bruno Munari, this lamp has been manufactured by Danese since 1964, and formed part of its foundation. The shade is made from a stocking-like, white elastic knitwear tube, attached to a stainless-steel cone at the top. Within the tube six aluminium rings of three different sizes are attached. When hung from the ceiling, the weight of the carefully positioned rings stretches the material of the tube into a scalloped sculptural form. There is also a freestanding version, Falkland Terra, in which the sleeve is suspended from a long rod within, which is attached to the base. Bruno Munari started his career as a graphic designer, and joined the Futurist movement, creating advertising in this style for such companies as Campari and Pirelli. Later, he designed a wide range of products including books, toys and furniture. The Falkland lamp is thought to have been inspired by the growing interest and technology surrounding space travel at that time, but Munari's works were also often inspired by nature, particularly in their structures and forms. The shape of the Falkland lamp is reminiscent of bamboo. He described this relationship as 'industrial naturalism', ie. the imitation of nature using technology and man-made materials. From this philosophy a flexible, lightweight, foldable and, most of all, beautiful lamp was created. Munari was also fascinated by geometry, especially the circle. In his book *Discovery of the Circle* (1965), he wrote 'the square is closely connected with man and his construction, while the circle is related to the divine', and this lamp is a successful example of his ideas.

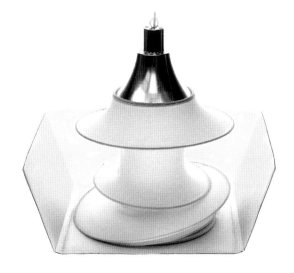

George Nelson

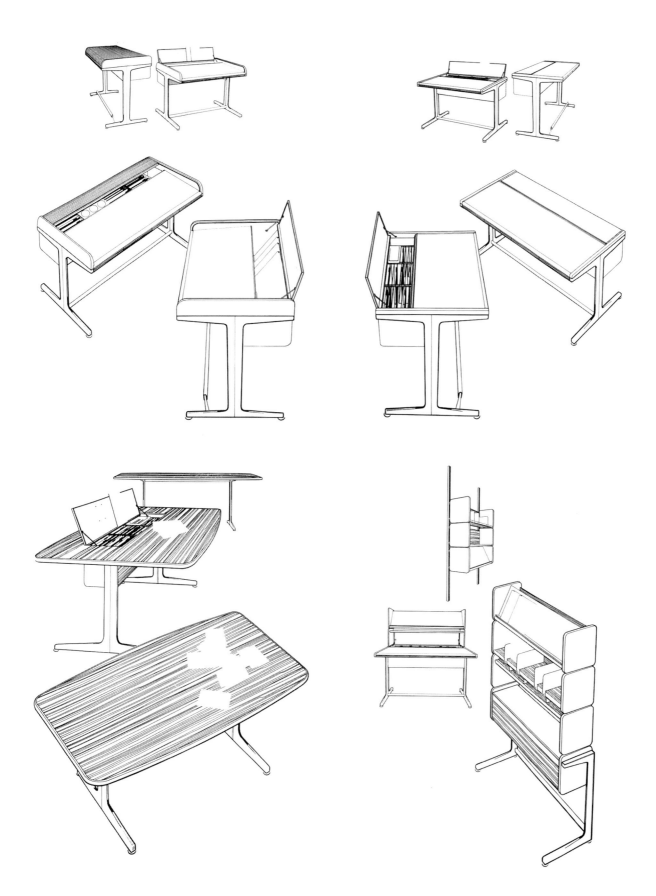

Action Office 1 (1964)
George Nelson (1908–86)
Robert Propst (1922–2000)
Herman Miller 1964 to 1970

**With storage space** for hanging files at the back and slim, pull-out drawers at the front, George Nelson's 1964 Action Office Desk was a wake-up call to the musty world of office furniture. The low Action Office Desk was only one component in a series of revolutionary designs that would alter the office space forever. The 'Action Office 1' was a concept devised by Robert Propst, an employee of Herman Miller, following three years of research into the culture of American offices. Propst's studies led him to conclude that the American office was 'a wasteland [that] saps vitality, blocks talent and frustrates accomplishment'. What the office needed, he concluded, was not just chairs and desks but something that is now taken for granted: an office furniture system. George Nelson, then Herman Miller's design director, was entrusted with transforming Propst's suggestions into coherent components, and so designed a sit-down desk, a high desk, a storage unit and a 'communications console'. The desks had roll-top covers that could be closed at the end of the day, and which were close to the desk surface to prevent in-trays from rising too high. A designated area for files kept information close at hand. The tall desk was intended for less formal meetings and times when employees needed to stretch their legs, while the communications console was a place to take private phone calls. All of the pieces have polished aluminium bases and wooden tops, and all are designed with contours rather than corners, to encourage a less aggressive office atmosphere. In 1965, Herman Miller claimed that the Action Office 1 was for 'the new breed of thinkers, writers, scientists, professionals and executives who are interested in personal productivity'. The Action Office 1 was produced by Herman Miller until 1970. Although it has, over the years, undergone various redesigns, it is George Nelson's original, elegant scheme that still inspires the most affection.

**For many furniture designers,** chairs are the ultimate test. For those trained as architects, chairs are little buildings that posit concepts they will explore on a larger scale. Industrial designers create chairs that explore new technologies and materials, while artisans often invest familiar form with visual subtleties. Helmut Bätzner's stacking chair realizes many of these goals. Launched at the Cologne Furniture Fair in 1966, it set a new standard for a multi-use stackable chair. Produced through the 'prepreg process' (i.e. using material pre-impregnated with resin, to make it tougher) and employing a ten-ton double-shell heated press, it was compression-moulded of fibreglass-reinforced polyester resin. This technology could form a chair in five minutes and required minimal finishing. The former carpenter turned architect and academic had produced the first single-piece mass-produced chair. Gracefully articulated rectangular planes form its back and seat. The compressed shell form exploits the curves where its legs meet the seat, removing the possibility of cracks and breaks. To add material and strength to the chair's legs, Bätzner triangulates their corners in a structure that inverts that of typical solid legs. The thinness of the chair's membrane and its subtly angled legs all facilitate stacking. Manufactured by what was formerly known as Menzolit-Werke Albert Schmidt, the Model No. BA 1171 Chair was distributed by the Bofinger Company and thus is sometimes referred to as the Bofinger Chair. Although it was discontinued in the 1990s, the chair's production process has since been used to produce countless plastic outdoor furniture designs.

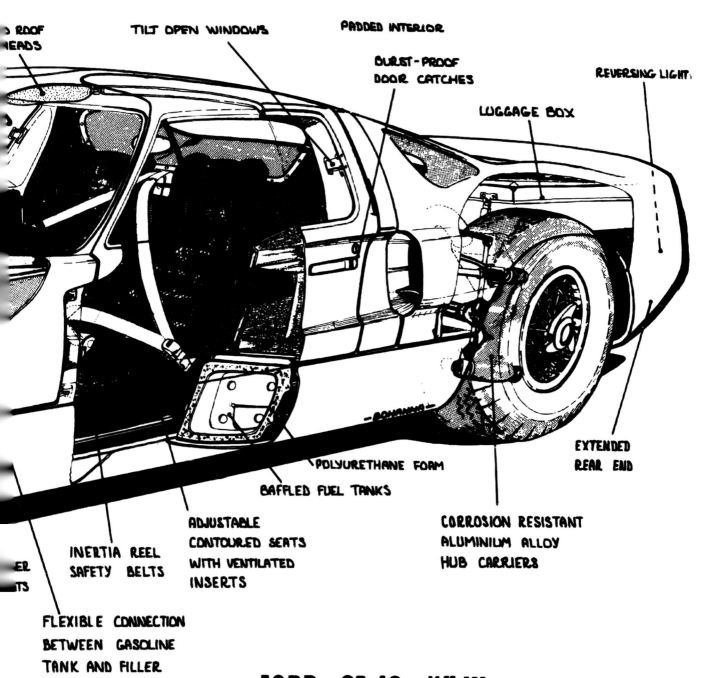

ROOF
HEADS

TILT OPEN WINDOWS

PADDED INTERIOR

BURST-PROOF
DOOR CATCHES

REVERSING LIGHT

LUGGAGE BOX

POLYURETHANE FOAM

BAFFLED FUEL TANKS

EXTENDED
REAR END

CORROSION RESISTANT
ALUMINIUM ALLOY
HUB CARRIERS

ADJUSTABLE
CONTOURED SEATS
WITH VENTILATED
INSERTS

INERTIA REEL
SAFETY BELTS

ER
TS

FLEXIBLE CONNECTION
BETWEEN GASOLINE
TANK AND FILLER

# FORD GT 40 MK III

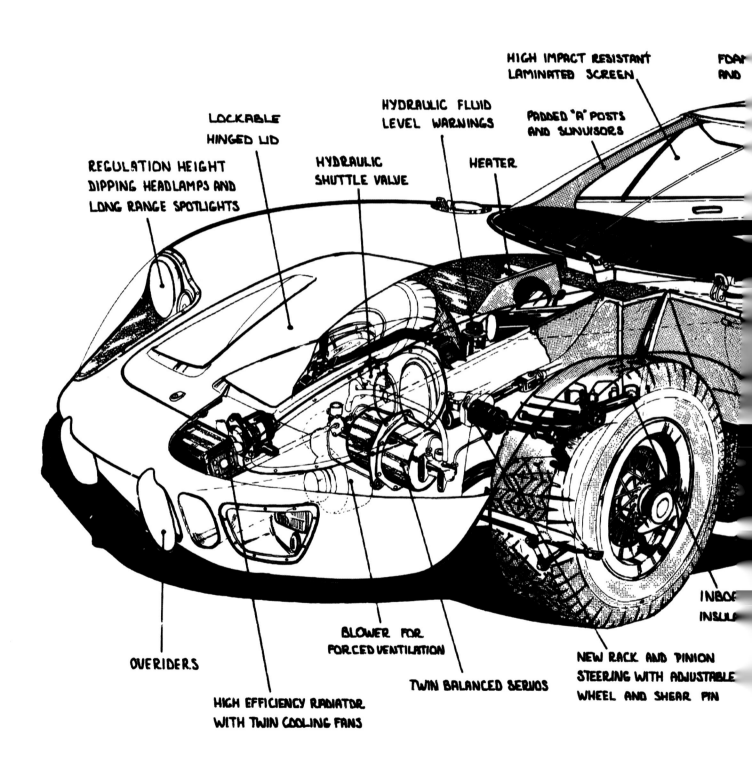

HIGH IMPACT RESISTANT
LAMINATED SCREEN

FOAM
AND

HYDRAULIC FLUID
LEVEL WARNINGS

PADDED "A" POSTS
AND SUNVISORS

LOCKABLE
HINGED LID

HEATER

HYDRAULIC
SHUTTLE VALVE

REGULATION HEIGHT
DIPPING HEADLAMPS AND
LONG RANGE SPOTLIGHTS

INBO
INSUL

OVERIDERS

BLOWER FOR
FORCED VENTILATION

NEW RACK AND PINION
STEERING WITH ADJUSTABLE
WHEEL AND SHEAR PIN

TWIN BALANCED SERVOS

HIGH EFFICIENCY RADIATOR
WITH TWIN COOLING FANS

**Rather like** all great sports teams, to make their mark on the popular consciousness racing cars have to win the big events. Ford took its GT40 into first, second and third at the 1966 Le Mans race, in France. Legend has it than when the company was rebuffed in an audacious bid to buy Ferrari, it promised to build a car that would beat the Italians instead. While this is very possibly true, Ford also had some legitimate business reasons for building the new supercar. According to the company's then executive vice president, Charles H Patterson: 'Our racing programme is… a prudent business investment. Our product improvements and sales records can be attributed to many factors, but we have no hesitation in stating that racing is one of them.' The company's bid to win Le Mans started in 1963 with the development of the Mark I GT40. Initial studies showed that all the essential components could be installed in a vehicle silhouette 396 cm (156 in) long and 102

cm (40 in) high  – hence the car's name – while its shape was developed to be as aerodynamic as possible. To keep size down to a minimum, for example, the car possessed two separate fuel tanks, each with its own filler cap. However, it still had to be relatively comfortable for a driver who would be in the cockpit for four hours at a time. Rather than having an adjustable seat, Ford created movable pedals that could be changed depending on the size of the driver. The Mark I was finished on 1 April 1964, just in time for the Le Mans practice later in the month. In the race itself none of the GTs made it to the finish line, and it would take another two years of development until the Mark II-A achieved the company's goals. Proof that the car's appeal was still intact came at the beginning of the new millennium when Ford revived the GT40 to widespread acclaim.

# 617

Superellipse Table (1964)
Piet Hein (1905–96)
Bruno Mathsson (1907–88)
Bruno Mathsson International
1964 to present
Fritz Hansen 1968 to present

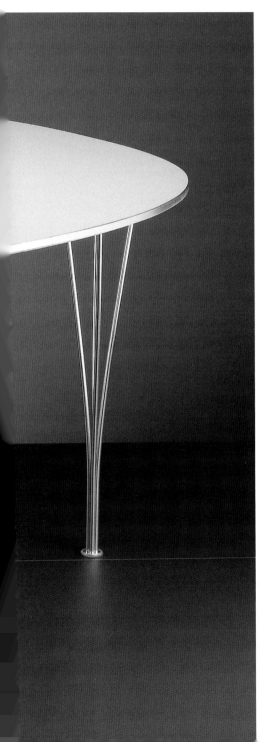

**At first glance** the Superellipse Table might appear a simple, straightforward design. On closer scrutiny, its incredible complexity becomes apparent. The table's shape, somewhere between a rectangle and an oval, is not the result of a designer's doodle but is the outcome of lengthy mathematical research. In 1959, Piet Hein, a Danish poet, philosopher and mathematician, was asked to design a town plaza in Stockholm to help ease the flow of traffic around the essentially grid-structured city. A circle or oval, he soon realized, would not prove space efficient and a rectangle would produce too many corners for cars to turn. The answer, he worked out, was to be found in the formula $(x/a)n + (y/b)n = 1$, where the exponent $n = 2.5$. This produced an entirely new shape, which he termed the Superellipse. Bruno Mathsson, a pioneering designer and craftsman from Sweden, soon saw the revolutionary potential in the Superellipse and began working with Hein to translate it into a table. Just as it had proved space efficient at Segels Square in Stockholm, the Superellipse also proved useful as a table in cramped city apartments. The additional advantage of the shape, though, was that it did not allow for the hierarchy of a 'head'. It was for this reason that the Superellipse was chosen for the 1969 Paris Peace Conference to discuss the future of Vietnam. Below the tabletop another ground-breaking design can be found: a self-clamping leg. The leg is made of metal rods that fit snugly under the table and have the advantage of being both rock solid and easily detachable for transportation. When first designed in 1964, the Superellipse was produced by Karl Mathsson's small family firm, Mathsson International, which is still producing it today. Four years after its design, Fritz Hansen began producing a similar table, attributed to Piet Hein with contribution to the base design by Bruno Mathsson and Arne Jacobsen.

# 616

**Nesso Table Lamp (1963)**
**Giancarlo Mattioli (Gruppo Architetti**
**Urbanistici Città Nuova) (1933–)**
**Artemide 1965 to 1987, 1999 to present**

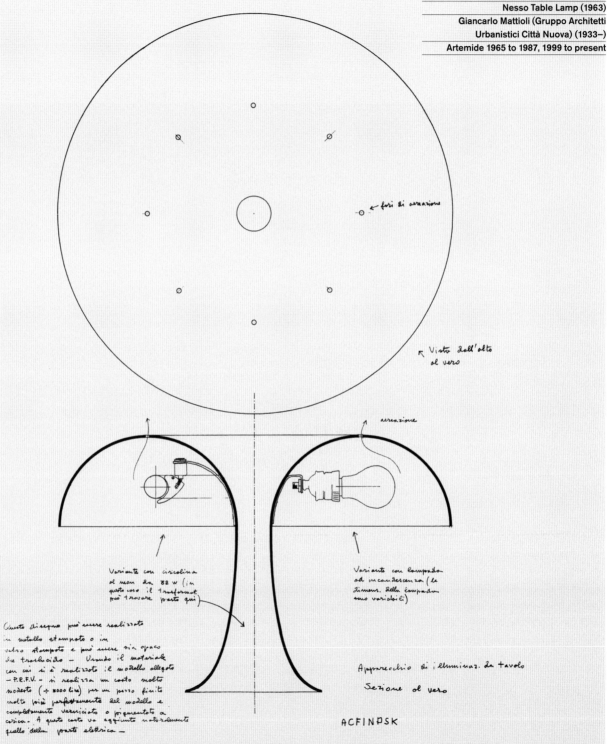

← fori di aerazione

← Vista dall'alto al vero

aereazione

Variante con circolina al neon da 32 W (in questo caso il trasformat può trovare posta qui)

Variante con lampada ad incandescenza (le dimens. della lampada sono variabili)

Questo disegno può essere realizzato in metallo stampato o in vetro stampato e può essere sia opaco che traslucido — Usando il materiale con cui si è realizzato il modello allegato — P.R.F.V. — si realizza un costo molto modesto (± 2000 lire) per un pezzo finito molto più perfezionato del modello e completamente verniciato o pigmentato a colica. A questo costo va aggiunto naturalmente quello della parte elettrica —

Apparecchio di illuminaz. da tavolo

Sezione al vero

ACFINDSK

**Winning a design** competition does not always lead to success but it did in the case of the Nesso Table Lamp, designed by Giancarlo Mattioli and Gruppo Architetti Urbanistici Città Nuova. A competition formed by the manufacturer Artemide and the cutting-edge magazine *Domus* in 1965 led to the introduction of the Nesso Table Lamp. The psychedelic 1960s was a time of great experimentation with plastic, especially in Italy, where there was an explosion in new design. Using the new plastic technologies and materials, Italian designers created everything from chairs to houses. Artemide was a leader in the design and manufacture of plastic furniture and lamps in the 1960s, which led to its involvement with the revolutionary design group, Memphis. The Nesso Table Lamp is a perfect example of the possibilities of plastic technology when used well. The form uses the translucent quality of plastic to its best advantage, creating a shape that glows from within, mimicking the glow of phosphorous. The Nesso embodies Italian style of the 1960s in its use of colour; bright orange and white were prevalent in all things plastic. The injection-moulded, translucent Nesso lamp is a very simple design statement. Uncluttered, formally pure, and unobtrusive, it happily compliments any interior, which explains why it is still in production, over 40 years since it was fisrt designed. The fact that it is both a wall lamp and a table lamp further enhances its flexibility. Artemide has recently introduced a smaller version of the lamp, named Nessino, which is manufactured in many transparent colours, including red, blue, orange, grey, and yellow. The transparency enhances the design, revealing the internal structure and the light sources. The Nesso endures as an icon of 1960s Italian design, outliving many of its contemporaries because of its clarity of purpose, and by the way it simply declares itself a lamp.

the UK's *Melody Maker* magazine. Among the millions who saw *Hard Day's Night* again and again was Roger McGuinn, guitarist with The Byrds. Inspired by the film and The Beatles' other output he put the 360-12 to work on The Byrds' records such as 'Turn Turn Turn' and 'Hey Mr Tambourine Man', which themselves did much to define the jangly sound of mid- to late 1960s Pop. The 360-12, like other Rickenbackers of the time, had a totally distinctive design that went back to the guitars of the mid-1950s, with their large, double cut-away tulip-shaped bodies and cat's eye slashes instead of the usual f-holes, a look which became the company's signature. Such was the popularity of the guitar in the wake of Beatlemania that a six-week waiting list stretched to six months. Meanwhile, the LA-based firm would often receive mail addressed to 'Rickenbacker, Liverpool, England', so strong was the association with the Fab Four in customers' minds. Although Rickenbacker guitars fell out of fashion in the 1970s, they were soon back in favour again with later users including Paul Weller, REM's Peter Buck, Lloyd Cole and The Smiths' Johnny Marr.

**The Rickenbacker's** place in rock 'n' roll legend is arguably down to owner Francis Hall's quick thinking when he heard that a bunch of mop-topped boys from England calling themselves The Beatles would be crossing the Atlantic for the first time in early 1964. Hall contacted The Beatles manager Brian Epstein and arranged a demonstration of several amplifiers and guitars at a New York hotel. Among them was the yet to be launched 360-12 string model. Although George Harrison was unwell, John Lennon was so impressed with the guitar he took it to the sick Beatle's room at the band's neighbouring hotel and the two bonded instantly. Thereafter, the 360-12's unique, chiming tone became a hallmark of The Beatles sound, announcing itself spectacularly in the opening chord of 'A Hard Day's Night' and used later on 'Ticket to Ride' and numerous other chart-toppers. Although Lennon had used an earlier 325 Rickenbacker for several years, the 360's unique sound and its prominence during the onset of Beatlemania in America and the band's film debut, *Hard Day's Night*, made it even more influential. It was dubbed 'the beat boys' secret weapon' by

**61-4**

Mercedes-Benz 230 SL Pagoda (1963)
Friedrich Geiger (1907–66)
Karl Wilfert (1907–70)
Daimler-Benz 1963 to 1967

Motor Type 230 SL, 1963–7

**By the late 1950s** Mercedes had re-established its racing credentials with the Gullwing, or the 300SL, and the 190SL, but by the turn of the decade the company realized that it had two cars appealing to the same market. To solve the problem the Mercedes design team took the practicality of the 190SL and the elegance of the Gullwing to create a light, stylish model that was the 230 SL Pagoda. This manual standard transmission, with large vertical frontal headlamps, had a 2.3 1 in-line six-cylinder engine, and a top speed of 200 kph (125 mph). Introduced in 1963 at the Geneva Motor Show, in many respects the 230SL was technically behind its legendary predecessor, the 300SL. Certainly its drive aped the less loved, but less expensive 190SL.

However, it was saved from ignominy by its exterior, particularly the detachable, 'pagoda-shaped' bowed, hard-topped roof. Typically, the curved top, designed by Daimler-Benz development engineer Béla Barényi, was no mere styling tick but was created for safety and structural reasons, although it perhaps took away the potential for higher speeds. Coincidentally, when in place it also allowed for an unusually large amount of headroom, as well as providing stability due to the lightness of the whole structure. The passengers were further protected by 'crumple zones' at the front and back of the chassis. This was the first model to have a removable hard top, a design feature which has been carried through to today's SL models. Despite this, in terms of pure

motoring, the 230SL is possibly best remembered for being the first of a successful trio of cars that shared the same styling but improved upon their performance with each subsequent model. It was initially succeeded by the 250, but this was only in production for three years before being replaced by the 280, which arguably stands at the summit of the series. Whatever the arguments surrounding the merits of the three pagoda models, they all sold extremely well, with 19,831 230SL models produced between 1963 and 1967. They have also managed to age well. Over thirty years after the last one rolled off the factory floor, the 230SL remains hugely sought after.

The Astro Lava Lamp and its various prototypes

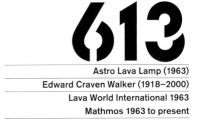

**Inspired by the design** of an egg-timer, Edward Craven Walker invented what we now call a Lava Lamp by using coloured wax in an oil-based solution. A bulb at the base of the lamp gradually heats the wax, causing it to rise and swirl in amorphous patterns. As the wax reaches the top, it cools and begins to fall, repeating the display and floating and revolving like an astronaut until the lamp is switched off. In 1963, Walker, through his UK-based company Crestworth, launched his first model, the Astro Lamp. By 1966, two American entrepreneurs who had seen the lamp at a trade show bought the rights to manufacture it in North America. The Astro Lamp was renamed the Lava brand motion lamp and was manufactured by Haggerty Enterprises, doing business as Lava World International. As sales increased, new models began to appear and it soon became an essential item in stylish homes. Embodying the mood of the 1960s, the lamp was a constantly changing piece of art, to be privately contemplated or enjoyed in the company of groovy friends. The lamp's serpentine movements and hypnotic patterns created an original visual experience that seemed to gel with the 'flower power' generation. Its fluidity echoed the free spirit of the hippy culture and the lamp's popularity continued to grow. In the 1990s Crestworth Trading was remarketed under Mathmos and, with a new-found trend for 1960s nostalgia, the lamp enjoyed a repeat of its original success. New lamps were developed and external designers were hired, such as Ross Lovegrove, who designed Fluidium, a modern version of the Pop classic Astro Lamp. In July 2000, the British Design Council officially declared the original Astro Lava Lamp a design classic.

Edward Craven Walker

# 612

Laminated Chair (1963)

Grete Jalk (1920–)

Poul Jeppesen 1963

**Grete Jalk**

**One special feature** of the Danish furniture industry, and one that was often cited as key to the seemingly miraculous growth of Danish furniture exports during the 1950s and 1960s, was the degree of formal collaboration that existed between furniture designers and cabinet-makers. It was an arrangement that allowed the designer a special freedom to experiment, notably in preparation for the exhibition of the Copenhagen Cabinet-makers' Guild, an important annual event at which new and trial designs were first presented to the public and the furniture trade. During the this period these exhibitions were known as the place to see the most challenging new design. To be sure, some of the more experimental designs were remarkable only for their outlandish improbability and were quickly forgotten, but others, such as Grete Jalk's Laminated Chair, exhibited in 1963 on the stand of the cabinet-maker Poul Jeppesen (now P J Furniture), were immediately recognized for their originality, visual flair and structural ingenuity. Jeppesen and Jalk had been collaborating since the mid-1950s and began experimenting with furniture made from wooden laminates in the early 1960s. The Laminated Chair is the best-known result of the collaboration and by far the most surprising. It is extreme and angular, and its sharply bent folds of plywood seem to involve compressing the material far beyond its natural limits. Jalk's *tour de force* succeeds in part through understatement: the separate elements of the bent plywood that form the seat and back are assembled with bolts in a straightforward and practical way (in its sobriety an approach characteristic of the Danish furniture industry) as if the chair were almost ordinary. Jalk called the design Laminated Chair in her personal presentation material but it is also referred to as the Rest Chair in official museum files, and only 300 were ever produced.

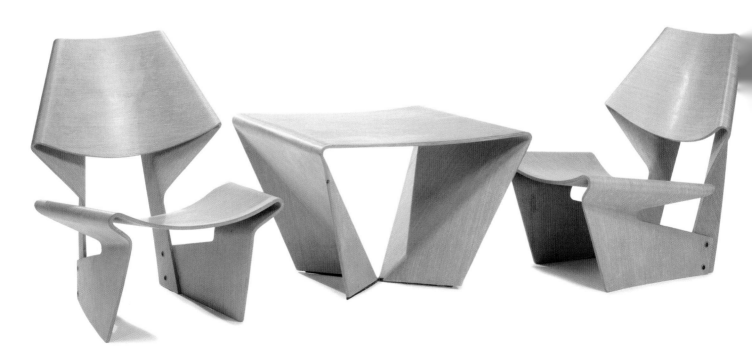

**611**

Chevrolet Corvette Sting Ray (1963)
Chevrolet Design Team
Chevrolet 1963 to 1976

**The Chevrolet Corvette** was initially created by a combination of the creative talents of the legendary Harley Earl and Robert F McLean in 1953, and still exists today. Yet it was not until the launch of the 1963 Sting Ray version that it truly cemented its position as an American icon. Obviously powerful but not quite as brutish-looking as the models that were to follow, the second generation Corvette was created by a combination of styling from Bill Mitchell and Larry Shinoda, and a chassis created by Corvette's chief engineer Zora Arkus-Duntov. The Sting Ray was based around work Shinoda, a keen racing enthusiast, had been doing on the 1960 Stingray Racer and the XP-755, and included features such as rotating hidden headlamps and the V-8 engine from the 1962 model. However, it was perhaps most notable for the thick bar that bisected the rear

window, earning it the nickname 'the split window coupé'. Interestingly, according to some critics, the 1963 model was the fussiest of all the Sting Rays: it had fake vent grilles in the bonnet as well as decorative gills in the front fenders. Yet the American public loved it and bought it in droves. In 1963 Chevrolet built more than 20,000 Corvettes; by 1966 that number had grown to more than 27,000. Shinoda continued his work on the Corvette, coming up with the third generation model in 1968, which was liked but never quite loved in the same way as the 1963 model. After leaving for Ford and working on the Mustang, he would return to the car once again in 1989 when he designed the Rick Mears Special Edition Corvette, a special model based on the 1984–89 production car.

Kodak Carousel Projector S (1963)
Hans Gugelot (1920–65)
Reinhold Häcker (1903–76)
Eastman Kodak Company 1963 to 1992

**Kodak first introduced** its innovative carousel format in 1961. The 'jump-proof', 'spill-proof', and 'long-play tray' design allowed up to eighty slides to be viewed in rotation and quickly became the standard in preference to its more cumbersome linear predecessors. This was the format on which Hans Gugelot and Reinhold Häcker created their innovative design in 1963, now recognizable as the model on which all others were subsequently based. The cast-aluminium housing makes for an extremely robust device, which could happily endure the sometimes severe environments in which it was used. It is a timeless piece of equipment design, which requires little or no instruction to use; all parts are clearly laid out in a very rational order with the operational controls easily identified in black. The principle functions of forward, reverse and load are managed by just two circular buttons at the rear of the machine, while the focus and height adjustments are made with rotary knobs at the front. For Gugelot, who had worked as a designer for Braun, and had taught at the influential Hochschule für Gestaltung, Ulm, this typified the efficient and rational approach to which he aspired. His rejection of styling in all its forms led to the development of a systems-based approach to industrial design, which has endured to this day. The Carousel Projector S was a very successful and much copied design. It sold in its thousands for over twenty years, while Kodak became the world's largest manufacturer of slide projectors. Production of its carousel range ceased in June 2004 among protest from fans the world over. Despite its efficiency and popularity, slide technology could no longer compete with digital projectors, which had become cheaper, lighter and more versatile.

You can ride anything with a MAKAHA! Well . . . almost anything. We don't suggest that you tackle the San Francisco heavies your first day out, but it'll out-perform any other board in the world. Just check out what they're doing in the photos above. It's the only skateboard designed by top surfers to look and handle just like a surfboard. Phil Edwards, Mike Doyle, and Mike Hynson ride MAKAHA. Why not drop into one of the friendly MAKAHA dealers listed here and give it a test ride yourself!

SOUTHERN CALIFORNIA: MAY CO., BROADWAY DEPT. STORES, BUTLER BROS., KERR'S, CLARK DRUGS, BULLOCK'S, ROBINSON'S. SAN FRANCISCO: MACY'S, EMPORIUM, ROOS ATKINS. OAKLAND: CAPWELL'S. NEW YORK: MACY'S. NEW JERSEY: BAMBERGER'S. MIAMI: JORDAN MARSH.

Please send me the Makaha skateboard for $12.95 ($13.95 east of the Rockies) postage included to:

name _____

address _____

city _____ state _____ zipcode

**Send Check or Money Order to
Box 1278, Santa Monica, Calif.**

"CHICAGO" Roller Skates

CHICAGO QUALITY ROLLER SKATE PARTS ARE USED EXCLUSIVELY ON MAKAHA SKATEBOARDS

Advertisement, 1960s

MAKAHA

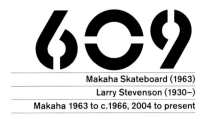

**Humanity's desire** to speed down hills of snow, water or concrete seems hard-wired, which might lead certain members of the generation raised on extreme sports to wonder what people did before the advent of skateboards. Long before the first professionally designed and manufactured board came on the scene, kids around the United States were constructing their own makeshift models with dismantled roller skate wheels and a simple plank of wood. The first commercial Roller Derby Skateboard hit the market in 1959 in a slightly evolved form, and appealed to boys and teens whose imaginations were already caught by the rise in popularity of surfing. The spread in appeal of 'sidewalk surfing', however, was largely due to a surfer-cum-publisher named Larry Stevenson, who saw that surfing had a stylish and money-generating popularity that could extend to land-locked areas far from the beach communities in Hawaii and California. Stevenson began publishing articles about the new sport in his magazine, *Surf Guide*, and organized team expositions and the first-ever skateboard contest. He expanded his surfboard company Makaha to include the design and sale of the world's first professional-quality skateboard in 1963. Replacing metal wheels with clay versions and altering the rectangular plank to a more surfboard-reminiscent curvilinear form, Stevenson's 24- and 18-inch models were the progenitors of the modern skateboard. Although Makaha sold in excess of $4 million worth of skateboards from 1963 to 1965, widespread incidents of injury, and in rare cases, death, put a damper on the sport's evolution in the mid-to-late 1960s. Hailed as a 'new medical menace' by the California Medical Association, skateboarding foundered in popularity across the country, only to regain interest in the early 1970s. In 1969, Stevenson patented the kick tail, a feature that added not only greater control for the rider, but also a means for creating tricks, and was widely copied, much to his chagrin. By this time, the skateboard's further evolution became piecemeal, with additions like a pressure-moulded fibreglass body by surfer Hobie Alter in 1973 and urethane 'Cadillac' wheels by boarder Frank Nasworthy the same year. The skateboard continues to evolve with technological innovations pioneered by manufacturers, but the spirit of the sport, and the cult that surrounds it, still has as much to do with the personal touches and customizations that die-hard proponents apply to their boards. As such, the skateboard has become the tabula rasa for a worldwide subculture's collective imagination.

**Everything about this chair** is youthful. Firstly, it is made precociously from paper with a strong colourful surface pattern, not really a serious, grown-up material or treatment for a chair. Secondly, its designer Peter Murdoch designed the original when he was still a student at the Royal College of Art in London. Finally, its conception in the early 1960s makes it truly a child of its time. In spirit, material and philosophy it is a perfect manifestation of the emerging mass-consumer culture of the period. In this decade notions of stability, longevity and the status quo were questioned and challenged. Both high and commercial culture were fused together in Pop Art. To be progressive in this period was to be mass-produced, instant, cheap, light, portable and throwaway. This chair caught the very essence of the period. The quintessential flat pack, the chair was literally the equivalent of the container it might otherwise have been packaged in: itself a flat sheet of laminated paper, die cut and folded into a three-dimensional shape in the same manner as a cardboard box. The lamination used three types of paper in five layers with a polyethylene surface coating. When folded it produced a structure that was durable enough to support a child's weight. It was ideal for high-volume production and could be produced on a single machine at a rate of one chair per second. Unfolded, 800 chairs stacked in a pile only 120 cm (4 ft) high, making for highly efficient transportation and storage. The chair was sold in its sheet form, eliminating assembly time from its production cost. It was then simply folded and assembled by the customer, without the need for special skills or tools. Despite all of this, the chair was not a long-term commercial success and production ceased after only a few years, yet it continues to remain important in rhetorical terms.

Barboy (1963)
Verner Panton (1926–98)
Sommer 1963 to 1967
Bisterfeld & Weiss 1967 to 1971
Vitra Design Museum 2001 to present

**Verner Panton** is renowned for his 'colourscapes', amazing psychedelic interiors formed from undulating stripes of concentrated colour. They were essentially lounges whose walls, floor and ceiling flowed seamlessly into each other, offering an improbable array of soft foam seating options covered in new stretch fabrics. The early 1960s saw many new materials and technologies become available and was, unsurprisingly, a boom period for Panton and his countless ideas for curvaceous, colourful furniture. The Barboy was designed during this period for the German company Sommer and manufactured until 1967 under the trade name 'Declina'. It is, like most of Panton's work, an attempt to reduce an object to an externally minimal form. Untypically though, it is made using a traditional technology from earlier in the century: formed plywood. The curved plywood components are carefully joined together to create a series of different cylinder compartments to house bottles, glasses, or corkscrews, which rotate around a pivot to one side of the main body. The Barboy was finished with a very high-gloss lacquer, available in red and violet, two of Panton's favourite colours, as well as black and white. Of the few more geometric pieces Panton designed, which included a family of cylindrical plywood seats and tables, also for Sommer, the Barboy remains the purest. It is perhaps this purity of form which has ensured the Barboy's survival. Production was taken over by another German company, Bisterfeld & Weiss, from 1967 until 1971. Finally, after thirty years out of production, it was reissued by the Vitra Design Museum, but only in black or white. The monochromatic options available on the reissued version probably also help it to sit happily apart from Panton's fantastical full-colour environments.

sportiva

*elegante*

SCHE

Dr.-Ing.h.c.F.Porsche KG · Stuttgart-Zuffenhausen · Printed in Germany · Juni 1967 · Entwurf Strenger · Foto Barth

*elegante*

sportiva

PORS

**Such was the Porsche** company's enormous success with its 356 model, its postwar car which took the firm through the 1950s, that the decision to create a follow-up car which would acquire a world-renowned status represented an enormous challenge. It was met head-on by a member of the third generation of the Porsche family, Ferdinand Alexander Porsche, better known by his nickname 'Butzi'. Until then the Porsche contribution had been primarily one of sophisticated engineering skills. The visual language of the cars had been provided by Erwin Komenda who had worked with Ferdinand Porsche since the prewar years. Butzi was the first member of the Porsche family to study design. On graduation he worked with Komenda in the body shop. His first challenge was to find a replacement for the 356, a challenge which was also being met by two other employees of Porsche, Heinrich Klie and the American stylist, Albert Goertz, who worked in the modelling department. The result of all their labours was the 911, launched in Frankfurt in 1963. The genius of the 911 lay in its respect for its predecessor combined with an updating which made it a car of its time. Re-utilizing all the well known and successful visual strategies, but pushing them forward at the same time, the 911 was an integrated, restrained, aerodynamic machine with nothing included in its design which was not integral to its high performance and the superior experience of driving it. The subtle changes of curve and line that were implemented served to remove it from the streamlined era of the 1930s in which the 356 had originated and brought it in line with the look of the day which was less bulbous and more refined. Until the twentieth-century, the Porsche company continued to rework this successful design, updating it to create new models.

Ferdinand Alexander 'Butzi' Porsche

**During the 1960s** the Canon Camera Company sought to introduce cameras that would appeal to a mass market. An earlier model, the Cine Canonet 8-mm still camera was launched in January 1961 with this specific aim. It was a compact type 35-mm camera with a fast f/1.9 lens and automatic exposure control, all for under ¥20,000. The low price had delayed the launch by six months, with competitors complaining that the price was too low to compete with. Upon its introduction, a week's worth of stock sold out in only two hours; within two and a half years 1 million Canonet cameras had been sold. The camera came with the slogan 'Anyone can buy it and anyone can take pictures with it' and the public appeared to agree. Having had such success with an amateur still camera, Canon turned its attention to the movie camera market, which at the time was a significant part of the wider photographic market. The first Canon 8-mm movie camera (and only the third movie camera to have been made in Japan) had been introduced in 1956 and had been awarded a G-mark Good Design prize by the Japanese Ministry of International Trade and Industry. The Cine Canonet 8-mm Camera was designed by the team behind the Canonet still camera and featured a simple, modernist design. This camera was brought to the public in September 1963 with a price of ¥27,800. Physically the camera was compact, making use of an electric motor, reflex viewfinder and new compact 2x zoom lens, which combined a focusing and zoom group of lens elements, making the camera pocketable. Sales were disappointing and it failed to do as well as the Canonet still camera. It was not as distinctive as expected and Eastman Kodak's introduction of the more versatile Super 8 format in April 1964 undoubtedly had an impact on the camera's success. Canon continued producing 8-mm and other format movie cameras until production was halted in 1985 when the video camcorder gained dominance in the market.

# Canon
## CINE CANONET 8

A compact cine developed by Canon engineers...
When it comes to packing big camera features into a
pocket size case, the Cine Canonet 8 represents a
revolution in design engineering.

Its zooming range is between 10 and 25mm. Film
is advanced by a micro-motor. The CdS exposure
meter is coupled to the lens diaphragm and geared
to filming speeds for automatic aperture setting. Built-
in battery checker eliminates power failure while filming. With full brightness viewing and focusing...right
through the lens.

A compact detachable grip with wrist strap is available
for easiest manipulation of the exposure.

All the finest of Canon's know-how in producing 8mm
cine cameras have been incorporated within slim
(32.5mm) and compact body...

You'll get thrill out of having this pocketable Canon
Cine Canonet 8.

Make the Cine Canonet 8 your traveling companion.

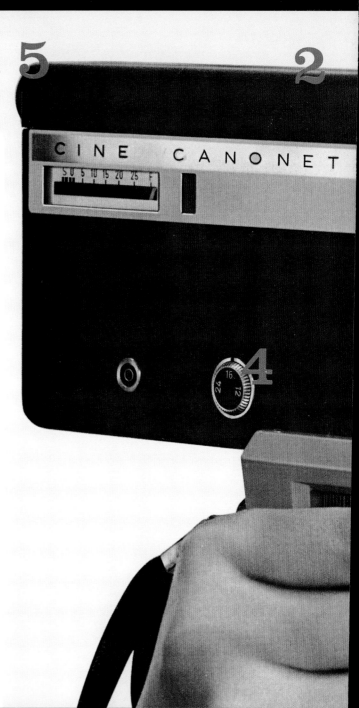

Samsonite Attaché Case (1963)
Samsonite Design Team
Samsonite 1963 to 1988

**The unassuming** outline of the Samsonite Attaché Case of 1963 disguises a revolution in the postwar design and use of luggage. Worldwide air travel was booming in the early 1960s and there was a growing demand for innovative luggage to respond to the liberated means of travel. The streamline, hard-shell casings with recessed locks and moulded handles were evocatively modern in style and in use of material. The pioneering design was lightweight by virtue of the use of injection-moulded polyvinyl chloride, a material allowing for uniform surface texture and colour, which proved highly durable. Various colours were available and the luggage was quickly accepted by a growing consumer base of business and pleasure-seeking travellers. The success of the Attaché and the fortunes of Samsonite relied on this design being carefully researched by designers Willard Axtell, Clair Samhammer, and Melvin Best, who looked at the perspectives of design,

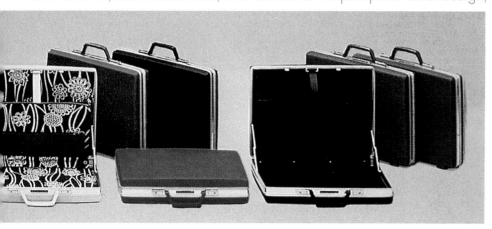

materials and process, as well as through an acute understanding of market needs. Further, the launch of the range was supported by a visually appealing advertising campaign and a solid distribution base to ensure the product reached the targeted market. By 1965 the Attaché and Samsonite (which was originally founded in 1910 by Jesse Shwayder and called Shwayder Trunk Manufacturing Company) were world-renowned. Following the success of the Attaché, Samsonite realized the Saturn suitcase range in 1969, marking another milestone through the utilization of a fully supported injection-moulded polypropylene shell. The company has grown and diversified with licensed international markets and a range of travel-based brands. The brand profile for design-led, innovative, high-quality luggage remains crucial to the core company's success and the design of the Samsonite Attaché Case remains a key reference in the way modern, hardside luggage is designed and produced.

exceptionally high quality, is produced by Tendo Mokko, a pioneer of moulded plywood products in Japan who also manufacture Sori Yanagi's Butterfly Stool of 1956. Fujimori's Zaisu was originally designed for the guest rooms of the Morioka Ground Hotel as part of his commission to design the interiors. Although the hotel has since been renovated and does not keep the original interior, the Zaisu has always been in production. It remains very popular, particularly for Japanese-style hotels and recently, for Japanese restaurants outside of Japan. It is now made in three different types of plywood – keyaki, maple and oak – and has been in production continuously. In the 1950s Fujimori was sent by the Japanese government, to study product design in Finland. His fusion of Scandinavian and Japanese thinking into a single object, has resulted in an innovative seating solution, and is a result of his enduring involvement in Finnish design institutions, directing the Japan-Finland Association for seventeen years.

**In the Japanese home** people remove their shoes upon entering. Traditionally, there are no chairs and people sit, with or without cushions, directly on the tatami floors. Tables are generally low and designed to be used for a low sitting position. In response to a desire for something to lean back on while sitting on the floor, and to add an element of formality and dignity, particularly, for senior figures or guests, the zaisu ('za' meaning to sit on the floor, and 'isu' is chair) was invented. This particular design by Kenji Fujimori

in 1963 has become recognized as the definitive zaisu – able to be stacked and inexpensively mass-produced. Although minimal in form, it is very comfortable to sit on, with the back shaped to support the spine. The hole in the bottom of the seat prevents the chair from slipping on the floor; it also reduces the chair's weight. The chair also tessellates beautifully, an important factor for Japanese houses. As rooms are usually required to be multi-purpose, it is important that everything, like the futon beds, can be packed away. This chair, of

**602**

USM Modular Furniture (1963)
Paul Schärer (1933–)
Fritz Haller (1924–)
USM U Schärer Söhne 1965 to present

## The USM Modular Furniture

system appears as a totally rational storage solution. The highly resolved furniture range is based on three simple components: the sphere, connecting tubes and steel panels. From these basic elements an infinite range of configurations may be realized and a host of storage needs satisfied. The spheres act as joints to link a skeletal framework constructed to the user's specification and panels enclose storage areas where required. The closed storage boxes may house drop-down doors or drawers, or merely be enclosed on two or three sides. The ingenuity of the system relies on Fritz Haller's ability to rationalize the design to this minimal component count without sacrificing functionality. The austere design is constructed to a very high quality, and whether coloured panels or open storage is specified the range exudes an extremely refined air. Fritz Haller had already developed a reputation for formalist architectural building systems inspired by the work of Mies van der Rohe when he was commissioned by Paul Schärer in 1961 to design a new factory for USM. The company had been founded in 1885 by Ulrich Schärer in Munsingen (hence USM) and produced sheet metal and construction. Haller's pioneering concept for modular flexibility in architecture allowed for both exterior and interior features, such as walls, doors and windows, to be dismantled and moved within a steel framework. Schärer was so impressed with Haller's architecture that he commissioned the architect to design a range of modular furniture for the offices. Thus was the Haller system born. The response to the system was such that Schärer and Haller realized they had a viable commercial product. The USM Haller system was launched in 1965 and soon transformed USM from metal manufacturers into makers of high-quality office furniture. The system typifies the qualities of a highly resolved design solution and has changed little over the last thirty-five years. Its timeless qualities, and spare decoration, provide use for both the home and the office. It generates a $100 million turnover in Western Europe alone.

# 6O1

Kodak Instamatic (1963)
EKC Research Division
Eastman Kodak Company 1963 to 1989

**The Kodak Instamatic range** of cameras was launched in 1963 with a new drop-in cartridge film, the Kodakpak cartridge, also known as 126. A range of cameras was launched to accompany the film, with the basic Instamatic 50 introduced in February and models 100, 300, 400 and 700 in March. Each camera had a plastic, moulded body, with the basic controls of shutter-release button and film advance set into the top. Each camera had provision for flash photography and the later models had automatic exposure. The model 400 had a low-light indicator in the viewfinder window and clockwork film advance. Compared to the traditional box camera – many of which had been updated during the 1950s and some which had stylized plastic injection-moulded bodies – the Instamatic range of camera was compact, taking advantage of the 35 mm film producing 28 x 28 mm negatives compared to the larger roll films used in box cameras. The idea of a drop-in cartridge was not a new one (cameras using them date from the 1890s) but roll film was more popu-lar and Kodak's range of cameras from the mid-1890s successfully made use of it. However, roll film was not without problems and amateurs frequently experienced difficulty loading it correctly. The 1950s saw a boom in camera sales and in amateur colour photography. There was also increasing competition from Japanese products, with 35 mm film gaining ground. In the late 1950s Kodak's 'Project 13', code-named 'Easy Load', was initiated to design a camera system – both camera and film – that would, in effect, be a 35 mm snapshot camera that was simple to use and capable of producing good results. This was completed in 1961. The camera and cartridge both made use of postwar plastic injection-moulding techniques. The cartridge would simply drop into the back of the camera and could only fit one way. The cartridge design formed a light-tight seal between the camera and cartridge. New fine-grain and faster film emulsions allowed the smaller negative size to be enlarged with no noticeable loss of quality and the cartridge eliminated all the handling problems associated with traditional roll film. The plastic camera bodies and high-quality acrylic lenses could be mass-produced. The concept was phenomenally successful and by 1970 more than fifty million Instamatic cameras had been sold, replacing the box camera at a stroke. Kodak licensed other manufacturers to produce cameras taking 126-cartridges and only discontinued the range in 1989. Kodak developed the concept further with the 1972 launch of the Pocket Instamatic, which took the smaller 110-cartridge. The later disc and APS formats failed to meet the success of the 126-cartridge.

Jucker Table Lamp (1963)
Afra Scarpa (1937–)
Tobia Scarpa (1935–)
Flos 1963 to 1995

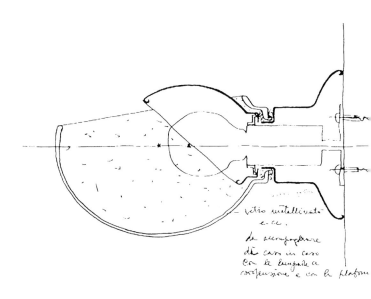

## The Jucker Table Lamp

neatly encapsulates the spirit of the 1960s and today remains as charismatic as a collector's item as it was when first showcased in 1963. Standing only 21 cm (8.3 in) high, the table lamp is comprised of an enamelled metal base and shade, painted head-to-toe in a choice of colours ranging from emerald green to red, white or black, all in tune with the strong 1960s palette. From the base the design mushrooms upwards to encompass a round, oversized bulb. The domed shade topping off the lamp is attached to a pivot, which allows it to move back and forth over the bulb. From this perspective, Jucker's appearance could be likened to that of a sleepy eye, with the shade being a heavy eyelid blinking over the light bulb, or eyeball. Whereas technical innovation was widely significant for 1960s design, Jucker owes more to other characteristics of the era – those of convenience, accessibility and informality. Of particular relevance, therefore, is this ingenious tilting shade. It moves around the bulb, enabling the light to be varied on a scale that grows from a subdued glow when the shade is pulled level, to a bright glare when the shade is pulled back to its farthest reaches. Simple, inexpensive and flexible: the Jucker Lamp proved attractive to the trend-driven modern consumer. The Jucker Table Lamp also typifies Tobia and Afra Scarpa's love of classic form over some of the more strident statements emerging at that time. In 1962 Tobia Scarpa joined Pier Giacomo Castiglioni in designing the founding models for the newly formed Flos company, a market leader in lighting-design innovation ever since. He continued working for Flos throughout the 1960s and for part of the 1970s, implementing designs around the latest halogen technology. Sadly, Jucker was taken out of service in 1995 as Flos's portfolio grew larger.

Pioneering plastics designer Eero Aarnio sought to design a chair that would generate a private space around it. The result was the Ball Chair (called the Globe Chair in the US), whose shape defined, in the simplest way, the space around the person sitting in it. Produced in moulded fibreglass on a painted aluminium base, with a reinforced polyester seating section, it was presented at the Cologne Furniture Fair in 1966. The fibreglass sphere is perched on a swivelling central leg, creating the illusion that the sphere is floating while enabling it to rotate 360° on its central axis. The upholstered inside, fitted with a red telephone, creates a cocoon, a warm private space within the home where the sitter can close him or herself off from noise, relax or have a private conversation. The design reflected the dynamic social style of the 1960s, and the Ball Chair immediately became a metaphor of its time. Featuring in films such as *Tommy,* influential interiors such as one of Vivienne Westwood's show-rooms and widely used on magazine covers from household to adult titles, from its launch in 1963 to the present day, the Ball Chair has been synonymous with the 'goodtime' lifestyle. It pays tribute to Eero Saarinen's Tulip Chair, which was the first to introduce a one-legged pedestal base as a device for clearing up the visual space taken by legs. It introduced the idea of a seamless flowing shape, which was achieved by painting the fibreglass shell and its aluminium base in the same colour. In a way the Ball Chair was a contemporary version of the traditional club chair, but Eero Aarnio's was the first one to really achieve, in a simple and honest way, a truly independent space, 'a room within a room'. And it is his treatment of the object as a kind of mini-architecture that makes this chair a very contemporary and influential design proposition. In 1990 all of Aarnio's fibreglass designs were licensed to Adelta and the Ball Chair, which was reissued in 1991, is still available on the market, with over sixty interior fabric colour options.

599

Ball Chair (1963)
Eero Aarnio (1932–)
Asko 1963 to 1985
Adelta 1991 to present

Eero Aarnio

# 598

**From the moment** a perfectly dressed and dashingly handsome Sean Connery emerged from his specially made silver birch Aston Martin DB5 in the 1964 film, *Goldfinger*, this already successful model was cemented in popular culture as an emblem of exciting, fast-paced living and 1960s style. The 007 version of the DB5 came fully equipped, with ejector seats, spinning extendable spikes on the wheel hubs, bulletproof windows and missile launchers lurking behind a no-nonsense grille. Although the other 1,021 models that were produced by Aston Martin between 1963 and 1965 did not come equipped with these unusual features, the car was, and still is, an enviable possession. The DB5's body is the essence of sleek and unembellished motorcar design, and aesthetically it has long been considered the most beautiful of the DB series. The DB5 also brought significant engineering improvements to its 1961 predecessor, the DB4. Its new six-cylinder engine increased the

car's capacity to 4 litres (1 gallon), giving the DB5 an impressive top speed of 230 kph (143mph) and the ability to go from 0 to 96.5 kph (0 to 60 mph) in just 8.1 seconds. Inevitably though, the DB5 remains most lovingly remembered for its starring role in *Goldfinger,* and *Thunderball* a year later. As Bond's Aston Martin streaked along in a flash of silver with machine guns blazing, it effectively inscribed itself into history as the eloquent and perfected symbol of late modaernity. The original 007 DB5, that Connery drove, was stolen from an airport hangar in Boca Raton, Florida, in 1997 where owner, Anthony Pugliese, was storing it, and sadly, it has never been recovered. However, before its disappearance, and as a nod to its influence in early Bond films, the DB5 made its comeback in the 1995 film, *GoldenEye*. The DB5 remains an extremely expensive collector's item today. The stylish convertible model is particularly sought after due to its rarity as only 123 were ever made.

**Richard Schultz** was indeed fortunate when after his graduation from the Institute of Design in Chicago, he was hired in 1951 by Knoll International to be the assistant to Harry Bertoia. The two worked together on all aspects of Bertoia's famous wire chairs, such as the Diamond Chair, including the design, prototyping and overseeing initial production. In those years Knoll was a particularly supportive environment for young designers and the experience that Schultz gained there would lead directly to the later successes of his career. Unhappy with the quality of most outdoor furniture, Florence Knoll, now Florence Knoll Bassett, asked Richard Schultz in the mid-1960s to design some outdoor furniture that looked new and would not fall apart after exposure to the elements. He experimented with corrosion-resistant aluminium for the frames and Teflon for the seating. After a period of intense research and development, he introduced the results as the Leisure Collection for Knoll in 1966 and it was an immediate success. The line consisted of eight different pieces, including tables and seating, but it was the Contour Chaise Lounge and the Adjustable Chaise Lounge that were the signature designs and they revolutionized the outdoor market. While most outdoor furniture was stylistically traditional, these new designs were regarded as a very fresh alternative, and the chaises in particular were so lightweight and airy as to be almost invisible in the garden. Sculpturally minimal and elegant, the most famous Adjustable Chaise had a cast and extruded aluminium frame with a polyester-powder-coated finish, cast-aluminium wheels with rubber tyres and Teflon mesh upholstery. Quickly recognized as an iconic design, its status was solidified when The Museum of Modern Art in New York purchased the Adjustable Chaise for its permanent collection, soon to be followed by other prominent museums such as the Louvre Museum, Paris, the Victoria and Albert Museum, London and the Vitra Design Museum, Weil am Rhein. No longer produced by Knoll, the line has been updated with new woven vinyl-coated polyester-mesh upholstery and reintroduced as the 1966 Collection by Richard Schultz Design.

**Richard Schultz**

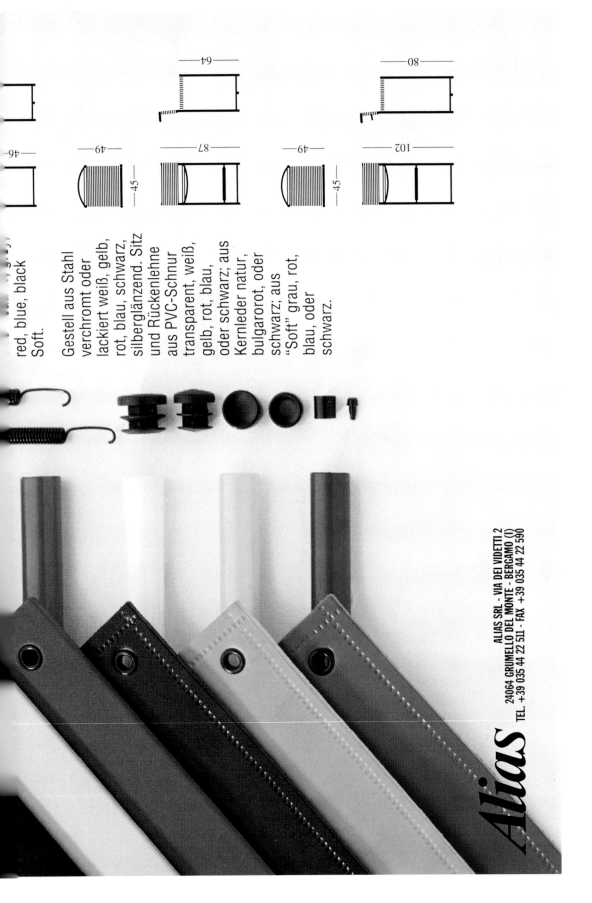

64

80

46

49

87

45

49

45

102

red, blue, black Soft.

Gestell aus Stahl verchromt oder lackiert weiß, gelb, rot, blau, schwarz, silberglänzend. Sitz und Rückenlehne aus PVC-Schnur transparent, weiß, gelb, rot, blau, oder schwarz; aus Kernleder natur, bulgarorot, oder schwarz; aus "Soft" grau, rot, blau, oder schwarz.

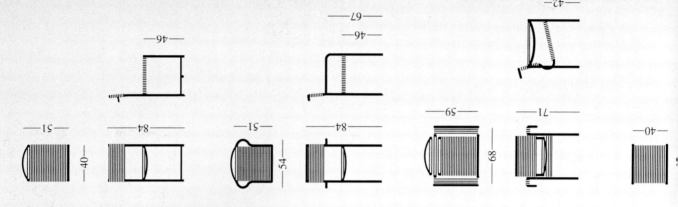

Struttura in acciaio cromato o verniciato bianco, giallo, rosso, blu, nero, argento brillante. Seduta e schienale in tondino di PVC trasparente, bianco, giallo, rosso, blu, nero; in cuoio naturale, rosso bulgaro, nero; in Soft grigio, rosso, blu, nero.

Structure en acier chromé ou laqué blanc, jaune, rouge, bleu, noir, argent brillant. Assise et dossier en fil PVC transparent, blanc, jaune, rouge, bleu, noir; en cuir naturel, rouge bulgare, noir; en Soft gris, rouge, bleu, noir.

Steel frame chromed or painted white, yellow, red, blue, black, bright silver. Seat and back in transparent, white, yellow, red, blue,

**Giandomenico Belotti,** Carlo Forcolini and Enrico Baleri founded the furniture manufacturer Alias in Bergamo, Italy in 1979. The company's first product was Belotti's Spaghetti chair, made from strips of coloured PVC that are stretched taut around a slender tubular-steel frame, which form the seat and back. The designer had originally conceived the design in 1962 under the name Odessa. When first exhibited in New York, the chair assumed its new name, inspired by the pasta-like strips that make up the flexible and tactile seat and back. The chair was an instant best seller and gave Alias the financial and moral boost that every newly formed manufacturer needs. The Spaghetti chair paved the way for subsequent releases from the company, which has always taken pride in creating products of timeless appeal, unaffected by current fashions. The simple, structural shapes employed by Belotti in this chair provide a clean-lined and uncomplicated framework for the unusual yet highly practical rubber-string seat. The graphic and light appearance does not distract from the all-important issue of comfort. The PVC flexes according to the weight and shape of the user, able to accommodate virtually anyone who sits on it. One could draw parallels with the rope seat constructions of Poul Kjærholm's PK24 Chaise Lounge and Hans Wegner's Flag Halyard Chair of the early 1950s, redefined by Belotti in a newer, more durable material. Today, the chair is available in a large variety of colour options. The frame comes in chromed steel or painted in a variety of colours. The PVC strips can be even be chosen to match the colour of the frame or bright translucent options can be specified.

Spaghetti (1962)
Giandomenico Belotti (1922–2004)
Pluri 1970
Alias 1979 to present

Giandomenico Belotti

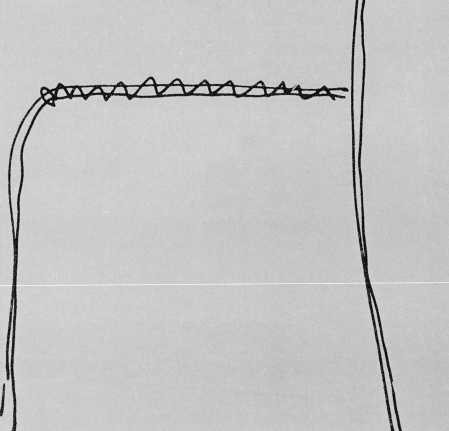

"FILVO"

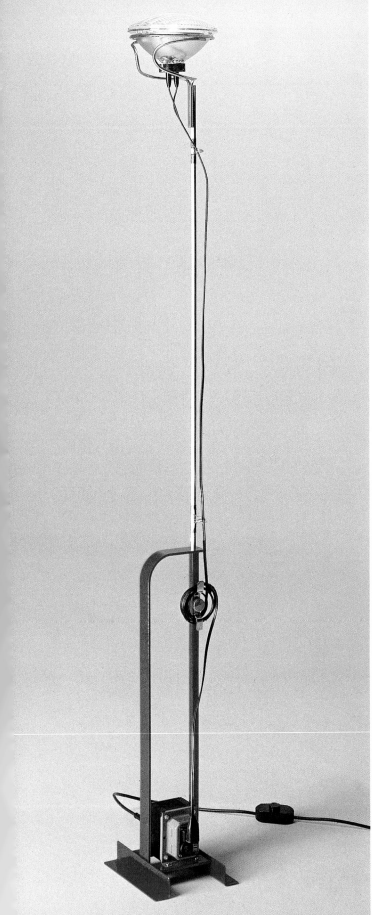

**The extendable Toio lamp** was produced
by the Castiglioni brothers in the early 1960s as part of
a series of 'ready-made' products. Borrowing a concept
associated with Dadaism, the Castiglionis used found
objects as the basis for industrial products. The brothers
chose anonymous engineered objects and components
as the starting-point for their products. This approach
to design also offered an antidote to the excessively
modern products of the 1950s and 1960s. The Toio lamp
is constructed almost entirely from ready-made components: a 300-watt car reflector bulb, attached to a metal
stem that is weighted by the transformer at the base
pedestal. The electrical wire is pinned to the stem by
fishing-rod screws. Products such as this one and the
Mezzadro and Sella stools, both from 1957, celebrate the
ingenuity of the mundane or everyday object, with the
minimum of intervention. The design writer Paolo Ferrarl
offered a system of classification for Castiglioni objects,
grouping together the 'ready-mades' into a distinct family.
The Castiglioni brothers developed an industrial style
which was at once humorous and thought-provoking.
Their work had its roots in the Italian Rationalist movement,
which was predicated on a functionalist approach to
design. Some of their work, particularly the lighting, was
an experiment in the design of products from minimum
means. Achille Castiglioni also championed an approach
to design that demonstrated a strong awareness of the
user. Products had to appeal on an emotional level, and
be as satisfying to use as to look at. The Toio lamp is
featured in major museum collections, including the
Victoria and Albert Museum in London.

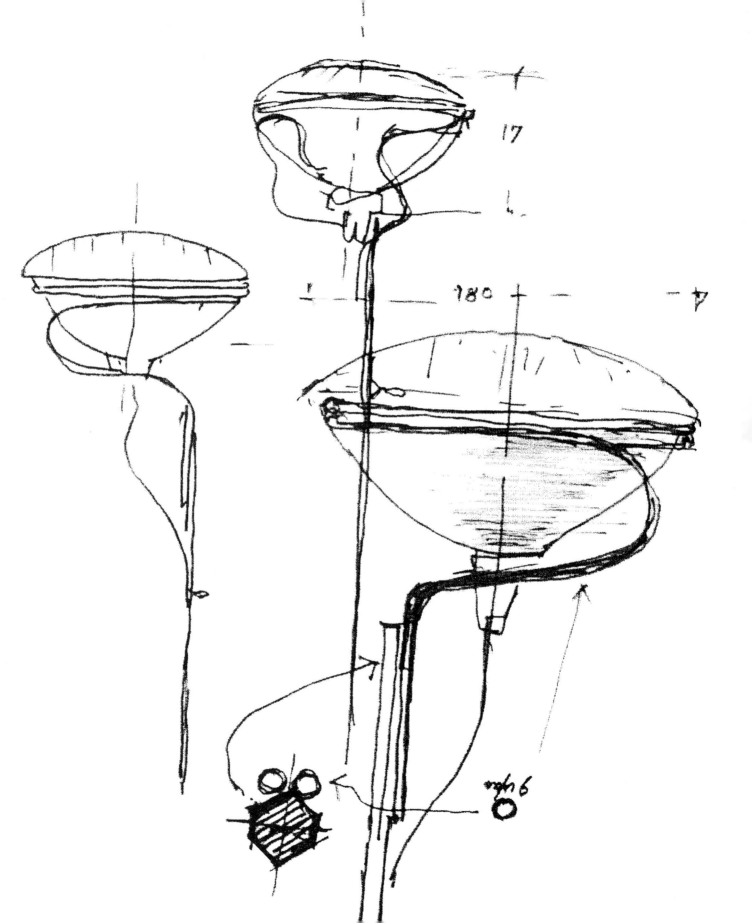

17

180

**In the 1950s and 1960s** the list of owners of Riva motor cruisers read like a *Who's Who* of the international jet set, with celebrity fans including Sophia Loren, Brigitte Bardot, Richard Burton and Elizabeth Taylor irresistibly drawn to the sumptuously streamlined style cruisers. The Riva brand became synonymous with glamour, luxury and exclusivity. This golden era of Riva, which saw the company's crafts feature in every fashionable resort from St Tropez to the Italian lakes, was achieved under the tutelage of Carlo Riva, the fourth generation of the boat-building Riva dynasty based at the family *cantieri* in Sarnico on Lake Iseo. Keen to modernize the traditional company in the early 1950s, Riva did so by launching a range of meticulously crafted pleasure boats to meet the demands of the emerging postwar glitterati. And top of the Riva sports boats range was the Aquarama, which went into production in 1962. The Aquarama has been described as a thoroughbred on water and came in three production models – the Aquarama itself, the Super Aquarama and the Aquarama Special. In many ways evolved and distilled from earlier Riva models, it had dual Chris Craft engines, giving it 185 hp and a top speed of 73 kph (45 mph), making the Aquarama a true power cruiser. Both powerful and easy to handle in the tradition of the Riva range, the Aquarama boasted refined handcrafted details that have been much copied but never bettered – details such as the design of the dashboard, instruments and helm, and the positioning of the controls, all clearly inspired by cutting-edge motor car design of the time by companies such as Ferrari. But perhaps the defining glory of the Aquarama was its elegant streamlined form. At just over 8 m (26 ft) long, it was articulated in plywood, using a process derived from aircraft technology. The hallmark Riva frame was built from heavier gauge mahogany sourced from Gabon and the Ivory Coast, with a silkier, smoother mahogany imported from Honduras for the fittings. No other power cruiser came close to matching the Aquarama's styling and quality. When it came to the end of its production run in 1966, after 784 units had been launched, it counted among its owners the Aga Khan, King Hussein of Jordan, Roger Vadim and Jane Fonda.

| | |
|---|---|
| Aquarama (1962) | |
| Carlo Riva (1922–) | |
| Riva 1962 to 1996 | |

**Carlo Riva**

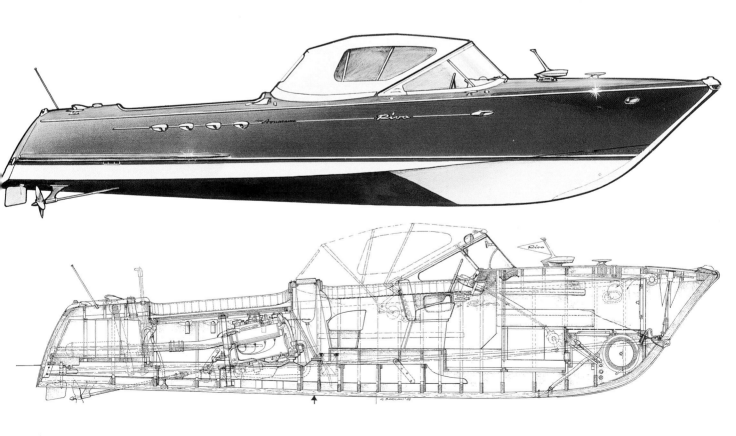

**Braun shavers** contributed to changes in the perception of personal hygiene equipment from the 1950s onwards. The Braun company led the field in design and innovation and introduced outstanding products that remained design milestones for decades. According to Braun's company history, this shaver was the starting point for making the company a global competitor in electric shaving. The SM3 Shaver, in traditional white and designed by Gerd Alfred Müller in 1960, was the turning-point, followed by the innovative and sales record-breaking Sixtant SM 31 in 1962, which redefined the notion of technological luxury. Designed by Hans Gugelot and Gerd Alfred Müller, under the direction of Dieter Rams, the Sixtant set production standards for years to come. Drawing on their Bauhaus heritage and its ideas of simplicity and durability, the designers aimed for 'timelessness' when designing the Sixtant. The Sixtant's volume and details follow the principles of functionalism, of simple, un-decorated and harmonious forms that express the object's use. The shaver's holding area is a smooth, 'clean' upright that curves gently outwards reaching its widest dimension as it meets with the metallic, detachable razor head. The subtle release latch and the operating switch placed elegantly on the opposite side are both positioned at the most convenient locations and least intrusive to the flow of the shape. The proportions of the shaver and considerations for 'overall measurements to fit the male hand' made it part of the rise of what was later seen as the birth of ergonomics, the science of the relationship between human beings and their working conditions. The modern electric razor, as created by Braun, born from the Good Form movement, heralded the strand of industrial design that championed the 'less is more' ideology.

# 592

Ring-Pull Can End (1962)
Ernie Fraze (1913–89)
Dayton Reliable Tool & Manufacturing
Company 1962 to present
Stolle Machinery (Alcoa) 1965 to present

**In the 1950s and 1960s** the Ring-Pull for aluminium drinks cans was the holy grail of the American beverage industry. Metal cans, and increasingly, aluminium cans, had enormous advantages over glass bottles in terms of weight, cost and storage space, but their widespread popularity was thwarted by the fact that they were not conveniently portable for the individual consumer. The consumer needed to carry a can-opener with him/her to get at the drink, which was at the time almost always beer, as soft drinks were still sold in bottles. The necessity for a self-opening can was evident, but the field was littered with unsuccessful prototypes, and the industry was wary of committing itself to something that might prove to be a failure with consumers while being more expensive to produce. However, after a picnic where he had been reduced to using his car bumper to open a can, tool-maker Ernie Fraze of Muncie, Indiana, set out to develop the pull-tab opener. He created a see-saw mechanism that used leverage to rip the can open along a pre-scored line. The rivet that held the lever to the can was attached by a process called cold-welding, and used only the material of the can itself. The idea was sold to Alcoa, despite its initial scepticism, and in 1962 the first 100,000 orders were placed by the Pittsburgh Brewing Company, which made the easier-to-use 'snap tops' an element in its advertising. From that point on, Fraze's invention continued to be refined by scores of individuals and companies. In 1965 the tab opening was replaced by the ring and, in a bid to reduce an enormous litter problem, the non-removable tab was developed in 1975 by Daniel F Cudzik. The tab-opening drinks can, thanks to its association with the enormous marketing clout of the beer and soft drinks industries, epitomizes accessibility and convenience, and the application of tremendous creativity to a mundane problem. On the other hand, the disposability of the can and the reputation that removable Ring-Pulls had as instant litter, has made it seem the epitome of waste. It is a product at the heart of our society, used billions of times a year.

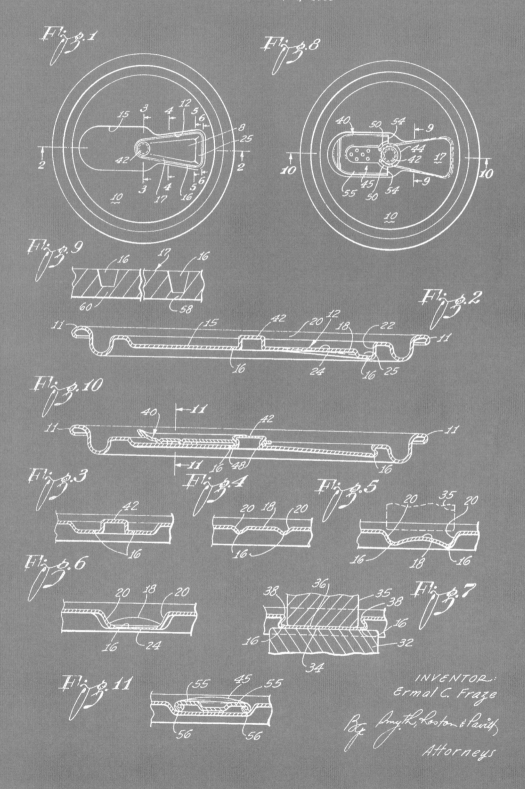

INVENTOR:
Ermal C. Fraze

By Smyth, Roston & Pavitt

Attorneys

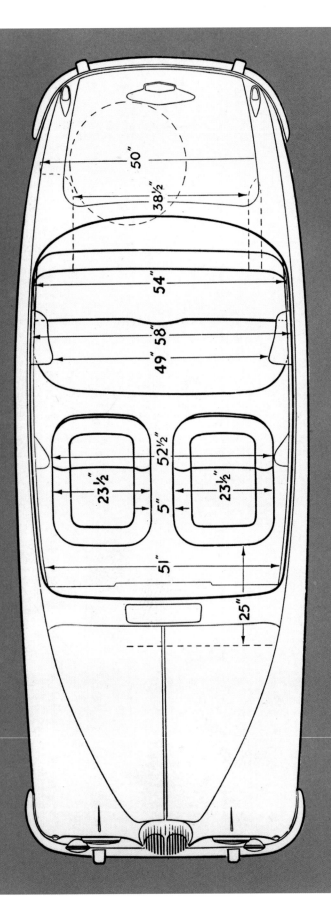

THE DAIMLER COMPANY LIMITED · COVENTRY · ENGLAND

*The issue of this catalogue does not constitute an offer. The specification described in this brochure varies for different countries, and The Daimler Company Limited reserves the right to amend specifications at any time, without notice.*

# Principal Dimensions

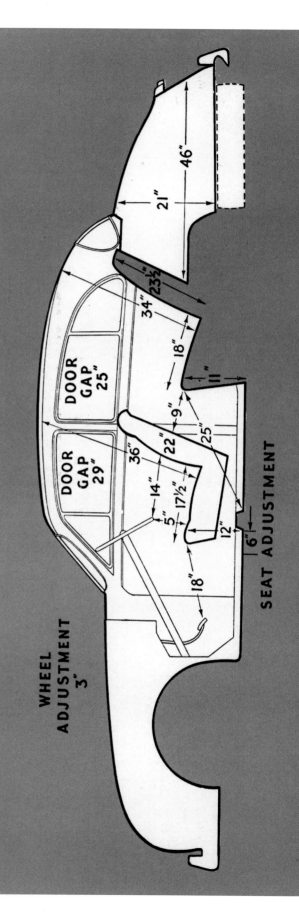

WHEEL
ADJUSTMENT
3"

SEAT ADJUSTMENT

DOOR GAP 29"

DOOR GAP 25"

46"

21"

23½"

34"

18"

11"

9"

25"

22"

36"

18"

14"

5"

5"

17½"

12"

6"

**There is a delightful** symmetry in the fact that the Daimler Mark II brought together two of Britain's best design engineers, both of whom started in the motorcycle business. Sir William Lyons, legendary founder of Jaguar, started building motorcycle sidecars in the early 1920s while Edward Turner's pre-World War II Triumph Speed Twin had a vertical-twin engine design that set the standard for British bike engines of the classic mid-century era. In the late 1950s, Turner turned his talent to car engines and designed a beautiful 2.5 l V8 engine for the short-lived Daimler Dart sports car. Meanwhile in Coventry, Sir William had built Jaguar into one of the great automotive brands of the postwar era and was intrigued with the idea of buying the Daimler marque. After all, the name went back to the very origins of the automotive industry, to Gottlieb Daimler, who invented the internal combustion engine at the end of the nineteenth century. In 1960 Jaguar bought Daimler and Sir William's first move was to insert Turner's V-8 engine into a Daimler-badged Jaguar Mark II. As successful as the Jaguar Mark II was, the light, sporting and very fast Daimler version was even more so. The beauty of the Mark II lies in the lines, which are pure Jaguar, with hints of both the XK series and the contemporary E-Type. But it is in the engine compartment that the Daimler really stands out. V-8 engines are American by tradition and birthright; heavy, overbuilt and under-powered. Taking advantage of his motorcycle experience, where low weight and high power are paramount, Turner made a compact V8 engine for Daimler, which transformed a luxury saloon into a sporting classic in the Mark II. There are very few differences apart from the engine between the Jaguar Mark II and the Daimler Mark II. For purists, the grille and boot handle had Daimler 'fingermarks', resembling a pastry crust pressed into place just before baking. Production of both the Jaguar and Daimler Mark II's ended in the late 1960s, as the British car industry began its downward spiral of decline.

**Self-taught and a practising** designer since 1956, Enzo Mari produced many beautiful designs during his collaboration with manufacturer Danese from children's toys to office furniture and accessories. The Formosa Perpetual Calendar is one of the most popular. A perpetual calendar in aluminium with mobile lithographic PVC pages, the Formosa's design is minimal, graphic and modern. Date, month, and day of the week are changed by switching the individual placards hanging on the metal back plate. The calendar's legibility, due to the clear typeface (the ubiquitous 'Helvetica' font) and grid formation, means it is still a relevant object for the office today. It is available in either a red or a black version and has been sold all over the world and translated into many languages. Since 1962 Mari has worked with Danese's signature material, plastic, initially developing a hatstand, umbrella stand and waste bin. By the end of the 1960s Mari's manipulation of plastic was so skilful that many of his designs acquired a sculptural quality, which helped to convince the public that the material could be tasteful rather than cheap-looking. Mari's path as a designer has always been thoughtful and provocative. His statement, 'Real design is about who produces rather than who buys', explains his attitude towards the product as the meeting of two minds between the designer/artisan and the manufacturer. Only in this way, he believes, can designers create products with strong values, objects that maintain throughout the years their cultural, social and economic purpose. Mari has always believed that mass production should compromise neither beauty of form nor functionality, and these theories have developed into an applied philosophy of 'rational design'. The Formosa Calendar's timeless appeal reflects this credo.

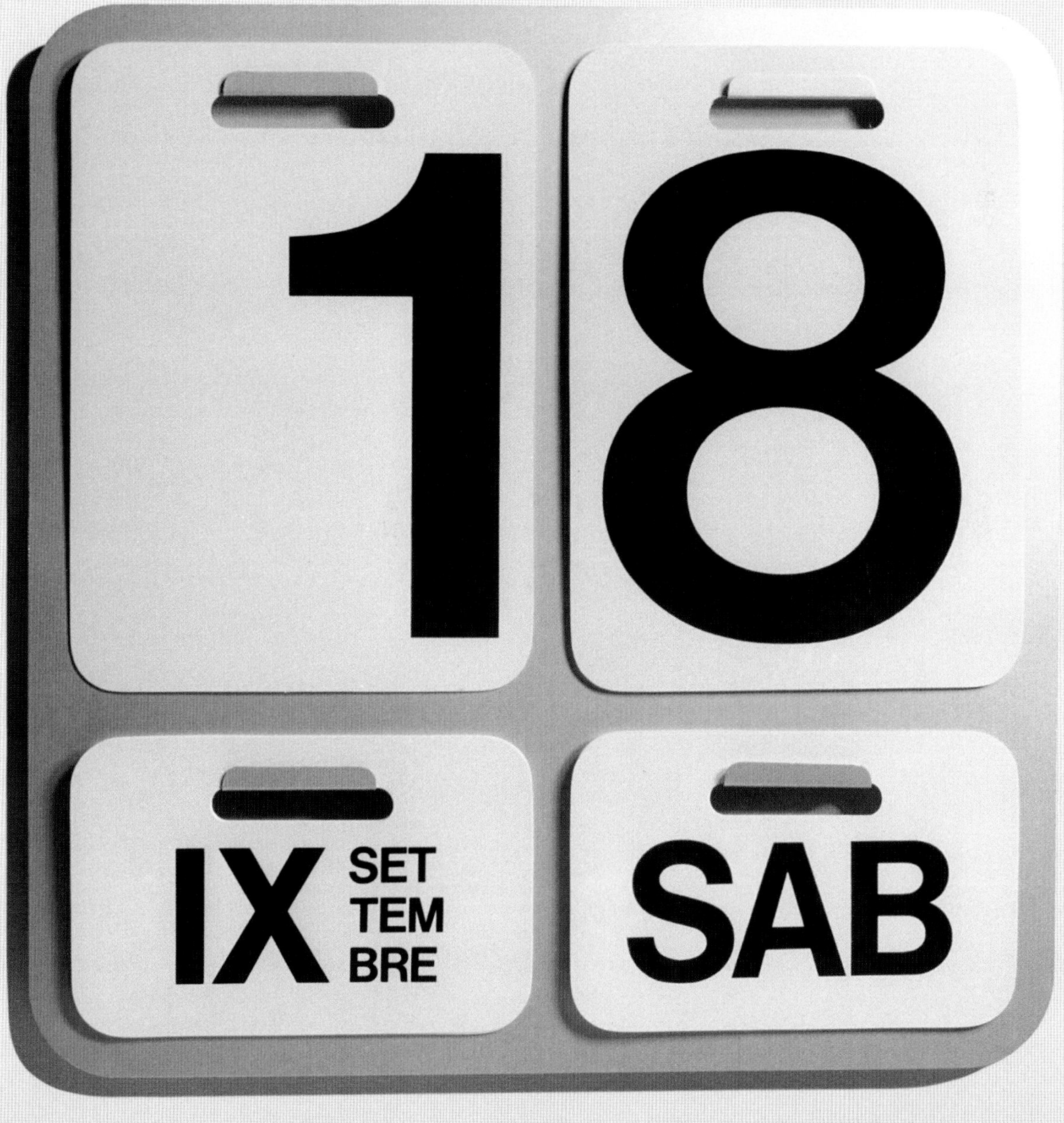
18
IX
SET
TEM
BRE
SAB

**589**

Sleek Mayonnaise Spoon (1962)
Achille Castiglioni (1918–2002)
Pier Giacomo Castiglioni (1913–68)
Alessi 1996 to present

**The Sleek Mayonnaise Spoon** was designed by two of the prolific Italian Castiglioni brothers, Achille and Pier Giacomo. The spoon was first designed in 1962 as a promotional item for the Kraft company, to accompany its mayonnaise product, and bore the company's logo printed on the handle. The Sleek Spoon was produced specifically to retrieve the last remnants of food from jars of mayonnaise, peanut butter and jam, all items produced by Kraft. The design is both clever and simple. The spoon features a narrow, curved tip, with one side of the bowl formed to the curvature of most jars, while the other is straight, allowing it to slide along the side of the container, maximizing the chance to scoop out every last bit of food. A further feature is a thumb rest on the handle, making it easier to grip. The design incorporated the use of Polymethylmetacrylate (PMMA), a flexible, hardwearing and hygienic plastic, to allow maximum movement for cleaning the inside of the jar. The Castiglioni brothers, in particular Achille, played an important role in the history of Italian design. They were allied to the ideals of Neo-Modernism, and their designs, such as the Sleek Spoon, exhibit a strong awareness of form, production and the user. The use of plastic and bright colours are characteristic of Italian domestic home-ware design and the 1960s Pop sensibility, combined with a strong element of fun, making it no surprise that the Alessi company reissued the Sleek Mayonnaise Spoon in 1996. Still in production by Alessi today, in a wide range of bright primary colours, together with a white/translucent colourway called 'ice', Sleek is the perfect domestic spoon: fun, practical and guaranteed to brighten up any kitchen.

**Today's technology** is on a ceaseless trajectory towards extreme miniaturization and dematerialization. Today, music is 'played' from iPods with 'no moving parts' and television broadcasts are streamed over tiny Nokia cellphones. This desire for ever-smaller embodiments of data emerged with the Philips Compact Audio Cassette, the inconspicuous, pocket-sized plastic envelope containing two spinning gears that attracted and repelled an infinite loop of magnetic tape. The audio cassette's genesis was due to a number of inventors and companies from different countries. In 1889 Valdemar Poulsen, a Danish inventor who expanded on American engineer Oberlin Smith's experiments with magnetic tape, created the Telegraphone, which could record messages. Poulsen had received patents in Denmark and the United States for a steel wire that would wrap around a cylinder under an electromagnet connected to a microphone. The BBC and the British Marconi Wireless Telegraph Company then bought the rights to a patent for steel tape recorders between 1931 and 1932, and these were used for radio services in Australia, Canada, France, Sweden and Poland. The German manufacturer AEG bought the rights to a patent for a paper coated with a magnetizable, powdered-steel layer, invented by Fritz Pfleumer, after which the company developed an accompanying recorder. But the classic integration of design and technology made its appearance in 1963, after numerous attempts to create a stereo tape in a cartridge format that even required a specific player. The Philips Cassette led the way in terms of interactive media, by means of its small cartridge, and introduced the possibility of home recording. It surpassed the capabilities of the portable transistor radio and gave individuals unprecedented possibilities for exchanging personalized data (music and voice) with ease. In its diminutive plastic shroud, the Philips Compact Audio Cassette embodied freedom, liberation and versatility. These characteristics contributed to the now iconic status of the Philips device and initiated the space in which we exist today, where bodies and data are inseparable.

**588**

Compact Audio Cassette (1962)
N V Philips Gloeilampenfabriken Group
Philips 1963 to present
Various 1964 to present

Mexico City Olympics Stadium, 1968, with 3,500 chairs

need for a multi-purpose side-chair at a very low price…(for) cafés and canteens, chairs for working at a table, seating in lecture halls and assembly halls…The differences demanded by these functions could be achieved by various stands or leg frames carrying a mass-produced seat-and-back unit.' Available in a host of colours and a variety of base options, the chair was an immediate success. On its launch in 1963 *Architects Journal* anticipated its success as 'the most significant development in British mass-produced chair design since the war'. The design sealed Hille's status as the most progressive furniture manufacturer in Britain and a true force within international markets. Its achievements supported development of other models, including an armchair and perforated Polo Chair, all based on the original. The Polypropylene Stacking Chair was licensed for manufacture all over the world. Despite the fact it was quickly copied, in excess of 14 million licensed chairs have been sold in twenty-three countries.

Robin Day with a mould for the Polypropylene Stacking Chair

**The familiar form** of Robin Day's Polypropylene Stacking Chair belies its significance in the history of furniture design. The simple shape of the single-piece shell, with deep-turned edge and finely textured surface affixed to a stacking base, remains the most democratic seating design of the twentieth century. Polypropylene has many advantages over traditional materials used in the furniture industry. It is incredibly durable, light and flexible; it requires little finishing and is well suited to injection moulding. Robin Day became aware of this new thermoplastic in 1960, when judging a competition for Shell, who had acquired the rights to its manufacture. Although at the time no-one had managed to overcome the technical difficulties involved in its manufacture, Hille supported Day's quest to realize the potential of the material. Development began in the early 1960s. The chair's design was influenced by anatomical demands as well as structural considerations to allow for integral fixing points and a minimal component count. Although polypropylene as a material was low cost, the tooling was extremely expensive and refinement towards production was a slow process of fine-tuning the shape, wall-thickness and fixing bosses. The development of the Polypropylene Stacking Chair was pioneering; with no precedents in the field of manufacturing, the process was arduous. Day envisaged the chair in a multitude of environments: 'This chair arose from the

**In the 1950s,** Spain found itself struggling. Burdened by protectionism and with little industrial development, the economy under Franco was stagnating. A design industry, whether modern or traditional, hardly existed, much as in northern Italy a decade earlier. Domestic design production was largely limited to individual craftsmen favouring regional histories and materials. Debate and discourse about modern design and architecture was stifled by officially sanctioned, highly conservative teaching. Despite this historical context, Miguel Milá was inspired to create a design of lasting relevance and modernity. Unlike many icons of design, the TMM Floor Lamp was praised from its very inception, and has since become an icon as one of the first products to be industrially designed in Spain. In 1956 Milá's maternal aunt Nuria Sagnier, commissioned a light from him. The resulting lamp, named TN, was an early precursor of the TMM Lamp and vaguely resembled it in form. It lacked elegance, however, because of its pronounced mechanism for adjusting the height of the lamp. Moreover, Milá replaced the cold, awkward metal of the TN with walnut for the TMM. The TMM, short for Tramo Móvil Madera, was designed in 1962 as one element in a competition entry to design a complete interior using economical, low cost furniture. The self-assembled, all wood structure supported an easily adjustable light with simply integrated cord light switch, an element Milá had used in a design from 1960. While the do-it-yourself packaging was not new in world design at that time, it was still novel in Spain. The timelessness of the TMM resides in its modesty of form and use of natural, warm materials, which together possess a serenity that allows them to coexist across space and time. It is a signature piece reflecting Milá's own insistence that he is 'a pre-industrial designer', a designer who willingly embraces the history and skills of traditional craftsmen and insists on a rigour that sees no discord between the modern and the sensual.

Miguel Milá

**Tandem Sling Chair installed in an airport waiting area, 1988**

**Public seating** is not the most glamorous of design commissions, but it is one of the most challenging. It has to be comfortable, sturdy, easy to maintain and attractive without being overwhelming in a large public space. The Tandem Sling Chair fulfils all the criteria, the sleek black and aluminium design remaining smart and contemporary more than forty years after it was first launched at Washington's Dulles International Airport. But then its designers, husband-and-wife team Charles and Ray Eames, were always up for a challenge. Their work spanned architecture, film, exhibition design and toys, but they are most remembered for their quest to create high-quality, yet affordable furniture. Long before ergonomics became a buzzword, one of their personal missions was to do away with the cushioning of traditional upholstery and search for different ways to create comfortable seating that would support the spine. In their quest they experimented with moulded plywood, fibreglass-reinforced plastic and bent and welded wire mesh. They turned their talents to aluminium after World War II when the aluminium industry was looking for new outlets for production after the demand for munitions had ceased. Thus began their Aluminium Group series, in which the Tandem Sling Chair was a late arrival, but capitalized on those early experiments to create a chair that was light and comfortable and resistant to corrosion. Eventually they developed an aluminium-frame chair on which the seating, foam pads pressed and sealed between two layers of vinyl for a durable, wrinkle-free finish, is suspended like a sling. The practicalities of the chair are numerous – the seats are wide and padded with an open seat-to-back angle to provide optimum comfort for tired passengers, and the support-beam design leaves plenty of space under the seats for luggage. The aluminium frame is joint-free for maximum strength and there are no stitch lines in the seat portion where dust can gather.

**The Acrilica lamp** combines technical innovation with sculptural form. It is made of cast acrylic set into an enamelled metal base, the light source being concealed in the base, so that the light itself is diffused through the clear acrylic curve. The method of light diffusion is the same as that used in exterior edge-lit perspex signage. The form of the light has no precedent in contemporary lighting products, and exemplifies the hybrid approach of one of its designers, Cesare 'Joe' Colombo, who saw his work as a marriage of artistic language and technical experimentation. The clear acrylic resin known as perspex or plexiglass was patented in 1934 by ICI. It was most commonly produced in sheet form and used as a substitute for glass. It could also be vacuum-formed and one of its early uses was in the cockpit canopies of Spitfire fighter planes during World War II. Its transparency and durability made it a useful component in light fittings from the 1930s onwards. However, in the 1950s and 1960s the material was developed for use in exterior signage, and it quickly became an integral component of the urban landscape of advertising signs and brightly lit branded displays. Having trained as a painter, Colombo moved into design when he inherited the family firm, a manufacturer of electrical equipment. At the same time, he developed an interest in finding applications for both new materials (such as reinforced plastics) and manufacturing methods (like injection moulding). His plastic furniture and product designs were among the most experimental and influential in the 1960s. His use of plastics helped to raise the status of these materials, showing them to be flexible and durable, with inherent aesthetic qualities. The Acrilica, developed with his brother Gianni, stems from previous experiments in the light-diffusing potential of perspex. The light is currently in production by its original manufacturer, O luce, for whom Colombo designed several products.

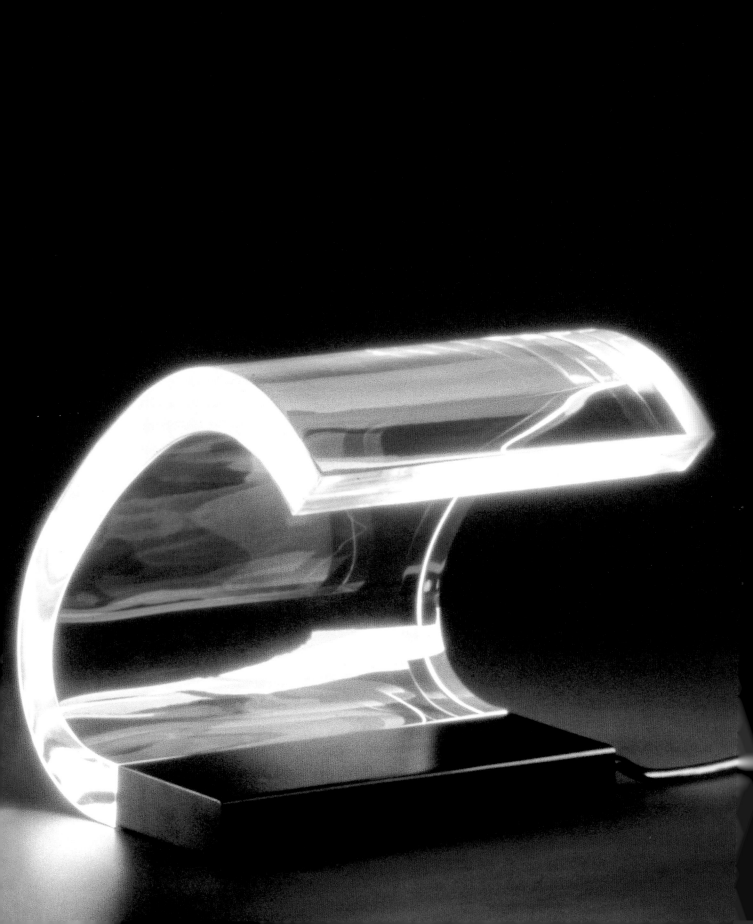

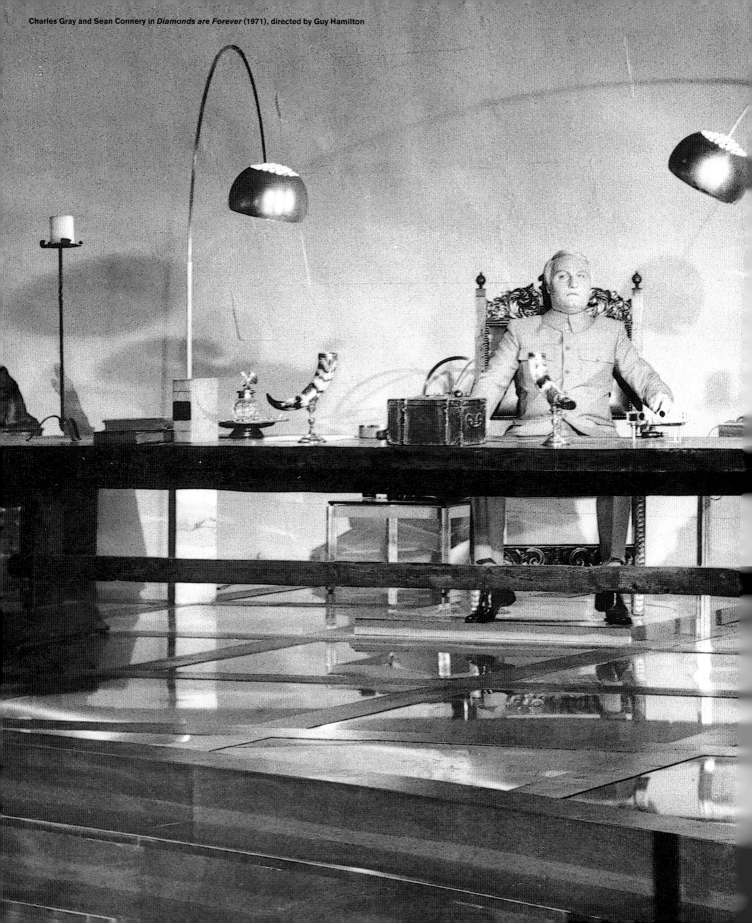

**Inspired by everyday products,** the Arco floor lamp was developed as a freestanding interior version of a standard street lamp, to obviate the need for built-in lighting in a room. Arco comprises an arching arm fixed to a rectangular base of white Carrara marble. The telescopic arm supports the light at a distance of over 2 m (6.6 ft) from the base and can be adjusted, allowing enough space for a dining table and chairs to be positioned comfortably under the shade. Simple adjustable mechanisms are a common feature of Castiglioni designs. The arm, made of satin-finished stainless steel, with a zapon varnished aluminium reflector, weighs over 45 kg (100 lb), but, helpfully, the designers incorporated a hole into the marble base to allow a broom handle to be inserted, enabling two people to lift it. The overall effect is both rational and pleasing, and is characteristic of the Castiglioni brothers' work, which questioned the basic form of useful objects and created solutions injected with humour and irony. The lamp complies with Achille Castiglioni's basic design philosophy, which was that objects should develop from an analytical approach to materials and technologies. The Arco floor lamp is successful precisely because its physical adaptability is so clearly articulated. Arco was produced during the Castiglioni's most prolific period of lighting design, from the late 1950s to the early 1960s, and is a product of their dual thinking. They chose to work with a select range of manufacturers with whom they built up a close and productive relationship over time. Flos, the producers of Arco, was one of their most respected collaborators. Together they redefined the nature and purpose of interior lighting, affording it a sculptural as well as a functional role. The Arco floor lamp has become one of the most admired design objects of the postwar period, and is a regular prop in films, television programmes and lifestyle magazines. Perhaps its most famous appearance was in the 007 film *Diamonds are Forever*.

**Max Bill**

**Swiss artist Max Bill** was one of the Modern movement's true Renaissance men, and his progressive modernist credentials are perfectly encapsulated in the simple, practical wristwatches he designed for German precision watchmakers Junghans in 1962. The Max Bill Wristwatch, part of a collection that is still in production today, also marks the beginning of the current trend to commission well-known product designers and architects to design watches – a discipline once the sole preserve of a company's in-house watchmaker. Bill was architect, painter and sculptor as well as stage, graphic and industrial designer. He played a major role in the emergence of the constructivist tendency in the Swiss school of graphic design in the 1930s and embraced the concept of Concrete Art, representing 'abstract thoughts in a sensuous and tangible form' in a series of artworks featuring grids, pure geometries and mathematical formulas. The clarity and precision of the Wristwatch collection makes it very much a product of the Ulm school ethos, which Bill co-founded in 1951. The watch designs – white and black faces with a diameter of 34.2 mm (1.34 in) – are characterized by a simple no-fuss digit configuration inside a polished stainless steel case featuring a seventeen-jewel Swiss hand-winding movement mechanism. The pared-down design of the watch recalls the earlier minimalist Wall Clock range that Bill designed for Junghans in 1956–7. Junghans and fellow German manufacturers Braun saw in Bill and the Ulm school an opportunity to associate their names with leading-edge designs.

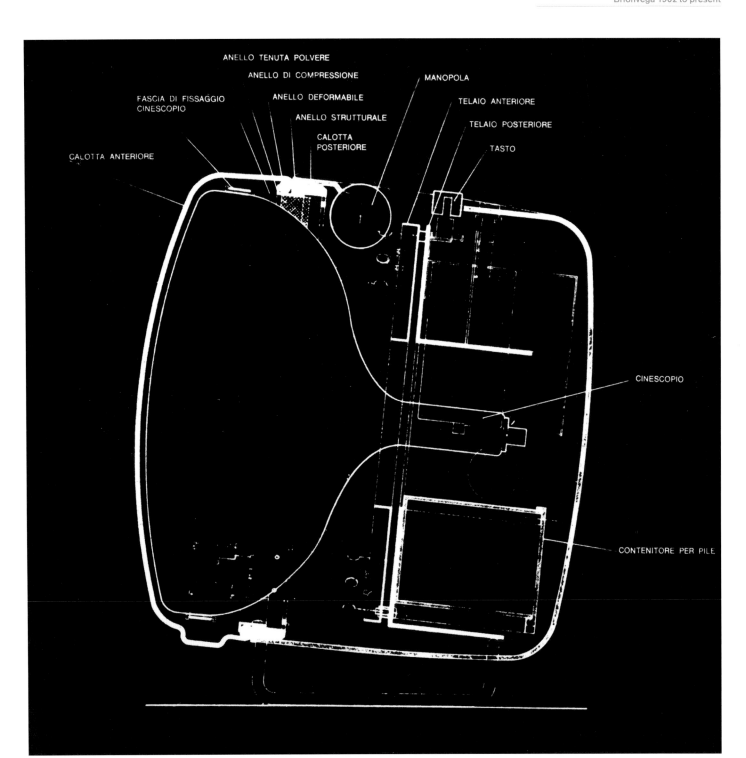

ANELLO TENUTA POLVERE

ANELLO DI COMPRESSIONE

MANOPOLA

FASCIA DI FISSAGGIO
CINESCOPIO

ANELLO DEFORMABILE

TELAIO ANTERIORE

ANELLO STRUTTURALE

TELAIO POSTERIORE

CALOTTA
POSTERIORE

TASTO

CALOTTA ANTERIORE

CINESCOPIO

CONTENITORE PER PILE

**The Italian-German design team** of Richard Sapper and Marco Zanuso was responsible for some of the most striking and innovative consumer products of the 1960s and 1970s, helping to establish the reputation of design-led European companies such as Brionvega, Terraillon and Siemens. The Doney 14 was one of the first commissions for Brionvega, which had only recently moved into television manufacture following the launch of the Italian television network in 1952. It takes some cues in its styling and celebration of portability from the Sony TV8-301 (the world's first direct-view transistor TV) of 1960. Both eschew the notion of 'product-as-furniture' popular at the time, in favour of a more high-tech, playful form whose dimensions are dictated by the picture tube itself. The Doney did away with the four mounting rings that were up until then the most common means of securing the cathode ray tube in the housing. Instead, it employed a band that ran around the picture tube, which helped to define the distinctive barrel shape and compact form. The internal workings were shoehorned into this tiny space around the tube and the whole lot encased in a single moulding. The large number of cooling vents necessary for this configuration were emphasized through the location of channel buttons and dials. There was such pride in the form of the object and its relation to the inner workings that the (much sought-after) first production models were in clear acrylic. The Doney won the influential and prestigious Compasso d'Oro award in 1962, and quickly established itself as a style icon. Available in black, white and orange, it is still often spotted in the styled photos of interior decoration magazines. It was updated and improved in 1967 and continued to sell well into the 1970s. Following its acquisition of Brionvega in 1992 its parent company, Seleco, decided to concentrate the brand name in its marketing of classic designs. 2001 saw the Doney relaunched, along with the Algol of 1964. These modern versions incorporate more recent innovations, including colour, digital tuning and a remote control, but demonstrate their lasting appeal as design objects.

A Millard, M Ives, A Collins, and C Groom in a four-man pursuit team, breaking a record at the Coventry CC, Butts Stadium, April 1963

Alex Moulton riding an original 'F' frame Moulton Deluxe, 1963–4

The Moulton Bicycle (1962)
Alex Moulton (1920–)
Alex Moulton Bicycles 1962 to 1975,
1983 to present

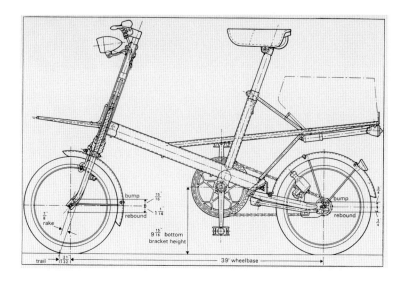

In 1970 Colin Martin famously rode a Moulton bicycle from England to Australia, covering 16,093 kilometres (10,000 miles) in 169 days of riding, doing an average of 96.5 km (60 m) a day. This was the world's first small-wheeled production bicycle, with suspension. Alex Moulton famously worked with Alec Issigonis as the suspension designer on several ground-breaking vehicles throughout the 1960s and 1970s, including the Mini and the hydrolastic suspension system on the Austin 1100. It was working on the Mini, with its winning combination of small wheels and suspension, which in part inspired the first Moulton Bicycle. One early prototype, again like the Mini, used a monocoque frame as well. The advantages of small wheels (16 as an alternative to the traditional 27 inch tyres) are their inherent strength and that their reduced size allows more space lower down on the bike for load

carrying. Importantly, this does not have a significant negative effect on the handling of the bike. The foreseeable disadvantages of increased rolling resistance and hardness of ride are solved by high-pressure tyres and suspensions. Moreover, the lower aerodynamic drag of small wheels means they will go faster with less effort. Achieving the right balance among these elements prompted the production of the first serious bicycle to break with the seventy years of proven success of the regular, diamond-frame bicycle. Alex Moulton worked extremely hard to develop his concept into a product, which during the 1960s, much like the Mini, became an icon of optimistic modern Britain, and prompted enough demand that most production was sub-contracted to British car manufacturers. The design was bought by Raleigh in 1967, but was taken out of production

in 1974, perhaps because it was in competition with some of Raleigh's own small-wheeled bikes, which, ironically, had been developed following the initial success of the Moulton. In just seven years of production Raleigh manufactured a quarter of a million Moultons. Alex Moulton later went on to develop a second generation of bicycles using the small-wheel-suspension concept, which have been in production since 1983. These are manufactured by his own company, Alex Moulton Bicycles, as well as under licence by specialist manufacturer, Pashley. The 'F' frame was the original design but from 1983 he produced the AM bicycles with a new frame called 'Space Frame'.

**There has been an ironworks at Fiskars** in Finland since 1649, but fine forging, such as the manufacture of cutlery and scissors, did not begin there until the 1830s. And it was only in 1971 that scissors were first mentioned in the company's annual report. Now the company has a whole plant sited at Billnäs devoted specifically to the production of scissors. The reason for this major turning-point in the company's business was the introduction of Olof Bäckström's now famous O-Series ABS and Steel Scissors, his orange-handled remodelling of the basic scissors, which he worked on from 1961 to 1967. The O-Series are the world's first scissors and pinking shears to have ergonomic handles made in ABS polymer. Their success led to new types of scissors being made, and created a profitable field of production for the company.

The success of this model is fairly easy to account for as they were the first scissors to be affordable and comfortable to use, which stayed sharp and cut precisely. Prior to the introduction of these scissors, the main problem was cost of manufacture. In order to keep the price down, most cheap scissors were made from two identical cast sections riveted together, often with simple painted metal loops for handles. These loops were usually the same size and shape for both the thumb and fingers of the cutting hand and could be remarkably painful to use. Comfortable scissors were not unknown, however. Any tailor would have had a comfortable pair (possibly even made by Fiskars, who were manufacturing such things at least as early as the 1880s) but these were expensive to produce because of their finely shaped handles, which had to be cast and polished. Bäckström's solution and prototype, remarkably close to some of the nineteenth-century tailor's scissors produced by Fiskars, was initially made in wood. For the final design Bäckström simply recast the comfortable handles in durable orange plastic and inserted the stainless-steel blades into them.

Neil Armstrong

Buzz Aldrin's bootprint from the Apollo 11 mission, 20 July 1969

**On 25 May 1961,** President John F Kennedy announced to Congress his plan to send an American to the moon by the end of the decade. Thanks to the many people who worked on NASA's Apollo programme, this goal was achieved on 20 July 1969, when Apollo 11 touched down on the lunar surface. And while much of the incentive for this programme was a result of the Cold War politics that dominated the era (many American histories of the voyage still celebrate beating the Soviet Union to the Moon just as much as they celebrate reaching it in the first place), Apollo 11 remains one of the twentieth century's greatest design and engineering feats. Launched via a Saturn V rocket, Apollo 11 was made up of three spacecraft: the command module *Columbia*, a service module and the lunar module *Eagle*. The command module, which provides about as much interior space as a large automobile, served as the primary living quarters for the three astronauts and housed an onboard computer developed at MIT; the service module contained oxygen, water and electric power for the command module; and the lunar module was designed to serve as a base while the astronauts were on the Moon. Many of the design features of the command module, manufactured by North American Rockwell, had evolved under the supervision of NASA's Max Faget (chief engineer of the Manned Spacecraft Center), from experience gained during earlier space missions. The blunt-end design came about following studies of the Mercury and Gemini spacecraft, and was engineered to accommodate the heat radiation on re-entry to the earth's atmosphere. Apollo would re-enter at a faster velocity than any previous spaceships). Similarly, the single command module hatch, which opened in five seconds by pumping a handle to activate a pressurized nitrogen cylinder, was designed in response to a fire that occurred in 1967 on a previous module, Apollo 1, in which three astronauts died, when the double hatch had taken 90 seconds to open. Despite this incident, and damage suffered by Apollo 11 en route to the Moon, the space capsule system is such a safe design as safety was one of the primary design criteria that many experts called for a return to the Apollo programme following the loss of the space shuttle *Columbia* in 2003. The Apollo programme cost $25.4 billion, but for that money, America got more than just a very safe spacecraft that enabled astronauts to jump about on the moon and take photographs of the earth. Arguably what really makes Apollo a superb design is the fact that the technology developed during the programme found many other uses. Among other things it found its way into the short-lived Skylab space station, the flight computer that was a driving force behind early research into integrated circuits, and computer-controlled machining (CNC) was pioneered in fabricating the Apollo's structural components.

# 578

Apollo 11 Spacecraft (1961–5)
NASA Design Team
North American Rockwell,
Grumman Design Team
North American Rockwell, Grumman
1966 to 1970

Aerial view of Apollo 11 on Transporter, 20 May 1969

Marquina 1961 (1961)
Rafael Marquina (1921−)
Various 1961 to 1971
Mobles 114, 1971 to present

Rafael Marquina

## Several generations of holidaymakers

travelling to the Costa Brava, north of Barcelona, will recognize Rafael Marquina's brilliant oil and vinegar cruets, which have been celebrated in Barcelona, and all over Catalonia, for more than forty years. While it is true that Marquina's design has only come to be recognized outside Spain relatively recently, the glass cruets are among the true gems of modernist design. The elegant simplicity of the Marquina 1961 set belies the sophistication of its design. A removable spout sits like a stopper in the flat-bottomed, conical glass. It is held in place by the friction of the ground surface of the glass. A little groove is cast into the side of the stopper to allow air to flow into the chamber of the cruet as the liquid flows out. If it did nothing more than that, it would be worthy of acclaim. But the flared neck of the glass acts as a funnel to catch drips, which re-enter the bottle through the air groove in the stopper, a brilliant solution to a perennial problem with all sorts of decanters, bottles, teapots and other pourers. A benefit of this non-drip solution to pouring is, of course, that rims of liquid do not gather on the bottom. Rafael Marquina is somewhat of a design polymath, crossing with ease into the worlds of architecture and fine art. And while his international legacy may be tied to these cruets, he is revered in his native Catalonia as one of the visionary modernists of the century.

THIS IS THE NEW JAGUAR XK-E!

# 576

Jaguar E-Type Roadster (1961)
William Heynes (1903–89)
Sir William Lyons (1901–85)
Malcolm Sayer (1916–70)
Jaguar Cars 1961 to 1974

**The Jaguar Cars Company** is a British institution, a rare combination of radical stylishness and tradition. Unlike Rolls Royce, but like Alfa Romeo it defines its contribution to tradition through its evocation of a level of quality and luxury which combines the best of the old and the new. Headed by one man, Sir William Lyons, until his death in 1985, the company evolved from being a sidecar manufacturer to a producer of stylish, streamlined cars which blurred the distinction between the race track and the road. Indeed the remarkable E-Type roadster of 1961, styled by Malcolm Sayer, took the idea of transferring the high performance racing car on to the road to create a car which was a total experience. Fun to drive its elongated, sculptural form enhanced its low, road-hugging character which was inspired by the race-track. The E-Type stood for youth and excitement. Available in a topless and a coupé version its sleek forms led to its being selected as the third car to enter The Museum of Modern Art in New York's permanent design collection. The lines of the E-Type bear close analysis: the tiny radiator grille and integrated elliptical headlights are positioned such that they do not interrupt the flowing form of the extended bonnet. No chrome extras disguise the clarity of the lines. The coupé version, perhaps the more superior design of the two models, features a curved rear line of which begins above the front window – the glass is subtly curved – and reaches in one continuous sweep down to the rear fender. A product of the youthful 1960s of which it was an integral part and a marker of the level of design sophistication achieved by that pioneering company, the E-Type sits among Jaguar's more grown up cars – the Mark X and the XJ6 among them. Alongside Burberry raincoats and Church's shoes it remains a symbol of Britishness.

575

Maya (1961)
Tias Eckhoff (1926–)
Norsk Staalpress/Norstaal 1961 to present

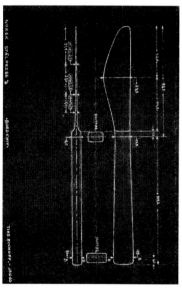

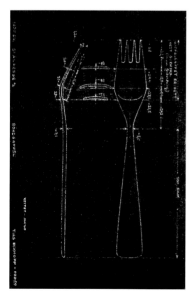

**Tias Eckhoff** was among a small group who helped to move Norwegian design out of the shadow of its neighbours during the 1950s. Eckhoff's designs, including ceramics, glassware and tableware, have an enduring quality that has seen many of them remain in production for several decades. Simplicity is a key aspect of his work, inspired, according to the designer, by a farmyard upbringing close to the cottage of the district's 'sovereign craftsman', where he spent much time during his child-hood, observing how big problems were dealt with through simple remedies. He also tempers a rational and scientific approach with a strong artistic sensibility that ensures his designs are beautiful as well as practical. His Maya flatware was the first product of a relationship with Norsk Staalpress (now Norstaal) that began when Eckhoff met founder Finn Henriksen at a trade show in the late 1950s. The collaboration would later yield a number of cutlery sets. Maya, created in brushed stain-less steel, and made from pressing stainless steel plates, embodies the Scandinavian pursuit of 'beautiful things for everyday use.' The relatively generous spoons and knife blades contrast with short handles in a 'sculptural' way that was also distinctively Scandinavian. There are thirty-five steps involved, from the initial stage to the final product, with the extremely difficult process of grinding and polishing done by hand by a number of skilled metalworkers. The design is one of the most complicated products which Norstaal creates, due to the distinctive streamlining. The design was still sufficiently radical for mainstream European and American tastes that overseas sales did not take off until the 1970s. Today, around 25 per cent of sales are from exports, mainly to the Far East and North America. Eckhoff has won a wide array of prizes domestically and internationally, including medals at the Milan Triennale in the 1950s and 1960s, and the 1991 Design Classic prize from the Norwegian Design Council and the Scandinavian Design Prize in 1992, both for Maya. The twenty-piece set, Norstaal's biggest seller, was modified in 2000 with the addition of a slightly longer soup spoon, dinner knife and fork, made to match dinnerplates of a larger size, and were resized by Eckhoff himself.

657

4751

1956

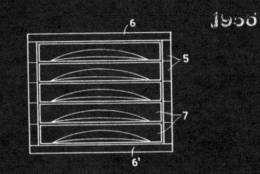

6
5
7
6'

Fig. 1

5
10
9
8'
9
8

Fig. 2

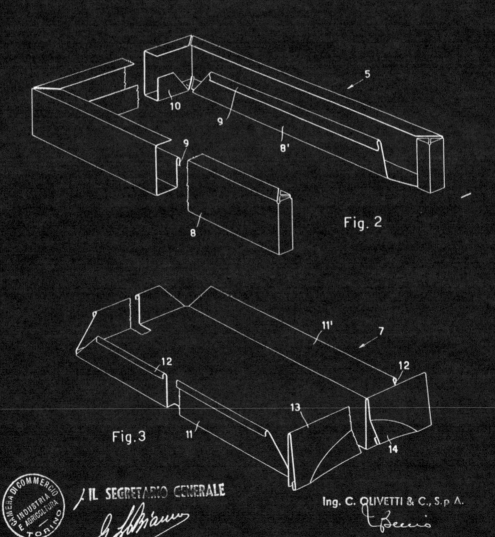

11'
7
12
12
13
11
14

Fig. 3

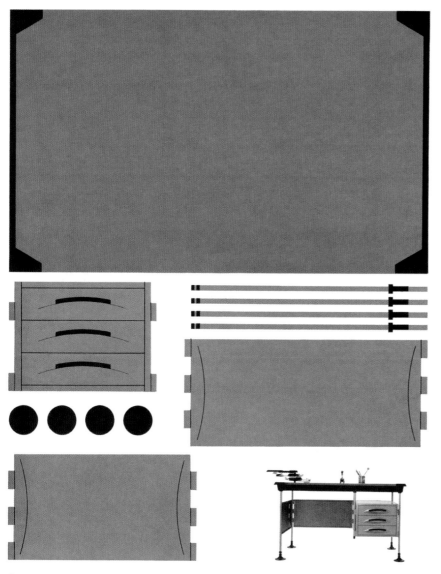

Ogni particolare dei mobili metallici Spazio riflette la perfezione tecnica, la solidità costruttiva, la semplice e razionale eleganza dei prodotti Olivetti. Spazio è l'arredamento Olivetti a elementi modulari componibili per la moderna organizzazione aziendale.

*Olivetti "Spazio"*

**Arredamenti metallici**

**Olivetti's Spazio Office System,** designed by BBPR (an acronym for the designers Banfi, di Belgiojoso, Peressutti and Rogers), was not so much a conceptually radical idea in terms of spatial configuration as it was an exciting and innovative example of unique, interchangeable product design. Comprised of elemental units manufactured from simple industrial products – steel sheeting, tubes and bars – these worked together to form a number of arrangements for office desks, shelves and units. This do-it-yourself assembly approach resulted in a number of highly complex, yet flexible and functional configurations, offering not only an extensive choice of organizational solutions for office environments, but also, with its four-colour series options, the opportunity to match each one visually to individual company requirements. Heavy steel elements that required complicated welding were replaced here by a system of threading, grooving or folding mechanisms that connected the standard modules. These surface tops (available with coverings in vinyl or cloth), drawers and the panels in their component sections relied on the tubular parts for both structure and support. The thin steel sheeting over large surfaces was given a gentle curvature to compensate for weakness; together with triangular component detailing, the system expressed itself visually as an informal and accessible office solution. This system was a high-quality product; because the basic elements could be manufactured with ease, the standardized process yielded production uniformity and precision. The Spazio System attempted to address the problems of noise and distraction in the open-plan working environment. Additionally, an increasing need to delineate individual space and to convey status was met through the system's limitless structural possibilities. Over twenty desk variations, combined with varying arrangements of independent drawers, adjustable shelves, small cupboards and hanging spaces, ensured individuality, privacy and a sense of hierarchy for its users. It was rightly awarded the Compasso d'Oro in 1962.

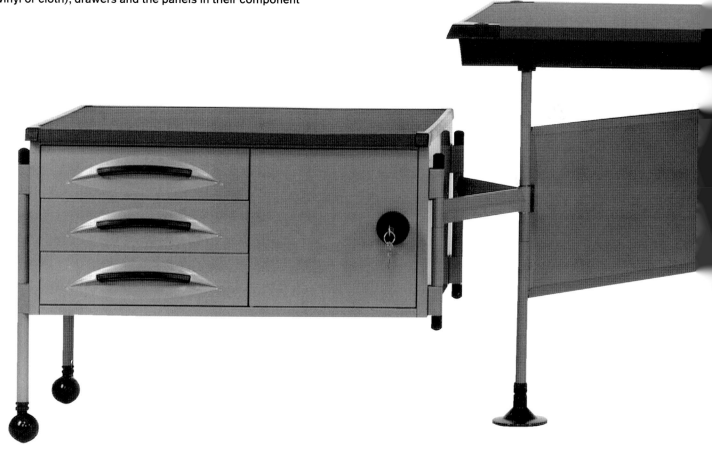

technical credentials, reliability and durability also exerted a magnetic pull on the car buyer of the time. Each vehicle, which contained a 300 hp engine, faced numerous tests and inspections to monitor the quality of the production process, and so convinced was the Ford Motor Company of its reliability that the model was accompanied by a 24-month/24,000-mile warranty, as opposed to the 12-month/12,000-mile warranty of its predecessors and competitors. The combination of sleek, streamlined elegance and solid dependability earned the 1961 Lincoln Continental many fans: Picasso had one. Most poignantly, it was the preferred presidential car of the Kennedy era, and the model in which the president was travelling when he was assassinated in Dallas on 22 November 1963.

# 573

Lincoln Continental (1961)
George W Walker (1896–1993)
Eugene Bordinat (1920–87)
Ford Motor Company 1961 to 1969

**The introduction** of the coolly understated, streamlined Lincoln Continental in 1961 heralded a new era in American car design and effectively brought an end to the earlier fashion of more flamboyant models, such as the chrome-festooned and razor-sharp fender-finned Cadillac that dominated the US car market at the time. The 1961 Lincoln Continental was a bold step for the Ford Motor Company. To attempt to introduce a car that flew in the face of prevailing trends was a risky move, but one that ultimately paid off. The 1961 Lincoln Continental's response to the ever more decadent styling of its competitors was to present a smaller model with clean, straight lines, with quality trim and accessories, in addition to a rational symmetry. The Lincoln achieved this effect by incorporating extremely flat body panels, outlined in a narrow stainless-steel moulding. In addition, side panels that were almost vertical dispensed with the usual mid-point bulge that characterized the finned and sculptured look of the popular Cadillac and Chrysler models. The 1961 Lincoln Continental came in two body styles: a four-door sedan and a four-door convertible, with a completely automatic soft-top. The four-door convertible version was the first of its kind in a decade, and proved extremely popular. The classic car also formed the basis of the quintessential stretch limousine design, which was achieved by essentially slicing the car in half, extending it and then refinishing the whole. As well as the simple, understated good looks of the 1961 Lincoln Continental, its advanced

**EJ 5-M**
**EJ 5-W**

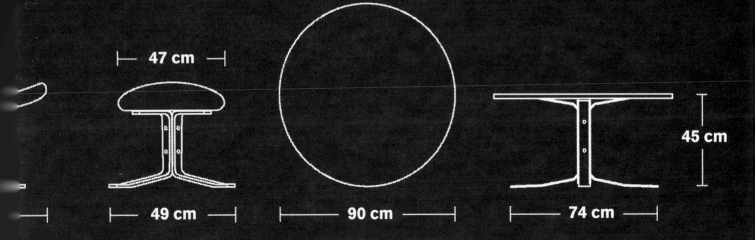

47 cm

45 cm

49 cm

90 cm

74 cm

**EJ 5**

**EJ 5-F**

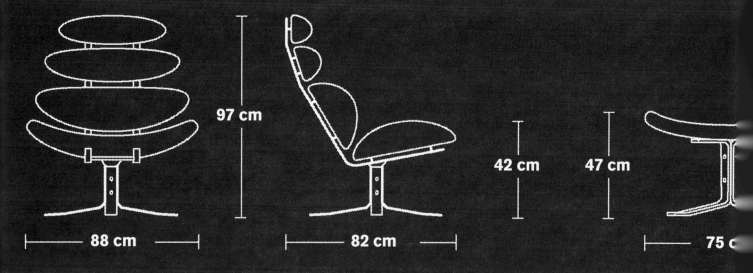

97 cm

88 cm

82 cm

42 cm

47 cm

75 c

**572**

EJ Corona (1961)
Poul Volther (1923–2001)
Eric Jørgensen 1961 to present

Poul Volther

## The EJ Corona chair,

designed in 1961 by Danish architect Poul Volther, is visually and structurally symbolic of tensions within the Scandinavian furniture industry in the early 1960s. Anticipating change, and poised on the cusp of a dramatic decade of design, the chair nonetheless responded to important ideological and manufacturing tenets of the previous decade. Its structure is defined by four graduated and curving elliptical shapes that seem to hover in space; indeed, its name, 'Corona', signifies its visual association with time-lapse solar eclipse photography. The forms are supported by a chromium-plated steel frame and pivoting base. The covering was initially manufactured in leather and later in fabric, which in turn enclosed neoprene-upholstered plywood seat and back elements. The frame of the original model was constructed in solid oak and produced in very small numbers by Danish furniture manufacturer Erik Jørgensen. By 1962 plywood had replaced the oak to afford larger-scale production. The influence of Pop art and design was certainly felt amongst Scandinavian designers in the 1960s, but the latter were far more reluctant than their Italian and British counterparts to forgo the tradition of high-quality production. The disposable ethic enthusiastically championed by other European manufacturers held less of an appeal for early 1960s Scandinavian furniture designers and producers. The visually organic legacy of Arne Jacobsen, and his innovative, single-seat shell constructions which supported high-density, rigid polyurethane, remained the template for avant-garde Scandinavian endeavour. The forms and signifiers of Pop certainly appealed, but a truthful use of materials (though now, in part, in synthetic forms), as realized in the EJ Corona chair, continued to convince Scandinavian designers such as Volther that quality production was the ideal. Today the extremely comfortable Corona Chair remains one of the Erik Jørgensen's most popular products.

Bell UH-1 'Huey' (1961)
Bartram Kelley (1909–98)
Bell Aircraft Corporation 1961 to c.1975

**Perhaps because of** an unforgettable
sequence in Francis Ford Coppola's film, *Apocalypse
Now,* but also because of its very ubiquity in the news
broadcasts and popular lore of the time, the Bell UH-1
is eternally linked to the Vietnam War. The name 'Huey'
was only a nickname, derived from the original US Army
designation, HU-1, for 'Helicopter Utility'. But the name
stuck, and with it, the reaction it provokes for the
Vietnam generation. The design lineage of the Huey
refers directly to a helicopter of an earlier era,
the Bell 47, primarily designed by Arthur Young.
Engineer and physicist Bartram Kelley was Arthur
Young's protégé on the design of the Bell 47, and a
key member of the Bell helicopter team. So when team-
guru, Arthur Young, took an early retirement to return to
an academic life as a philosopher, it was inevitable that
Kelley should take up the reins. The timing could not
have been better. The push was on for the next
generation military helicopter, the Model 204, and
Kelley was perfectly placed to do the design
engineering. The 204 would ultimately bear fruit as the
Huey. The major leap forwards for the Huey was
Kelley's choice of a Lycoming turbine engine for the
new chopper. Designed by Dr Anselm Franz, who led
the German race for a jet engine during World War II,
the turbine engine had a number of distinct advantages
over piston engines for helicopter use. Unlike recip-
rocating engines, turbine engines spin effortlessly
around an axis at high speed, creating smooth,
vibration-free power. The army originally ordered the
Huey for the role of medical evacuation, or 'Medevac',
to use the military jargon. Later, it was developed into a
highly effective platform for all sorts of weaponry, from
missiles to machine-guns. And it was in this latter role
that it achieved its greatest fame in the Vietnam era.
The Huey, in all its manifestations, is one of the most
influential and successful rotor aircraft of all time. Over
its twenty-three-year production period, over 16,000
were built, many of which are still in service.

## Reinhold Weiss's HL 1/11 Portable

HL 1/11 Portable Fan (1961)
Reinhold Weiss (1934–)
Braun 1961 to 1965

Fan is not only a functional and stylistic gem but also a symbol of the alliance between the increasingly progressive industrial design manufacturers Braun, the leading exponents of the rationalist approach to design from the mid-1950s to the late 1960s, and the ultra-modern Hochschule für Gestaltung at Ulm in Germany. The plastic and metal air-conditioning fan at 14 cm (5 in) across, a favourite gadget of John F Kennedy on his presidential travels, was the first portable air-conditioning fan that Braun produced. Its freestanding form is typically functional, yet beautifully refined, with its smooth encased 'engine' at one end and circular, striated louvre arrangement allowing for optimum air circulation at the other. Its combination of technical bravado and rational first principles with one eye on the mechanics of mass production firmly encapsulates the Braun philosophy of the period. Established in 1921 as a radio manufacturer, the Braun company was successfully taken into a new design era in the postwar period by the founder's sons Artur and Erwin, who developed a wider range of innovative and high quality products that put the Braun brand on the global map. In 1960 the Braun product line comprised four main categories, each with a principal designer: Dieter Rams at radio and hi-fi, Richard Fischer at shavers, Robert Oberheim at photographic equipment and Reinhold Weiss at the helm of household and personal care appliances. A graduate of the Ulm school, Weiss brought a sober sensibility as well as honest clarity to a range of now immediately recognizable products. But sadly, the HL 1/11 Portable Fan is no longer in production.

in the United States. Identifying motorcycle designers is always tricky, particularly in the design-by-committee world of British and Japanese bike manufacturing. But the two men most closely associated with the Gold Star are Val Page, one of the great designers of British industry, and development engineer, Roland Pike, who took the Goldie to its ultimate expression in the DBD34 series. At the heart of the Gold Star is its engine, with aluminium cylinder and cylinder head, and characteristic swept exhaust pipe. These project an image of toughness and speed, qualities that contributed handsomely to the Gold Star's success. By the end of its life in 1964, the Gold Star DBD34, together with some of its off-road siblings, were among the most beautiful BSAs ever produced.

**While steep-banked** motor-racing tracks are usually thought of as American, one of the most famous in the world was Brooklands, in Surrey, just south of London. Many speed and distance records for cars and bikes were set at Brooklands, and if a rider achieved the rare feat of lapping at 160 kph (100 mph) or greater, the British Motorcycle Racing Club awarded him a gold star. In 1937, BSA rider Walter Handley had several done

several hundred laps of Brooklands riding an experimental 500cc Empire Star. In 1938, celebrating that Brooklands triumph, BSA introduced the M24 Gold Star, the first in a line of sporting Gold Stars that was to become one of the most celebrated in British motorcycling history. The Gold Star evolved in several ways over its lifetime, particularly after the end of World War II.  The postwar decade was, in many ways, a golden age of British motorcycle

design and the 'Goldie', as it was known, took its place alongside the Manx Norton and Matchless G50 as one of the greatest 500cc single-cylinder machines ever made. The Norton and Matchless, however, were genuine race bikes. The Gold Star was principally a sporting road machine, capable of being ridden to work during the week, and in races, motocross and trials at the weekend. It was this versatility that guaranteed its success both in Britain and

**The intricate criss-crossing** of rattan stems and the circular, cocooning shape lend Isamu Kenmochi's lounge chair the appearance of a nest. Called variously the Rattan Chair, the Lounge Chair or the 38 Chair, it was originally designed for the bar of the New Japan Hotel in Tokyo, as part of Kenmochi's brief to update the Yamakawa Rattan Company's range of products. Kenmochi was a Japanese architect and designer who studied under the German architect Bruno Taut. He toured the United States in the 1940s. When New York's Museum of Modern Art purchased the Rattan Chair for its permanent collection in 1964 it was an historic moment for modern Asian design. The contrast of the unconventional shape of the Rattan, and the traditional methods used to make it, was not only recognized by MoMA: Kenmochi was also awarded the coveted Japanese G-Mark award in 1966 and the G-Mark Long Life award in 1982. The construction of rattan furniture is a wonderfully simple procedure that starts with the harvesting of good-quality rattan, a solid timber vine. The rattan is first steamed until it becomes pliable. It is then fitted to a jig, to form the required shape, and left to cool. Although Kenmochi was a staunch supporter of traditional construction techniques he was also an avid researcher into cutting-edge production methods, particularly those of aircraft construction. Despite this he never used metal for his furniture; woods indigenous to Japan (such as rattan) were the only materials Kenmochi used. It is the billowing, airy appearance of the Rattan Chair, a true break from convention, which has made it an enduring design that is still produced by the same company today, albeit with slight variations. Indeed, it proved so successful that Kenmochi subsequently added a sofa and stool to the Rattan range, as it suits both commercial and domestic interiors.

## The Table Type Soy Sauce Bottle for

Kikkoman combines practicality with a creative modernist design that owes much to Raymond Loewy's streamlined design style. As a form, the bottle designed by Kenji Ekuan is reassuringly familiar yet mildly exotic. Ekuan's design manifests practical, sturdy elements in the wide base, ensuring stability. The flowing, tapering form suggests a teardrop and gives the bottle a soft, organic shape. However, this is sharply contrasted at the top by the bold, red flat-topped cap, which, ingeniously, has a double opening ensuring against drips when pouring. The innovation behind this well-known soy sauce bottle is in Ekuan's vision of designing a bottle that could be placed directly on the table. The Kikkoman Soy Sauce bottle was intended to be used as part of a table-top condiment set. It is Ekuan's forward-thinking ideas that have paved the way in the discussion of brand identity and contemporary design in Japan and Ekuan is a founding member of the GK Design Group in Japan. The first members of this company had all studied outside Japan as part of a government initiative by the Japanese Ministry. It was decided that design was of utmost importance to Japan since the country depended on processing, manufacture and export for its livelihood. Designers were given the opportunity to study abroad in West Germany and America, and brought back knowledge of Western processes and standards. GK Design was officially established as a company in 1957, and its influence is apparent in the praise the designs received in the press of the day – indeed they were seen as evidence of the new westernization phenomenon. The successful cruet design exemplifies longevity. Made in robust, dishwasher-safe glass, the bottle is refillable and virtually unbreakable. This is married to its enduring form: its unique appearance and striking red cap are intended to set the product apart from the competition, making it instantly recognizable and a pleasing item for any modern kitchen.

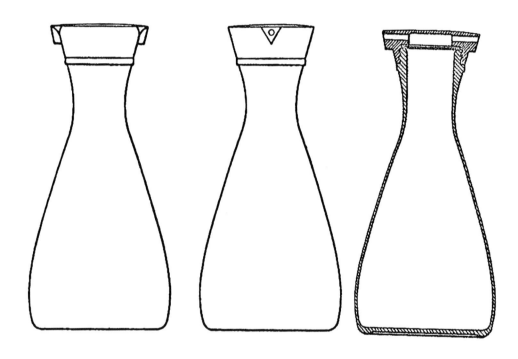

**566**

Mixing Bowls (1960)
Sori Yanagi (1915–)
Uehan-Shoji 1960 to 1978
NAS Trading Company 1978 to 1994
Sato-Shoji 1994 to present

**When Sori Yanagi,** renowned for his Butterfly Stool, started to design this set of five mixing bowls he started with actual size models rather than with drawings, saying, 'When you make an object that is to be used by hand, it should be made by hand.' A process of making numerous experimental models determined the size and the shape of each bowl. The smallest bowl, designed for making dressings or sauces, is 13 cm (5.1 in) in diameter. The next bowl, designed for mixing three eggs, is 16 cm (6.3 in). The 19 cm (7.5 in) bowl can be used as a serving bowl, while the 23 cm (9 in) bowl, the only one with a round form, can be held firmly under the arm to mix ingredients for baking. The largest bowl at 27 cm (10.6 in) is useful for washing vegetables or can be used as a wine cooler. The bottoms of all the bowls are flat and extra thick, making them heavier than conventional oncs and contributing to their stability. Made of stainless steel, the surface is a matt brushed finish. The edges are carefully rolled over so they do not catch washing up tools or debris. Originally the bowls were designed for the Uehan-Shoji Company, but since 1994 they have been made by Sato-Shoji, known by their 'Martian' trademark. In 1999 Yanagi designed strainers to fit each bowl using punched stainless steel sheets. His rediscovery by a younger generation in recent years has seen these bowls and strainers become one of the bestselling ranges of kitchenware in Japan, appreciated for their functionality and their beauty. For Yanagi, who was heavily influenced by the Bauhaus, the form of these bowls simply follows the use.

# 調理器具

使いやすくあきのこないシンプルなデザインを心がけています。素材は丈夫で清潔な18-8ステンレスを基本にして用途に応じパンチング材、エキスパンドメタル、ブルーテンパ材、鉄鋳物、耐熱強化ガラス等を使用し、使いやすく耐久性があるものとなっています。

## 耐熱ガラスボール

使いやすくシンプルなデザインのガラスボールです。調理から盛りつけ保存まで幅広くお使いいただけます。耐熱強化ガラスを使用しているため電子レンジからオーブンまで使え、ショックに強く、割れにくいのが特徴です。チタンコーティングが施されているので汚れが着きにくく、汚れが着いても簡単に落とせます。別売のステンレス製パンチングストレーナーと組合せて使えるよう、大きさを揃えてあります。直火での使用はできません。

16cm ¥1,365
φ160 × H68 0.6L

ふた19cm ¥1,155
φ192 × H18

19cm ¥1,575
φ192 × H85 1.2L

### 耐熱ガラスふたについて

ふたは19cmのみですが、ボール19cmと16cmにお使いいただけます。本体と同じ耐熱強化ガラス製なので電子レンジ、オーブンで使用できます。直火での使用はできません。

オーブン　食器洗浄機　電子レンジ

23cm ¥2,310
φ240 × H102 2.0L

## ステンレスボール

このステンレスボールは18-8ステンレスを使用しており、大変丈夫で清潔です。料理の専門家や多くの家庭の主婦の意見にもとづき、良い研究を重ねてデザインしたものです。用途に応じ、小（13cm・16cm・19cm）ははまりこむ様に底が絞ってあり、中（23cm）はミキシングしやすい様に深めに曲線が工夫され、大（27cm）は洗い桶にも使える様大きめになっております。

13cm ¥893
φ132 × H50 0.4L

16cm ¥1,155
φ158 × H65 0.7L

19cm ¥1,418
φ185 × H77 1.2L

23cm ¥1,943
φ231 × H119 3.4L

27cm ¥2,415
φ272 × H117 4.2L

## パンチングストレーナー

パンチング加工された18-8ステンレスは目詰まりしにくく洗いやすく丈夫で清潔です。接地面の少ない断面形状で水切りの良い設計になっています。

### 手付きパンチングストレーナー

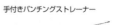

19cm ¥2,415
φ193 × 300 × 90

27cm ¥3,150
φ276 × H103

23cm ¥2,625
φ238 × H86

19cm ¥1,890
φ193 × H69

16cm ¥1,470
φ164 × H63

パンチングストレーナーは、ステンレスボール・耐熱ガラスボールと組合せて使えるようにサイズを設定してあります。ただし13cmのボールに合うストレーナーはありません。

# 565

**Humble everyday objects** are often the unsung heroes of design. A perfect example of this is the small Plastic Ice Cream Spoon developed in the 1960s to accompany individual pots of ice cream. Plastic was still a relatively new material at the time, but due to breakthroughs in manufacturing techniques and as well as chemical composition, the opportunities for the material seemed endless. The 1960s saw the market flooded with affordable plastic goods. These new plastics were perfect for household objects. No longer were they brittle and dark in colour; the new plastics were brightly coloured, flexible and with the added appeal of being hygienic and easy to clean. The Ice Cream Spoon, although disposable, replaced the wooden spatula and was instantly adopted as the preferred cutlery utensil. The 1960s saw the emergence of the ice cream stand, which sold ice cream in tubs as an alternative to the cone or wafer. With no wafer or edible receptacle provided, a spoon was needed, and the ingenious solution was a lid with a spoon that sat in the top. The spoon was designed with a square flat bowl for ease of packaging, a wide handle for ease of use and the flat front to scoop into the frozen food. Industrial moulding techniques in manufacture allowed for such objects to be made quickly, cheaply and in large numbers. While the spoon was intended to be disposable, and despite this not being an age where recycling, sustainability and environmental concerns were at the forefront of the public's mind, these small desirable objects were often washed and kept, later to be found in kitchen drawers and picnic baskets.

# 56-4

Moon Lamp (1960)
Verner Panton (1926–98)
Louis Poulsen 1960 to c.1970
Vitra Design Museum 2003 to present

**An early light** by Danish designer Verner Panton, the Moon Lamp is a complex, abstract hanging form made of ten metal rings of diminishing size, fitted onto mobile bearings so that each ring can be rotated. The rings act as shutters for the light, which is diffused between them and reflected from the shiny surfaces. The quality of light can be adjusted by moving the rings. The first versions were produced in white lacquered aluminium, and later in plastic. The lamp has the added advantage of being able to be packed flat for transportation. Verner Panton produced some of the most innovative furniture and lighting of the postwar period. Exploiting the properties of new materials such as acrylic, foam, plastic and glass fibre-reinforced polyester, he created playful, organic forms that made vivid use of colour and soft and reflective surfaces. His work is closely connected to the Op and Pop Art movements of the late 1950s and 1960s. His lamps incorporated mirrored materials, clear and coloured plastic fittings, and even metal chains and shell discs. Panton's vibrant and futuristic interiors of the 1960s used lighting as a fundamental element, literally built in to the fabric of the room and melded with the furniture. He trained as an architect, and was closely connected to some of the key figures in Danish Modernism. As a student, Panton was taught by the influential lighting designer, Poul Henningsen, who introduced him to the idea of product design as a radical (as well as commercial) area of design practice. Henningsen's lighting, which combined an industrial sensibility with a sensitivity to the technical and ambient possibilities of light, was clearly a central influence on the development of the Moon Lamp. Henningsen's PH series of lamps (produced by Louis Poulsen from 1924) uses a similar shuttering system of overlapping leaves to eliminate glare. The Moon Lamp was included in a major retrospective of the designer's career by the Vitra Design Museum in 2000, which also holds Panton's archive and a substantial collection of his work, and have put it into production since 2003.

Timo Sarpaneva

A black cast-iron cooking pot lined with white enamel, the Sarpaneva Cast Iron Pot is both modern yet friendly and familiar, its shape in part taken from the simple forms of Finnish folk traditions. These historic roots are emphasized further by the pot's detachable wooden handle to facilitate lifting the pan off the stove and carrying it to the table. Sarpaneva was true to the tenets of Scandinavian Modernism, where the human being rather than the machine was placed on a pedestal, and believed that good design sold at reasonable prices could improve the overall quality of life. His pot is an important piece since it is an example of something modern that wasn't necessarily new – a very different position in the Modernist debate to that of the Bauhaus. The design of the pot celebrated a modern way of life rather than adhering to a strictly industrial language of form, and was radical in its concept, rather than in its style. In it, Sarpaneva anticipated a more relaxed, modern way of eating, where the utensil used to cook a dish could also be used to serve it, and opened the way for oven-to-table ware. Sarpaneva preferred to work in ways that revealed the high quality of his country's craft tradition, believing that, 'If you are not familiar with the traditions you cannot renew them.' The pot was made using traditional cast-iron techniques, which Sarpaneva had direct experience of: cast iron has been used as a material for kitchen utensils in Finland for centuries. Moreover, his grandfather was a smith from the Finnish countryside. Sarpaneva saw tactile pleasure as an important part of the design process. Equally important was his interest in the ways that natural forms could be mimicked in the man-made objects that surround us. He explored these principles in many different materials, including textiles, glass, ceramics and metal. The Sarpaneva Cast Iron Pot was originally manufactured by Rosenlew & Co, and won numerous awards, including the 1960 Milan Triennale. It was so beloved that it was reproduced a few years ago on a postage stamp as one of the cult objects of Finnish design, to be followed by its reintroduction by iittala in 2003.

Sarpaneva Cast Iron Pot (1960)
Timo Sarpaneva (1926–)
Rosenlew & Co 1960 to 1977
iittala 2003 to present

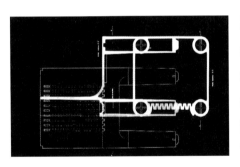

**In 1957** Italian designer Marco Zanuso formed a collaboration with German designer Richard Sapper. One of their first and most successful projects was a small, stackable child's chair in non-reinforced plastic for Kartell in 1964. The designers had initially thought about using laminate, but rejected the idea because of safety issues and because the varnish would have scratched easily. The final design, with its injection-moulded polyethylene ribbed seat section and separate injection-moulded legs on rubber feet is, in effect, the first large object ever produced in this material. The patents for polyethylene had expired in the mid-1960s, thereby lowering the material's cost. This piece was light and playful, and was manufactured in several bright colours. It was toy-like enough for a child's room, and heavy enough to be stable. The designers collaborated closely with Kartell in order to create larger legs to provide extra stability. It could be stacked but also linked sideways to create a ziggurat-like structure. The chair was one of the designs in the 1960s responsible for convincing people that plastic was a viable and appropriate material for the modern home and was rightfully awarded the prestigious Compasso d'Oro prize. Kartell manufactured the chair until 1979, when it was discontinued because the size of the average child had changed so much over the years that the measurements of the original chair had become obsolete. Nonetheless, the chair is a reflection of Zanuso's constant need throughout his career to experiment with a broad spectrum of materials, from bent metal to lush upholstery and sleek industrial plastic.

**561**

Ox Chair (1960)
Hans Wegner (1914–)
AP-Stolen 1960 to c.1975
Erik Jørgensen 1985 to present

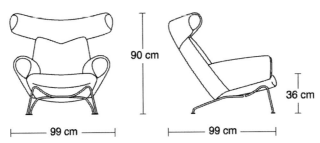

90 cm

36 cm

99 cm

99 cm

**The large, tubular 'horns'** and general bulk of this chair, especially when seen in profile, have provided it with its English name of Ox Chair. In Danish it is called the *Pållestolen* which translates as Bolster or Pillow Chair. Together, both names help to give an idea of the comfortable freestanding mass of this large easy chair, one of Wegner's favourite designs. It is claimed that this design has no precedents, but the form is related to the English wing armchair, one of the 'timeless types' of furniture much studied and adapted by the followers of Kaare Klint. The Ox Chair looks very much like a chromed-steel and leather update of this traditional form. In this design Wegner follows through a number of ideas that preoccupied him throughout his career. Firstly, the chair was intended to be situated towards the middle of a room, away from any wall, so it would be presented as a sculpturally whole object that can be viewed in the round. Secondly, and not surprisingly for a furniture designer, Wegner was concerned with comfort. Clearly the abundant, but firm, padding of the Ox Chair goes some way to providing this, but Wegner was especially aware that the sitter should be able to adopt a number of different seating positions. Wegner envisaged a comfortable lack of decorum and sitters are encouraged to slouch, sit asymmetrically and to swing their legs over the arms. The Ox Chair has a monumental quality that would dominate a room. A more slender version, without the horn-like protuberances, was produced as a companion piece.

Hans Wegner

# 560

Viscontea Cocoon Lamp (1960)
Achille Castiglioni (1918–2002)
Pier Giacomo Castiglioni (1913–68)
Eisenkeil/Flos 1960 to 1995, 2005 to present

**George Nelson's** experiments with metal-frame lamp structures inspired Achille Castiglioni to produce a series of decorative lamps for Flos in the 1960s, all luminous sculptures in which the white steel-wire frame was formed and then sprayed with cocoon, a film of plastic polymers, or spun fibreglass produced in the United States. The Viscontea Cocoon Lamp is one of this series, incorporating lights sprayed with the plastic polymers whose form is defined by the metallic structure. Castiglioni's career was inextricably linked with light manufacturer Flos since its beginnings, making it just one of Italy's many design success stories. The focus of Italian design of the postwar era was on invention, made possible by experimentation with new materials such as plastics, foam rubber and new variants of plywood. Entrepreneurial manufacturers keen to cash in on new low-cost materials were seen as the perfect employers for out-of-work architects and designers, and Flos was no exception. While Flos had produced earlier designs by the Castiglionis, it was the Viscontea which made the company's name by using cocoon. Italian importer Arturo Eisenkeil had started researching possible new applications for this material and, noticing a gap in the market, decided to collaborate with Dino Gavina and Cesare Cassina to create Flos, a company to produce lighting fixtures using this fibreglass. The company was originally established in Merano, Italy, the hometown of Eisenkeil, and the first cocoon lights to be created were the Viscontea, Taraxacum and Gatto by the Castiglioni brothers. The polymer would spray cobweb-like filaments that created a permanent, but flexible, membrane that was waterproof, and would resist corrosion, dust, oil, gas, and even liquids such as citric acid, alcohol and bleach. Cocoon, used for any type of surface or material, could revert back to its original shape after bearing a heavy load. This remarkable material is still used today for a wide number of applications, such as sealing outdoor walkways, or spraying ceilings in order to protect them. Flos eventually discontinued their production once their individual cocoon licence expired but resumed it in 2005.

Rams, a talented young designer, should fulfil his interests and passions not only for their company, but also for others. Rams met Niels Wiese Vitsœ through the designer Otto Zapf, who established Vitsœ + Zapf in 1959 specifically to create Rams' furniture designs. Zapf left the company in 1970, after which Rams and Vitsœ became acquainted with Mark Adams. Adams founded Vitsœ in London in 1985 and, as managing director, he brought the production and corporate business to London, where the 606 Universal gained its rightful international audience. The co-operation between Braun and Vitsœ remained, as Rams designed the Audio 1 Sound system in 1962, with its turntable, tape recorder, radio and speaker, specifically for the 606, following the same measurements. The first versions of the 606 were even in the same colour palette as such Braun products as the SK4, with off-white and beech lacquered doors and drawers. This understated approach was reflected in Rams' interest in the ordinariness of things, that 'the shelving system…should be like a good English butler. It should be there when you need them, and in the background when you don't.'

**The reductionist outline** of the 606 Universal Shelving System is based on geometric simplicity with minimum decoration. Its strength as a timeless design rests with this style, married with strong practical characteristics. The 606 is a wholly flexible shelving and storage system, composed of sheets of anodized aluminium, 3 mm (0.12 in) thick, which hang from an extruding wall-mounted aluminium track with 7 mm (0.04 in) aluminium pins. The system can be readily dismantled and moved, and easily accommodates the addition of more components from the range. Its multi-functionality is due to the host of components that may be arranged within the basic structure, including drawer sets, cabinets, hanging rails and shelves, all of which are designed to a series of standardized dimensions. The idea for the shelves developed when Dieter Rams, first employed by Braun in 1955 and later to become its executive director until 1995, responded to Erwin Braun's observation that people were increasingly transforming their domestic environments into modern spaces. Rams then suggested that he design an exhibition room for Braun to display its products along with his furniture. Both Erwin and Arthur Braun felt that

606 Universal Shelving System (1960)
Dieter Rams (1932–)
Vitsœ 1960 to present

Dieter Rams

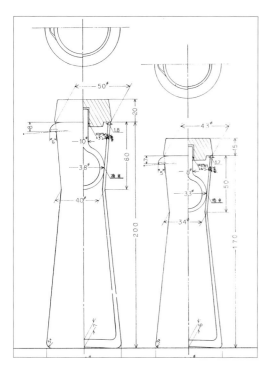

**This condiment set** was continuously in production up until 2003, since it was designed in 1960. The bottles were originally designed as part of a series of glass products by Saburo Funakoshi, a leading Japanese glass artist, for his one-man exhibition at the Matsuya department store in Tokyo, aiming to exemplify the superior quality of Japanese exports. Funakoshi then became head of the design department of Hoya Crystal, which became renowned for elegant crystal glass products and tableware produced in large quantities, as well as for decorative, handmade limited collections. Funakoshi remained with the company until his retirement in 1993. The set consists of containers for soy sauce, salt and mustard, and is made in two different sizes: 150 ml (0.26 pt) and 240 ml (0.42 pt). Funakoshi intended the larger bottles to be used to mix oil, vinegar and other seasonings at the table, allowing salad to be dressed freshly. To achieve this, the bottle has a special stopper. The top part, made of wood, is fixed to a glass ball by a short glass rod. To mix the contents, the user holds the bottle firmly, pushing down on the stopper with finger or thumb. The glass ball seals the neck of the bottle, allowing it to be shaken vigorously without any liquid escaping and ensuring that the top part of the bottle remains clean. The shape of the bottles makes reference to traditional Japanese pottery and lacquered tableware, but Funakoshi improved on these designs with his innovative opening, which prevented the liquid from spilling onto the outer surface. Earlier tableware was accompanied by a tray for this very purpose. The glass balls are hand blown by skilled craftsmen, and each has an irregular-shaped void within, giving the products a charming human touch. The set was first granted a G-Mark, the Japanese Good Design Award, in 1964 and was then further honoured in 1980 with a Long-Life Design Award for twenty years of excellence. Combining elegant use of material qualities with a practical design solution, this product reinterprets traditional forms, leading it to become a popular item for both industrial and domestic tableware.

**Having built a reputation** on the development of transistor technology for portable radios, Sony turned its attention in the late 1950s to the their use in television. Although narrowly beaten by the Philco Safari as the first all-transistor television, the TV8-301 nonetheless represented a significant milestone as the first direct-view transistor TV and the first Japanese TV to be sold in the United States. The Philco model was a clever design, but one that never really caught on; it achieved its slim shape and genuine portability by having its picture tube mounted vertically. This projected the image on to an angled concave mirror which, while magnifying the image, gave a rather narrow and uncomfortable field of vision. Sony's tube, by comparison, was mounted horizontally, but allowed the image to be viewed from all angles. Prior to the development of transistors, televisions were bulky items whose reliability was let down by valve technology that tended to require replacement on a regular basis. Not only that, but they tended to be conceived, design-wise, as furniture. Sony's consummate flair for the design of miniature appliances led it to the product's unusual shape – largely dictated by the dimensions of the 20 cm (8 in) picture tube. At only 6 kg (13 lb) this machine was truly portable, running from either AC, 6V DC or rechargeable batteries. The interior, with the picture tube and chassis, was designed first, and the exterior laid out around it, along with a hood on the top, acting as a visor to reduce glare. Contemporary advertising in the United States sang the praises of the space-age nature of the design, including its 'space-age' reliability and compactness as well as its 'space-age' alkaline battery pack. If anyone was still in any doubt, it also had a picture of a rocket on the screen. Because of its high price, the TV8-301 did not capture a huge market share. Televisions were still considered a luxury commodity at the time, and larger, cheaper sets represented better value for money. Despite this expense and a questionable record for reliability, it did have its fans, among them, it is reputed, President Kennedy. History does not relate what they might have been watching, but a high proportion of US consumers would have been enjoying *Bonanza,* the biggest TV hit of the era. Sony continues to develop the market for increasingly personal, miniaturized TVs to this day, with intermediate product innovations including the LCD Watchman in 1988 and the aptly named 'Tummy TV' of 1965.

George Nakashima

**In an era** when bent plywood and metal were the materials of choice for most furniture designers, George Nakashima unashamedly celebrated wood in its most naked state. Although the Conoid Chair is more refined than many of his designs (his tables, for instance, were often just slabs of unsquared wood on legs), the richness and texture of the woods used are still very much in evidence. When the Conoid was first introduced in 1960 it was greeted with derision by many in the furniture industry, who claimed it to be both unstable and unsafe. Time, though, has proved these accusations wrong, as Nakashima's intimate knowledge of joinery made for an impressively solid chair, with a cantilevered construction that was not as precarious as his critics claimed. The Conoid Chair, which was produced in a wide range of woods, including East Indian rose and Japanese cherry, was conceived on Nakashima's estate in New Hope, Pennsylvania. Just three years earlier he had completed the building of an incredibly complex but softly shaped studio, which he named the Conoid Studio.

Its concrete-shell roof is said to have inspired Nakashima's Conoid collection, which included tables, benches and desks in addition to the dining chair. George Nakashima was born in America to Japanese parents, both of whom were descended from Samurai families. Nakashima took his Japanese heritage seriously and had a great interest in Buddhism and Shinto, both faiths that encourage a deep reverence of nature. Equally influential on his furniture designs was the American Shaker style; indeed, Nakashima often referred to himself as a 'Japanese Shaker'. While most American furniture designers were preoccupied with testing technological limits, Nakashima encouraged a more spiritual, craft-based approach. Yet his style was entirely modern, as was his core belief in functionality, so it is no surprise that of all the designers working in the 1950s and 1960s there are few whose work is as in demand today as George Nakashima's. Nakashima's New Hope studio is now run by his daughter, and it still produces and sells numerous Conoid Chairs.

In 1960, brothers Achille and Pier Giacomo Castiglioni were commissioned by Aldo Bassetti to design the interior of his Splügen Bräu beerhouse and restaurant located on Corso Europa in Milan. Housed on the ground floor of a building designed by Luigi Caccia Dominioni was a spectacular, warm-coloured open space made more intimate with various tiered seating levels. The Castiglioni brothers designed several of the fittings specifically for the project, including this pendant lamp, which hung gracefully above each table in the from the high ceiling. The shade is made from thick, corrugated polished aluminium with a highly polished spun aluminium reflector. The ribbed body aids heat dispersal from the silver-domed bulb that lets off an indirect but concentrated light source onto the subject below. At Splügen Bräu, the general overhead supplementary lighting reflected off the polished surface of the shade, helping to accentuate the presence of the hanging light and its eye-catching ripple effect. Unfortunately, the Splügen Bräu restaurant was destroyed in the early 1980s. However, many of the furnishings were subsequently produced. In 1961, leading Italian lighting manufacturer Flos put the Splügen Bräu Lamp into production, which continues to enjoy commercial success today. The Servofumo Ashtray and Servopluvio Umbrella Stand were also produced by Flos until 1970 when Zanotta took over production, followed by the Spluga high-backed bar stool in 1986. Eventually, Alessi also released reproductions of the beerglasses and bottle openers in 2001. The legacy of the Splügen Bräu project lives on today through this product collection, and later proved to be one in a long list of influential projects by the Castiglioni brothers. Their functional purist approach was always lifted with a playful twist and continues to inspire designers around the world.

**Splügen Bräu beerhouse, Milan**

# Until now we were merely the most accurate watch in the world.

The movement in the Accutron watch you buy is just like the one we sent to the Moon with the Apollo 11 astronauts. The Accutron timer left on the Moon has been designed to provide accurate pulse signals for a period of a year without any further help from Earth. And it will do just that after being blasted off, sent through space, landed on the Moon and having withstood the uncertainties of the lunar environment.

## Accutron® by Bulova
# The most accurate watch in the universe.

Every hour of the day, an American Airlines plane is in the air. Every day, these "Flagships" fly 50,000 miles — twice around the world — by Bulova Watch Time!

Accutron Space Watch (1960)
Max Hetzel (1921–)
Bulova Watch Company 1961 to 1977

**The Accutron Space Watch** was the world's first electronic watch, and revolutionized the watch-making industry. Invented by Max Hetzel, the watch was launched to great acclaim in 1960; never before had a watch at any price been available that was so accurate. In the 1950s the best mechanical watches could rely on a primary moving element with a frequency of around 2 Hz, or two 'beats' per second. The Accutron did not feature a traditional spiral balance spring and escapement mechanism that ticked, which had been the staple mechanism for watch-makers for over 450 years. Instead, the Accutron had a miniature electrically excited tuning fork movement with a frequency of 360 Hz, which kept time to an accuracy of within two seconds per day or one minute per month and produced the watch's distinctive hum and sweep second hand. Cased in steel, gold or platinum, the number of component parts was dramatically reduced to a mere twenty-seven, of which only twelve were moving parts. By comparison, the most efficient self-winding watches of the era contained about one hundred and thirty-six parts, with twenty-six of them moving. Production began in November 1960 and the watches were introduced to the public in 1961. The Accutron proved extremely profitable for Bulova, which manufactured nearly five million tuning fork watches before ceasing production in 1977 to concentrate on quartz watches. During the seventeen years that tuning fork watches were made, they were the most accurate production timepieces on earth, and in space. In 1960 NASA asked Bulova to incorporate Accutron technology into its equipment for the Space program. An Accutron watch movement sits on the moon's Sea of Tranquility today, in an instrument placed there in 1969 by Apollo 11 astronauts, the first men on the moon. The Bulova Accutron was used on a total of forty-six missions of the US Space Program and went on to become the White House's official gift of state, as announced by President Lyndon B Johnson.

Joseph Bulova

Accutron Spaceview featured in *The Saturday Evening Post*, 1962

# Why you should wear
# ACCUTRON †
## instead of a watch

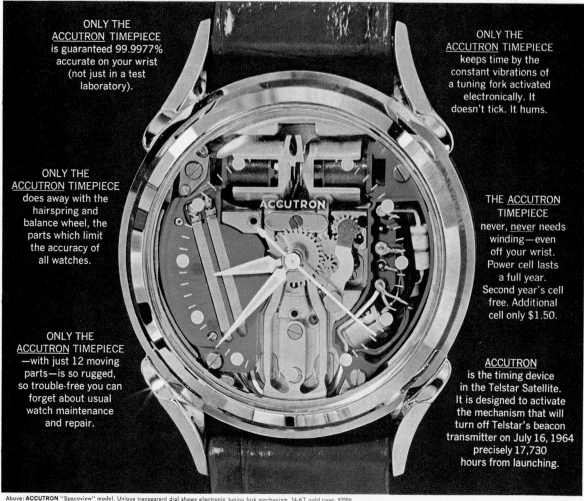

ONLY THE ACCUTRON TIMEPIECE is guaranteed 99.9977% accurate on your wrist (not just in a test laboratory).

ONLY THE ACCUTRON TIMEPIECE keeps time by the constant vibrations of a tuning fork activated electronically. It doesn't tick. It hums.

ONLY THE ACCUTRON TIMEPIECE does away with the hairspring and balance wheel, the parts which limit the accuracy of all watches.

THE ACCUTRON TIMEPIECE never, never needs winding—even off your wrist. Power cell lasts a full year. Second year's cell free. Additional cell only $1.50.

ONLY THE ACCUTRON TIMEPIECE —with just 12 moving parts—is so rugged, so trouble-free you can forget about usual watch maintenance and repair.

ACCUTRON is the timing device in the Telstar Satellite. It is designed to activate the mechanism that will turn off Telstar's beacon transmitter on July 16, 1964 precisely 17,730 hours from launching.

Above: **ACCUTRON** "Spaceview" model. Unique transparent dial shows electronic tuning fork mechanism. 14-KT gold case. $250°

## ACCUTRON† by BULOVA

### The only timepiece guaranteed 99.9977% accurate on your wrist.
### It makes the finest watches—even electric watches—obsolete.

♁ Symbol of accuracy through electronics

ACCUTRON† is the registered trade mark of the Bulova Watch Co., Inc.        ©1962 Bulova Watch Company, Inc., New York, Toronto, Bienne, Milan. *All prices plus tax—waterproof when case, crystal and crown are intact.

Pon Pon (1960)
Aquilino Cosani (1924–)
Ledragomma Design Team
Ledraplastic 1963 to present
Ledragomma 1969 to present

Helmut Lang advertising campaign, Spring/Summer 2003

Advertising, *Topolino* magazine, 1971

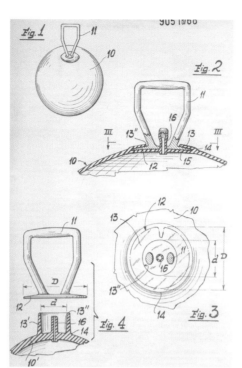

# Recently the 1970s-era

Spacehopper, a product derived from the original 1960 Pon Pon, appeared in an advertising campaign for fashion designer Helmut Lang, grinning madly and decked out in a deconstructed 'wetsuit skeleton'. The unlikely convergence of couture and the ubiquitous red-orange hopping ball formed a surreal portrait of innocence and experience, the very ingredients of nostalgia, which this artefact evokes in just about everyone of a certain generation. In distinction to scooters, bicycles and skateboards, the Spacehopper was a study in going nowhere fast. Bouncing onto the scene in the early 1970s in the UK and the USA, the Spacehopper was nothing more than a large, robust balloon with handles that prevented one from flying off while in motion, although the motion was admittedly more vertical than horizontal. Perhaps not surprisingly, the Spacehopper was born in Italy, the country that had bred legions of groovy inflatable furniture in the 1960s. The brainchild of an Italian manufacturer named Aquilino Cosani, the large inflatable toy was made of resilient vinyl with a special patented process that allowed for the seamless addition of the handle, which received an Italian patent in 1968 and a US patent in 1971. Although Cosani had released the round jumping ball he called Pon Pon in Italy in the mid-1960s, the Spacehopper received its most enthusiastic audiences in the UK and USA, where its vaguely Satanic horns and black-stencilled facial features amused – or scared – children. Although there were a number of versions out on the market (not all, one would guess, sanctioned by Cosani) the most popular, pear-shaped version was distributed by the British toy company Mettoy. How Mettoy got the idea for its bouncing toy is shrouded in corporate mystery, although one Spacehopper fan site on the Internet spreads the apocryphal tale that Mettoy's marketing manager took a summer holiday in Italy and saw local kids hopping down the street on shipping buoys. (Cosani's patent also applied to the formation of nautical buoys.) Although the Spacehopper fell out of favour by the late 1970s, deposed, one assumes, by the smoother, fleeter roller skate, Cosani continued to improve on his original Pon Pon, and released a softer-handled model called Hop in the 1980s, which is still manufactured by his Italian company in response to a recent fad that could best be termed 'Spacehopping Yourself Slim'.

**After his initial training** with the Danish silversmith Georg Jensen, Jens Quistgaard worked largely for the firm of Dansk, producing a range of domestic objects such as ice buckets, salt and pepper mills, candlesticks, furniture and so on. This ice bucket is one of his most popular and best-known models and illustrates the straightforward sense of quality and the appearance of craftsmanship he achieved through using smooth wooden surfaces, simple, well-balanced shapes and sound modern methods of construction. Although Jens Quistgaard's Teak Ice Bucket is most closely related in form to the simple vernacular wooden pail, somewhat paradoxically the shape is more likely to be recognized, in the museum world at least, through ceramic versions from the eighteenth-century Arita kilns in Japan or nineteenth-century Staffordshire. However, Quistgaard's influences, especially regarding his use of wood, are usually felt to come from his training as a carver, Viking longboats and the Scandinavian craft tradition. Certainly, his use of staves in this design might bring to mind the overlapping planks of longboat hulls or the construction of wooden wagons, and the areas of plain wood with clearly visible grain suggest associations with traditional craftsmanship. Whatever the actual sources, the piece repeats one of the fundamental principles of Danish design, articulated by Kaare Klint, of basing a modern object on a successful historical model. Quistgaard's use of a hidden interior liner made of plastic, as this was an object for use in the modern home, helps to complete the artistically restrained but highly successful fusion of ideas from the past with those of the present for which Scandinavian design has been so widely acclaimed.

# 551

| |
|---|
| Time-Life or Walnut Stools (1960) |
| Charles Eames (1907–78) |
| Ray Eames (1912–88) |
| Herman Miller 1960 to present |

**This design is attributed** primarily to Ray Eames and was initially commissioned for the lobby of the Time-Life Building in New York. Conceived as stools or low occasional tables, the tops and bases are identical and only the turned sections in the centre of the three variant designs differ. Of all designs by the Eameses, these stools seem closest to a craft aesthetic. They are turned from solid blocks of walnut, an age-old technology that enhances the individual character of each piece of timber. This stands in contrast to the highly finished and engineered quality of most other Eames designs. Ironically perhaps, they are machine-made, like all Eames products. Before her marriage to Charles Eames, Ray Kaiser had practised as an artist. Although the complexities of their collaboration are difficult to untangle, it is often rather simplistically considered that Ray's artistic talent balanced Charles's more technical expertise in architecture. Undoubtedly the forms of these Walnut Stools were inspired by 'ethnic' art, an unusual source for the Eameses but a familiar reference point in twentieth-century avant garde art and, by the 1950s, a signifier of 'good taste' in a modern interior. Many works by Charles and Ray Eames are easily identifiable because they are part of a progressive design experiment. Whether they are rendered in plywood or fibreglass, the organic forms of a whole series of chairs are related. The Time-Life Stools stand alone as the only solid timber designs in the Eameses' vast oeuvre. They do not seem to fit with the Eameses' programmatic approach to design that is so familiar to us, and perhaps their singularity is the exception that proves the rule.

Sanluca (1960)
Achille Castiglioni (1918–2002)
Pier Giacomo Castiglioni (1913–68)
Gavina/Knoll 1960 to 1969
Bernini 1990 to present
Poltrona Frau 2004 to present

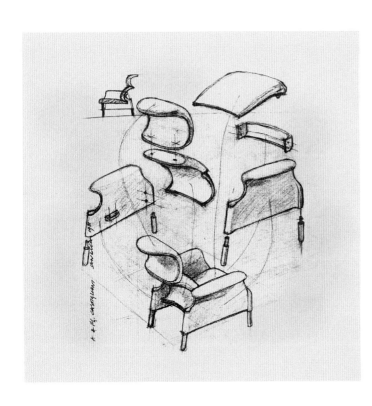

**At first glance** the Sanluca looks like an old-fashioned chair. Seen from the front it resembles its inspiration, a seventeenth-century Italian baroque chair, but it lacks its predecessor's unwieldy appearance. This is because it was also influenced by the futuristic sculpture of Boccioni. The use of hollow, modelled panes gave the chair a spacious and aerodynamic look, updating the chair to the present and beyond into the future. This witty paradox is characteristic of all Castiglioni designs and Sanluca turned out to be the inspiration for generations of chairs to come. The concept of the Sanluca was revolutionary. Instead of building a frame, which was then upholstered, the Castiglioni brothers used pre-modelled and pre-upholstered panels, which would be fixed to a stamped metal frame. This industrial technique was common in the manufacture of car seats and saved a lot of time in production. Achille and Pier Giacomo Castiglioni hoped that their chair could be machine-made like car seats, and thus mass-produced. Unfortunately, this was not the case. The chair's complicated construction meant it could only be produced by hand. Following preliminary sketches, a final, life-sized prototype was made in wood, plaster and clay, in order to decide on proportion, shape and comfort. The chair consists of three parts: seat, back and sides that were made from pre-formed metal and covered with polyurethane foam of various thickness. The legs were made of rosewood. The most beautiful version of the Sanluca has space between the legs, which are upholstered, unifying the total shape. The original chair, commissioned and produced by Gavina in 1960, and later by Knoll International from 1960 to 1969, came in leather or cotton. In 1990 Bernini reissued the chair with minor technical adjustments, supervised by Achille Castiglioni, to make it more comfortable. In 1991 Castiglioni designed a matching ottoman. The Bernini version is available in natural, red or black leather.

Achille Castiglioni

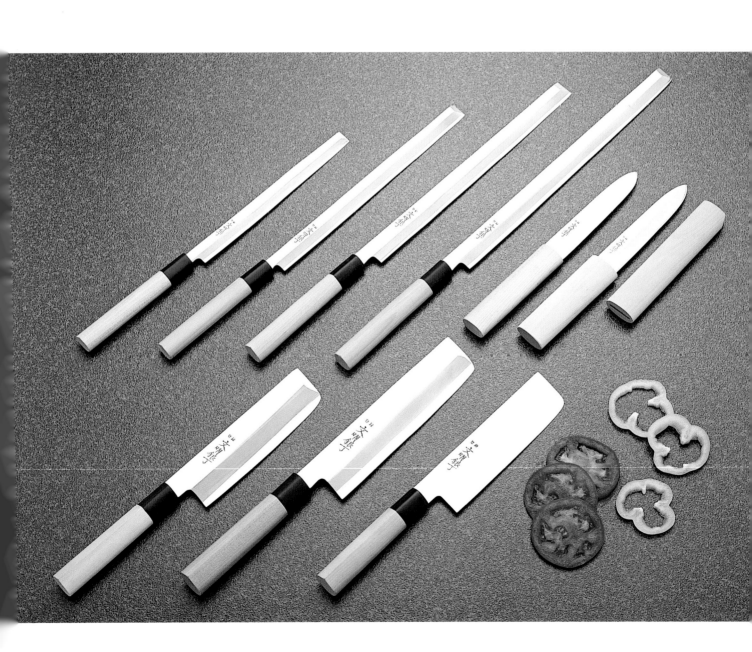

**An amalgamation of tradition** and modern technologies, this beautiful knife, influenced by samurai swords, was developed for preparing Japanese cuisine. The Bunmei Gincho Knife (its name means 'the civilized silver one') was first produced in 1960 by the Yoshida Kinzoku Company, later shortened to Yoshikin. Part of a set of six knives, each designed for a specific purpose, the knife design, generally known as 'yanagiba', the willow-leaf shaped knife, is designed particularly for the preparation of raw fish cuisine, or sashimi, that requires a very sharp cut. Yoshikin was inspired by medical scalpels to use high-grade stainless steel containing molybdenum, which is highly corrosion-resistant and easy to maintain. Previously, high-quality Japanese cooking knives had, like samurai swords, been made of ordinary steel, which provides a sharp edge but is vulnerable to rust. The Bunmei Gincho Knives were the first Japanese-style professional knives to be made of stainless steel and soon they became renowned for their high quality. They were awarded a medal by the Japanese Catering and Hygiene Association in 1961, and were later purchased by the Japanese imperial household. In subsequent years the knives were marketed worldwide and the reputation of the product continues to the present day. The factory is located in Tsubame, an area renowned for the production of metalwork and the Japanese equivalent of Solingen in Germany. Since 1983 the company has also manufactured the world-famous Global Knives, including a yanagiba-type knife. These knives, made of one piece of stainless steel, can be put in the dishwasher, unlike the Bunmei Gincho range. With its wood handle and plastic blade junction, the Bunmei Gincho Knife requires a little more care. However, its affinity to its use and elegance make it the perfect knife with which to prepare beautiful Japanese food.

**5-48**

Trimline Telephone (1960–4)
Henry Dreyfuss (1904–72)
Western Electric Company/AT&T
1965 to 1995

**When the sexy,** streamlined Trimline Telephone was introduced in the United States in 1965 it immediately became an American success story. New York's Museum of Modern Art selected it to be part of its permanent collection in that same year. It also changed the face of telecommunications design at the time, and its legacy has endured. Indeed, the model set the benchmark for the cordless and mobile phone technology that has become an intrinsic part of the current communications revolution. The Trimline Telephone was designed by Henry Dreyfuss Associates. Dreyfuss, along with Raymond Loewy and Norman Bel Geddes, was one of the great industrial designers of the twentieth century. Dreyfuss played a pivotal role in the evolution of the telephone, and was responsible for designing, among other things, the first push-button phones. The Trimline, however, truly revolutionized the telephone, and justified the ten years of research it had taken to develop. Its innovative characteristics included a receiver, transmitter and dial combined into a single element nested into a compact base, and it came in both desk and wall models. This first dial-in-handset allowed people to dial a new call without having to return to the base. The fact that it was constructed of four components – handsets, desk bases, wall bases and cords – meant that the Trimline was also easy to assemble, and the hybrid network tucked away inside the handset resulted in fewer conductors, which in turn made the cord more pliable. Its plug-in terminal had a practical implication in that parts would be easier to replace. Dreyfuss had researched and published extensively on the subject of design relating to the human figure, a study which would become known as ergonomics. Its curved, contoured and coloured form meant that not only was it extremely good-looking, it was also easy to hold and light to handle. After thirty years of production, more than 100 million Trimline phones had been sold or leased, and one of AT&T's bestsellers.

As the V8 engine is to American cars, so the V-twin is to American motorcycles. It is the ubiquitous engine of a century's worth of Harley-Davidson and Indian motorcycles. Indeed, in its somewhat lumpen presence, the V-Twin more or less defines the American motorcycle design standard. But what of British motorcycle design? What is the standard bearer? The answer, for once, is simple. The Triumph Bonneville and its signature vertical twin engine, designed by Edward Turner, is the defining British motorcycle of the twentieth century. The 1950s and 1960s were the glory years of British motorcycle design, and indeed, of British motorcycling. Triumph was its heart and soul, and it is a delicious irony that the recent renaissance of British motorcycle design should be led, again, by Triumph. Edward Turner designed the vertical twin engine in the mid-1930s and with it, the Triumph Speed Twin. This was the mould from which all subsequent Triumphs emerged. Like Harley-Davidson in the United States, Triumph knew it had a winner, and it changed its design in tiny increments, sure of its position as the leader of the

European industry. Such was Triumph's strength, particularly in the American market, that rivals like Harley-Davidson adjusted their production to match the power, lightness and the very European agility of the T120 Bonneville. This position held throughout the 1960s, and the late, unit-construction Bonnevilles – where the gearbox is integral with the engine – are considered by many to be the very peak of Triumph's achievement. But change was in the air in the form of superior Japanese designs, from lightweight runabouts (the Honda C100 Cub being the best) to the first true superbike, the Honda CB750. The Japanese caught Triumph, and to be fair, the rest of the British industry, completely off guard, with production methods, technology and marketing that looked forward half a century. Countless books have been written about the inability of British motorcycle manufacturers to respond to the Japanese revolution in motorcycle design. But from the perspective of the early twenty-first century, it is worth recognizing the enduring qualities of the T120 Bonneville.

**5·47**

T120 Bonneville (1959)
Triumph Design Team
Triumph 1959 to 1983

## 5-46

Panton Chair (1959–60)
Verner Panton (1926–98)
Herman Miller/Vitra CH/D 1967 to 1979
Horn/WK-Verband 1983 to 1989
Vitra 1990 to present

**The Panton Chair** is deceptively simple – an organically flowing form that makes maximum use of plastic's principle characteristic which is its infinite formal adaptability. The back of the chair flows into the seat, which in turn flows into an undercut base. The whole integrated shape creates a stacking, cantilevered chair, highly distinctive in its complex but autonomous unity. This was the first whole chair made of an unjointed continuous material that was intended to be realized both in serial and mass production. This, however, was not easily achieved and the history of the chair's manufacture contains many more turns and revisions than its elegantly sensuous form. Panton first exhibited a prototype of what became known as the Panton Chair at the start of the 1960s. It took until 1963 to find visionary manufacturers, Vitra in Switzerland, in partnership with Herman Miller in the United States. Initially Herman Miller had reservations about the production of the chair but Rolf Fehlbaum of Vitra finally backed the project and Panton produced ten further hand-laminated fibreglass-prototypes. Eventually the first viable chairs emerged in 1967 as a limited edition of 100 to 150 pieces using cold-pressed fibreglass-reinforced polyester. Since its original production debut the chair has undergone several more manufacturing halts and changes to resolve structural fatigue and improve manufacture. In 1968 the chair was remade in plastic baydur polyurethane and was included in the Herman Miller collection. In 1970 Vitra switched again to a more economical thermoplastic injection-moulding with ABS plastic and continued production until 1979, when the licence was returned to Panton. In 1983 Horn, in Rudersberg, produced the chairs. Then from 1990 Vitra began producing them again, but now in injection-moulded polypropylene and as a less expensive version than the earlier models. The Panton Chair was originally marketed in seven bright colours. These colours and the chair's informal flowing shape captured and epitomized the Pop Art culture of the period. As such the Panton Chair was much used in media imagery and rapidly began to represent the 'anything is possible' technical and social spirit of the 1960s.

**The most telling insight** into what makes the Mono-A Cutlery set deserving of its status is that, in the forty-five years since it was first designed and manufactured in Germany, it remains free from significant alteration. Measure that against today's less exacting standards, where fashion emphasizes obsolescence and disposability over endurance, and this achievement is all the more significant. Mono-A, the first design of what later became an extended series, was the perfect embodiment of late 1950s Modernism and, as such, remains a timeless representation of flatware from the period. Cut from standardized sheet metal, the crisp one-piece knives, forks and spoons made for a rather austere statement. Yet this was nonetheless attractive to a young postwar Germany busy embracing the democratic design ideal, along with all its trappings. Even when the strict utilitarian brief of the Mono-A was softened by the addition of teak and ebony handles, in the new Mono-T and Mono-E series, respectively, the resultant tableware remained as moderate as the original 'A' design. Introduced to add comfort and to increase the product range, the Mono-T and Mono-E versions may have been a degree more sophisticated, yet they remained uncomplicated in spirit. Peter Raacke, the cutlery's designer, was a young German gold- and silversmith who identified more with the ideals put forward by the Bauhaus movements than with the emerging postwar bourgeois restoration of the day. Raacke adhered closely to a refined purism that instilled in his tableware a classic appeal, impervious to the changing fashions of the early 1960s. And herein lies the essence of Mono's persistent commercial success. Mono continues to be bought by a twenty-five to thirty-five year old market looking to make a once-in-a-lifetime purchase, to which they can add pieces as their entertaining needs evolve. It remains as optimistic and modern a statement today as it did when it first appeared in 1959, and now stands as Germany's best-selling cutlery design. Since its introduction, Mono has been honoured by the German Post Office with its own stamp, in addition to receiving over fifteen international design awards, including the Busse Long Life Award in 1999.

Mono-A Cutlery (1959)
Peter Raacke (1928–)
Mono-Metallwarenfabrik Seibel
1959 to present

Peter Raacke

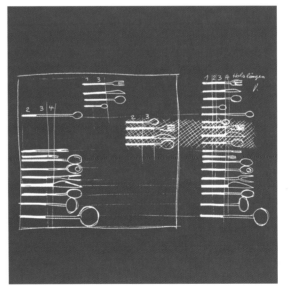

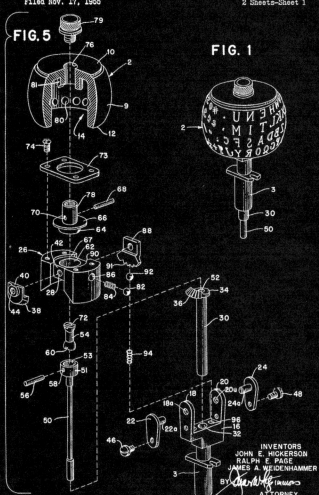

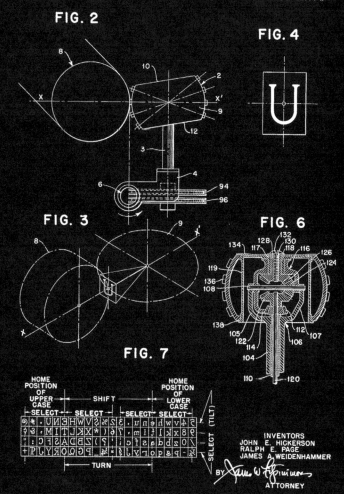

July 21, 1959          J. E. HICKERSON ET AL          2,895,584
SINGLE ELEMENT PRINTING HEAD

Filed Nov. 17, 1955                          2 Sheets-Sheet 1

FIG. 5

FIG. 1

INVENTORS
JOHN E. HICKERSON
RALPH E. PAGE
JAMES A. WEIDENHAMMER

BY

ATTORNEY

July 21, 1959          J. E. HICKERSON ET AL          2,895,584
SINGLE ELEMENT PRINTING HEAD

Filed Nov. 17, 1955                          2 Sheets-Sheet 2

FIG. 2

FIG. 4

FIG. 3

FIG. 6

FIG. 7

INVENTORS
JOHN E. HICKERSON
RALPH E. PAGE
JAMES A. WEIDENHAMMER

BY

ATTORNEY

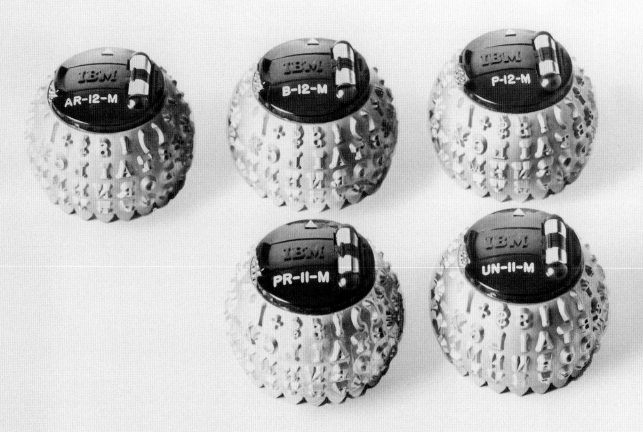

**Through his tutors** Walter Gropius and Marcel Breuer at Harvard, as well as the writings of Le Corbusier, American designer Eliot Noyes became heavily influenced by the International style and modern European design in general. As director of corporate design at IBM from 1956, he sought to engender a coherent and unified approach to design that would be fêted by both employees and clients alike, emulating the approach of Marcello Nizzoli for Olivetti and, later on, the work of Dieter Rams for Braun. He achieved this by employing prominent designers with a sympathetic approach, including Eero Saarinen, Marcel Breuer, Charles Eames, George Nelson and Paul Rand, and giving unambiguous guidelines on corporate design implementation through his *Design Practice Manual*. A prime example of this policy in practice is the IBM Selectric Typewriter, designed by Noyes in 1959. Contemporary advertising celebrated not only the looks, but also the speed and accuracy of the Selectric, which was the first to incorporate what was popularly known as the 'golfball' type-head. This moves over the paper on a head-and-rocker assembly, doing away with the need for type-bars and a moveable carriage. The ink delivery was also improved, being housed in a cartridge that was a simple matter to change. Noyes took advantage of the reduction in moving parts by creating a slick, crisp, sculptured housing, which also lent the machine a more high-tech feel than its predecessors. The ability for users to change type styles and coloured cartridges was a huge hit, as was the 'stroke storage', which meant that the head could not jam as in a conventional machine. This desirability, along with the fact that all the innovations were sewn up with watertight patents, ensured that the Selectric remained a unique product for over a decade.

**Up until the introduction** of the Princess design by Western Electric in 1959, the telephone was unlikely to have been considered as anything other than a practical home or office fixture. By the mid-1950s however, with the changing pace of domestic life placing greater emphasis on the convenience and versatility of design, Bartlett Miller, head of marketing at Western Electric, realized that the postwar increase in demand for telephone services was a marketing opportunity waiting to be exploited. Miller wanted to reposition the telephone, both physically and sociologically, by transporting it from the hallway to the bedside table and marketing it as a lifestyle accessory to a largely female audience, who were growing ever more fond of chatting on the telephone as a means of entertainment. In 1956, Miller enlisted the design skills of the increasingly celebrated designer Henry Dreyfuss in order to realize his vision. The ambitious marketing manifesto developed to accompany the introduction of the Princess Telephone upped the stakes for Dreyfuss and the AT&T design team. This unit had to satisfy a hungry market looking for convenience, but it also had to sell, and in large quantities. Dreyfuss's first move was to simplify the unit into a lightweight and streamlined plastic entity that shed a whole 1.3 kg (3 lb) in weight from the previous model. The familiar standard-issue black colour was replaced with a modern pastel-based palette that included white, beige, pink, blue and turquoise. Most significant, perhaps, was the addition of a light into the keypad, which illuminated when the telephone was in use and which could also be used as a bedside nightlight. 'It's light, it's lovely, it lights' rang the marketing motto that accompanied Dreyfuss's design. Although the design experienced technical teething problems, it went on to establish itself as a symbol of American postwar design and marketing that was embellished upon further by AT&T in the form of updated models, and mimicked by countless competitive manufacturers.

**left and right: Sales brochure, 1960**

**Although synonymous** through countless movies with mountain excitement, the Ski-Doo Snowmobile was originally intended as a practical vehicle for rescue services, trappers and anyone else travelling over snow in remote parts of Canada. In fact, the first two hand-built models helped Oblate missionary Maurice Ouimet reach his comrades in often isolated areas in Ontario, after he received them as a gift from his friend Joseph-Armand Bombardier. Since then, some two and a half million Ski-Doo Snowmobiles have been produced. The concept of a one-man snowmobile had been Bombardier's dream since boyhood. Displaying a clear gift for mechanics, he had designed his first snow vehicle by the age of fifteen. Founding Bombardier Snowmobile Limited in 1942, he would design and market tracked snow-going vehicles for various industrial uses, including an enclosed twelve-passenger model the B12 built since 1942. But it was the development of lighter motors and his son Germain's creation of a new track with metal rods built-in that let him realize his ultimate goal. The first Ski-Doo Snowmobile, equipped with wooden skis and a helical spring suspension, was marketed between 1959 and 1960 and sold for $900 Canadian dollars. It included an all-rubber track and a centrifugal clutch with only six moving parts. Powered by a four-stroke Kohler engine, its maximum speed was 40 kph (25 mph). Just 225 units were made in the first year, but demand grew steadily, with more than 8,000 units produced in 1963–4. Bombardier formed a subsidiary to make the fibreglass hoods that eventually replaced the original steel hoods. By 1968 Ski-Doo SUPER Olympic 300 cc models were robust enough to take a US expedition to the North Pole. The Ski-Doo Snowmobile remains ever popular, mainly in leisure markets. The Bombardier business, meanwhile, became a giant in air and ground transportation.

EXCITING EXCURSIONS

ENJOYABLE FOR ALL AGES

IDEAL FOR LINESMEN AND PATROLMEN

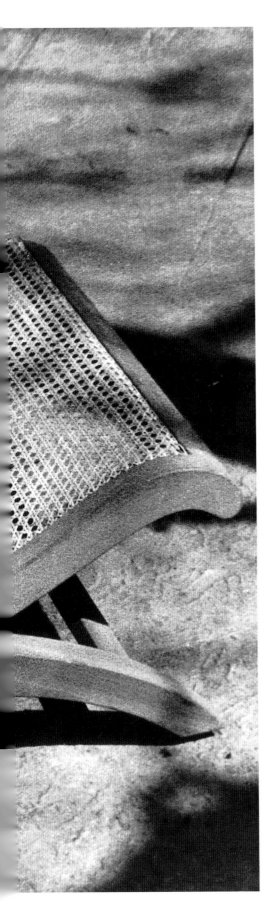

Clara Porset

**The deep,** swooping seat of Clara Porset's Butaque chair gives the piece a true sense of grandeur. Yet despite this rather stately feel, the chair also displays an admirable economy of line, making it unashamedly modern. Clara Porset, born in Cuba but a naturalized Mexican, developed the chair following extensive research into the history of Latin American culture. The 'Butaque', a type of chair has existed in Mexico ever since its introduction by the Spanish in the sixteenth century and it is believed that the Spanish developed this particular style from seating used in antique cultures. Porset's refined Butaque, then, is a chair design with an ancient pedigree. Porset's personal history is almost as tangled as that of the Butaque chair, whose origins are still being debated today. She studied in the United States and Europe (she applied to join the Bauhaus in 1933 but, since it was on the verge of collapse, was directed towards Black Mountain College in South Carolina, USA) and trained in art, decoration and architecture. When Porset returned to Mexico in 1936 she set about initiating a more professional approach to design, on a national level. She set up systems of referencing the culture of Mexico, and paying homage to designers, working closely with numerous architects including, most famously, Luis Barragan. Indeed Porset worked extensively for Barragan, making bespoke furniture to fill his houses. It is due to this close alliance, and the fact that Porset's Butaque chair can still be seen in many of Barragan's houses, that many think the chair design is his. Although her work is little recognized in the United States today, Porset had a high profile in New York in the middle of the twentieth century. The Butaque Chair, of which Porset developed various versions, was at one point distributed by Artek-Pascoe. The UN building, in Manhattan, is known to have put in an order for a number of Butaques at one point, but the manufacture and productions are relatively unknown.

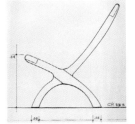

David Hemmings and Verushka in *Blow Up* (1966), directed by Michelangelo Antonioni

Nikon F Camera (1959)
Nippon Kogaku Design Team
Nippon Kogaku 1959 to 1971

**The Nikon F Camera** was one of the most influential cameras of the twentieth century and did more to enhance the reputation of the Japanese photographic industry than any other camera marque. Its design built on the technical advances of the 1936 Kine Exakta, the first true 35 mm single lens reflex camera; the Contax S, with a built-in pentaprism; the Asahi Optical Company's Asahiflex IIb (1954), with an instant-return mirror; and the original Pentax single lens reflex (1957). The Nikon F defined the look of the single lens reflex camera and set the course of camera design for the next thirty years. Launched in 1959, the Nikon was manufactured to a high physical standard: the eye-level viewfinder gave a 100 per cent view; the camera came with a range of accessories, including a four-frame-per-second motor drive; and it was immediately available with lenses from 21 mm to 500 mm. The Nikkor lenses, especially, were recognized as being of exceptional quality. A defining feature of Nikon's design, which few other manufacturers attempted, was that all previous Nikkor lenses would fit subsequent models, a feature which continues to the present day. Compared to contemporary press cameras, the Nikon was small and light, making it ideal for work in difficult environments, especially in the combat situations for which it became known. Minor mechanical changes improved the Nikon F, until the Nikon F2 was launched in 1971. Between 1959 and 1974 when production ended, 862,600 Nikon F cameras were made, lead by key designer Masahiko Fuketa. It had been used by many of the legendary names in photography, including Don McCullin, W Eugene Smith, David Duncan Douglas, Alfred Eisenstaedt and nearly every photographer on *Life* magazine from 1960 until its close. It was also standard equipment at *National Geographic* and *UPI* and appeared in such films as *Blow Up*, *Apocalypse Now* and *The Bridges of Madison County*, which all helped reinforce its status. The Nikon F2 and subsequent Nikon models continued to develop the company's reputation for quality and design. The company's current range of cameras was seen as the standard throughout the 1970s and 1980s and remain popular. As camera design moved into the 1990s and increasingly used printed circuits and with the more recent advance in digital technology, Canon's EOS range edged ahead of Nikon in popularity.

**The inspiration** for the Barbie Doll came from Ruth Handler observing her daughter, Barbara and her friends playing with paper dolls, projecting stories onto them as cheerleaders, college students, and career women. She instantly saw the importance of this role-playing activity, and recognized the gap in the market for an adult fashion doll. Ruth and Elliot Handler and their partner Harold 'Matt' Matson, who had founded Mattel in 1945 (Matt + Elliot), presented Barbie, the Teen-Age Fashion Model at the 1959 American Toy Fair, New York and the doll went on to sell over 351,000 units in its first year. It was the first of its kind on the market, as only baby or toddler dolls had existed previously. Barbie Doll's proportions would be an impressive 39-18-33 inches if she were life size, and from the beginning it became clear that the Barbie Doll's wardrobe was as important as the doll itself. This was not only paramount to the Barbie Doll's design, but also became a very useful device to update her through changing times, adapting her wardrobe, hair style, make up and accessories to the ongoing fashions in order to keep her competitive. What set Barbie apart was that she addressed a new kind of play, which allowed girls to project themselves into adulthood through her. Some believe that Barbie is in fact modelled after Lilli – an adult German cartoon character (created by Reinhard Beuthin in 1952) and doll – who appeared in the daily newspaper, *die Bild-Zeitung*, often scantily clad. Barbie was originally 29 cm (11.5 in), and weighed 0.3 kg (11 oz), and was first sold with a black-and-white striped swimsuit, gold earrings, and most importantly, had movable arms and legs, and a head that could turn from side to side. Ken (named after the Handler's son) was introduced in 1961, as her male companion, and Midge, a freckle-faced friend, came along in 1963. The success of the Barbie Doll was due to factors such as television advertising (as TV's became popular in homes across America), her novelty as a toy onto which young girls could project their future hopes and dreams onto, a definition of femininity that reflected this 'perfect' body, and an air of independence that has been of utmost influence. She has had five facelifts, numerous careers, and has been able to mirror the trends amongst teenagers – remaining an enduring archetype throughout the decades.

Lambda Chair (1959)
Marco Zanuso (1916–2001)
Richard Sapper (1932–)
Gavina/Knoll 1963 to present

**Automobile construction** methods are a recurring influence on Marco Zanuso's work, and can be seen in particular in his Lambda Chair for Gavina (designed with Richard Sapper). But although the design adopts methods of working sheet steel typically used in car manufacture, the inspiration to use this technique was purely architectural. Commissioned by Olivetti to work with Edoardo Vittoria on new headquarters in São Paulo in Brazil, Zanuso studied a way to create vaults out of reinforced concrete for the roof of the factory, a technique that he transferred to his furniture design. Preliminary sketches of the chair, originally to be made in sheet steel, show the influence of his Olivetti work. Eventually, though, the Lambda prototype was cast out of polyvinyl, which tapped into the availability of new thermo-setting materials and would later permit the mass production of similar products. Zanuso wanted to create a chair out of a single material, but did not know what shape the design would take. The cylindrical pillars of the factory influenced the idea for the Lambda's empty leg, enabling Zanuso to maintain the continuity of the chair's general shape and the way its lines alternate from horizontal to vertical. Zanuso says, however, that the chair's ultimate appearance, which looks as though it was inspired by a plant, actually developed almost on its own and was probably 'a subconscious act'. Throughout his career, Zanuso consistently managed to create design that represented both innovation and comfort. All his pieces carry an underlining concern with pioneering the use of new and different materials as well as testing market accessibility. As with most of Zanuso's designs, the research into the chair was long and complex, but it has provided a blueprint for future plastic chairs that is still widely used today.

**The simple, grey plastic** Portable Phone Radio TP1 of 1959 was perhaps the ultimate expression of legendary German designer Dieter Rams's belief in uncluttered, uncomplicated product design. The record player is barely larger than the 7-inch records it plays and is pared down to its key elements, with just a single fader switch acting as the only visible means of controlling the device. The player is so minimal that the speaker was housed in an auxiliary unit within the radio. The Portable Phono Radio TP1 also reflects the growing trend towards miniaturization in the late 1950s. In the same year that Rams's scaled-down record player hit the shelves, Sony started selling one of the smallest television sets in the world, exploiting speedy progression in transistor technology. Designed just four years into Rams's career at Braun, the record player marks a distinct progression from his earlier, more elaborate designs. Just at the start of his career at Braun, Rams designed the Phonosuper SK4 with fellow Braun designer Hans Gugelot. The TP1 is perhaps the culmination of Rams's work in the Neo-Functionalist tradition. Its focus on geometrical simplicity and lack of clutter is typical of the style, which developed in the 1950s in contrast to the highly decorative and chromed designs emerging from the US during the same decade. Rams would later apply this philosophy to the iconic Braun electric razors, alarm clocks and calculators of the late 1970s and early 1980s. But the purity and simplicity of the TP1 set the standard for a style that dominated product design up to the 1990s.

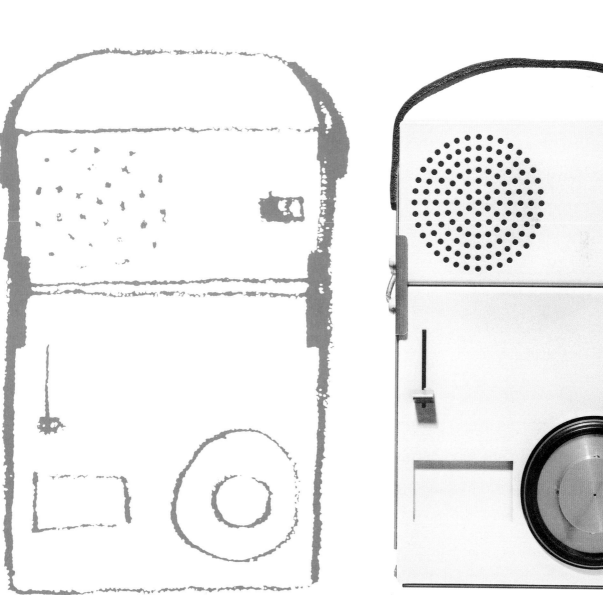

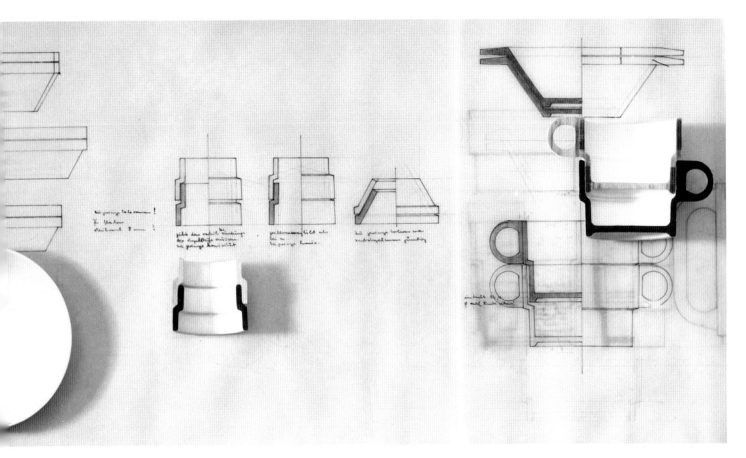

was used for the sides of all bowls and plates, and a vertical interlocking arrangement for the cups, pots and jugs. These rules of form were in turn implemented across the entire range. The set consisted of cylindrical jugs, bowls, plates, cups and saucers in a variety of sizes. The design allowed all the different pieces in the set with the same diameter to be interchangeable and stacked, regardless of their type. Manufactured in chip-proof porcelain, this tableware is extremely tough and hard-wearing. Since first being manufactured by Rosenthal in 1959,

this modular table service has become an archetype and been widely imitated. It presents a model for how rational modernist design ideals can be success-fully implemented to produce an enduring, attractive and extremely practical set of tableware that is widely adopted in both domestic and commercial settings.

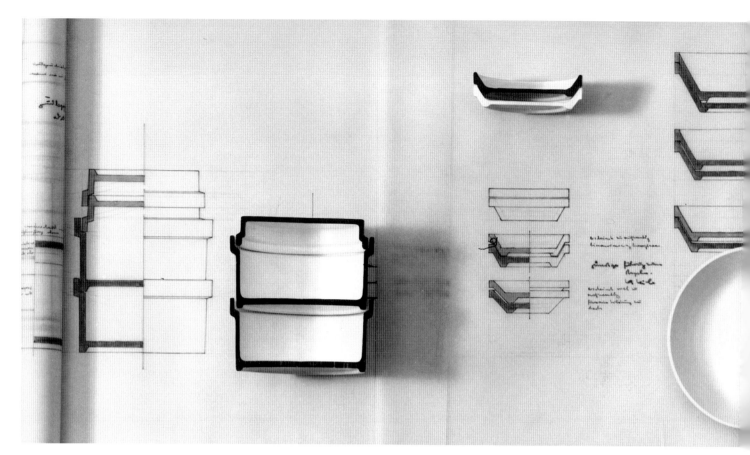

## Hans 'Nick' Roericht's TC 100

tableware was designed for his diploma graduation project at the Hochschule für Gestaltung at Ulm, where he was a student from 1955 to 1959 under Tomás Maldonado. Roericht's design explicitly illustrates the design philosophy of the Ulm school, which openly encouraged 'system design'. The design is based on high levels of research into both use and manufacture, resulting in a striking product within the parameters of a rationalist design idiom. Economical use of materials, space and visual codification was the aspiration for

all rational Modernists. Roericht's research method was thorough. Despite being sold for domestic use, the tableware was ostensibly designed for more utilitarian, institutional-based usage. Roericht surveyed existing patterns and shapes, together with the needs and demands made by the users of ceramic tableware in institutional environments. The success of this set lay not only in its modern styling and ease of use, but in its consideration of mass storage. A homogenized system produced a tableware set that was based on two modular forms: a constant angle

**This radio** has proved enduringly popular, as its many comebacks attest. Bush faced increasing competition from the growing number of rival portable radios, and looked to reclaim the market by creating its own product. The first incarnation of this enduring design, the Bush MB60, first hit the scene in 1957, just a year after Elvis had his first hit single in the United States with *Heartbreak Hotel*. The battery-operated portable radio, made possible by the carrying handle, capitalized on the emerging teenage market of the 1950s. The TR82 Radio became the classic British radio and sold well, allowing teenagers to own a slice of popular culture in America during a time of postwar austerity. But soon the valve technology housed within the cream plastic and chrome shell was sounding dated compared to the new, transistor-based radios like the Sony TR610 of 1958. So the MB60 was re-launched as the TR82, with a virtually identical look and with

all-new transistor technology inside, which meant it could be played louder and with more clarity. The look of the radio certainly owes more to the American school of curves, chrome and luxury than the stark minimalism of electronic goods being developed in Germany at the time. The radio dial, on the front of the set, looks more like the speedometer of a 1950s Cadillac, topped with metal trimming and a slow-pointer for the dial, from which the

stations could be selected. The aluminium chassis provides the structure underneath, over which the plastic case sits; the 'B' model with brown sides, and the 'C' with blue sides, both with chrome trim. The Bush TR82 Radio still has mass appeal. The radio, complete with modernized electronics, can be bought on the high street once again, as part of Bush's Nostalgia Audio product range. It was relaunched in 1997, of the same size as the original, now with the trim painted around the dial. The original two waveband buttons on the top of the set has another added in order to accommodate the addition of the VHF band. Bush Radio certifies that the reproduction has strictly followed the original design, and now incorporates better technology, but many enthusiasts and collectors prefer the original.

**After a brief period** of involvement with furniture design in the immediate postwar period, Vico Magistretti spent most of the 1950s developing a successful architecture practice. In 1959 he designed the clubhouse for the Carimate Golf Club near Milan; the chair he designed for its dining room would have a major impact on his career. Although he has continued to design extraordinary buildings, Magistretti has been best known as a designer of objects since Cassina began production of his Carimate 892 Chair in 1963. The chair is still very popular and is produced by De Padova today. The Carimate 892 Chair was inspired by the traditions of simple country furniture, while at the same time respectfully challenging and carrying them forwards. Much of Magistretti's success can be attributed to his belief that good product design is dependent on respectful collaboration between designers, enthusiastic manufacturers and talented craftsmen. Along with the vision of certain manufacturers, he has credited the network of highly skilled craftsmen still active in postwar Milan with playing a central role in the development of the Italian design phenomenon. He has acknowledged that many designs were made possible only because of the extraordinary skills of these craftsmen. The design references the turned wood chairs with woven rush seats that have been popular for centuries in Europe, but is brought into the present somehow free of the burden of stylistic historicism. This is accomplished by Magistretti's design process, which relies on simple but powerful concepts and functional problem solving as opposed to stylizing. In this case his approach results in a transcendent object with a clear logic and no unnecessary decoration. The frame is made of solid beech with legs that are thicker where the seat rails join into them, directly addressing the primary structural problem of the chair by adding mass only where it is needed. Of the many extraordinary qualities of the Carimate Chair, it is perhaps the brilliant red finish that makes the traditional associations and the conceptual simplicity come together into a brilliant design.

**The little C100 Super Cub**, known universally as the Honda 50, may well be the most important and influential motorcycle design of all time. A big claim for such a little motorcycle, but in its forty-five years of continuous production this small wonder has sold over 35 million units, almost the number of Model T Fords and Volkswagen Beetles combined. As a design, it is a combination of innovative engineering, high-tech production and all-round practicality. The principal imperative was borrowed from Vespa, which was to provide good weather protection in the form of leg shields; a step-through frame, so that women could ride it even when wearing skirts; and a maintenance-free engine, hidden from view. The production is a marvel of materials technology, using plastic in the leg shield and front mudguards, and pressed steel for the backbone frame and forks. But the heart of the motorcycle, and perhaps the single most important reason for its success, is the tiny, 49 cc engine. Honda had long been drawn to four-stroke engines, which were at that time heavy and hard to start. Two-stroke engines, which do not use the heavy and complicated valve mechanism of a four-stroke, were, and to an extent still are, preferred for small capacity motorcycles. Vespa, the historic market leader in scooters and mopeds, used a typically smoky, noisy two-stroke for its eponymous scooter, and with great success. But Honda's tiny four-stroke, with a horizontal cylinder, overhead camshaft and an automatic clutch in an all-enclosed engine case, was quiet, easy to start and operate, economical to run and seemingly easy to maintain. It was, and is, a brilliant piece of engineering miniaturism. Aside from its obvious design and mechanical merits, Honda's success depended on breaking through into the difficult US market at a very challenging time. The 1950s were a car decade. Motorbikes, when they were thought of at all, were considered to be nasty and dirty, like their riders. Sanitizing the little Honda was achieved with the help of a famous advertising campaign, whose message, 'You meet the nicest people on a Honda', struck a loud and reverberant chord in American pop culture. The rest, as they say, is history. Honda is now a dominant force in automotive manufacturing around the world. And it is no exaggeration to say that it owes much of its success to the little Honda Cub.

Honda C100 Super Cub (1958)
Soichiro Honda (1906–1991)
Honda Design Team
Honda 1958 to present

Soichiro Honda

**Kijkt u er ook
zo van op als u een
lettertang ziet waar géén
Dymo op staat?**

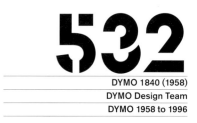

**532**

DYMO 1840 (1958)
DYMO Design Team
DYMO 1958 to 1996

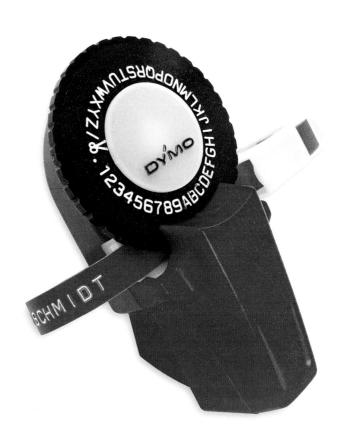

DYMO LABEL WRITERS WERE INTRODUCED IN THE LATE 1950S AND FOR NEARLY THREE DECADES WERE THE SIMPLEST AND EASIEST WAY TO CREATE PERSONALIZED LABELS. THE DEVICE BECAME KNOWN FOR THE EMBOSSED STRIPS OF LETTERING IT PRODUCED, WHICH WERE FAR MORE ICONIC THAN THE SIMPLE DESIGN OF THE PRODUCT ITSELF. THE BODY, PRODUCED IN MANY DIFFERENT COLOURS, FEATURES A ROUND PLASTIC DIAL, WHICH INCLUDES ALL THE LETTERS OF THE ALPHABET, SITTING ON TOP OF A HANDLE WITH A TRIGGER. THE DIAL IS TURNED TO THE APPROPRIATE LETTER AND THE TRIGGER PULLED TO EMBOSS THE LETTER ON A STRIP OF VINYL THAT AUTOMATICALLY FEEDS OUT OF THE TOP. THE SIMPLICITY OF THE PRODUCT AND ITS EASE OF USE WAS PART OF THE REASON IT WAS SO WIDELY USED IN OFFICES, HOMES, SCHOOLS AND INDUSTRY. THE DISTINCTIVE EMBOSSED LETTERING COULD BE SEEN ON EVERYTHING FROM FILING CABINETS TO NAME TAGS AND FROM SCHOOL TEXTBOOKS TO CONTROL PANELS IN POWER STATIONS. THE ORIGINAL DYMO LABEL MAKER HAD A LIMITED INFLUENCE ON LABEL MAKERS THAT FOLLOWED OWING TO STRIDES IN TECHNOLOGY, WHICH MEANT THAT LED SCREENS REPLACED THE CLICK-WHEEL AND CONVEN-TIONAL KEYBOARDS COULD BE INCORPORATED INTO SMALL DEVICES. IN ADDITION, THE ADVENT OF THE HOME COMPUTER ALLOWED FOR LABELS TO BE EASILY CREATED BY ANYONE, EVEN WITH A STANDARD PC. HOWEVER, ITS LASTING INFLUENCE MAY BE SEEN IN ITS LEADING TO THE DEMOCRATIZATION OF PUBLISHING, WHICH HAS FOUND ITS MOST RECENT EXPRESSION IN DESKTOP PUBLISHING PROGRAMMES, THE INTERNET AND DIGITAL PHOTOGRAPHY. ITS ENDURING POPULARITY IS ALSO DEMONSTRATED BY THE FACT THAT A COMPUTER FONT, CALLED 'DYMO', IS NOW AVAILABLE THAT PERFECTLY MIMICS THE DISTINCTIVE RAISED WHITE TEXT ON THE VINYL RIBBON. IN THE COMPUTER AGE THERE IS STILL A NOSTALGIC FONDNESS FOR THIS SIMPLE BUT INCREDIBLY USEFUL PRODUCT.

Bristol Type 192 'Belvedere' (1958)
Bristol Design Team
Westland Helicopters 1958

**The design of the** Bristol Type 192, known as the 'Belvedere', was based on the earlier Bristol Type 173, which was the first helicopter specifically designed for commercial operation, particularly passenger transportation. This helicopter could carry up to ten people, a capacity that increased to thirty as it was developed by Bristol in response to specifications from the Royal and Canadian navies. The result was the Bristol Types 191 and 192 with their characteristic dual engines and propellers. The Bristol 191 was a ship-based craft, and only three were built. The Bristol 192, launched with an inaugural flight on 5 July 1958, saw a larger production of the helicopter for RAF use. The Bristol Type 192 was the world's first heli-copter with true twin-engine safety, that is, it could fly with one engine out. In its initial configuration this aircraft had a purely manual system of control and wooden rotor blades. By 1960 this had been upgraded to power controls and with metal blades as standard. The production Bristol 192 had an all-metal, skinned fuselage and an anhedral tailplane, compared with the dihedral one of its predecessors, and had instrumentation that enabled night flying. Twenty-six of these helicopters, called the 'Belvedere', were ordered from Westland Helicopters, who had by now taken over the project, and were used for some years as a military transport with 66 Squadron from September 1961, not only in Britain, but also in the Middle and Far East. The 'Belvedere' was withdrawn from service in March 1969 to be replaced by the twin-rotored Chinook. However the developments the 'Belvedere' marked in helicopter aviation continued to drive the technology, specification and engineering in the field long after it was removed from production.

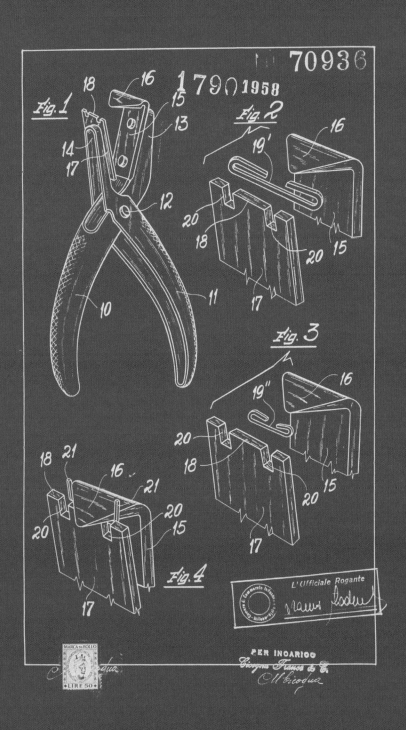

**The price of perfection is** is that the design is likely to fall victim to plagiarism. And so, if imitation is the sincerest form of flattery, the Zenith 580 staple remover is without doubt one of the most admired desktop designs of the past fifty years – so plentiful are the imitations. Designed in 1958 in Voghera, Italy, by Giorgio Balma, the world-famous stationery brand, the jaw-like grip of the staple remover leaves little doubt about the equipment's physical prowess, or the manufacturer's claim that it can remove any staple, big or small. Made from nickel-coated iron, it could almost be mistaken for a set of heavy-duty pliers. The handles, which are ergonomically engineered for comfort, are also spring-loaded for added control. In turn, the handles are joined by a bolt from where they extend to incorporate the jaw area comprised of a flat plate and a pointed-looking beak used for hooking and then extracting the staples. Balma Capoduri & Company – Zenith's parent company – was founded in 1924, and the first independently branded Zenith line of products, comprising a tray and related accessories for copying letters, was rolled out at Milan's trade fair during the same year. The company has since become known for their office equipment, much lauded for its simple durability and timeless design. The bespoke finish of the staple remover in particular has established it as the definitive model in its class. The stapler's individual components are separately tested before assembly – a painstaking process, but one that must be discharged before Zenith agrees to attach its famous life-time guarantee. The Zenith staple remover will undoubtedly go on to enjoy many more years of success as a simple statement of high-quality manufacturing and a style of brand building that is as understated as the product which defined it.

**Often the best designs** emerge when even the slightest attention and creativity is applied to the humblest and most everyday objects. Such is the case with this attractive Liquid Container designed in 1958 by Roberto Menghi and manufactured by Italian tire manufacturer Pirelli. The handle at the top, integrated into the container rather than a separate element, and moulded to suggest the impression of fingers, immediately says 'lift me'. The curves are both economical and with the silky finish of the plastic, some-what sexy. They suggest intrinsic quality, almost luxury, in a product that is cheaply mass-produced in its thousands. And the completeness of the design, with that now ubiquitous integrated handle, suggested security in a way that assembled products might not; an important feature when one is dealing with the trans-portation of flammable fuels. It is very much a product of the 1950s, when heat-moulded plastics were becoming more widespread in domestic design and being used in hundreds of applications whereas metal had once done the job. Thermoplastics, notably polymers such as polyethylene, proved to have a variety of advantages over metal, especially when it comes to holding liquids. They did not rust nor have weakening seams that could leak, and were much lighter which was a crucial benefit since liquids are heavy. Also, they offered designers a greater toolbox of geometries to play with, and allowed gentle curves that permitted far easier pouring and more comfortable lifting. And, most importantly, they were cheaper than metal. The sudden availability of these materials spawned a great deal of experimentation in all fields of product design, especially at Pirelli which was rapidly diver-sifying into a myriad of plastic-related products. Roberto Menghi's track record in architecture and industrial design was ideally suited to the job he was given. His products, which often return to plastics and resins as materials, display a geometric approach to ergonomics; using plastics and mass-production techniques to mould an object to its user and its purpose in ways not previously examined. This was either thanks to the shortcomings of pre-existing materials or the utilitarianism of war. The Pirelli Liquid Container is a prime example of this approach. Variants on the design are so numerous and widespread that many may not even consider it a 'design' at all. This alone renders it a definitive standard.

Chups were launched internationally in the 1970s and it was only a matter of time before they became the world's leading lollipop brand. In 2002 Chupa Chups launched the Chupa Chups MAX, a flavour-filled hard candy exterior combined with an inner filling of gum or chewy fillings, adding even more surprises to their already well-rounded selection. Chupa Chups now come in a range of over forty tasty and unique flavours, ranging from the traditional cola, chocolate and vanilla to a myriad of ice cream, fruit and super-sour, and the more exotic chilli (available in Mexico), mango and lychee flavours. Today Chupa Chups produces over 4 billion lollipops a year which can be purchased in more then 150 countries. The sweet is popular with teenagers and adults and has even become an accessory for some celebrities. The Chupa Chups delectable flavours and superior packaging together have created *the* archetypal lollipop.

# 528

Chupa Chups® (1958)
Enric Bernat Fontlladosa (1923–2003)
Chupa Chups Group 1958 to present

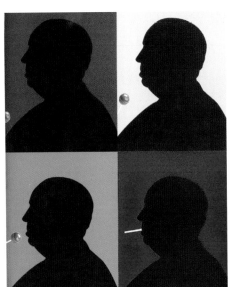

## As a lollipop whose history

mentions its arrival into space in 1995, together with Russian cosmonauts on the MIR spaceship mission, it is no wonder that the success of Chupa Chups is universal. The origins of the lollipop are generally vague, although George Smith, an American, claimed to have invented the modern-day lollipop in 1908 by placing a stick on the end of a hard lozenge. However, during the Depression the demand for Smith's sweet declined, and he stopped producing them. In 1958 a Catalan, Enric Bernat Fontlladosa, launched the Spanish version of the traditional sweet on a stick, calling it Chupa Chups. The name was derived from the Spanish verb *chupar*, meaning to suck or lick. Having been born into a family of sweet manufacturers, Enric observed that there was no candy that specifically catered for children, although children were the largest consumers of sweets. By adding a stick on to the end of a sweetened ball, children could easily grasp the stick and neatly devour the sticky treat, and thus Chupa Chups were born. With innovative packaging consisting of an inner transparent wrapper sealing in the flavour of the lollipop and an outer wrapper, with its roseate logo, Chupa Chups were easily recognized and quickly purchased. It was the self-proclaimed genius and surrealist painter, Salvador Dalí, who designed and created the now recognizable floral logo, with its scroll-like script, in 1969. Chupa

## Such an appealing product obviously needed an appealing appearance.

The original 1958 design showing a little girl with pigtails seemed to fit the bill perfectly, but Chupa Chups' spectacular success both in Spain and abroad soon called for a more universal design.

And thus, some years later the company began to consider a change. In search of new ideas, the advertising agent entrusted with the project and Enric Bernat decided to pay a visit to the world-famous artist Salvador Dalí. In barely an hour, the artist sketched on a piece of newspaper what would become the basis of the Chupa Chups logo. This change would play a major part in making the Chupa Chups brand name a universal image.

Apart from the novel idea of being on the end of a stick, another great Chupa Chups feature was its round shape. This adapted it perfectly to the mouth and, when swirled, got the taste-buds busy and enhanced its flavour tremendously.

Chupa Chups lollipops were initially placed on a wooden stick. As a result of timber shortages in Spain, the company went further afield and negotiated with a Central European company the necessary supply for the 3 million wooden sticks needed daily by the factory. The popularisation of plastic as a raw material is coming years would mean the eventual switch to this material.

"If you can be the first to do something, and you do it after due consideration, it's always an advantage". These words of Enric Bernat reflect an important aspect of Chupa Chups culture. The constant search for new materials and systems to perfect the original idea would be present in all aspects of the company's development, and would ensure Chupa Chups' pioneering position in the sector in the years to come.

**(Anatomy of a Chupa Chups lollipop)**

(A great idea)

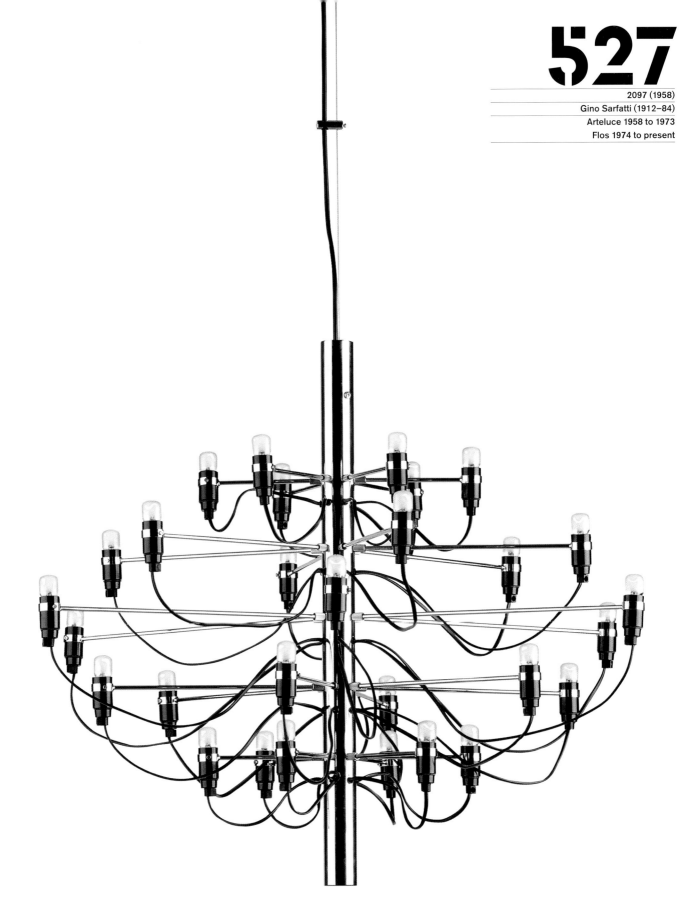

**With the 2097** hanging lamp for Arteluce, Gino Sarfatti has taken the traditional candelabra form and provided it with an innovative modern twist, not only in terms of novel design solution, but also in its technological inventiveness. Gino Sarfatti is one of the most important figures in Italian postwar lighting design, being responsible for around 400 lamp designs for Arteluce, the company he founded in 1939 that was eventually sold to Flos in 1974. Model 2097 is an important exemplar in the Arteluce canon, principally because it takes the most flamboyant and fussiest of lighting forms, the chandelier, and reinvents it within a modern idiom. The hanging lamp is refined and rationalized, comprising only a central structure of steel with brass arms, which results in a simple suspension fixture. The connecting flexes and bulbs are exposed and these raw, unadorned features are intrinsic to the beautiful symmetry and integrity of the piece. Although Arteluce was pioneering in its approach to developing a new and simplified lighting language to suit new industrial production methods, this did not compromise the integrity of its products. Indeed, model 2097 does not pull any punches when it comes to honouring its *raison d'être*, namely to explore and provide movement of light in space, in this case by providing a beautiful diffused light. Model 2097 currently forms part of a series of re-editions by Flos, of classic production pieces. It continues to endure because it forms an elegant modernist take on the traditional chandelier typology, and embodies the pioneering designs of Arteluce. In many ways 2097 marks the end of an era, and the new age of lighting design characterized by an obsession with the possibilities of new materials such as plastic, and ever more futuristic, space-age forms.

# 526

Eames Aluminium Chair (1958)
Charles Eames (1907–78)
Ray Eames (1912–88)
Herman Miller 1958 to present
Vitra 1958 to present

This group of chairs is arguably one of the most outstanding ranges to be produced in the twentieth century. Such a claim is based on the very high-quality material specification combined with exceptional comfort – comfort derived in turn from careful ergonomics and formal configuration rather than bulky padding. The level of comfort emerges from the Eames's declared intention to develop contoured, body-shaped forms of support rather than approximate platforms for sitting. Each chair in the range consists of a sheet of flexible, resilient material tensioned between two side frames in cast aluminium. The material forms the seat and back support and is held under tension by bow-shaped stretchers (also in cast aluminium) fixed under and behind the fabric. The underside stretcher forms the link to the leg pedestal. The general principle is similar to the army camp bed or the trampoline. The specific genius of the chairs lies in the sophistication of the side frame profile which controls the form and provides all of the facility for attaching membrane, stretchers and optional arms. This cast profile is formed in section like a symmetrical double T-beam (one 'T' on top of another). The symmetry of the components allows the same profile to be used for both the left and right frames of the chair. The double T-form creates a profile with a continuous running groove on both sides. The outer groove accommodates the fabric and the inner groove provides location for the bow-shaped lateral stretchers. The lower element of the double 'T' section creates a stiffening rib and is used to fix optional arms. Herman Miller first produced the original Aluminium Group (sometimes called the leisure or indoor/outdoor group) in 1958. In 1969 a further variant of the system was produced that added 50 mm (1.9 in) thick pads onto the basic membrane and was called the Soft Pad Group. Both ranges are still made today and are now produced by Vitra.

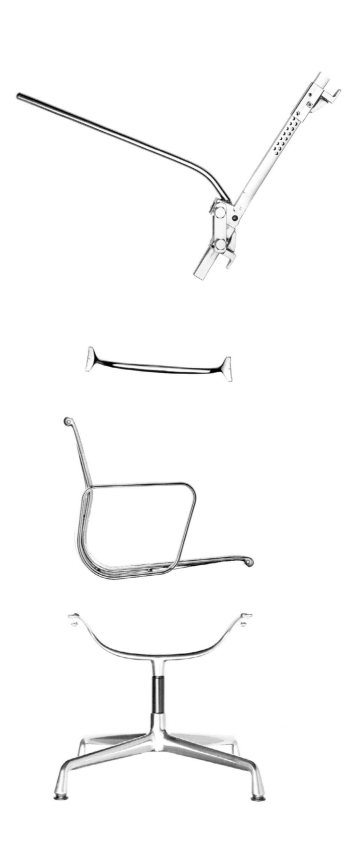

to capture this sense of vastness and set it on a tabletop. Originally conceived as part of a research programme undertaken by Mari, which produced numerous variations on the iron beam, the Putrella Dish proved the most durable design. Indeed the Putrella's shape, a flat base with two gently upturned ends, soon became something of a signature for the designer, who employed it in a later product, the Arran Tray for Alessi. Although virtually identical in form, the Arran is made from thin, polished steel rather than thick, scuffed iron. Although the idea of altering a product that is pre-manufactured could hardly be described as new, Mari seems to have created something of a masterpiece within the genre. Like all of the best radical designs it completely changes our approach to an everyday product such as the iron beam, and means we can never look at it in quite the same way again.

# 525

Putrella Dish (1958)
Enzo Mari (1932–)
Danese 1958, 2002 to present

**By giving a chunk of raw iron beam,** similar to the T-beam, a gentle upward curve on either side, Enzo Mari succeeded in creating a sophisticated, beautiful product out of a material commonly used as a building component in load-bearing structures. Mari, a designer always seeking to challenge the status quo, once described his approach to design thus: 'I take an industrial object, a pure, lovely object, I make a small change, I introduce a discordant element, that is design.' The Putrella Dish, made for Danese, could not be a better example of this attitude, although, unsurprisingly, it is not among Mari's most commercially successful designs. Although often described as a fruit bowl, the Putrella has no prescribed function. Despite being such a small product it appears almost monolithic, as if too significant to be reduced to merely holding fruit. By using iron, a material we normally see on a much larger scale on building sites and railways, Mari has managed

**Luigi Caccia Dominioni's** P4 Catilina Grande chair is an important product of the period when Italian design first became influential on a truly international scale. A smaller version of the chair, the Catilina Piccola, was initially introduced at the 11th Milan Triennale in 1953, and then used the following year in an exhibition in Como for the sculptor Francesco Somaini. Azucena, a company that Caccia Dominioni set up in Milan in 1947 with Ignazio Gardella and Corrado Corradi Dell'Acqua, was one of the many design-led furniture manufacturers that emerged from the 1940s onwards. Like many such companies, it was a vehicle for architects who, faced by a relative lack of commissions in the postwar period, found themselves drawn to interiors and furniture. Their work would mark a shift away from an artisan-driven, craft-based tradition, instead combining an experimental use of materials, modern methods, cutting-edge production techniques and a bold approach to form with a reliance on skilled labour, which meant the furniture retained high quality. The Catilina's steel structure is typical of the impulse to experiment with

both materials and form that had become especially marked by the late 1950s. The chair also underlines the Italians' stylistic departure from the straight lines of mainstream European Modernism. The curved back frame, in metallic grey powder-coated cast iron, supports the oval seat, comprised of black polyester lacquered wood, with either a leather or red mohair velvet cushion, or even the owner's own material. The design has been revisited over the years, but only to alter the size of the chair, making it available in a smaller version for tables, a steel version and a low, armchair-like version. The graceful arch of the frame was centred on the idea of bending an iron bar into a sweeping ribbon, which gently curves only by a few centimetres, creating a comfortable and sinuous back and arm rest. Caccia Dominioni would continue to design furniture and other products for Azucena, while the Catilina in a way became an archetype of Italian design, and has been in production ever since.

Luigi Caccia Dominioni

**This much-imitated design** is the product Sony used to launch itself onto a global market and to establish its reputation for innovation, miniaturization and quality. Sony anticipated the potential for transistors in consumer products earlier than anyone else, and had already achieved considerable success with portable radios, using technology licensed from Western Electric in 1954 (who considered their only potential application to be in the manufacture of hearing aids). The TR-55 was the first of these. Despite being beaten in the race to produce the first transistor radio by Texas Instruments (under the Regency brand), Sony's TR-55 was the first to be produced in any quantity, providing the company with its first export. This was followed by the TR-63 in 1957, which Akio Morita, the vice-president, was so keen to be able to describe as 'pocketable', that the sales force was provided with shirts with over-sized breast pockets. Following the success of this model, the TR-610 was launched almost simultaneously in the United

States and Japan, where it sold for 10,000¥ (the average annual starting salary) in 1958. Smaller still than its predecessors, and available in four colours, red, black, ivory or green, its plastic body has a distinctive contoured shape and a novel kickstand/handle. This combination of elements proved highly desirable, and quickly established the TR-610 as the archetype for all pocket radios of the era. Although previous models had incorporated the Sony name (famously devised by Morita and co-founder Masaru Ibuka as a compression of the Latin sonus and the then-slang 'Sonny-Boy'), the TR-610 was the first product to incorporate the now-ubiquitous logotype by Yasuo Kuroki. The company never looked back. By the end of the year it had changed its name from Tokyo Tsushin Kogyo Kabushiki Kaisha to Sony Corporation and was listed on the Tokyo Stock Exchange.

**Kristian Vedel's Egg Cups** are so futuristic they could be likened to a flying saucer. Measuring a modest 11 cm (4.3 in) in diameter, this melamine design is composed of a cup and saucer moulded into a one-piece unit that, depending on your perspective, seems to hover from the elevated base. The lines of the saucer taper upward from the squared-off base to form a rim so fine it is almost sharp. The Egg Cups are stackable and were originally produced in a range of colours of which red, white and black proved to be the most popular. Danish-designed homeware between the1950s and 1970s was characterized by a rational, pared-down simplicity and a heightened quality mark, and Torben Ørskov was among the key manufacturers of the day. Forming part of the Gourmet Series, which included salad servers, bowls, cruets and candlesticks, the Egg Cup, as designed by Vedel, is one of Ørskov's most memorable items. Always a company obsessed with bringing the highest quality design to everyday objects, Ørskov became famous for issuing its designers with a rigorous brief that often promoted a degree of innovation in manufacturing. At the time that Vedel designed the Egg Cup, the company had been experimenting with melamine, a recent material more closely associated with industrial manufacturing. Vedel explored further the finishing techniques that had been heralded by Ørskov's Salad Servers by Hermann Bongard, Jug and Bowl designs, all of which featured a finish superior to any previously achieved in melamine. Vedel employed the same contrasting brushed and polished effect to the Egg Cup, consequently adding a satisfying tactile quality. Just as melamine proved the contemporary material of choice for many manufacturers of the late 1950s and early 1960s, in its turn it gave way to new substances as the decade progressed. Yet unquestionably Ørskov's period of experimentation with melamine was a significant influence on the modern day penchant for plastic as a material for design. In the twenty-first century, the Egg Cups, along with a number of other of Vedel's designs for Ørskov, are honoured at Denmark's Kunstindustrimuseet (The Danish Museum of Art & Design).

**In some instances,** great objects are not so much original as they are lucky in terms of timing and technology. The clearest case in point is the Hula-Hoop, a concept that had been alive since ancient Egypt, when children would weave together giant rounds of dried grapevines to swing around their waists. But it was the convergence of postwar plastics and pop culture that led to the twentieth-century's most profitable fad object. Two California inventors named Richard P Kerr and Arthur Melin, who had already made their name developing the design for a must-have slingshot for boys, were inspired by tales from a visiting Australian about how children in his country twirled hoops around their waists in fitness class. Intrigued with the idea of marketing a toy in the United States using this idea, the two created a prototype which was tested by children in their neighbourhood. The swaying motion necessary to keep the circle going reminded Kerr and Melin of Hawaiian hula dancers, and a name was born. In this particularly American swords-to-ploughshares scenario, it was contemporary thermoplastic research that enabled the inventors to fashion a hoop that was cheap and lightweight enough to become a cult phenomenon among children, teenagers and adults. The material itself, a Phillips polyolefin plastic called Marlex that was easily coloured for visual appeal, became a hit due to the popularity of the Hula-Hoop. Though the Hula-Hoop was banned in some countries due to potentially suggestive hip rotations, the retooled creation soon found its way into the popular imagination, featured in a four-page story about the phenomenon in *Life* magazine, and onto prime-time television. In their first four months of business, Kerr and Melin sold 25 million hoops through their company, Wham-O, which became a major player in the toy industry with other objects such as the Frisbee.

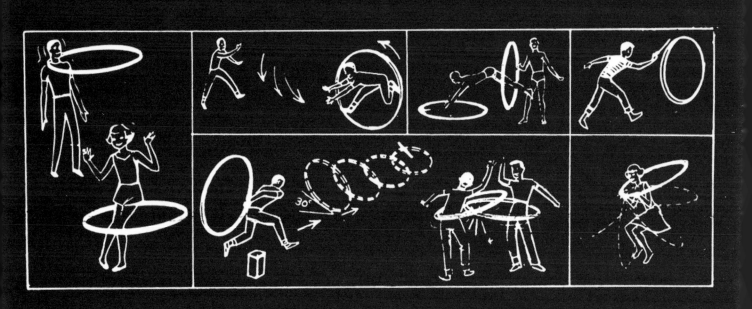

**The Ferrari 250 GT,** so named for the capacity of each of the twelve cylinders in its mighty 3-litre engine, was not one car but many. Between 1954 and 1962 the company launched no fewer than thirteen variations on the theme, finishing with the Berlinetta Lusso. Of these thirteen models, the short wheelbase (SWB) variant proved to be one of the best loved. Like all the best grand tourers, the coupé design was equally at home thundering along the open road or gobbling up the racetrack, where it enjoyed considerable success. Along with the car's 235 kph (147 mph) top speed and its ability to surge to 96 kph (60 mph) in just 6.6 seconds, its appearance is the root of its appeal. The sweeping, clean lines of its body are a stand-out embodiment of Ferrari's long-standing relationship with Battista 'Pinin' Farina. By the early 60s, Farina and Pininfarina, the manufacture, would be Ferrari's standard body designer and the bond has lasted beyond Enzo Ferrari's death in 1988 to this day. The exterior, notably its gracefully curvaceous nose, may have been stylish, but it was also efficient. In tests in Pininfarina's wind tunnel, the 250 GT managed a drag coefficient low enough to make many of today's designers envious. This, and the aluminium bodywork used for the racing cars, helped make the 250 GT a competition success. Its best-in-class showing at 1959's Le Mans and Stirling Moss's victory in the 1960–1 Tourist Trophy at Goodwood were just two triumphs. Moss was to describe his 250 as 'a very well mannered, well balanced car, especially good for Le Mans or any other circuit where one could give it its head.' Ferrari only made 167,250 GT SWBs in three years. Rarer still would be the 250 GTO, of which only thirty-nine were produced from 1962. Owners include Pink Floyd drummer and racing car collector Nick Mason, who bought his well before the price peaked.

**Poul Henningsen's PH Artichoke lamp,** with its spiky cascade of copper-toned louvred shades, is one of the twentieth century's most striking pieces of lighting. It is by far the grandest of Henningsen's many designs for light fittings and represents the culmination of several decades of work. As an architect and committed Modernist, Henningsen began to be interested in the scientific and rational design of lighting in the 1920s, winning numerous awards in the process, including a gold medal at the Paris 'Exposition des Arts Décoratifs' of 1925. His PH series of lamps was produced by the manufacturer Louis Poulsen Lighting in Copenhagen and was especially popular with other architects for use in their own buildings. In general, Henningsen was concerned to eliminate glare from light sources without the use of a gauze or filter, and attempted in all of his designs to ensure that his lamps produced a softened and even distribution of reflected – not direct – light. To this end most of his designs involve a series of concentric parabolic-section cowls – usually painted white on the reflective surface – that enclose the bulb, preventing it from being viewed directly, but nevertheless allowing out a maximum of reflected and thus mellowed light through the interstices in the design. Henningsen calculated the shapes of the shades with great precision, producing a series of diagrams cleverly demonstrating the path of light rays through them and the subsequent even dispersion of light about a room. In the PH Artichoke lamp Henningsen follows his basic theories, but the shades – instead of being solid rings – are opened up and broken into a dynamic series of separate overlapping flaps. These are made from copper, painted white on the underside, and help to emphasize the warmth and mellowness of the light that is emitted. Overall, they work in exactly the same way as Henningsen's more usual light shades – evenly reflecting light about a space – but transform the lamp into a singularly impressive and dramatic sculptural artefact.

Poul Henningsen in a demonstration room designed for Louis Poulsen Lighting, 1939

# 518

**Desk (1958)**
Franco Albini (1905–77)
Gavina 1958 to 1968
Knoll 1968 to present

Franco Albini

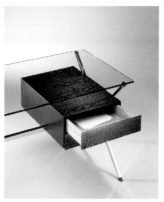

**Franco Albini worked in** a number of fields, including architecture, product design, urban planning and interiors, in the neo-rationalist style established in Italy in the 1920s and 1930s, which sought to unite European Functionalism with Italy's classical heritage. Hallmarks of the architectural style included strict geometric forms and the use of state-of-the-art materials such as tubular steel, traits still clearly visible in Albini's 1958 minimalist Desk. A 1990 US retrospective of his work characterized Albini's approach as a 'rigorous Minimalism [which] illustrates that innovative and profound work can occur by restricting and clarifying the limits of exploration rather than assuming that invention only occurs when those limits are expanded.' Albini was particularly preoccupied with the fine balance between space and solid forms, which the desk exemplifies. By using raw materials he quotes the tradition of the artisanal, and simultaneously uses minimal forms. The 1.28 cm (0.5 in) polished plate glass rests on a frame of chrome-finished square steel tube. The 'floating' drawers, of ebonized oak wood or white lacquer, have an open rear section where magazines or small books can be placed, making the entire structure multi-functional. The desk was first produced by Gavina from 1958 but found a wider market through Knoll, which bought Gavina in 1968. Knoll manufactured work by leading Europeans on a royalty basis, crediting them by name. Albini's designs, among others, figured in corporate as well as domestic interiors and quickly became icons of the Modernism that embodied good design. Florence Knoll would later issue an occasional table design that drew heavily on Albini's desk, using the same glass surface and *cavalletto*, or 'saw horse' legs. The pared-down quality of the desk's design, with its complete absence of ornamentation, means it remains effortlessly modern today, and Knoll still produces it.

**517**

| | |
|---|---|
| Cone Chair (1958) | |
| Verner Panton (1926–98) | |
| Plus-linje 1958 to 1963 | |
| Polythema 1994 to 1995 | |
| Vitra 2002 to present | |

the design of the interior, and all the elements – walls, tablecloths, waitresses' uniforms and the upholstery of the Cone Chairs – were red. Interest in the chair was enormous: Danish businessman Percy von Halling-Koch, owner of the furniture company Plus-Linje, saw the chair at the opening of the restaurant and offered to put it into production immediately. The Cone Chair caused controversy almost as soon as it was launched. When a number were photographed for *Mobilia*, the Danish design magazine, in 1961, Panton draped naked shop mannequins across them. In New York the police ordered it to be removed from a shop window when large crowds gathering to see it caused a traffic jam. Panton continued to add other designs to the Cone range, including a Barstool (1959), Footstool (1959) and chairs made of fibreglass (1970), steel (1978) and plastic (1978). Polythema was the only manufacturer to produce an acrylic and leather version. The range, now produced by Vitra, continues to inspire a new generation of consumers almost fifty years from its creation.

Verner Panton

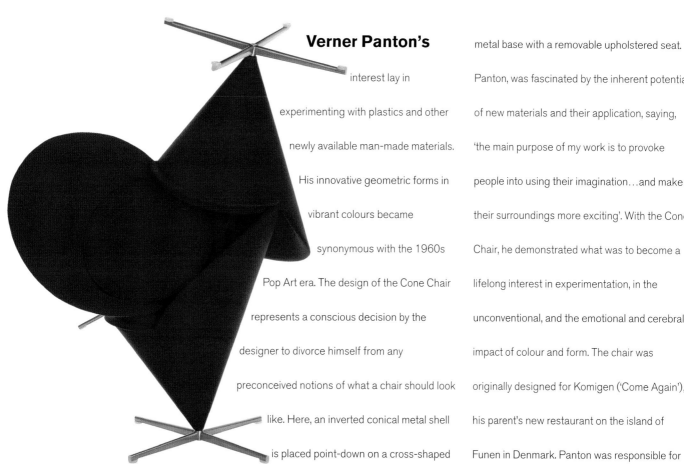

## Verner Panton's

interest lay in experimenting with plastics and other newly available man-made materials. His innovative geometric forms in vibrant colours became synonymous with the 1960s Pop Art era. The design of the Cone Chair represents a conscious decision by the designer to divorce himself from any preconceived notions of what a chair should look like. Here, an inverted conical metal shell is placed point-down on a cross-shaped metal base with a removable upholstered seat. Panton, was fascinated by the inherent potential of new materials and their application, saying, 'the main purpose of my work is to provoke people into using their imagination…and make their surroundings more exciting'. With the Cone Chair, he demonstrated what was to become a lifelong interest in experimentation, in the unconventional, and the emotional and cerebral impact of colour and form. The chair was originally designed for Komigen ('Come Again'), his parent's new restaurant on the island of Funen in Denmark. Panton was responsible for than black. The phone's form is also innovative, with a curving body that rises to mould round the raised dial. The handset is straighter than a traditional handset, but the earpiece and mouthpiece are very prominent, so it fits snugly behind the phone's body when it is placed in the cradle. Nizzoli was perhaps inspired to try his hand at telephone design by the recent popularity of the curving Ericofon designed in 1956. The Table telephone 2 + 7, for all its ingenuity, and the convenience it provided, is one of the least well-known of Nizzoli's products, even if introduced having numerous lines, a phone message, and the ability to put a caller on hold. Interestingly however, it failed to achieve the popularity of his era-defining typewriters designed for Olivetti in the 1950s.

# 516

**Table telephone 2+7 (1958)**
**Marcello Nizzoli (1887–1969)**
**Giuseppe Mario Oliveri (1921–)**
**Safnat 1958 to c.1960**

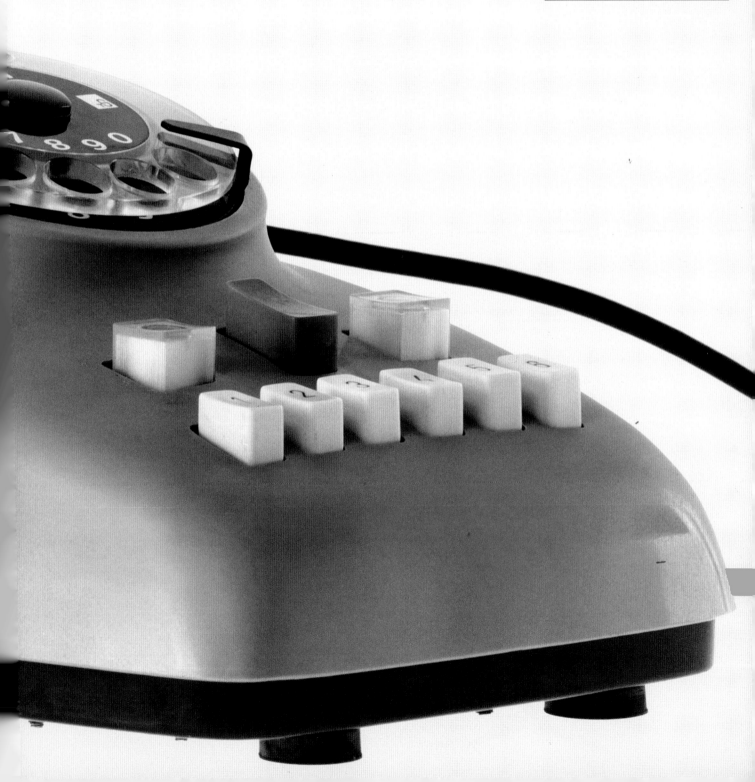

**The Table telephone 2 + 7** represents a rare departure into telephone design for Italian designer Marcello Nizzoli. A former painter and graphic artist, Nizzoli was part of the elite group of Italian designers who emerged in product design during the post-war period. In 1959 Nizzoli collaborated with Giuseppe Mario Oliveri to bring his famous sculptural style to the design of telephones. His distinctive approach is evident in the design of the Table telephone 2 + 7. The crisp and logical placement of the buttons and the dial is reminiscent of a small typewriter or calculator, placing all the components on to the same surface. The phone mechanism is contained in a single, sculptural form, complete with a ring dial housed in the base. Its name comes from the number of buttons, as it was a telephone that allowed the user to take two external calls and up to six internal calls. The external calls could be taken on the two larger white buttons, which would light up as a call came through. The user could then put the caller on hold using the red button in the middle, while the numbered buttons beneath were used to access various departments within the company, such as sales, marketing, administration and so forth. When on hold, the Table telephone would even play music, a novelty at the time. In the evenings a message was recorded to alert the caller that the office was closed, making the apparatus a forerunner of the answering machine. Most importantly, its mint-green colour marked it out as the first office phone to be produced in a colour other

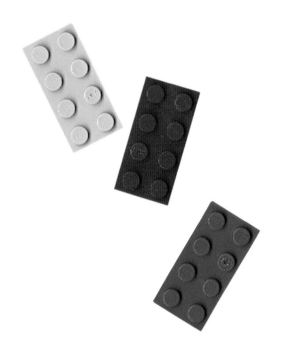

Ole Christiansen & Godtfred Kirk Christiansen

## The simple, modular building brick

admired by parents and enjoyed by children across the globe illustrates successful design attributes. Beyond the marketing machines and company evolution, the stud-and-tube LEGO brick offers enormous opportunities for imaginative play and stimulation. The bright colours and durability of the injection-moulded plastic provide for ready acceptance by children, while parents appreciate the easy cleaning and long lifespan. The design is often considered fundamental in the development of a child's dexterity and interactive playing models. Ole Christiansen's design evolved from his manufacture of wooden toys in Billund, Denmark, in 1932. He named his company LEGO in 1934 after the Danish 'Leg godt', meaning 'play well' and purely by coincidence, the Latin translation of this phrase is 'I put together'. His company grew quickly and, through acceptance of modern manufacturing technologies, LEGO was the first Danish company to invest in injection-moulded plastics. The Automatic Binding Brick was the precedent of today's LEGO and was introduced in 1949 using the new material technology. Soon plastic toys accounted for more than half the company's output and, by 1958, the brick had evolved into the stud-and-tube LEGO brick we know today. Godtfred Kirk Christiansen, son of the founder Ole, was responsible for this particular interlocking system, creating an extensive product development programme. LEGO continually added new features, characters and themes to the range and to expand to international markets. The LEGO brand was universally adopted and the first LEGOLAND was built in Billund in 1968 – by 1974 five million visitors had passed through its gates. The LEGO brick proves that a well-conceived design can transcend age, gender and even culture, as proven by the company's figure that approximately 320 billion LEGO elements have been sold since 1949.

with size and went on to influence a generation of vehicles that became known as 'muscle cars'. When it was introduced to the US market in 1958 originally as a show-car, its vernacular defied the postwar European trend for small, economically minded vehicles. Cadillac had long been America's luxury vehicle of choice and Chevrolet introduced the Impala as a potential rival in this market. It was priced accordingly,

becoming Chevrolet's most expensive model and yet, despite the elevated price tag, the public reacted with enthusiasm. Performance was key to the Impala's success. It launched Chevrolet's Super Sport 'SS' signature brand and became a symbol of performance for the early 1960s. The introduction of a 409 cubic inch V8 engine in 1961 sparked a horsepower race between America's three big manufac-

turers – Chevrolet, Ford and Chrysler – for nearly a decade. Throughout its life, the original 1958 Impala was consistently embellished upon, upgraded and refined. It was taken out of service in 1969 when competition from the market for smaller cars diverted people's attention away from full-size performance. It remains a collectable car, fetching high prices at auction.

**The most striking aspect** of the Impala is its distinctive form: wide, long and low. Straight lines dominate the car from front to back and yet, despite its hefty proportions, it remains surprisingly aerodynamic in essence. Chevrolet's crossed-flag emblem embellishes the front of the bonnet between two large air vents sitting above a wide chrome grille. Round double headlamps flank the grille to left and

right, and tell-tale chrome work is a feature through-out the exterior, especially the hub-caps and fenders. Coupé-style windows without frames, and a broad windscreen and back window give the cabin an open feel. But the most striking feature about the car is the highly distinguished tailpiece. The car's rear end is a masterpiece of design: decadently sweeping tail fins, cat's-eye-shaped rear lamps,

bat-wing fenders and a huge deck lid could at the time be rivalled only by the Cadillac. While some cars are remembered for heralding technical innova-tions and others for defining an era, the Chevrolet Impala Coupé found fame on its looks alone. So much so that it is now recog-nized as an archetypal example of US car design of the late 1950s and early 1960s. The vehicle embodied America's obsession

**Arne Jacobsen's Swan Chair,** made from a moulded lightweight plastic shell supported on a cast aluminium base, was, like its companion the Egg Chair, designed for the SAS Royal Hotel in Copenhagen. The earliest versions of the Swan had a set of legs made from laminated beech, but these were soon replaced with the far less pedestrian aluminium swivel arrangement that now lifts the seat from the ground. When it is viewed from the side it becomes clear how the Swan Chair got its name, with the chair's arms and back forming the bird's wings and neck. However, the sources that lie behind one of Jacobsen's most popular designs are harder to discern. On the one hand the Swan evolves from his own work: for instance, the shape of the Swan's seat and back is actually quite closely related to one of the Series Seven chairs and also to some of Jacobsen's other preliminary designs and models for plywood furniture. The arms, too, have echoes in earlier designs. In this way the Swan represents a culmination of many of Jacobsen's own thoughts on seating design, with the moulded plastic allowing him a freedom of expression denied by the much less malleable medium of plywood. But, on the other hand, Jacobsen was also influenced, often more generally, by the work of his contemporaries. In this context must be cited the pioneering work of the Norwegian designer Henry Klein on the moulding of plastic chair seats (Fritz Hansen used Klein's patented technique) and the internationally influential work of Charles Eames and Eero Saarinen on shell and fibreglass seating. In the Swan Jacobsen deftly combined and improved on ideas from all of these sources, fusing them with such meticulous attention to detail that he succeeded in creating something so distinctive that it has come to define an era.

**If proof were needed** that influential statements are not the preserve of grand-scale design, then the diminutive G-Type Soy Sauce Bottle would put forward a substantial argument. Designed in Japan in 1958 by Masahiro Mori, who was hired by the Hakusan Porcelain Company, this unassuming ceramic bottle grew into a national tabletop icon on the back of a low price-point, national distribution and the promise of a drip-free pouring experience. Good design and mass-market appeal were, it seemed, no longer mutually exclusive. Standing only a few inches tall, the bottle's crisp outline has been kept free from handles or any other superfluous detail. In place of a handle, the bottle is picked up by pinching the high waist that sits just below the lid. Tilt it forward and a smooth flow of soy sauce quickly emerges from the right-angled spout. Apart from the lid, which is set into the bottle to expose an elegant rim, and an attractive ceramic glaze that reflects light to a flattering effect, the design trades on its practicality alone. Masahiro Mori drafted the G-Type design at a time when the majority of Japan's designers were focused on chasing the growing technological tide. Mass-produced electronic goods had long since stolen the limelight from Japanese arts and crafts. But while Japanese families were transfixed by advances in household technology, there remained a need for life's basic tools. Mori's design dictum was refreshingly realistic, citing that the number one criteria for a good design is that it is commercially successful. Backed up by the marketing and distribution savvy of the Hakusan Porcelain Company, Masahiro Mori marched out into the market place to swiftly establish the G-Type as a national design emblem. In 1960 it became the first design to receive the coveted Good Design Prize. In 1961 it won the G-Mark award for ceramics, and seventeen years later, in 1977, after sales had long since passed the 1 million mark, the design was awarded the Long-selling Good Design Products Prize. G-Type continues to be sold in vast quantities throughout the world today and its influence lives on in countless contemporary Japanese tableware designs that exemplify G-Type's utilitarian heritage.

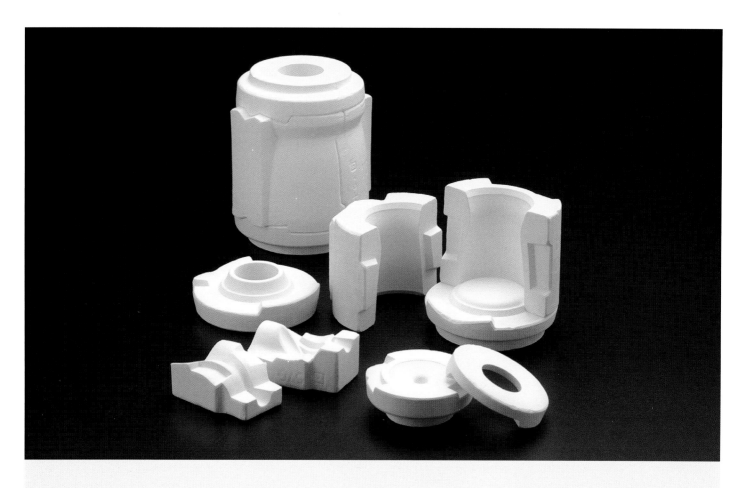

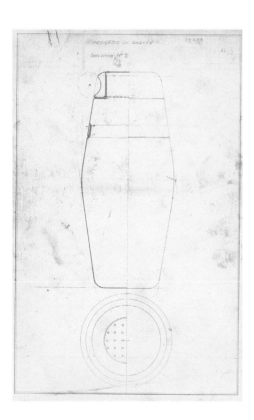

**This groundbreaking product** was first produced by Alessi in 1957 under the name Alfra (Alessi Fratelli), which was the name of the company from 1947 to 1967. General manager Carlo Alessi (eldest son of founder Giovanni Alessi), who had designed many of the firm's products during the 1930s and 1940s, was making a deliberate move away from in-house design towards the use of outside professionals. Mazzeri and Massoni, from nearby Novara were the first of these (later joined by Anselmo Vitale), who began working with the company in 1955. This coincided with a period of experimentation by Carlo's younger brother, Ettore, in the cold-pressing of metals, and stainless steel in particular. The Model 870 Cocktail Shaker was a huge technological challenge from a production point of view because its extremely deep and narrow shape required not only innovation in the progressive technique of cold-forming, but also an intermediate annealing cycle to prevent the material from cracking. In overcoming this, the firm did much to establish its reputation for technical expertise and helped cement its move away from traditional production in nickel, brass and silver plate towards stainless steel. The shaker was part of a complete bar set, which included an ice bucket, tongs and spirit measure. The ice bucket and shaker were available in two different sizes, the latter in 25 cl and 50 cl. Their flawless, highly polished finish was fairly unusual at this time, and has become an enduring feature of Alessi products ever since. This laborious hand-finish can account for up to 30 per cent of the cost of some larger pieces, but sets the company apart from competitors in the field. The set, which became known as Programma 4, was exhibited at the prestigious Milan Triennale the same year. This was another significant first for the company, in that it had never exhibited its products publicly before. From this point on, Alessi began to distance itself from its beginnings as a manufacturer of high-quality catering equipment for the professional trade, and deliberately courted a design-aware audience for its products. The hi-tech nature of the materials and design was emphasized in particular, with subsequent collections, being associated with the potent contemporary symbols of glamour and modernity: international travel. In common with the general Alessi policy of 'once introduced, never withdrawn,' the complete set of Programma 4 is still in the catalogue forty-five years on, with the Cocktail Shaker selling up to 20,000 units every year.

510

Sportster XL (1957)
Harley-Davidson Design Team
Harley-Davidson 1957 to present

## The postwar American period

was one of boom and optimism and this mood, helped by the end of the Korean War in 1953, spawned a golden age of industrial design and production. British industry in the 1950s was emerging from a post-war slump of its own, and motorcycle manufacturers, particularly Triumph, with its light and quick sporting machines, waged a successful assault on the enormous US market. In response to Triumph's theft of its market share, Harley-Davidson had to look beyond its somewhat prewar designs, to a lighter, sportier look. The result of this battle in a competitive market was the Harley-Davidson Sportster XL, introduced in 1957.

It was a bold new step for Harley-Davidson, and gained success over a period of time. The new bike was certainly lighter, and handled like a European bike, and within a couple of years, Harley-Davidson took care of the engine's power needs and the Sportster line became one of Harley-Davidson's perennial favourites. Like so many Harley-Davidson models, it all starts with the engine. The general styling followed the K and KH models from the early 1950s, but the engine was entirely new, with overhead valves to replace the side-valves of the K bikes, of unit construction for simplicity, and with hemispheric ('Hemi') combustion chambers. The word 'Hemi' has almost mythical

status among American motor-sport fans and there is no doubt that Harley aimed to attract a younger, sportier crowd with its new bike. The XL was the first Harley model to have a formal name, with 'Sportster' cast into a polished stripe on the primary chaincase. The engine would eventually come to be known as the Shovelhead, for the shape of the rocker covers, but the original was known simply as the Sportster. With its hot-rod lines and bold colours, the Sportser caught the imagination of the most critical demographic of all: young rockers in search of a machine to represent the way they presented themselves – cool, fast and desirable.

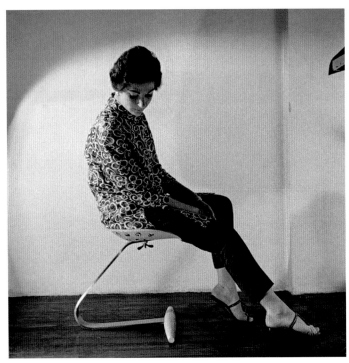

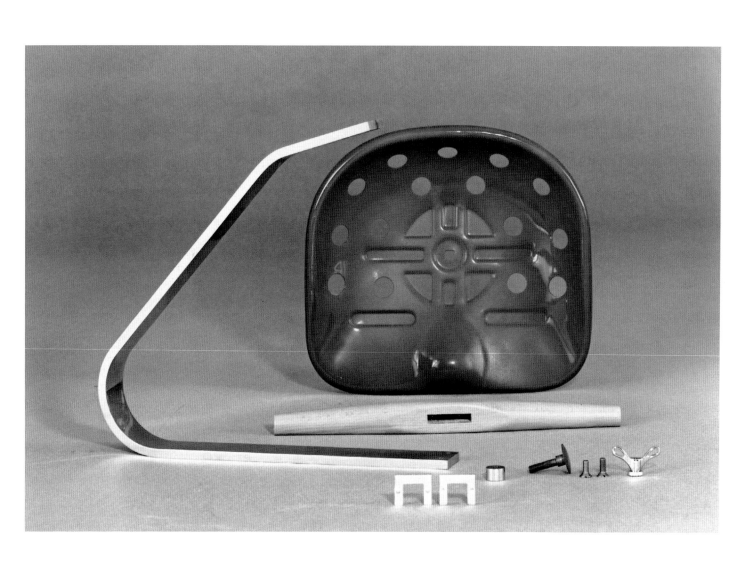

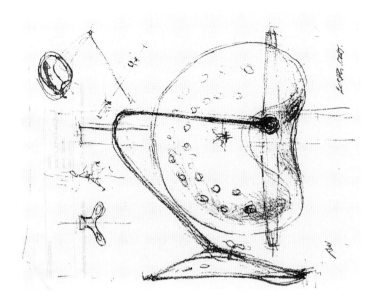

# 509

**Mezzadro (1957)**
**Achille Castiglioni (1918–2002)**
**Pier Giacomo Castiglioni (1913–68)**
**Zanotta 1970 to present**

**At first sight** this is a strange and puzzling chair, which appears to sit outside of mainstream, rational, Modernist design culture. Its importance lies in its challenge to and rejection of, a strictly integrated, formally coherent modern design style. The design apparently favours something more informal and engages in poetics referencing the artistic and psychological as well as the pragmatic. In fact, it is an entirely rational piece but one in which the rationalization is constructed in parts. Rather than developing a simple, seamless whole, each element is considered separately. Each function is analyzed in a search for its most essential manifestation in performance. Castiglioni asks first what is the most basic, comfortable seat form and concludes that it is the tractor seat. Similarly he searches for the most optimal sprung suspension and produces the single cantilevered bar. Finally, he asks what is the most rudimentary stabilizer and finds it to be, quite simply, a log or length of wood. This therefore, is not an arbitrary collection of elements randomly cobbled together. Each part has its own logical integrity. The assembled result produces a deliciously ambiguous tension between explicit formal discontinuity and implicit functional continuity. The first version of Mezzadro was exhibited in 1954 at the 10th Milan Triennale within the theme of 'Art and Production'. In 1957 the current version was shown at an exhibition, organized by Castiglioni, at the Villa Olmo in Como. However this piece was so avant-garde that it was not until 1970, some sixteen years after its conception, that it first went into production. In product terms it anticipated the arguments against formal, reductive rationalism that the designer, Robert Venturi, was to propose for architecture in Complexity and Contradiction in Architecture (1966), by more than a decade. Paradoxically both simple and complex, Mezzadro has high and predictive status, a latent catalyst eventually reshaping the design landscape of the latter half of the twentieth century.

**508**

KS 1068 Dustpan (1957)

Gino Colombini (1915–)

Kartell 1957 to 1976

**Gino Colombini** developed this highly practical dustpan using polystyrene, a rigid, durable and easy-to-process material that can flex slightly under the inevitable strains demanded by its function. Replacing traditional dustpans made up of separate components, typically wooden handles and metal pans, the lightweight KS 1068 could be manufactured in one piece by the fast process of injection-moulding plastic, which also opened up the option of production in a variety of appealing colours. Moreover, the intelligence of the design of the dustpan lies in its upright end, which allows the user to remain standing straight while brushing the detritus into the base. Along with many of Colombini's other product introductions, this affordable alternative earned considerable commercial success. Colombini started his career in the offices of architect Franco Albini in Milan, where he worked from 1933 to 1953. Albini was against frivolous novelty-driven designing, opting instead to employ ordinary mass-produced materials and simple technical solutions. This design approach was to hugely influence Colombini during his time as technical director of Kartell, the Milanese manufacturer of plastic objects. Colombini, under the directorship of founder Giulio Castelli, was instrumental in the early growth of the business. Kartell was targeting the new and relatively unknown possibilities of plastics and was able to create colourful and curvaceous forms through injection-moulding, thereby gaining a unique market share. Colombini explored the technical limitations tolerated by the various sorts of plastics and allocated the appropriate production technique in the manufacture of everyday items such as lemon squeezers, colanders, carpet-beaters, umbrella stands and children's lunch-boxes. While customers were still tentatively approaching the mass-market introduction of plastics in the early 1950s, Kartell helped win over consumers with these small, inexpensive products that stretched the preconceived limitations of the material for domestic use.

**Isamu Noguchi** was a true interdisciplinary practitioner. As well as being a sculptor and designer, Noguchi worked on public art projects, stage design and architecture and collaborated with such figures as choreographer Martha Graham, architect Gordon Bunshaft and composer John Cage among others. Noguchi's career as an artist began as a studio assistant to the sculptor Constantin Brancusi in Paris in 1927. It was a defining experience for him and defined his interest in the use of natural materials and the development of simple, organic forms. Alongside tradition he embraced modern design with the work of Richard Buckminster Fuller, whose ideas consolidated connections between organic structure and architecture. The Prismatic Table brings all these influences together and was designed as a result of Noguchi's experiments with sculptures of folded and bent aluminium that began in the late 1950s. Originally designed as a prototype between April and May 1957 for ALCOA (Aluminium Company of America) and conceived as part of the advertising campaign for its 'Forecast' programme that explored new uses for aluminium. It was originally designed in black, but was advertised as having multicoloured interchangeable elements. Its faceted design combines Noguchi's exploration of new materials and science and technology and has been likened to the traditional Japanese art of origami. This table was Noguchi's last piece of furniture design. Its modernist style is simple and appealing and in 2001 it put into production for the first time, in black and white, attracting new devotees to Noguchi's work.

**Italian designer Enzo Mari** has long thought that the focused intensity of a child at play has much in common with the creative process. This makes sense for a designer who once stated, 'I want my work to be my play,' and who dedicated much of his early career to creating games like 16 Animali that were sought out by children for their whimsical qualities and by design aficionados for their formal mastery. A puzzle that cleverly renders the shapes of monkeys, snakes, camels, elephants, alligators and the like out of a continuous cut in a single rectangular piece of wood, 16 Animali was created by Mari as 'a game that, unlike most of the games produced, would not be easily consumed by the child.' Intended for a pre-literate age group, 16 Animali also serves as a book without words that can be arranged and rearranged to tell stories about the world as children see it. Mari's game was commissioned in 1956, during a period when he was doing design research and development for the Milanese department store La Rinascente, and collaborating with his wife Iela, whose specialization was visual perception and communication in early childhood. While studying Scandinavian wooden games, Mari was taken by the idea of creating a menagerie of animals that was formed by one line. Mari, who had been greatly influenced by the rigours of rationalist thought as well as the tenets of Gestalt psychology, sought to create a design that incorporated maximum meaning through a minimum of elements, essentially taking naturalistic forms and rendering them into symbols. After more than thirty sketches and three prototypes, Mari hit on the final version, which challenged children to successfully distinguish each animal. Elephants had trunks and snakes had tails, but Mari's amusement was in differentiating the forms with the least number of elements required. One year later the design manufacturer Danese picked up production of the puzzle, which first appeared in wood but ended up costing too much to manufacture, making the original version a collector's item. The company experimented with producing the game in a more durable plastic foam, which proved cheaper and easier to make and became a commercial success. A later collaboration with Elio Mari saw the creation of 16 Pesci ('fish') a polyurethane puzzle of various fish forms. In 1997 Alessi reissued the original wooden game in a limited edition of shock-proof polystyrene.

**505**

Flatware (1957)
Irving Harper (1917–)
George Nelson Associates
Carvel Hall 1957 to 1958

surface layer that maintains its finish for years without polishing. The restaurant industry had long appreciated stainless steel for its low maintenance and durability, but stainless-steel flatware did not become popular in the home until the mid-twentieth century, as it was considered too industrial. The flatware designed for Carvel Hall is consistent with Nelson's approach to designing products that suit the technical capacities and marketing needs of his manufacturing clients. Designer Irving Harper had worked with such designers as Gilbert Rohde and Raymond Loewy before joining George Nelson Associates and remaining there for sixteen years. Harper retired in 1983, but remains a key consultant to Maharam for reproduced fabrics, which were originally designed by the Nelson office.

**This six stainless-steel** place settings consisting of six pieces each,
along with a ladle and serving knife was designed by Irving Haper and
George Nelson Associates for the Carvel Hall cutlery manufacturer in 1957.
George Nelson Associates was a beehive of activity dependent upon the
talent of many designers, Irving Harper, who was primarily responsible for
the Carvel Hall Flatware project. Although not the most recognized of the
many famous designs to have emerged from the offices of George Nelson
Associates, the Carvel Hall Flatware remains highly collectable. The graceful
lines of the pieces created an elegant option for homeowners who found
silverware either too costly or too time-consuming to polish. The flatware is
made from 18/10 stainless steel, which contains 10 per cent nickel and 18
per cent chromium, and which reacts with oxygen to form a protective

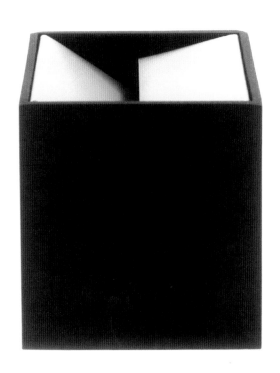

Painter, writer, designer, graphic inventor, educator, philosopher –
Pablo Picasso once called Bruno Munari the new Leonardo. His playful, poetic, subversive and original approach to life and design is present in his posters, poems, lights and in his graphic books for children. Munari's Cubo Ashtray is deceptively simple and rational from the outside: a shiny melamine plastic box. Within it, though, sits a discreet second element, a removable, folded grey anodized aluminium-sheet insert. This resolves all the niggling functional issues of an ashtray – a place to rest or safely extinguish a cigarette, a lid to conceal ash and contain odours – with Munari's characteristically inventive and economic means. Munari's aim was that every facet of the design process had to maintain a relationship with the senses: 'When you confront an object you have to touch it, smell it, listen to it.' Or not in the case of the Cubo, for Munari was anxious to avoid what he described as the 'aspect of a small garbage can'. Designed in 1957, the ashtray and was one of the first products created by the Italian company, Danese, also established that same year. Cubo was amongst the first products created by Danese, and led to a life-long collaborative partnership with Munari. Danese was particularly interested in working with people like Munari because of the links that could be made between art and design. As a company, they aimed to pursue the production of geometric and minimal objects, using sophisticated materials, in an effort to move away from the artisanal to the industrial. The initial design for the Cubo Ashtray was three times the height that it is today, in which the cigarette would eventually be extinguished. However Munari opted for the shorter square shape because he wanted the function to be evident by its form. It was originally available in orange and red, but now in white and black in either 6 cm (2.36 in) or 8 cm (3.14 in). The first edition (1957–9), was a painted black antiscratch steel model, with anodized aluminum in a natural colour, while the second edition, from 1960, saw the launch of coloured melamine models with an anodized aluminum ashtray in an opaque grey colour. The ashtray, achieves Munari's fundamental stance for objects that are 'aesthetically functional'.

**George Nelson** was a leader in establishing good design in America. His Pretzel Chair showcases a number of principles central to Nelson's beliefs. In his catalogue essay from the 'Design Since 1945' exhibition at the Philadelphia Museum of Art in 1983, Nelson states, 'In problem solving, the limitations are more important than the freedoms.' With the Pretzel Chair Nelson conceived of a chair utilizing minimal components while achieving a sound structure so lightweight that it could be lifted with two fingers. Bending laminated wood produced the desired result, a unified structure inherently strong that required minimal material. Backrest and arms created one graceful tapering form. Legs became an elegant system negating the need for stretchers. The structure echoed the system devised centuries earlier by Windsor Chair makers, but here was the minimalist progeny. The use of laminated bent forms, rather than steamed solid forms, allowed a much stronger and lighter contemporary chair with fewer parts that could be more reliably mass-produced. An early environmentalist, he viewed nature as a resource for understanding methodologies of efficiency and problem solving. He paralleled these systems in his own design principles. Nelson defined clear distinctions between the internal necessities and the language of materials as the core logic of design practice, distinct from 'style' which he considered more about the look of things. His article in *Life* magazine in 1945, describing his ground-breaking designs for his new concept of 'wall systems' caught the attention of DJ DePree, founder of Herman Miller, who persuaded Nelson to work as his design director. Nelson played a key role in defining the company's principal design tenets, still relevant today. The Pretzel Chair was originally available as a side chair and one with arms. The latter is far more succinct as a complete form, representative of Nelson's belief in the idea that design is a process of linking everything together. A close cousin is Paul Goldman's Plycraft Chair, which derives its inspiration from Nelson's chair, but adds a one-piece bent ply seat and back. Paul Goldman was subcontracted by Herman Miller to produce the original Pretzel Chair, and attributed his Plycraft version to Norman Cherner as a ploy. Though Plycraft achieved great commercial success, it was not the lightweight chair or the original concept that Nelson intended with the source, the Pretzel Chair.

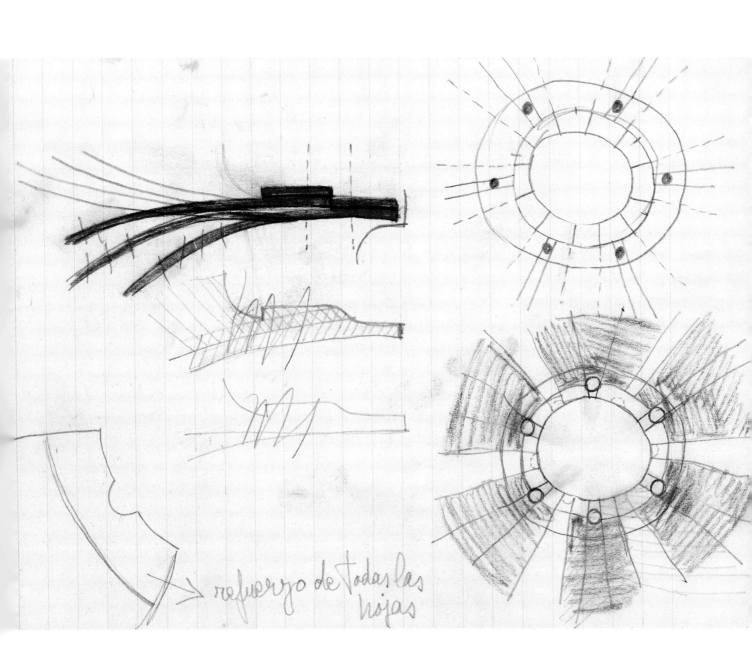

refuerzo de todas las hojas

**Modern in both appearance and materials,** and richly organic in form, the Lámpara de Techo is playfully architectural. Hanging low from the ceiling, two sets of bent plywood strips are affixed to metal washers at the top and base. These form inner and outer layers, which are staggered so that the glare of the bulb is contained, while a softer light is allowed to seep out from between the gaps. This gives a sense of both containment and space, allowing a play of light and shade within the body of the lamp and drawing attention to its physicality as a 'little world' in itself. Its spherical form is a generous 39.5 cm (16 in) at its widest point and the lamp has an idiosyncratic yet unobtrusive presence, which produces an intimate and congenial atmosphere. Josep Antoni Coderch i de Sentmenat's desire to 'contain a complex plan within a simple envelope' is a paradigm that seems to apply directly to this lamp, even though his principles were more directed towards his architectural work. Coderch opened his architectural office with Manuel Valls in 1942, amid a post Civil War Spain that was culturally disorientated and ready for change and development. He qualified in 1941 (his studies had been interrupted by his fighting for the Nationalists in the war) and became one of the first to champion modernist architecture in Barcelona during the 1940s. Coderch also sought to use his work to reintroduce, and therefore to give new relevance to, the traditional landscape of his region. He wished to create architectural spaces that the individual could both identify with and comfortably dwell in. He first gained international acclaim at the 1951 Milan Triennale with his design for the Spanish Pavilion. Admirers included Gio Ponti, who both influenced Coderch and used his *Domus* magazine to bring the young architect's work to a wider audience. While many of Coderch's early works are privately commissioned, single-storey houses, he embarked on larger building projects later in his career, including the extension to the Barcelona School in 1978, which Coderch himself had attended. The year 1951 also saw the erection of his La Barceloneta apartment building, a design sympathetic to the locality composed of ingeniously arranged living spaces and using for the first time his innovative louvre system; a modern adaptation of the traditional Mediterranean window blinds that became a trademark of Coderch's practice. On a smaller scale, similar principles of space are at work in his famous and much-loved hanging lamp from 1957.

**In 1923** the already successful British bicycle and motorbike producer Triumph branched out into the growing motorcar trade. However, the Triumph Motor Company's first attempts failed to find a niche market and were a comparative commercial failure. These difficulties led in turn to bankruptcy in the late 1930s and a takeover by a steel manufacturing company; but when Triumph's key factories were virtually wiped out in German bombing raids on Coventry during World War II, the company found itself yet again on the brink of financial ruin. Help came in 1945 in the form of Sir John Black, owner of the Standard Car Company, who acquired the brand with the intention of launching the Triumph as his company's top-of-the-range model. The unveiling of the early TR prototype at the Earl's Court Motor Show in 1952 was a success and proved to Black and his design team that they were on the right track. One year later the Triumph TR2 was on the market, closely followed by the TR3 and TR3A. The TR series marked a revolution in sports car design, embodied in the TR3A model produced from 1957 to 1961. The last of the traditional side-screen TRs, it differed only in small details from the TR3, featuring a full-width front grille and reshaped front wings along with improved breaks and exterior door and boot handles. The TR3A had all the appeal of a classic sports car: a powerful four-cylinder overhead valve engine, sweeping curvaceous bodywork, racing headlights, shiny grille and leather upholstery, yet it com-bined these attributes with a certain sense of fun and naive charm. Most importantly, here was a car capable of top speeds of over 160 kph (100 mph), with a price the middle classes could afford. The era of the sports car as the exclusive plaything of the very rich was well and truly over. Added to this was its reliability, easy handling and innovative introduction of the disc-braking system. Triumph had struck gold and the TR series continued right into the 1980s with the TR8. The TR3A is still hugely popular with vintage collectors, not just as a slice of British motoring heritage but also because the car is a pleasure to drive and parts for repair are, due to continued interest, still comparatively easy to source.

Hanging Chair (Egg) (1957)
Nanna Ditzel (1923–2005)
Jørgen Ditzel (1931–61)
R Wengler 1957
Bonacina Pierantonio 1957 to present

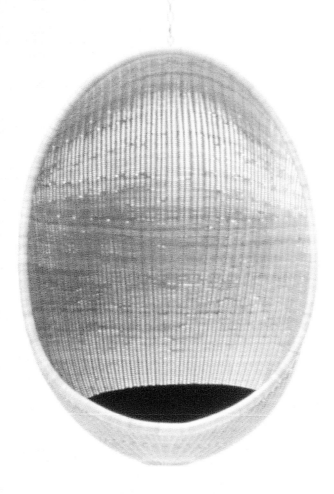
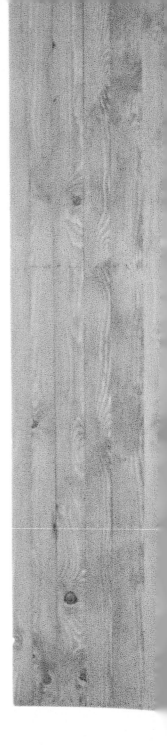

**To Nanna Ditzel,** chair design had the potential to be both practical and poetic. After meeting her first husband, Jørgen Ditzel, at school, they began working together, producing multipurpose furniture for small spaces. Experiments with wicker led to the Hanging Chair or (Egg), which could be suspended from the ceiling. In an interview conducted in 1992 Nanna Ditzel maintained that for many years she had been attempting to create 'lightness, the feeling of floating' in her furniture design. This is important in helping to understand a design such as the egg-shaped Hanging Chair of 1957, a design in which she came very close to realizing her ideal. To appreciate the significance of the design it is also important to recognize its distance from the dominant, rather sober ideas of the day and to see how far away it was from the mainstream of contemporary Danish furniture design. With the Hanging Chair, not only did Ditzel tap into a free and easy spirit several years ahead of the rest of the world, but she also started to move the direction of Danish furniture design away from what she recognized as its overused and dogmatic Functionalism. Ditzel has been dubbed the 'First Lady of Danish Furniture Design', as a nod to her long-standing contribution to textile, jewellery and furniture design. She was born in Copenhagen, studied cabinet-making at the School of Arts and Crafts, and later studied furniture design with Kaare Klint at the Royal Danish Academy of Fine Art. After their marriage in 1946 the Ditzels set up their own design studio and worked together until Jørgen's death in 1961.

**499**

Kitchen Machine KM 3/32 (1957)
Gerd Alfred Müller (1932–91)
Braun 1957 to 1993

**In the early 1950s** Artur and Erwin Braun set a new direction for the company founded by their father, Max, when they introduced a rational, systematic design programme that would mark its output for several decades. Beginning with a number of radios, Braun developed a less-is-more house style marked by geometric simplicity devoid of any decoration and cast in muted colours. The company created a corporate image that extended across products, logo, advertising and packaging. This new direction was accelerated with the establishment in the middle of the decade of an in-house design department, headed by Fritz Eichler, which drew heavily on the sober, scientific approach to design advocated by the Hochschule für Gestatung in Ulm from 1953. Gerd Alfred Müller joined Braun in 1955 and designed some of its best-known products, perhaps the most famous of which was the Kitchen Machine, which consolidated the move the company had made into the domestic appliance market with the Multimix blender of 1950. The Kitchen Machine, finished in white polystyrol plastic, was a multi-purpose unit with accessories including a blender, coffee mill, meat chopper and shredder/slicer. It capitalized on strides made in electric motor technology, which had turned the early hand-operated kitchen gadgets into food mixers and processors. In the United States these ungainly, factory-like tools were beginning to be trans-formed into more stylized items, hiding the motor from view. Braun moved in this direction as well, so that appliances such as the Kitchen Machine could be displayed in the kitchen when not in use, instead of being stowed away. The Kitchen Machine was first displayed at the 1957 Milan Triennale and was an immediate success, leading to its influence on future generations of similar machines.

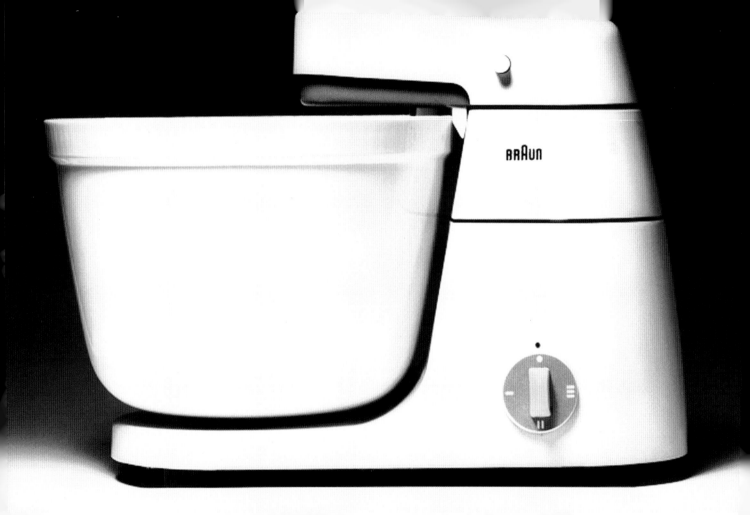

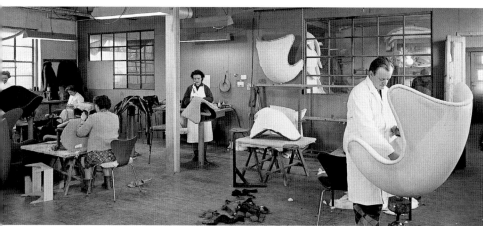

Fritz Hansen factory, c.1959

**Arne Jacobsen's** Egg Chair, so-named because of its resemblance to a smoothly broken eggshell, is a modified, International Style version of the Georgian wing armchair that offers a variety of seating positions and a protective cocoon to anyone who sits in it. Along with the same designer's Swan Chair, the Egg was originally designed for the SAS Royal Hotel in Copenhagen. It was intended to be used in the guest rooms and in the lobby where chairs were clustered to help provide a more intimate and relaxing atmosphere. It is not often recognized that in this work Jacobsen owed an enormous debt to the Norwegian designer Henry Klein. Klein was a pioneer in the development of furniture made from shaped plastic shells and held key patent rights for the moulding process he had developed and that was used under license by Jacobsen's manufacturers, Fritz Hansen. Furthermore, Henry Klein's own chair design from 1956, Model 1007, bears such a clear resemblance to the Egg Chair that it seems inconceivable Jacobsen was unaware of it. Despite the similarities with Klein's design, Jacobsen took a number of steps forward, particularly in making full use of the sculptural possibilities Klein's moulding process allowed. But what is most impressive about Jacobsen's work is his clever fusion of several functionally distinct components of the Egg Chair – notably the seat, the back and the armrests – into a clearly unified aesthetic whole, covered in either leather or fabric. The labour intensive and skilled hand-tailoring that is required to fix the covering to the frame means that only six or seven chairs were produced per week, even today. Since its first appearance in the SAS Royal Hotel, the Egg has developed an independent life as a prop and a symbol in films and advertisements. Perhaps its association with an expensive hotel in one of the world's major cities has helped it to develop an alluring and cosmopolitan sophistication. Whatever the case, nearly fifty years on from its conception, it still seems a chair made for the future.

**497**

| |
|---|
| Daffodil & Jonquil Chairs (1957) |
| Erwine Laverne (1909–2003) |
| Estelle Laverne (1915–97) |
| Laverne International 1957 to c.1972 |

their showroom on 57th Street, New York was ground-breaking in the way that the furniture was shown as if it were art. They displayed textiles, tableware and art by other designers and artists alongside their furniture in a mix of applied and fine art that would be familiar today but that seemed advanced in the 1950s. Despite the superficial similarities with contemporary furniture produced by Knoll and Herman Miller, the Lavernes, who produced and retailed their designs themselves, were operating at a more exclusive part of the modern furniture market.

**Several mid-twentieth-century** design concerns are epitomized by the chair designs of Erwine and Estelle Laverne. One of the defining preoccupations of designers in the 1950s was to capture a sense of organic growth. Bud-like, rounded and voluptuous shapes proliferated, which stood in direct contrast to the attempts by earlier designers to make their products appear machine-like. A second preoccupation was with new materials, and particularly with those modern substances that literally dematerialized objects. The Laverne's 'Invisible Group' of furniture dates from the late 1950s and captures all these concerns. Without a doubt, the Lavernes owed a debt to the work of Eero Saarinen, whose Tulip Chair of 1955 introduced a one-piece moulded, bulb-shaped seat and back upon a slender pedestal base. The names of the Lavernes' chairs also evoke the flower-like shapes of the chairs themselves. They are all variants on the same shape, with different seat and back proportions. Importantly, the Lavernes introduced the idea of transparency, predicting Pop design by a decade. The totally clear structure of the Jonquil Chair, right down to the transparent pedestal, is a tour de force of plastic moulding, and is more audacious than Saarinen's earlier design. The furniture appeared simultaneously natural, organic, futuristic and machine-made. Both Estelle and Erwine trained as painters before founding Laverne Originals in 1938 and

Fig.1

Fig.2

49800

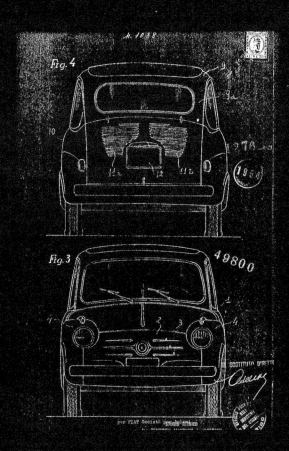

Fig.4

Fig.3

49800

**Following the continuing success** of Dante Giacosa's little 500A ('Topolino') automobile in the years from 1936 up until those following the end of the World War II, Fiat sought to repeat it with a follow-up design. The 500 was launched in 1957: acting as a powerful symbol of the newly democratized Italian society and of the enhanced mobility of the Italian population, it played a key role in Italy's economic reconstruction of those years. Building on his engineering and styling successes of the prewar years, Giacosa reinforced his ability to think across both aspects of car design – engineering and styling – as part of the same problem. Once again this 'joined-up' process resulted in an integrated whole. The 500, which came hard on the heels of a slightly larger 600 model, took the idea of the miniaturization of the car for Italy's narrow, medieval side streets to new limits. In spite of its small size the

space inside this little automobile amazed people who could not believe that a family of four could fit inside it. Marketed as the 'nuova' (new) Fiat 500, the new model had an even more integrated body-shell than its predecessor, its wheel arches having almost completely disappeared, its rear end having been truncated and its bonnet considerably shortened. Gone was the large radiator grill, replaced now by small vents and a badge. The headlights had been fully integrated within the body-shell. The car's body, free from chromed highlights, moved as near to a simple sphere as automobile engineering could make it. Like the 'Topolino' the new 500 proved a huge commercial success and by 1975, when it went out of production, 3.6 million units had been produced. Through the 1960s it was a familiar appendage of Italy's urban landscape and, for many families, became a second car, sitting alongside the more substantial Alfa Romeo in the garage.

**The highly stylized and organic form** of the AJ Cutlery designed in 1957 by architect Arne Jacobsen is instantly striking and a key example of functionalist design. Whilst being sculptural in form, it reveals Jacobsen's concept of cutlery in both shape and material as a design and product for ergonomic use and mass production. A stringent streamlined form is sustained through each piece, which in turn consists of a single strip of stainless steel, with no additional ornament or decoration. Originally consisting of twenty-one parts, the canteen included soup/bouillon spoons for right- or left-handed use. Arne Jacobsen was known as a perfectionist, and an influential Modernist who worked with a personal overall architectural vision and design style. Reflecting his minimalist beliefs, he approved of the 'less is more' idea that was being declared as the new modern credo by many contemporary European architects. It was for his Scandinavian Airlines System (SAS) Royal Hotel project that Jacobsen designed the AJ Cutlery. The cutlery was part of an overall design scheme that included the hotel interior, furniture and exterior. The project produced a number of other now famous designs including the Swan and Egg Chair. All were devoid of ornament, but included strong silhouettes, clean lines and a refined sculptural presence. The styling of the AJ Cutlery was far more unusual and exaggerated than had been seen in the designs of his contemporaries. However, there was a downside to Jacobsen's futuristic forms; the Royal Hotel staff allegedly misunderstood the cutlery forms and they were poorly received by the hotel visitors. In fact, the entire canteen design was soon replaced in full at the hotel with cutlery that had been designed elsewhere. But the futuristic styling was clearly acknowledged through its selection to be the cutlery of choice featured in Stanley Kubrick's science fiction classic *2001: A Space Odyssey.*

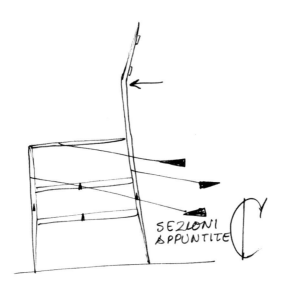

SEZIONI
APPUNTITE

**Gio Ponti's** Superleggera chair, Model 699, is visually and literally lightweight. Constructed in ash, the spare frame enjoys a transparency while the structure is clearly defined. The 699 Superleggera is the culmination of a series of experiments by Ponti to realize a modern design based on historical precedents. The traditional lightweight wooden chair made in the fishing village of Chiavari provided the model for this modernist updating. As simple as the Superleggera may appear, Ponti began to develop models based on the Chiavari Chair as early as 1949. Cassina produced at least three designs that show the chair's development and demonstrate a refinement and modernization of the vernacular tradition. In 1955 Ponti returned to the project, aiming to create a smaller version than its predecessors. The Superleggera is superficially an unassuming chair, with minor mid-century overtones. On closer inspection it displays beautiful fine lines and carefully considered details. The triangular sections and tapering lines of the leg and back supports reflect the desire to reduce weight both physically and visually. The rear legs rise and pay homage to comfort through the tilted back support, and the cross braces curve gently to accommodate the sitter. All the timbers are reduced to their minimum without compromising structure. The seat is finely woven cane, again to avoid weighty upholstery. It is functional from the selection of a lightweight timber through to its structure. From the outset the chair's success was recognized: it was shown at the Milan Triennale in 1957 and won the Compasso d'Oro prize, and remains a highly influential design today. It is still produced by Cassina, testament to its enduring appeal and to Ponti's design legacy.

**At the end** of World War II, the growing commercial airline industry was yearning to put wartime aviation technology, particularly the turbojet engine, into civilian use. In 1952, the British De Havilland Aircraft Company introduced the Comet, a beautiful and elegant design that was, however, underpowered and fatally flawed. The Russian Tupolev Tu-104 was not far behind, but, being a Soviet design, had limitations of a geopolitical nature. In the United States, the Boeing company in Seattle, under company boss William Allen, took the bold step of directing all the company's design resources, and $16m in cash (an enormous sum then) to a four-engine, long-range jet liner with both military and civilian applications. The prototype was called the Dash 80, and flew first in 1954. Its success drew the interest of the military but civilian airlines were still wary. All that changed on an August day in Seattle, Washington. The occasion was the Gold Cup Hydroplane races, held on Lake Washington, a short distance from the runway of the Boeing factories in Seattle. William Allen had arranged a fly-past of the Dash 80, with company test

pilot Alvin 'Tex' Johnston at the controls. As well as an assembled group of military brass, Allen had brought along a number of influential civilian airline executives, so there was a high level of interest. Tex Johnston's fly-past, at a medium low height, at first seemed normal. But unannounced both to the guests and to Boeing's executives, Tex pulled up the nose of the aircraft and executed what are perhaps two of aviation's most famous barrel rolls (or 'aileron' rolls). The crowd was suitably impressed. Under the direction of chief engineer, Maynard Pennell, the Boeing 707-120 prototype was bigger, more powerful and 160 kph (100 mph) faster than the Comet and was clearly the jetliner of the future. Pan Am was first to fly the 707-120 commercially, initiating a transcontinental service in October 1958. A transatlantic service quickly followed, and soon the 707-120 became the very symbol of the jet age. The key in-novation of the 707-120 was its speed, flying faster than the fastest of its contemporaries. It also had tremendous range and passenger payload. Depending on the Boeing's configuration, it was able to carry 147 passengers over 5,000 nautical miles. A total of 1,010 Boeing 707-120s were made during its two-decade production run, and many of these are still flying today.

**The development** of the potential for products and manufacture had a huge impact on product design from the 1950s. The Lemon Squeezer KS 1481 by Gino Colombini marks this move in the design and production of domestic products from this date. Gino Colombini designed the iconic Lemon Squeezer while he was head of Kartell's technical department from 1953 to 1960. The Italian company was founded in 1949, and was using exceptional treatments of the character of plastic, exploiting its potential as an inexpensive and lightweight alternative to materials (in particular metal) for the production of utilitarian domestic household goods. Amongst Colombini's many achievements in design was, most notably, his innovation in the field of plastic, which earned him recognition in the form of the prestigious Compasso d'Oro awards in 1955, 1957, 1959 and 1960. The 1959 award was given for the Lemon Squeezer. Manufactured in low-pressure polyethylene plastic, this simple, brightly coloured utilitarian example of design illustrated design ingenuity. It was acclaimed for representing popular household products and the trend towards using synthetic materials in small kitchen products. With its broad appeal and ease of use the Lemon Squeezer was important for taking a familiar object traditionally made in metal or glass and presenting a new product in keeping with the mood for modern items that employed up-to-date technologies. The styling was in keeping with the modern postwar Italian design. But most importantly, the new material meant it was easy to clean and along with the introduction of the large beaker into which the juice would collect, the squeezer offered improvements and practicality to this traditional object. The Lemon Squeezer by Colombini is therefore a quintessential piece of modern design, which adheres to classic traditions of form and use.

Gino Colombini

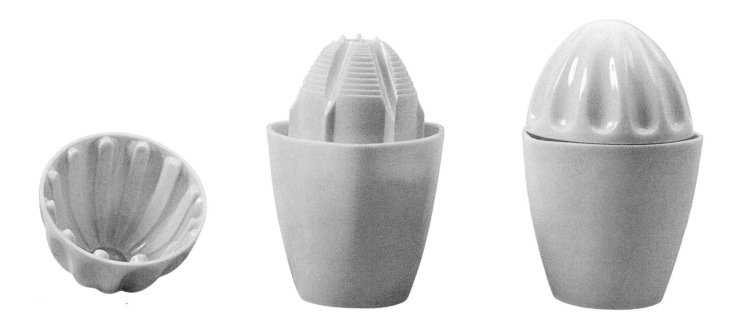

**Extendable both** in height and width, the modular LB7 Shelving Unit was the

culmination of architect Franco Albini's experiments in flexible furniture. Since opening

his first architectural office in Milan in 1930, Albini concerned himself with the structure

of furniture as well as buildings, developing a raw, industrial aesthetic that was

exemplified by the LB7. As early as 1936, Albini was investigating how to make

maximum use of minimal spaces (a problem still much discussed today). His 'Room

for a Man', an interior design concept created for the 1936 Milan Triennale, employed

numerous pieces of multi-functional furniture (a ladder leading to a bed, for instance,

that also served as a coat rack). It was these early experiments that led directly to

Albini's more widely distributed designs of later years, such as the extendable LB7.

Created for Poggi in 1957, the LB7 could be wedged into any room, with its feet pressed

against both floor and ceiling, making maximum use of any space available. The

shelves could be slotted in practically anywhere, allowing the user to configure the

unit to their own particular needs. With such an adaptable set up, very little space was

wasted. Despite looking industrial, the LB7 unit was largely handmade. The same is

true of all of Albini's furniture output as he did not trust the quality of machine-made

goods. The materials used to make the LB7 were walnut, rosewood and brass,

seemingly luxurious materials today, but relatively inexpensive in 1957 and all readily

available to furniture designers. In the frugal postwar era, Albini made a point of using

easily sourced, often local materials to make his furniture. Albini's practical attitude

towards furniture design was vastly at odds with many of his more style-obsessed

contemporaries, yet while they are largely forgotten today, the pioneering work of Albini

is still roundly admired and fetches a fortune at auction.

LB7 Shelving Unit (1957)
Franco Albini (1905–77)
Poggi 1957 to present

**490**
Trabant P50 (1956)
VEB Sachsenring Automobilwerke
Engineering Team
VEB Sachsenring Automobilwerke
1958 to 1962

KLEINWAGEN MIT GROSSER ZUKUNFT

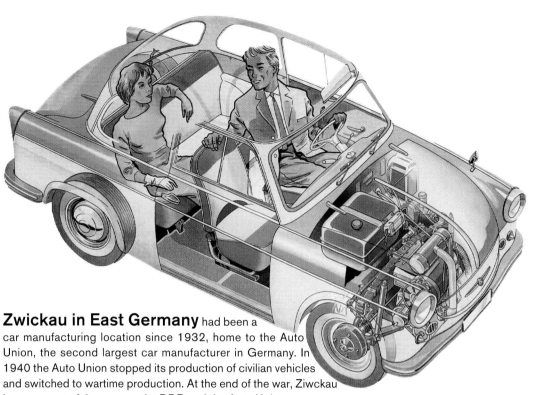

**Zwickau in East Germany** had been a
car manufacturing location since 1932, home to the Auto
Union, the second largest car manufacturer in Germany. In
1940 the Auto Union stopped its production of civilian vehicles
and switched to wartime production. At the end of the war, Ziwckau
became part of the communist DDR and the Auto Union was expro-
priated as its management moved to Bavaria. From the ashes of the
Auto Union, the IFA, the state-owned group that managed all vehicle
production in East Germany, formed the Sachsenring plant, dedicated at first to producing much-needed trucks and tractors. Car
manufacture resumed soon afterwards, with the further development
of some of the Auto Union's prewar models, such the IFA F8 and
F9. In 1955, Sachsenring introduced the P70, the first car with a
Duraplast bodywork, created as a way to cut on the import of
expensive steel. Made from a Phenolic resin reinforced with cotton
or wool, Duraplast is easily shaped with a moulding process and,
although much derided, it proved to be a reasonably better shield
than other Western hatchbacks in impact tests. The P70 led to the
development of the Trabant in 1956. A smaller car than the P70, and
originally designed to be a three-wheeled motorcycle, the Trabant
featured a 500 cc twin cylinder, two-stroke engine, an inner shell and
floor panel made of steel covered with Duraplast panels. Economic
in terms of fuel consumption but modest in its performance, the
Trabant could achieve a top speed of 120 kph (75 mph). Demand
far exceeded production, and underpaid workers from the Eastern
Bloc would wait years to receive their much dreamt of 'Trabbi'. The
Trabant P50 was replaced by the P60, a model with minor restyling
but with a 600 cc engine. The P601 emerged in 1964, having
undergone a major redesign to gain more interior and luggage space.
Subsequent Trabant designs remained basically unchanged, although
many improvements were carried out in the engine and mechanics of
the car. Trabants were exported within the Eastern Bloc and in a few
Western countries such as Holland, Belgium and South Africa. With
the fall of the Berlin Wall Sachsenring underwent financial troubles
and closed in 1991. Today the Trabant has achieved the status of
collectible car, much loved and sought after by many aficionados of
this little, unpretentious design.

available in a choice of fabric, leather or naugahyde cushions with a rosewood ply base. However, because of the scarcity of rosewood the current five-ply designs are now available in walnut, black cherry, or black-stained wood. It comprised three plywood shells, over which leather cushions embrace the structure. Charles Eames described the chair as having the 'warm, receptive look of a well-used first baseman's mitt'. The accompanying Ottoman, with one plywood shell, has a four-star aluminium swivel base. While the earlier Plywood chairs had just two shells, the Lounge Chair uses a third in order to support the reclining sitter. Rubber and steel shock mounts connect the shells and allow them to bend independently of one another. The leather cushions were originally filled with duck feathers, down and foam, while today's versions are filled with Dacron and foam. Eames claimed his customers could receive the chair in an early flat-pack form and assemble it single-handedly with a screwdriver. He supported this claim in the stop-motion film 'Eames Lounge Chair' of 1956. Although Charles and Ray Eames firmly believed in, and attempted to create furniture for, a wider public, the Lounge Chair was quite expensive to manufacture, owing to the combination of factory-production and hand-skilled labour, and the large number of individual pieces of which it is composed. But its welcoming form and stubborn elegance have assured its position amongst the most collected design pieces, remaining as popular today as it was when first produced.

489

Lounge Chair (1956)
Charles Eames (1907–78)
Herman Miller 1956 to present
Vitra 1958 to present

**The Lounge Chair** was originally designed as a one-off bespoke creation rather than a production piece, and is often perceived as the twentieth-century recreation of the traditional English club chair. However, because of its overwhelming popularity Charles Eames set about adapting the design for production. In doing so he deployed the same meticulous moulding techniques that he had developed earlier for the 'plywood group' range. Eames had been exploring the possibilities of creating furniture with interlocking pieces of moulded plywood for nearly a decade, and this idea finally took shape with the Lounge Chair. The prototype was made by Don Albison at the Eames Office, and the design was so successful that the Lounge Chair was eased into production in 1956. The early designs were

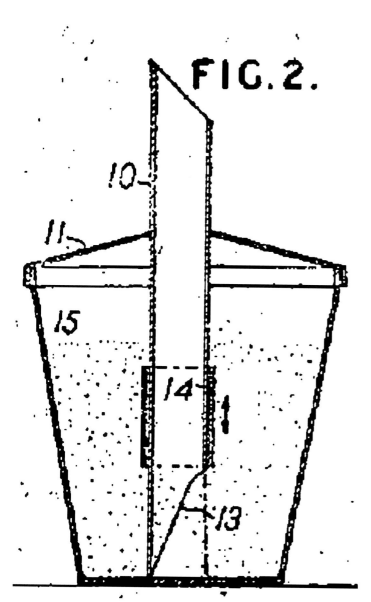

FIG. 2.

10

11

15

14

13

**Long a part of the classic** American diner made famous in the 1950s, the simple glass-and-metal sugar pourer has a surprising origin in central Germany. It was the brainchild of an inventor from Hanau, Germany, named Theodor Jacob, who patented a 'dispenser for granulated materials such as sugar', creating a model of simplicity and material modesty in 1956. Although American inventors had been working on the sticky problem of hygienic and accurate sugar dispensing since at least 1917, no one had been able to come up with as straightforward a solution as Jacob. America had seen a dizzying array of patents for flanges, funnels and flaring holding chambers that would expedite the serving of sugar without tacky tables, unsightly clumps and wasteful portions, but it was Jacob's concept of minimally moving parts that would become the ubiquitous diner accoutrement for decades to come. Jacob's simple design comprised a glass container sealed with a threaded, screw-on metallic top and a metal tube that reached into the depths of the vessel. Bevelled at the bottom, the tube allowed for an exact portion to be dispensed each time the container was turned upside down. Bevelled oppositely at the top, the dispensing tube was covered with a small self-closing flap, providing further assurance of the sugar's purity and non-contamination. In a cleverly concealed detail, Jacob added an additional moving sleeve that slid down the tube and over the lower bevel to allow restaurant management to regulate the dose of sugar even more precisely if thrift was an issue. In a final detail that in retrospect seems prophetic of the coming wave of commercialism, Jacob concluded his patent application with one additional note: 'The outer wall may also be used for advertising purposes.'

Marshmallow Sofa (1956)
Irving Harper (1917–)
George Nelson Associates
Herman Miller 1956 to 1965, 1999 to present
Vitra 1988 to 1994, 2000 to present

**When it first appeared** in 1956 the bold outline, easy-to-clean surfaces and see-through structure of the Marshmallow could hardly have contrasted more sharply with the heavily upholstered, dust-gathering bulky sofas that dominated so many living rooms of the period. Bright in colour, playful in shape and name and somewhat resembling a wide-open waffle-iron, the Marshmallow seemed already to be looking forward to the coming Pop era. With its round balls of colour held together as if by a molecular structure, it also relates to George Nelson's earlier design for a Ball Wall Clock (1947) or to Charles and Ray Eames's Hang-It-All Coat Rack (1953). Irving Harper, staff designer from 1947 to 1963 at George Nelson Associates, designed the Marshmallow Sofa during a weekend, as he has said in his accounts. Like the Eameses, Harper liked to exploit the decorative possibilities of scientific and biomorphic imagery. Ironically, given that he and his colleagues had fought so hard against the 'stylization' of the modern machine-age aesthetic, he recognized that the growing postwar interest in the biomorphic and organic had spawned a new style, 'with which we must now cope whether we like it or not'. He was concerned with qualities of silhouettes and the lack of weights, qualities he was most likely considering when designing the Marshmallow Sofa. The Marshmallow was marketed as suitable 'for lobbies and public buildings' as well as for domestic use. The cushions could be interchanged for a new look or in order to equalize wear. Its unitary construction system meant that it could be made available in a variety of sizes and customized colour combinations. However, this caused production to be labour-intensive, leading to its interesting history of manufacture.

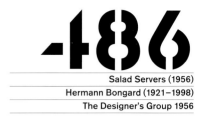
**Norwegian designer** Hermann Bongard first made a name for himself with graphic glass design. An early employment at Christiana Glassmagasin brought Bongard to the attention of Hadeland Glassworks, in the 1940s Norway's most influential glass producer, for whom he created designs until 1955. Bongard's design ambitions were already diverse and at this time, alongside his glassware design, he was also producing work in ceramic, wood and wicker. Bongard was particularly interested in the reinvention of traditional Norwegian handicrafts, using the British Arts and Crafts movement and the work of William Morris as inspiration. These Salad Servers were designed by Bongard in 1956 and produced by The Designer's Group in New York. The simple servers are an example of Bongard's graphic application of a traditional craft technique. While obviously modern, with a fluid and sculptural shape, the basic design and honesty of material is more than a nod to age-old Norwegian craftsmanship; the servers' function is also clear. By the early 1950s Hermann Bongard was an internationally recognized name. He played a significant role in the 'Design in Scandinavia' exhibition of modern household objects, which toured the United States between 1954 and 1957. His talents were recognized in 1957 when he was awarded the Lunning Prize, like Kaj Franck and Hans Wegner before him, the prestigious Scandinavian design award for contemporary design. Bongard then went on to become a professor of graphic art at the National College of Art and Design in Oslo and to produce graphics and art work for Norway's national bank, Norges Bank.

**PK22 was designed** when Poul Kjærholm was in his early twenties, and posited the central concerns that placed him among the great innovators of the Danish Modern movement. The lounge chair comprises a remarkably elegant, cantilevered seat frame encased in an envelope of leather or cane, and balanced on a polished stainless-steel sprung base, which constitutes its legs. Two flat arcs of cut steel provide both structural stability and the response to the experience of sitting in this lounge chair. Like many chairs of its kind from that period, this one forgoes cushions and upholstery in favour of surfaces in tension. The structure of its steel frame, however, maintains the perception of an unusually light gathering of planes and lines. This chair is an exercise in finely wrought minimalism and stands as an exemplar of the sustainable design strategy that demands economy in the use of materials. Kjærholm remains a favourite among rigorous modernists for his dedication to transparency in construction and use of materials that are readily comprehensible and profoundly considered. Through his masterful use of cantilevers and bent steel he takes the key furniture innovations of the first decades of the twentieth century and refines them into further innovations. His furniture was among the finest examples of the International Style and PK22 is one of its early and most articulate expressions. PK22 was initially issued by Ejvind Kold Christensen and has been reissued by Fritz Hansen. Kjærholm worked with Fritz Hansen for only a year, during which time he created a number of prototypes. He then collaborated exclusively with Ejvind Kold Christensen from 1955 until his death in 1980. Fritz Hansen gained rights in 1982 to reproduce the renowned 'Kjærholm Collection', of which the PK22 affirms its place as an elegant example of Danish Minimalism.

**485**

PK22 (1956)
Poul Kjærholm (1929–80)
Ejvind Kold Christensen 1956 to 1982
Fritz Hansen 1982 to present

Every so often an example of industrial design comes along that is so strongly associated with the cultural DNA of a city that it even becomes a part of the country's national identity. The Austin FX4 is one such design. Just as the Checker Yellow Cab typifies New York, the Austin FX4, or 'black cab' as it is more commonly known, takes its place alongside the red pillar postboxes and double-decker buses that punctuate and define London's cityscape. The FX4 is unmistakable as a gently rolling landscape of elongated black curves surrounding a passenger cabin that is considerably broader than that of a civilian car. The passenger area, which is separated from the driver's cabin by a screen, expands to accommodate up to five passengers, in a bench-like seating system that allows three people to face forwards and two to face backwards. The doors, which open backwards to ease entry, are another distinctive feature of the Austin, as is the orange 'for hire' light perched on the roof, the almond-shaped rear lights and the rather earnest-looking round front headlights found either side of a tall rectangular front grille. Bright chrome bumpers and hubcaps establish the car's outermost extremities, to the front, the rear and the sides. Aside from the Austin FX4's obvious charisma, its iconic status is also due to the technical innovations it heralded when it replaced the FX3 taxi design in 1956. The FX4 introduced fully hydraulic breaks and improved driver instrumentation, as well as a 7.62 m (25 ft) turning circle perfect for London's narrow streets. Its design would remain largely unchanged, apart from minor cosmetic improvements, for almost four decades, awarding it the second longest life of any passenger car after the Land Rover. Even with a limited annual production of only 2,000 vehicles, other models could not compete. By 1967, 97 per cent of all licensed London cabs were Austin FX4s. Production of the FX4 was superseded in 1997 by the TX1, an improved design that could meet the demands of the twenty-first-century city dweller in offering child seats, electric windows, air conditioning and an improved driver's cabin. Yet the distinctive body shape of the FX4 is faithfully imitated in the newer models, ensuring that the unique design will live on.

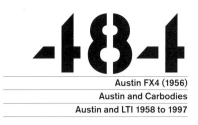

Austin FX4 (1956)
Austin and Carbodies
Austin and LTI 1958 to 1997

THE AUSTIN TAXI

Austin of England

**483**

'5027' (1956), Kartio (1993)
Kaj Franck (1911–89)
Nuutajärvi-Notsjö 1956 to 1988
iittala 1988 to present

**The different pieces** of utility glass – tumblers in two sizes, a bowl, two types of carafe, a vase and a candleholder – that comprise the Kartio range were all originally designed by Kaj Franck in the 1950s for the Finnish company Nuutajärvi-Notsjö. It is only more recently, in 1993, that they have been assembled into a single range and marketed under the name Kartio. Kaj Franck was well aware of the significance of colour in design, using it, for instance, as a means of enlivening a basic form, but the use of colour in his glassware has been something of a vexed issue, largely because of cost and the difficulty in achieving consistency from one batch to another. Over the years, the number of different colours in which the pieces were available has changed. Now, iittala, the current manufacturer, produces the set in six colours, including clear, smoky-grey and four different shades of blue, but the palette is limited, creating an overall monochromatic feel. Originally though, Nuutajärvi, a firm well known in Finland and abroad for its coloured glass, sold the set of six tumblers outside Finland as a multicoloured harlequin set. It was one of its most influential and popular lines, primarily for this use of colour. IKEA, for instance, now sell a comparable set made in plastic. Although the designs for the individual components of Kartio were produced over a period of time, with only a vague intention that they be used together, they nevertheless form a sensible product grouping. Each piece is linked to the others by a simple but all-pervasive structural clarity and follows Franck's fundamental approach to design of constructing a balanced object from one or two elementary geometric shapes.

**The highly acclaimed** Mirella sewing machine revolutionized the traditionally conservative field of sewing machines, utilizing a rationalist design style to transform the domestic landscape. The Mirella sewing machine encased the mechanical and electrical components within a plastic shell. The design was a result of extensive ergonomic research and the machine's sophisticated appearance was enhanced by a fashionable use of colours such as ivory, pink and apple green. Because many households still had limited access to electricity, the design also featured a hand crank, enabling users to operate the machine without power, and thus creating a truly portable sewing machine. Designer Marcello Nizzoli trained at the Art Academy of Parma. Upon graduating in ornamentation, design and architecture, he joined the radical Italian Futurist art movement, exhibiting paintings and textiles before moving increasingly into the field of industrial design and applied arts. In 1936 Olivetti appointed Nizzoli as chief designer of all its typewriters, a role he continued after the war. A truly multi-disciplinary designer, Nizzoli continued to work with other manufacturers and clients, designing acclaimed posters for Campari, as well as working for Necchi on a series of radical sewing machines. His design input to the firm was recognized when the Mirella won the prestigious Compasso d'Oro award in 1957. Nizzoli's enormous contribution to Italian design, and in particular his seminal design of the Mirella, has been rightly acknowledged through the sewing machine's inclusion in New York's Museum of Modern Art's permanent design collection. Necchi continues to dominate the market through a commitment to progressive industrial design. The company's extensive range of domestic and industrial sewing machines helps to produce everything from clothes and shoes, to home furnishings and boat sails.

Lamino Chair (1956)
Yngve Ekström (1913–88)
Swedese Möbler 1956 to present

Yngve Ekström

**In late 1999,** on the eve of the vaunted new millennium, Sweden's most renowned interior design magazine *Sköna Hem* polled its readers for the century's best Swedish design object. The overwhelming response was Yngve Ekström's Lamino Chair, the tall-backed, slightly reclined armchair that had an older generation reminiscing about how it had been at the top of their list for wedding gifts and graduation presents, while younger readers recalled the Lamino as the place where they snuggled up in parents' laps to listen to fairy tales. At first glance, the sinuous armchair is similar in genre to those created by other Scandinavian masters like Bruno Mathsson and Finn Juhl. Formed out of pressed laminate from a variety of woods, including teak, beech, cherry and oak, and lined most often in sheepskin upholstery, the Lamino possessed the pleasing form and utility that came to mark Scandinavian Modernism. But Ekström was shrewd as well as stylish, and designed the Lamino using a construction that would ensure easy shipping throughout Sweden and as well as to a secondary market in the United States. Customers bought the chair in two pieces, and were responsible for screwing the seat to the arms and legs themselves using a hexagonal key that was included in the packaging. The tool that was provided not only made the job easier, but ensured that the chair be properly and firmly placed together. Much to Ekström's retrospective regret, the device was never patented, and a door was opened to a competitor named Ingvar Kamprad, who went on to furnish a large portion of the First World with his knockdown, screw-together IKEA furniture. Despite this oversight, Ekström and his brother Jerker built a healthy and iconic modern design company dubbed Swedese around the Lamino Chair and its brethren, Laminett, Lamello and Melano, while remaining in the small town of Vaggeryd in Småland. With more than 150,000 Lamino Chairs having taken up residence since its introduction in 1956 – and it is still being manufactured – the chair continues to be a household name that has only increased in style and sentimental attachment.

*The Italian Job* (1969), directed by Peter Collinson

and chrome trim that his American counterparts were espousing at this time in creating what Harley Earl has called 'holidays on wheels.' In sharp contrast Issigonis adopted a minimal approach, preferring to create a utility object which people could adapt and add to as they wished. Launched in 1959 the Mini, the name given by the public to his creation, quickly developed a character of its own and became the object of desire for many women who had not felt at home in big, lumpy cars and for significant members of the Pop generation who wanted a neat, efficient little car to accompany their upbeat, urban lifestyles. Only three metres long, and only one point two meters wide and high, the Mini was smaller than the Fiat 500. Its minute size was displayed in *The Italian Job*, where theives make their getaway by driving through narrow alleys, sewers, over rooftops, through viaducts, and still manage to escape. It was loved for its basic utilitarian character and its low price and running costs.

Mini (1956)
Alec Issigonis (1906–88)
Morris/Austin 1959 to 2000

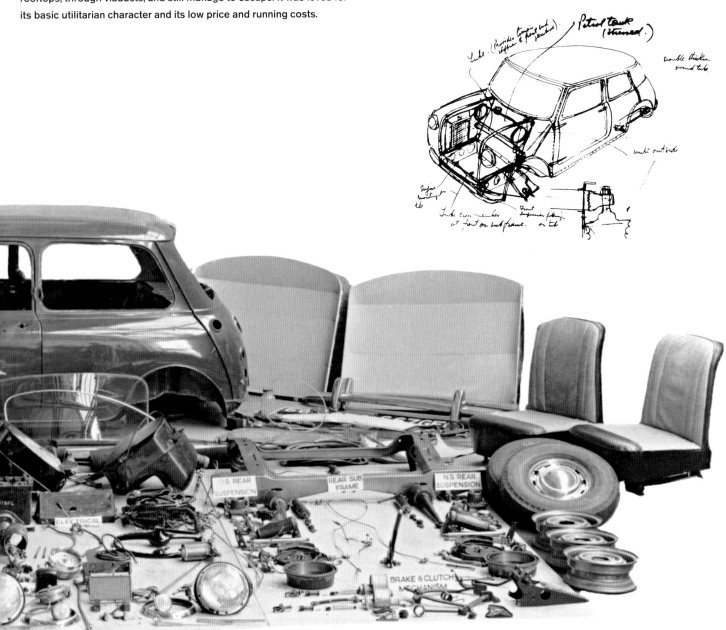

Alec Issigonis

**Like Dante Giacosa's** work for Fiat in the years after 1945 that of the engineer-designer, Alec Issigonis, for the British Motor Corporation focused on the challenge of creating the smallest possible four-person car. Inspired by the fuel shortage created by the Suez crisis (26 July, 1956) and competition from bubble cars the result – the Mini of 1956 – solved the problem admirably. The simple utilitarianism of the car has resulted in its becoming a classic. Such were Issigonis' significant engineering skills, honed through his earlier experiences at Humber and Morris Motors, that he approached the problem of the miniaturization of the car from the inside out: in order to make the largest possible internal space he placed the engine in a new position; he pushed the wheels to the extreme limits of the body; and he found a new space for the gearbox. The exclusion of any fancy extras meant that four passengers could sit with ease in this tiny car. The body was seen as little more than a container

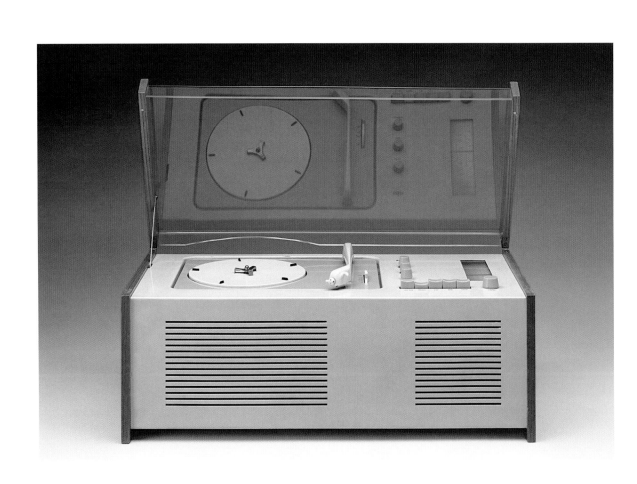

**Dieter Rams**

**By 1955 Gugelot** had already designed a series of rationalized radio sets for Braun that were exhibited in a revolutionary installation at the 1955 'German Radio, Television and Phono Show' in Düsseldorf by his friend Otl Aicher. The stark, modern setting was distinct from other decorative booths at the fair and increased Braun's appeal to the urban intelligentsia. Until this point, most domestic technology was 'buried in furniture' but Gugelot's starting-point was the product and its simple and honest use. Following the exhibition, Erwin Braun saw an opportunity to develop a low-cost radiogram, called the SK4, with the project originally given to Dieter Rams and his colleague Fritz Eichler. Rams had originally joined Braun as an architect, and this was one of his first design programmes. However, after struggling to find a feasible solution, Eichler asked his friend Gugelot to join the project. Gugelot's knowledge of manufacturing simplicity was extensive. He came to the project having designed the first modular storage system for the German firm Bofinger and had introduced the use of melamine for furniture. His initial suggestion for the project was to involve a wrapper of sheet steel, sandwiched between two wooden panels. The componentry was now entered from the bottom, rather than from the back, and there was now no need to place it against a wall, as each side was presentable. The design also included a perspex lid, an influential first. Originally it was prototyped in sheet steel, but sound vibrations caused problems. The perspex lid liberated the product even further, with its transparent honesty. The SK4 continues to resound simplicity. Nowadays such approaches in modern hi-fi design are rare. Today's products might involve sheet steel or perspex, but there is a backward step in terms of their use. Useful functions have now been taken over by marketable features. With the SK4, the sound is allowed to take front seat, with the product in the background. The irony perhaps is that the SK4 merged with its surroundings more successfully than contemporary 'furniture' solutions produced by competitors.

# The creation of the Kitchen Scoop

did not make headlines when the Vollrath Company launched it in 1956, yet this streamlined design is an immediately recognizable design, found in many of today's most stylish kitchens. Vollrath was founded in Wisconsin, USA, by the visionary Jacob Johann Vollrath at the turn of the twentieth century. Vollrath realized the potential for enamel-coated porcelain and glazed cast-iron kitchenware, already popular in Germany. Durable and inexpensive, his products were enormously popular in the US and sold to the public service industry as well as domestic kitchens and top restaurants across the country. The introduction of stainless steel in the early half of the twentieth century heralded a breakthrough in kitchenware, and cutlery was among the very first items to exploit this new technology. In 1930 the Chrysler Building in New York was completed, with its upper arches clad in stainless steel. It was not long before stainless steel was being used for a number of consumer products as well as for structural purposes. Known for being rust-resistant and non-toxic, as well as zinc- and lead-free, it was an ideal material for kitchenware. When Vollrath expanded his line to include stainless steel kitchenware products, he could not have known that his name would become synonymous with quality stainless steel domestic products. The Kitchen Scoop combines the durability and clean appearance of stainless steel with a simple yet unique design, making it an ideal utensil for use in a demanding kitchen. Multi-functional, the scoop's clever design allows for transferring liquids or solids without spillage. The scoop's aerodynamic lines and cutting-edge modernity created a design object with everlasting beauty and function, even inaugurated into The Museum of Modern Art's permanent collection.

**477**

Butterfly Stool (1956)
Sori Yanagi (1915–)
Tendo Mokko 1956 to present
Vitra Design Museum 2002 to present

Sori Yanagi

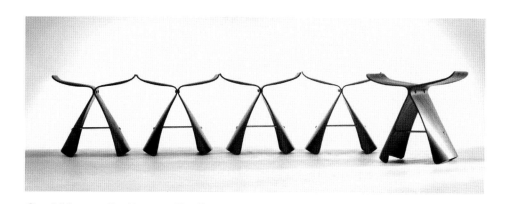

**Sori Yanagi's Butterfly Stool** is, in many ways, simplicity itself. It is constructed of two identical plywood forms, connected under the seat by just two screws. An additional threaded brass rod acts as a stretcher and gives the stool stability. Nothing else is required to make the piece of furniture. The name derives from the profile of the seat, suggesting a butterfly in flight. The Butterfly Stool was designed at a pivotal moment in Japanese history. In the early 1950s Japan was fast emerging as an industrial nation after its defeat in World War II. In 1952 Yanagi and others founded the Japanese Industrial Design Association to promote the role of designers within industry; a clear sign of renewed national confidence. Yanagi had been exposed to European Modernism in the 1940s, when Charlotte Perriand had been invited to visit Japan to advise Japanese designers and Yanagi, a French language student, accompanied her. This encounter may have influenced his approach to chair design, although Yanagi developed a more organic approach to form than Perriand's style of Modernism. Japanese interiors had been increasingly Westernized since the 1860s and Yanagi was not the first Japanese designer to design furniture that was essentially Western in form. Bent plywood was a technical innovation that had been developed by American and European designers and manufacturers, so the compound curves of the moulded plywood shells that make the stool can be seen as part of a global trend in mid-twentieth-century furniture design. The elegant, spare form of the stool may be superficially similar to contemporary, reductive modernist design in the West, but it derives from a Japanese design sensibility. The outline of the stool is reminiscent of both Japanese calligraphy and the shape of the gateways to Shinto shrines known as Torii, as well as of the wings of a butterfly.

rolled off the production line every hour. Total sales of 35,000 secured the Skyhawk 172's position as the world's bestselling four-seat aircraft in general aviation. Notwithstanding the huge advances in aeronautical technology of the last thirty years, the Skyhawk's enduring success is the level of respect it continues to command. Today the Skyhawk remains a rite of passage for trainee pilots, just as it has done since 1956.

eponymously named Cessna Aviation Company introduced the Skyhawk 172 in 1956, and it quickly

gained a loyal fan base on the promise of low maintenance and ease of use. Its highly reliable flying

characteristics included the large flaps, the fixed landing gear, billed as 'Land-o-matic' at the time of

its launch, and a low stall speed, making it popular with both fledgling and amateur pilots. In its first

year alone 1,100 aircraft were produced. At the peak of production in the 1970s a new Skyhawk

**476**

Cessna Skyhawk 172 (1956)
Cessna Aircraft Company
Cessna 1956 to present

the front section of the cabin and the rear is given over to two seats within a glazed canopy, with side windows making up a 360-degree view. The wings are mounted straight across above the cabin; below is the permanently fixed landing-gear, which gives the Skyhawk an almost toy-like appearance. What remains to be a highly influential aircraft, could more easily be mistaken for a plaything than the linchpin in aeronautical tutorage it has come to represent. Clyde Cessna's

**Despite its diminutive size** and relatively naïve technical credentials, the Cessna Skyhawk 172 remains one of the most influential and widely recognized aircraft of the twentieth century. The single-engine design is based around a small cabin, no bigger than a family car, which allows a maximum of four people including the pilot to sit in comfort. Because weight had to be kept to a minimum, the interior is fairly spartan. A windshield mounted above the control panel dominates

**475**

Ribbon Chair (Model CL9) (1956)
Cesare Leonardi (1935–)
Franca Stagi (1937–)
Bernini 1967 to 1970
Fiarm/Elco/Bellato 1970 to c.1973

**Performing a thick,** undulating loop, the fibreglass body of the Ribbon Chair is a starling concept by two of the most audacious Italian designers of the 1960s. According to Cesare Leonardi, the Ribbon Chair was conceived with Franca Stagi in 1956 whilst attending a lesson at the University of Florence. The first prototype was made of *scagliola* (a plasterwork imitating marble) and a metallic net making it almost impossible to move it around, but the sheer beauty of their design made them part of a group of designers who initiated the aesthetic of excess that was to characterize the most daring Italian designs of the 1960s. It took eleven years before the chair got into production. A second prototype in condensed cardboard was attempted in 1960 and in 1964 a patent was granted to the two designers. But it was a chance meeting with the manufacturer Bernini that led to the use of fibreglass and the subsequent industrial production. Bernini was known for the sweeping lines and almost theatrical shapes of its furniture. Woodwork has been a Bernini speciality since it was founded as a carpenter's workshop in 1904, but in the 1960s the company became swept up in the rush towards using new materials. With

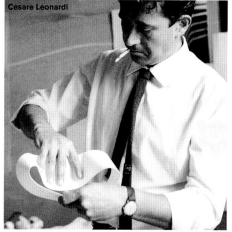

Cesare Leonardi

the frugality of the postwar years receding, the reductionist tendency that was so prevalent in most of the major designs of the 1950s began to ebb away. Youth culture was rampant and, as a mark of their break from the past, people wanted new designs. Using recently developed techniques and new materials, such as the fibreglass used for the Ribbon Chair, Leonardi and Stagi delivered the kind of eye-catching designs that were in demand. The Ribbon Chair was an adaptation of the cantilevered -base design developed at the Bauhaus around forty years earlier, but used the new material – plastic. The chrome-plating of the steel base also had echoes of earlier designs, and is something that will forever be associated with the 1950s. The form of the chair, however, and its unabashed use of significant quantities of fibreglass, was something no one had ever previously dared attempt.

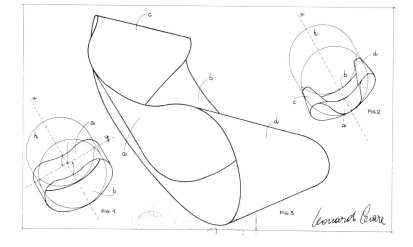

Wall Clock (1956–7)
Max Bill (1908–94)
Junghans 1956–7 to 1963,1997 to present

**Swiss designer Max Bill** originally trained as a silversmith before studying under Walter Gropius at the Bauhaus school in Dessau. A painter, sculptor and architect, when he designed the Wall Clock he was the director of architecture at the Hochschule für Gestaltung in Ulm, which he had helped to found. The clock provides an excellent example of art and technology fused for mass production. As with all of Max Bill's work, it incorporated an obsession with precise engineering and proportions. Designed between 1956–7, with a mineral glass face and quartz movement housed in a slim aluminium casing, the style of the Junghans Wall Clock has influenced clock designs ever since. After World War II aluminium had become cheaper and more readily available and Bill was able to make use of its many desirable qualities. The use of aluminium was immediately suggestive of cutting-edge precision and fresh, modern efficiency. Bill was able to produce a design that was at once a simple and unobtrusive office clock, and a smart, almost exquisite piece of art. In contrast to the side of the casing, the thin aluminium circle around the front of the clock face is highly polished, as are the hands, adding to the impeccable appearance. Bill, influenced by Le Corbusier, employs the simple and direct principles of functionalist design, stripping the wall clock of any superfluous detail. His emphasis on lines over numbers preceded the minimalist style would soon dominate the world of design. The clock has only minute and hour hands, with the minute hand moving very slightly, pulsing each second. 'Junghans' is in small Bauhaus lettering in the centre of the clock face. Bill's skill as a silversmith combined with a meticulous attention to measurement and mathematical proportions ensure the clock displays clarity and precision and contains all the essential elements for a great design, built to stand the test of time.

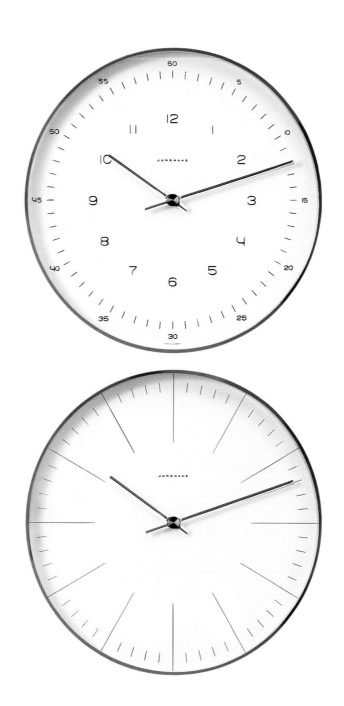

**The Spalter Vacuum** Cleaner was designed to be a lightweight, portable domestic appliance. It had a sleek, curvilinear shell made of bright red plastic and was designed to be slung across the user's back with a leather strap, like a bag. Its creators, the Castiglioni brothers, always welcomed the opportunity to reinvent familiar objects by subtly redefining and improving their design. They shared a belief that the contemporary designer's job was to redesign everyday objects and urged designers to try to find the Principal Design Component, or PDC, and build upon it, then investigate the technologies and materials available to develop and produce it. In devising this small vacuum cleaner, the Castiglionis drew on the design of compact, easily portable models initially produced. The motor and electrics are housed in a lightweight shell made of nylon, which is elastic, shock-proof and a good insulator, attached to the usual flexible tube. The model is shaped to rest snugly against the user's flank or can be slung from the shoulder by its leather strap. The strap can also be fixed with a clasp to become a handle when the cleaner is held horizontally, or used to hang it up when not needed. The cleaner has no wheels, and simply slips along the floor. The body of the cleaner is divided into two parts: one part contains the fan and motor, the second holds the removable filter and collects the dust. It is emptied simply by opening the casing, raising the filter cover and shaking out the dust. Immediately after World War II, many designers were eager to experiment with the new technologies and materials which had been developed by the defence industry and were now available for other purposes. This helped to foster a new generation of manufacturers who relished the opportunity to collaborate with enthusiastic young designers to develop innovative products for receptive post-war consumers. Spalter was notable during this period for its use of innovative materials and miniaturized components. The Castiglionis spent their careers observing or imagining a real need by the consumer and designing an innovative and satisfying solution. However, the Spalter Vacuum Cleaner was largely neglected by the market, which ignored its innovative qualities. It was perhaps too innovative for its day; commercially it was unsuccessful and it was in production for a very short time.

**Spalter (1956)**
**Achille Castiglioni (1918–2002)**
**Pier Giacomo Castiglioni (1913–68)**
**REM Enrico Rossetti 1956 to c.1960**

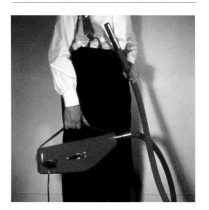

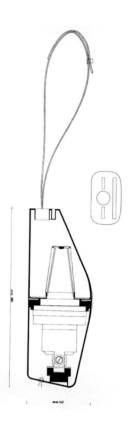

**Although the Model A Chair** is one of most successful and familiar chair designs of the twentieth century, its origins are far removed from the glittering world of designer glamour. In fact, the Model A was born in a seemingly humble plumber's workshop in France. In 1933, the French industrialist Xavier Pauchard added a sheet-metal division, named Tolix, to his successful boiler-making workshop. A year later, Tolix, based in Burgundy, France, released the Model A outdoor chair, part of a range of buckled, sheet-metal furniture fabricated according to Pauchard's designs. Built around a tubular frame, with a central back splat and elegant, tapered splay legs, the A56, a version of the Model A with arms modified by his son Jean Pauchard in 1956, combines functionality and decoration with a shiny, modern, jet-age style. The decorative piercing on the seat allows for drainage when the chair is used outside, while elegant grooves on the chair legs give stability when stacked. In addition to the basic steel finish, the Model A is available in twelve colours, achieved using an epoxy-polyester thermosetting paint. Yet, ultimately, it is perhaps the chair's simplicity that makes it such a success: in the end it is little more than a metal stool with a simple backrest and arms stuck on top. And so successful was Xavier Pauchard's original design that Tolix continues to produce the updated A56 to this day.

AJ Door Handle (1955–6)
Arne Jacobsen (1902–71)
Carl F Petersen 1956 to present

**The curvaceous** shape of Arne Jacobsen's famous door handle invites the user to grasp it. The gently arched lever of the handle fits snugly in the palm of the hand, while the thumb settles into the designated depression at the handle's base. If ever a last word has been said on a subject, it is surely Danish architect Arne Jacobsen's definition of the door handle. Simply known as the AJ Door Handle, it was designed in 1955 for the SAS Royal Hotel in Copenhagen, where it can still be seen. The AJ has been a consistent best seller for manufacturer Carl F Petersen for the past five decades. Anticipating the trend for ergonomic design that was to follow years later, Jacobsen studied the shape of the hand and designed his door handle accordingly. Originally the handles were made in white bronze, a metal that did not discolour or need to be polished, but today they are available only in satin nickel and brass. Responding to demand, Carl F Petersen has also begun to sell the handle in two sizes, with the larger one for exterior doors and the smaller one for interiors. Although mass produced, the handles are still finished by hand. The door handles were not Jacobsen's only project for the hotel. At the time he was architect for the entire building, overseeing almost every aspect of the hotel's design, including the furniture, textiles and light fittings. Such attention to detail made the hotel one of the most outstanding achievements of twentieth-century architecture and design.

Arne Jacobsen

It is obvious that the new Citroën has fallen from the sky inasmuch as it appears at first sight as a superlative object. We must not forget that an object is the best messenger of a world above that of nature: one can easily see in an object at once a perfection and an absence of origin, a closure and a brilliance, a transformation of life into matter (matter is much more magical than life), and in a word a silence which belongs to the realm of fairy-tales. The D.S. – the 'Goddess' – has all the features (or at least the public is unanimous in attributing them to it at first sight) of one of those objects from another universe which have supplied fuel for the neomania of the eighteenth century and that of our own science-fiction: the Déesse is the first and foremost a new Nautilus.

Roland Barthes, 'The New Citroën', *Mythologies*

**Paris Motor Show, 1956**

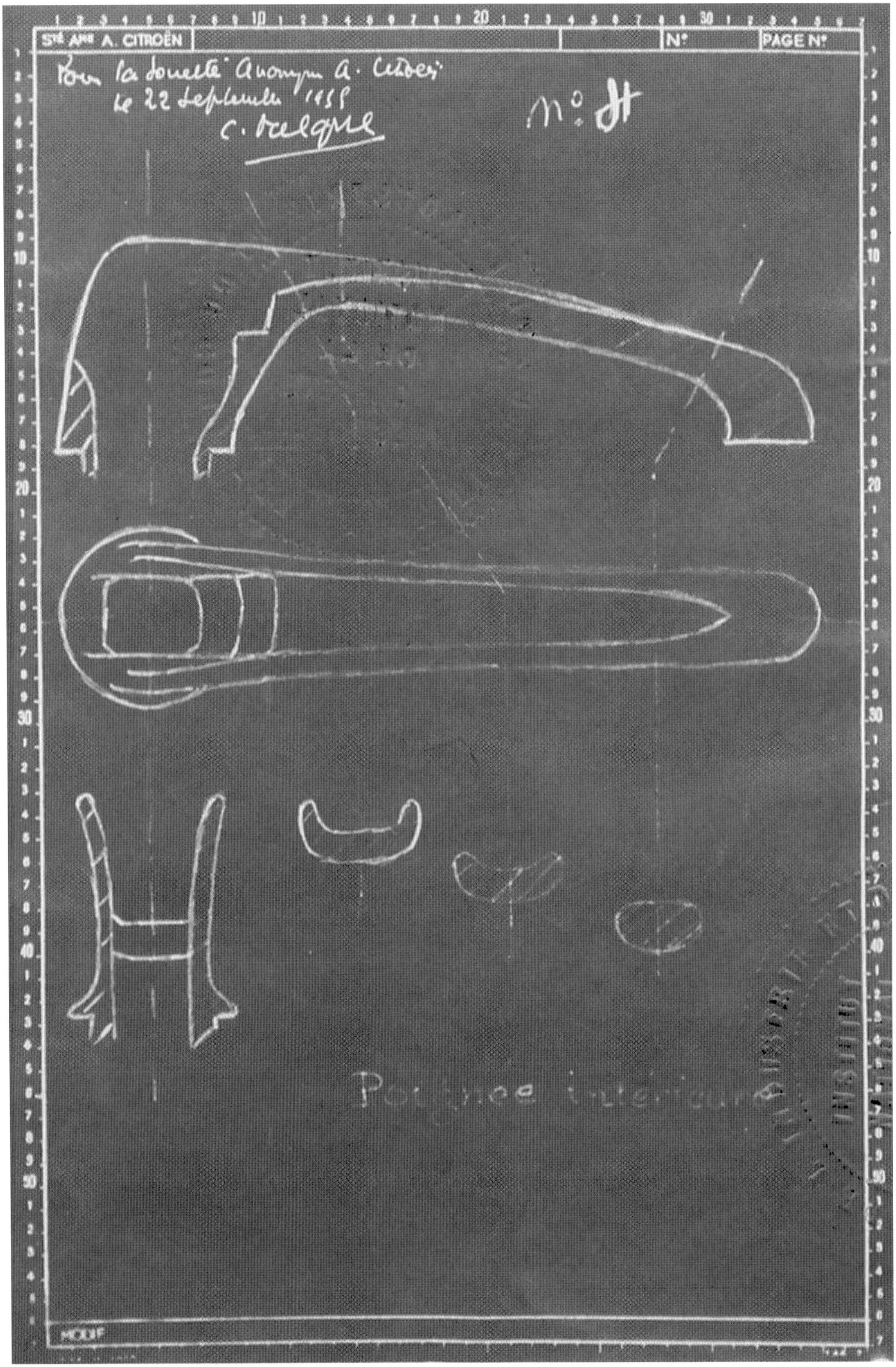


Patent for the door handle

Citroën DS 19 (1955)
Flaminio Bertoni (1903–64)
Citroën 1955 to 1975

**Citroën's DS model** is one of the mid-twentieth century's most magical cars. Its very name (the letters DS spoken in French spell out the word 'déesse', which means 'goddess') reinforces this fact. The intention behind its creation was Citroën's reputation for radicalism and to move beyond its earlier significant achievements – the Traction Avant of the 1930s and the 2CV of 1948 in particular. The DS was the result, once again, of Citroën's decision to combine the skills of the sculptor, Flaminio Bertoni, (who had worked on the 2CV), with the technical expertise of its engineers. The most striking feature of the DS is its uncompromising sculptural profile, which links the front with the rear in a single sweep, without any details interrupting the dramatic effect of this aesthetic decision. This is facilitated by the elimination of the radiator grille, by the integration of the headlamps into the form, and the introduction of subtle curves into both the front and the rear windows. The perfection of the finish and seamlessness of the form of the DS inspired the French cultural critic Roland Barthes to compare it to a Gothic cathedral as an equivalent symbol of high cultural achievement for its time and to see it as a 'purely magical object'. The sensation created by the DS of being taken over by magical forces is reinforced by the most striking technical characteristic of this outstanding car – specifically its hydro-pneumatic suspension. Designed to cope with the variable quality of French roads this technical detail allows the car to rise up into the air, a motion that makes the passenger feel that the car is about to take off, like an aeroplane. At a time when air travel was capturing the imagination of the masses the DS translated that sense of awe on to the road.

Flaminio Bertoni

**469**

Children's Highchair (1955)
Nanna Ditzel (1923–2005)
Jørgen Ditzel (1931–61)
Kolds Sawærk 1955 to ? Snedkegaarden

Lulu & Vita Ditzel, 1956

**Humane,** sensual and practical, this wooden high chair with simple vernacular lines is in the best tradition of Danish modern design. Indeed, it was the first modern highchair and sits comfortably among other modern pieces, for while it is child-friendly it is not child-like. It is a simple construction, but remarkable because it expresses so effortlessly what it is. Nanna Ditzel designed the highchair in 1955 with her husband, Jørgen Ditzel. It was made on the birth of her twin daughters. She wanted something that would complement her modern dining-room furniture and believed that all ages could benefit from more practical design. Her thoughts on chairs in general were that it was 'very important to take into account the way a chair's appearance combines with the person who sits in it.' The high chair was no exception. Ditzel's aim was that the child could sit at the same level as the table. The footrest is height-adjustable, and the front bar can be pressed out so that the front of the chair is open, allowing the child to get in or out independently as he or she grows older. The chair is also height-adjustable so that children can use it as they grow. This reflected the couple's design philosophy: to produce furniture that would expand, subdivide or serve a dual purpose so to appro-priately furnish a small apartment. The high chair is made using traditional cabinet-making techniques, but in such a fashion that it can be mass-produced. It has laminated wood on the back- and side-rests, and all parts are glued. The physical points of contact are important and these have rounded surfaces to the touch. It was originally made in beech or oak by Kolds Sawærk and is now produced by Snedkergaarden.

## During the early 1950s,

Heinz Nordhoff at Volkswagen wanted to introduce a new sports car to complement the VW Beetle Cabriolet and act as a flagship car to reinvent the Volkswagen image, and to provide an attractive and affordable car for an increasingly demanding car-buying public. The Wilhelm Karmann factory in Germany, which had exclusively built the Beetle Cabriolet from 1949, was contracted to design a sports model based on the Beetle chassis. In 1952, after Nordhoff rejected all of Karmann's designs, Dr Wilhelm Karmann began discussions in confidence with Luigi Segre, commercial director of cutting-edge Italian automotive design firm Carrozzeria Ghia, to develop ideas for presentation to Volkswagen. Carrozzeria Ghia, already contracted by auto design firms Alfa Romeo, Renault and Chrysler, produced a design for Karmann not dissimilar to the 1953 Chrysler D'Elegance. It has been suggested that, as both Chrysler and Volkswagen design projects were being directed concurrently, Chrysler design features had been transferred to the new VW prototype. Using a standard 1952 Beetle chassis, Ghia completed the VW Karmann-Ghia Coupé prototype by

September 1953, only five months after its conception. In November 1953 it was accepted by Volkswagen as a competitive and marketable sports car. To ensure cost-effectiveness, Karmann manufactured the body, assembling it with Volkswagen mechanical components and engineering, and a Beetle chassis. The Karmann Ghia combined the Beetle's small 36 hp flat four engine – which disqualified it from being a sports car, despite its beautifully curved and sporty appearance – with progressive aerodynamic design, giving enough power to allow maximum speeds of 150 kph (94 mph). Its good suspension and low cost relative to other 'image' cars, such as the Porsche 356A Speedster and Ford Thunderbird, added value, making the Karmann Ghia an economical, reliable and desirable option for car buyers. Mass production of the Karmann Ghia began in June 1955 and it was an instant success, selling over 10,000 in the first year. In 1958, Volkswagen released a convertible model and sales rose to 18,000 per year, peaking at 33,000 in the late 1960s. With over 365,000 coupés and 80,000 convertibles produced, the Karmann Ghia was a commercial success in both Europe and the USA.

© VOLKSWAGEN OF AMERICA, INC.

# The care and feeding of a Pussycat.

The Volkswagen Karmann Ghia only has the looks of a $5,000 car, not the tastes.

It's a Pussycat.

Sporty on top; economical underneath.

You can keep one going for the same price you'd pay to keep a VW Sedan going.

Just remember these easy-to-remember suggestions.

When stopping for gas, no need to stop at a premium pump. (A Pussycat runs great on regular gas. At, say, 30c a gallon, $3 will stretch into about 300 miles.)

And at, say, 50c a quart for oil, a change won't cost more than $1.50. (It only takes 2½ quarts.)

Keep water off your mind, and always forget to put in antifreeze. (The engine is air-cooled; it can't boil or freeze.)

Also, a Pussycat is very easy on tires. (40,000 miles should pass before you even have to think about new ones.)

And most important, when trouble comes up, head down to a Volkswagen dealer and get charged Volkswagen prices for repairs. (It uses the same mechanical parts that a Beetle uses.)

That's our Pussycat.

It costs less than $2,500, but it may upset the whole ritual of new car buying.

The "good deal" comes after the sale.

**The Volkswagen**
**KARMANN GHIA** Ⓥ

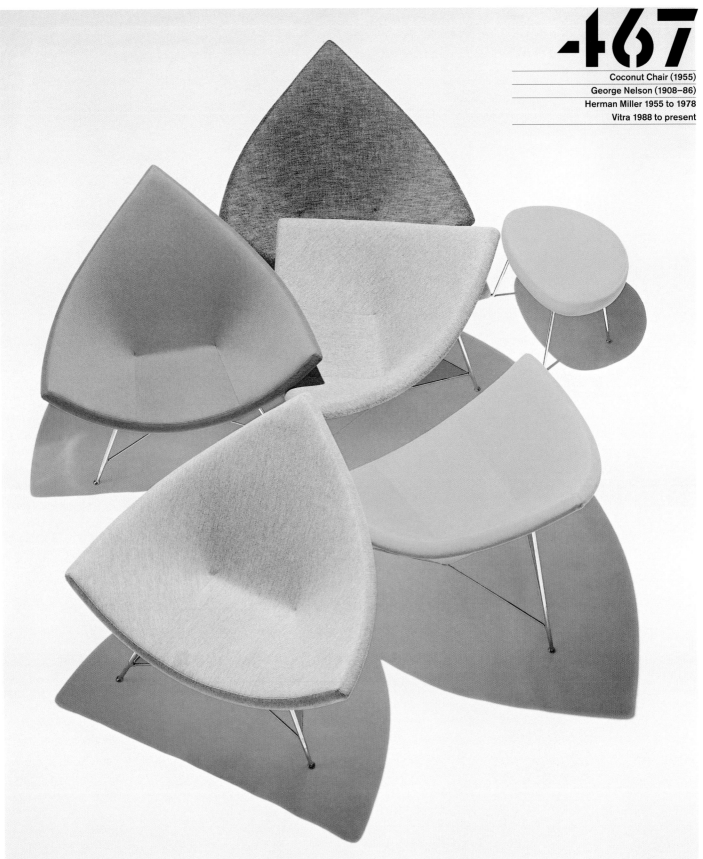

Coconut Chair (1955)
George Nelson (1908–86)
Herman Miller 1955 to 1978
Vitra 1988 to present

**Advertisement, 1967**

**Manufacturer Herman Miller's** advertisements and brochures to promote George Nelson's Coconut Chair made great play with the sculptural qualities of the design. From the side the coconut 'segment' appears to float lightly in space. Lit and photographed from above, groups of chairs clustered together create interlocking patterns and cast strong geometrical shadows, conjuring up the impression of a sphere that has shattered into neat, uniform shards. Although its strong visual presence was clearly of great importance to Nelson and to Herman Miller (of which Nelson was design director from 1946 to 1965) the chair also fulfils the equally desirable aim of allowing the sitter the freedom to occupy almost any position they choose on or 'in' the chair. The conventional arrangement of seat, back and armrests is replaced by a much more open composition of curves. Nelson was committed to a more flexible use of space, both in the home and in the office. His designs, teachings and writings contributed greatly to changing fashions in interior design and to the demand for more sculptural forms of furniture. In the open-plan spaces of the new homes of postwar America, with their built-in units and adoption of storage systems, a chair was likely to occupy uncluttered, open space rather than be pushed into a corner or against a wall. It must therefore have character and shape, and be attractive from all sides. Reminiscent of the contrasting 'wiry lines and heavy shapes' that Nelson enjoyed in the paintings of Joan Miró and the mobiles of Alexander Calder, the Coconut Chair becomes as much a piece of sculpture as an object of utility. If the chair does appear to float on its 'wiry' supports, this is entirely deceptive. Made of sheet steel and upholstered in foam rubber with a fabric, leather or artificial leather cover, the shell is heavy and cumbersome. The most recent version, with a moulded plastic shell, is now much lighter.

American contemporaries it exuded innocence and a sense of fun. It achieved this by combining the best of American styling with the best of European car design of the era. Three years later a much more substantial four-seater model with a wide roof was introduced to make the Thunderbird available to families.

This was a much boxier version which earned it the categorization of a 'personal luxury car.' Increased numbers were produced and bought but something of the original was sacrificed in the process, never fully to return.

## The Ford Thunderbird,

conceived along European lines mainly by Franklyn Hershey, with Bill Burnett and William F Boyer, in Ford's postwar styling studio, was originally intended to compete with General Motor's highly successful Corvette roadster. It quickly proved to be a much more adaptable car with a much greater longevity. In fact, through the numerous changes it underwent – from sports car to luxury family saloon, Ford's Thunderbird can tell the story of American car styling in the second half of the twentieth century. When it was revived in 2002, the designer of the new model, J Mays, set out to capture the spirit of the original 1955 little two-seater, as it was felt that the simple appeal of the early model had been lost over subsequent remodellings. The 1955 Thunderbird was a sleek, stylish little two-seater automobile, with a V8 engine, which came either as a convertible or with a removable fibreglass roof. Its most characteristic features included its round headlights, its egg-crate radiator grille and the porthole window in the roof. The shape of the wheel arches, which revealed the front wheel but half concealed the rear wheel, and the restrained front and rear fins also contributed to the elegance of its body shell and its general appeal. In contrast with many of its gargantuan

Emerson Transistor Pocket Radio - Model
838 (1955)
Emerson Radio Engineering Staff
Emerson Radio & Phonograph Corporation
1955 to 1956

**Proudly described by its manufacturer** as a 'transistor pocket radio', the 838 sought to capitalize on a rapidly expanding market for consumer electronics and an increasing fascination with technology in postwar America. In fact, this generous label only told part of the story, as its two transistors were, in fact, outnumbered by three miniature valves. Although not the first portable radio to incorporate new semiconductor technology (this was the Regency TR-1 launched in 1954), the cost was still prohibitive in a competitive market. The Emerson 838 was still an expensive purchase at $44 (including both the 4-volt 'A' and the 45-volt 'B' batteries), when the cheapest transistors at this time were around $2 each. As a compromise, certain manufacturers wisely decided to produce hybrid sets, which were able to offer improvements in performance while still being acceptable to consumers in terms of price. The 838 is a perfect example, therefore, of a 'bridging' or 'transitional' product that exists in the gap between one era and the next. The housing is essentially the same as its predecessor, the all-valve 747, with a silver or gold reverse-printed facia and bright red dial and surround. Contemporary reviews describe the 838 as having louder and better sound reproduction than its competitors, as well as a longer battery life. This performance, along with its price, and national advertising campaign, ensured that it was a great success during its brief appearance on the market. It was followed by the 856 in 1956, again in the same housing, which this time incorporated three transistors and two valves. This incremental development took place for several years before transistors became cheap and reliable enough to be used in place of miniature valves. By the early 1960s, radios that more accurately fitted the description of both 'transistor' and 'pocket' were commonplace.

Herbert Matter

No. 150 Chair. From the collection of **Single Pedestal** Chairs **and** Tables Designed by Eero Saarinen

**KNOLL ASSOCIATES, INC.** FURNITURE AND TEXTILES     575 MADISON AVENUE. NEW YORK 22

Eero Saarinen designed the Pedestal Chair for Knoll Associates.
See it at the Museum of Modern Art in New York or
Knoll Showrooms in 28 countries.

Knoll Associates, Inc., Furniture and Textiles, 320 Park Avenue, New York, New York 10022.

the slum of legs. I wanted to make the chair all one thing again. All the great furniture from the past, from Tutankhamun's chair to Thomas Chippendale's have always been a structural total.' The Tulip, however, has a reinforced, rilsan-coated aluminium swivel base, for strength, and a seat made of a moulded fibreglass shell, but because both have a similar white finish the chair appears to be made of one material. The base and shell are made in both black and white, with a removable foam cushion, with a zippered cover, fastened with Velcro. The upholstery either comes with a seat cushion, or with an upholstered shell covering both back and seat. The chair is still in production and available from its original manufacturer, Knoll. It was awarded The Museum of Modern Art design award and the Federal Award for Industrial Design, both in 1969, establishing its place in design history.

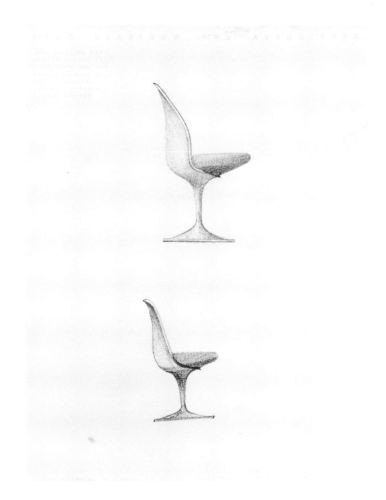

**The Tulip Chair's** nickname is clearly derived from its resemblance to the flower, yet the creative impetus behind the design was not to copy a form from nature, but was the result of a variety of complex ideas and production considerations. This chair is part of a series called the pedestal group, which also includes a large dining table, side tables, stools and side chairs that all share this basic one-pillar support. Like many of the American and Scandinavian designers of the post-war period, Saarinen rejected the geometric austerity of pre-war German design. Instead, he turned to what he thought was a more humanistic approach, often featuring soft, organic forms. This chair's stem-like pedestal was a result of Saarinen's keen interest in combining the overall form with the actual structure of the chair and thus creating a better sense of unity. He states, 'The undercarriage of chairs and tables in a typical interior makes an ugly, confusing, unrestful world. I wanted to clear up

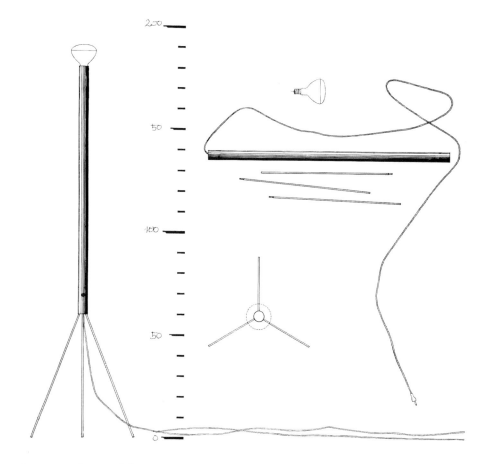

# 463

Luminator Lamp (1955)
Achille Castiglioni (1918–2002)
Pier Giacomo Castiglioni (1913–68)
Gilardi & Barzaghi 1955 to 1957
Arform 1957 to 1994
Flos 1994 to present

**A conscious drive** to rebuild the Italian economy after World War II led to Italian industry investing in low-tech objects, which could be exported easily. A series of products were developed that embraced this idea, while capitalizing on aesthetic appeal as a potent marketing force. The Luminator Lamp was one of these designs. Conceptually, it embodied the modernist dictum and confirmed the Castiglioni brothers' commitment to minimalist design. The reduced design is based around a metal tube whose diameter is the width of the socket for the pressed-glass reflector lamp. The Luminator was the first domestic lamp to use the latest tungsten bulb with a built-in reflector at the top. The simplicity of the design enabled the manufacturing costs to be kept low. Apart from its three-legged stand, the only other feature was the wire that came from the tube base with the switch attached. The success of the design lies not only in its elegance but also in its structural stability, and as such, came to embody postwar Italian design. It was exported in large quantities and contributed to the economic revival of the country. Yet, despite its modern styling, the Luminator was not entirely without historical precedent: this style of indirect photographer's lighting was first suggested for domestic use by Pietro Chiesa with his Luminator of 1933. In a form of tribute, the Castiglionis adopted the same name for their own breakthrough approach to contemporary lighting design.

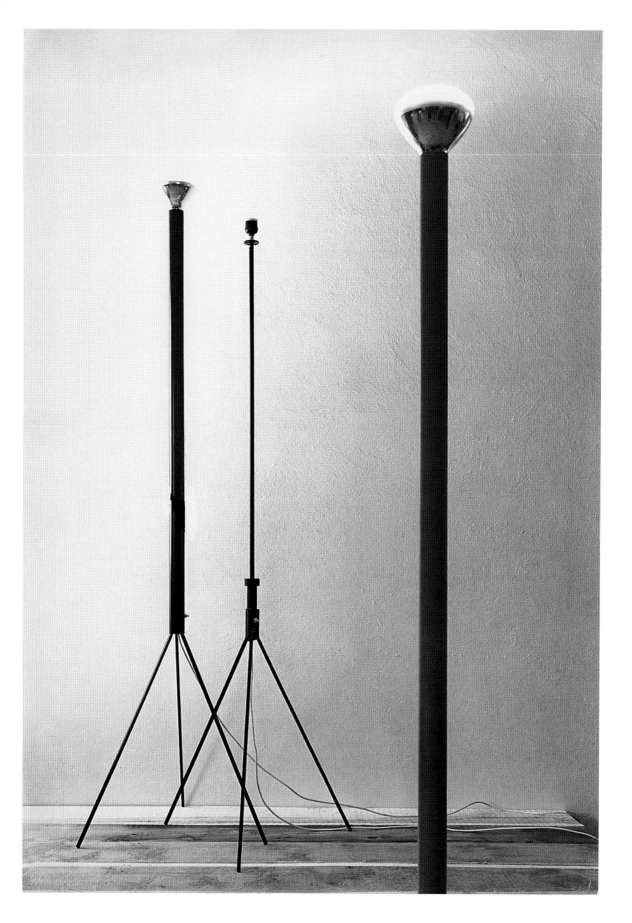

Ingeborg Lundin's Apple Vase, designed for the eminent Swedish glass manufacturer Orrefors, is one of the best-known decorative glass designs to have come out of the 1950s Modernist era. The highly accessible design remains appealing to both experts and novices alike, who are still drawn to the deceptively simple statements made by Scandinavia's free-blown glass movement. The Apple's plump proportions and naïve outline are almost cartoon-like in appearance. So perfect is the design's execution it is as if Ingeborg Lundin was asked shut her eyes and to imagine the perfect apple shape, free from blemishes and imperfections, and then to replicate this in glass. Certainly, the design's technical credentials are as lofty as those of the designer who implemented them and Lundin has long since been acknowledged as a highly influential figure in the history of Swedish glass design. Until Lundin's arrival at the Orrefors factory in 1947, male designers had dominated both Orrefors and Swedish glass design. Lundin, the first of Orrefors's female designers, soon offered an alternative voice to the overworked designs and extravagant showpiece statements that surrounded her. By contrast, Lundin worked with a distinctly youthful spirit that played on novel shapes, slight symmetries and made inspirational use of engravings. During the 1950s, Lundin was at her most prominent, and her free-blown designs such as her hourglasses, which appeared as the centrepiece of the glass section of the H55 exhibition in Helsingborg, began to receive accolades the world over. But her fame was solidified when she premiered the Apple Vase at the 1957 Milan Triennale. The air-filled bubble design, which was originally produced in colourless glass and later with a yellow and green underlay, proved a compelling statement against the formalities of decorative glass design.

Apple Vase (1955)
Ingeborg Lundin (1921–1992)
Orrefors 1957 to 1987

Ingeborg Lundin

Porsche 356A Speedster (1955)
Ferdinand 'Ferry' Porsche (1875–1951)
Porsche 1955 to 1959

## The son of Ferdinand

Porsche, the designer of the VW Beetle, Ferry Porsche was the creator of the Porsche 356 Speedster, one of the most beautiful cars of the mid-twentieth century which is still widely admired today. Considered by many people to be one of the most perfect combinations of engineering and styling the 356 Speedster demonstrates the way in which, at its best, car design is not just a process of creating pleasing forms but of developing a complete automotive experience in which the 'ride' is indistinguishable from the look and the feel of the car. For the way in which it manifests this fusion the 356 Speedster is still a benchmark car which has not been surpassed. The original, aluminium-bodied version of the car was created just after World War II. Ferdinand Porsche died in 1951 and his son took over the mantle of the name. By 1955 he was already producing all-steel 356s in his Stuttgart factory and had established his cars as leaders in their field. Visually they were characterized by their sleek, streamlined, yet restrained, body-shells – their close relationship with the ground, their high quality ride, and their strong character. While this aesthetic was seen as simple, it simultaneously demonstrated a commitment to quality and a level of luxury. Ferry Porsche's success also lay in his success in eroding the distinction between racing cars and sports cars. His cars were fast but they were also stylish. The Spanish word 'Carrera' (which means 'race') was used as a name for a model launched in 1955 – but the car was at home either on the race track or on the road. The status of 'myth' can be applied to the 356, a reputation which was enhanced by the fact that the young American actor, James Dean, was killed while driving one. By the late 1950s Porsche was looking for a new model and, although it went on to create other classics, such as the models 911, 904 and others, the Porsche 356 Speedster has never been displaced from its position at the top of the pedestal.

Chair No. 3107 (1955)
Arne Jacobsen (1902–71)
Fritz Hansen 1955 to present

**The hour-glass form** of the plywood seat of Arne Jacobsen's Chair No. 3107, often known as the 'Series 7' chair, places it firmly in the era of the wasp-waisted New Look: the 1950s. Jacobsen was originally inspired to develop a light stacking chair constructed from a moulded plywood seat supported on thin metal rod legs by the work of Charles Eames. The widely successful Ant Chair of 1952 was Jacobsen's first attempt in that direction, with Chair No. 3107 representing a further stage of development. It is a stronger, more durable and more stable modification of the three-legged Ant. The number of copies and illicit versions of Chair No. 3107 that continue to proliferate testify to the lasting popularity and success of this model. In Britain this chair gained widespread attention through a 1963 photograph by Lewis Morley of Christine Keeler, notorious for her involvement in the government scandal that became known as the Profumo Affair. Rather ironically the chair that Morley used as a prop, in lieu of any clothing, was an unlicensed variant and not, officially at least, one of Arne Jacobsen's designs, however close it was to the original. But the combination of Christine Keeler's pose and Arne Jacobsen's Chair No. 3107 have become inextricably linked and now appear to be universally recognized. In the early 1960s Lewis Morley, in a deliberately mocking and ironic way, photographed several other celebrities, including David Frost and the playwright Joe Orton, in positions similar to the one adopted by Christine Keeler. But neither the photographer nor the designer can have been prepared for the avalanche of similar photographs that continue to this day.

Christine Keeler, 1963, by Lewis Morley

Automatic Rice Cooker (1955)
Yoshiharu Iwata (1938–)
Toshiba 1955 to present

Advertisement, 1955

**Yoshiharu Iwata's** Automatic Rice Cooker for Toshiba was one of the first home electronic products to bring a recognizably Japanese style to an area of design mainly inspired by imported Western products, making it a milestone in Japanese industrial design. The most striking features of the original Rice Cooker are its simple shape and pure white finish. Iwata, who went on to become general manager of Toshiba's design division, took his inspiration from the traditional Japanese rice bowl. The white colour not only recalls the simple, glazed finish of a porcelain bowl, but also reflects the rice held within. The white body combined with an aluminium lid, black handles and a black plug connection, which acknowledges rather than denies its electronic aspect, became the design template for all subsequent electric rice cookers. It stands at 24 cm (9 in) high, with a diameter of 28 cm (11 in) and a capacity of 1.1 l (2 pt). Toshiba's Rice Cooker was not the first on the market. Many of Japan's leading electronics companies had launched similar products, but these simply replaced the external heat source with an electric coil, and the rice still had to be watched during

cooking. Iwata's design offered a completely automated system with a timer switch that would cook rice perfectly. Overcoming the technical difficulties inherent in this technology was an arduous task, and it was over five years from initial designs to products on shelves. The Rice Cooker was an instant success when it appeared in 1955, with Toshiba soon producing 200,000 cookers a month. In less than four years, half the homes in Japan owned a Toshiba Rice Cooker. By 1970, annual output had passed the twelve million mark. Itawa's design remained unchanged for nine years, and was credited with heralding a revolution in Japanese food culture and home lifestyles, helping to free people from the tyranny of time-consuming cooking.

**Vacheron Constantin**, based in Geneva, currently holds the distinction of being the world's oldest watchmaker. Since its creation by Jean-Marc Vacheron in 1755, the company has set the benchmark for timepiece technology, pushing the boundaries of mechanical innovation while elevating the craft of watchmaking to a fine art. The ultra thin wristwatch of 1955 perfectly embodies this Vacheron Constantin philosophy and is a milestone in watch design. Vacheron Constantin designs have recorded many historical moments, including the Wright brothers' first powered flight of 1903. The ultra thin Vacheron Constantin was not designed as a glamour model, but rather as a simple, slimline timepiece, and the result is eminently practical and wearable. The dimensions of the movement are a principal constraint in watchmaking and the Vacheron Constantin ultra thin was one of the first models to push the

*The world's thinnest watch*

Thin as a coin, and no larger, the Vacheron & Constantin "Extra Flat" contains the 120 parts of an intricate precision mechanism. To technical mastery is here added the quiet beauty of a designer's dream come true. Presented on the occasion of the Vacheron & Constantin bicentenary.

**VACHERON** ET **CONSTANTIN**

*The "Extra Flat" comes in a de luxe leather wallet.*

IN GENEVA SINCE 1755

'Extra Flat' Advertisement, 1955

envelope to the limit to create a flat movement. The extreme thinness of the movement – an astonishing 1.64 mm (0.65 in) – is a technical *tour de force*: it includes a unique escapement and regulator innovation, which dispenses with the need for the shock protection and adjustment mechanisms that are normally required after cleaning and lubrication. Other dimensions include a 33 mm (1.3 in) diameter, a 30 mm (1.2 in) dial opening diameter, a 1.6 in (39.7 mm) total length on the lugs, and a total thickness including the spherical glass case of 4.8 mm (0.19 in). Painstaking research, development, testing and honing produced the ultra thin Vacheron Constantin movement, and the watch was initially more of a meticulously handcrafted work of art than a mass market model. Yet the technological breakthrough of the ultra thin Vacheron Constantin continues to influence and inform watch design.

**Max and Moritz** salt and pepper shakers are discreet and visually reticent, yet are perfectly proportioned in every way. Made in glass with stamped stainless-steel tops, they are held together in a stainless-steel boat in a satisfying play of forms. The small, waisted vessels are a pleasure to hold and were intended to be personal. They make the contents seem precious, as opposed to being simply a condiment. Wagenfeld must have been inspired by two popular, rambunctious German cartoon characters, Max and Moritz, created by Wilhelm Busch in 1865, who were the feature of his book, *Max and Moritz: A Juvenile History in Seven Tricks.* From the mid-1950s to the mid-1960s Wilhelm Wagenfeld worked with one of the biggest metal manufacturers of cutlery, stamped metal and glass, WMF (Württembergische Metallwarenfabrik Geislingen). In the Max and Moritz salt and pepper shakers he created an archetype that became synonymous with the company. He also created a wide range of products that became well known worldwide, but it was for these salt and pepper shakers that WMF received numerous awards, and have continually produced them since their introduction. For Wagenfeld, mass production had a responsibility towards making objects that served their users, and raised the user's level of connection to the thing itself and the experience of using it. He wanted to lead 'the buyer to a consciousness of everything necessary for survival', and make him 'more demanding and at the same time less pretentious'. The bigger the production, Wagenfeld believed, the greater the need for this, and thus the more thought needed to go into the product's design and manufacture. In this capacity, Wagenfeld saw an important cultural role for industry and mass production. To that end, Wagenfeld preferred unobtrusive design. He wanted to convince by use, rather than by visible design features. Therefore these shakers have large, plug openings instead of a screw-top, a feature first used in 1952 and quickly adopted by Wagenfeld. The plugs were more economical to produce, and more convenient to refill. Design was not 'turning out wrappings' but an exploration of the DNA of a thing and its use in the hand. He was interested in the idea of the archetype-made-modern within a timeless design, achieved with these shakers.

weil Pfeffer u. Salz-
streuer
_mit_ Untersatz bedürfen
mehr getauft werden!
17/1

LONDON TRANSPORT

RM5

LONDON TRANSPORT BUS

TYPE: 'ROUTEMASTER'

SCALE: 7mm = 1 foot.

DRAWING N . B5

The red Routemaster Bus (RM to aficionados), has been a symbol of London for more than fifty years. Despite the introduction of countless other models, it remains the standard by which all buses are measured and is still the favourite of tourists, drivers, conductors and commuters. A A M Durrant was Chief Mechanical Engineer for London Transport from 1945 to 1965 and headed the design team which included Douglas Scott. Scott was not only one of the first professional industrial designers in the UK, but was also the founder of the subject at the Central School of Arts and Crafts, London (now Central Saint Martin's). Scott was first asked to work on the project in 1954, following successful previous projects in 1946 and 1949. London Transport wanted to improve on these existing designs through weight-saving and improved comfort, while providing a vehicle that would be acceptable to both drivers and passengers. Scott created a model from Plasticine, and smoothed the edges to create a form that appeared more compact than its boxy rivals, and was easier to clean than its predecessors. While much of the character of the vehicle stems from this shape, other features were never part of the original plan. Scott proposed doing away with the traditional half-cab, installing fibreglass seat frames, rubber flooring and fluorescent lighting. The half-cab was reinstated following protests from the Transport and General Workers' Union, while other elements were edited out to keep costs down. Hence the bus retained such cherished elements as the soft light from the tungsten filament bulbs, the nicotine yellow ceiling and the maple floor. The famous colour, which blends so well with the streetscape of post-boxes and Jubilee Kiosk phone boxes, almost fell victim to Scott's inclination to reduce further weight and cost. Some early models were finished in bare aluminium because the weight of the paint calculated to over 150 kg (330 lb). This was evidently a step too far towards the American streamlined aesthetic, and the buses were swiftly painted red. As a result of these constraints, the production model, produced until 1968, already looked somewhat dated at its launch, but it was a subtle transition for a public who were still used to trolleybuses. Unfortunately it was not a transition to anything else: the Routemaster was the last public vehicle to be designed specifically to cope with navigating the narrow London road network. All subsequent models, beginning in 1970, were less satisfactory multi-purpose models not nearly as well suited to the job. Since 2003, the Routemaster has been withdrawn, due to its lack of access for the disabled, and the much-loved bus will no longer be seen careening down London streets save for a few historic routes.

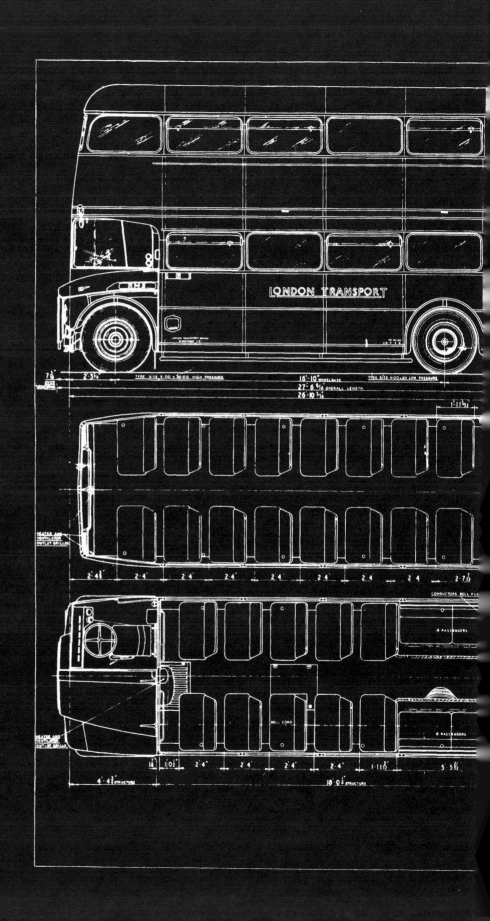

Rocking Stool (1954)
Isamu Noguchi (1904–88)
Knoll 1955 to 1960
Vitra Design Museum 2001 to present

Isamu Noguchi

**The sculptor Isamu Noguchi** did some of his best designs for Knoll. Noguchi blended his sculptural vocabulary with the functionality of furniture to a degree that is unique to American postwar design. When he designed the Rocking Stool, and matching Cyclone Low and Dining Tables, around 1954, Noguchi took traditional African stools as inspiration. But instead of using one piece of wood like the original stools, he combined wood for the stand and seat with five V-shaped metal wires. He used the metal wiring to build a very stable 'cyclone-like' construction. Its aesthetics matched the designs by the likes of the Charles and Ray Eames and Harry Bertoia for their work with steel bases and chairs. It was available in walnut and the less common birch version. The combination of materials gave the stool a very modern look, perhaps too modern, since the stool was in production for only five years. Many of Noguchi's innovative designs were not understood by the American public. The tables, however, which were inspired by the same construction principle as the stool, have had more success and are still in production today. The stool was in production from 1955 to 1960, and now re- introduced by Vitra Design Museum.

Garden Chair (1954)
Willy Guhl (1915–2000)
Eternit 1954 to present

**The Garden Chair** is so called because it is made of a continuous ribbon of asbestos-free cement fibre-bond, with no added fixings or supports, moulded into a sinuous and elegant looped form. Using a single slab of cement – the same one used for roofing and wall façades – the chair represents an incredibly brave and inventive use of an industrial material. Both lightweight and immensely strong, the chair has a surprisingly tactile surface that is smooth and warm, yet incredibly hard

Experiments with asbestos cement at Eternit: (left to right) Robert Haussmann, Noser and Willy Guhl

wearing. Willy Guhl's Garden Chair represents a successful tension of opposites: lightness combined with strength, robustness combined with a graceful elegance, utility combined with luxury. Guhl had first begun experimenting with ergonomically shaped chair forms after participating in the 'Low Cost Furniture Design' competition at The Museum of Modern Art in 1948. But it was not until the early 1950s when the company Eternit approached the Kunstgewerbeschule in Zürich, where Guhl was professor, that he was introduced to concrete. Eternit was looking for new ideas for using its eponymous product, a fibrated concrete that was machine processed in slabs and had hitherto been used mainly for building houses. The school's professors were appalled by the idea of using concrete, except for Guhl, who embraced the possibilities of working with a single industrial material to create a complete and articulate chair form. The width of the chair is determined by the width of the existing slab, which is moulded into shape while the material is still moist. This straightforward process ensured that the chair could be effectively and economically mass-produced. Originally called the Beach Chair, the Garden Chair was designed as a rocking chair for outdoor use. A technical development in the material made this possible. Eternit fibre cement had originally used asbestos, but was replaced by cellulose fibre, which allowed for thicker dimensions and Guhl modified the design of the chair to accommodate the material. At the same time he developed a table with two holes in the surface to hold bottles and glasses, which fit perfectly inside the Garden Chair for storage. Although indoor use of the chair is common, today Guhl makes it clear that the chair was in every respect designed for outdoor use. 'People send me pictures of their chair, they paint flowers on them, they upholster them – it's their chair, let them do with it as they want, but I still wouldn't put it in my living room.'

KS1146 (1954)
Gino Colombini (1915– )
Kartell 1954 to 1965

**This humble looking** bucket hardly seems the stuff of revolution but in 1954, it turned the world of homewares on its head. Until then plastic had never entered the domestic sphere; it was an industrial product used for making insulating cables and naval equipment. Giulio Castelli was the first to exploit the commercial possibilities of plastic for domestic use. He was the student of Nobel Prize Laureate Giulio Natta, who had invented a thermoplastic material, isotactic propylene, which was commercially marketed as plastic. In 1951 Castelli had the vision to commission Gino Colombini to create an object with the specific purpose of bringing plastic into the home. The result was this bucket, the first item produced in plastic by Kartell, and which won the prestigious Compasso d'Oro prize in 1955. Gino Colombini was employed as the company's technical director, and he brought to the position all the experience he had gained working in the studio of Franco Albini, one of Italy's most innovative architects. Colombini immediately saw that he had to keep his designs simple and coherent. Customers would be perplexed enough by the new material, so there was no need to create overly elaborate designs. He knew as well that the design must not appear too industrial, as people would not want to bring them through the front door. The KS1146 bucket is made of plastic, with its steel handle dip-coated in PVC to make it softer and more inviting to the touch. The bucket's cover has two shallow spaces for holding cloths, soap or anything wet that the user would want to keep from the floor. Structurally, the bucket is something of a resourceful reflective design. Where many buckets' sides will begin to bow out under the weight of too much water, Colombini added reinforced ribbing at the base and mouth of the bucket to give it the necessary strength. Colombini and the Kartell staff put in three years of research and development before launching the company's first product line. With no precedent of domestic plastic design before him, Colombini shaped from this infinitely malleable material a collection of designs that would soon be seen all across Italy.

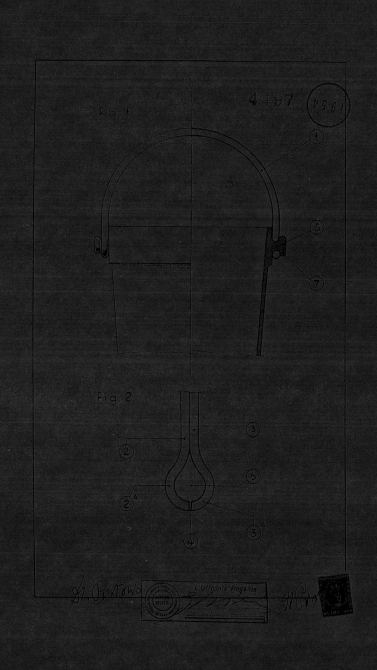

Fig 1

Fig 2

**When Philip Rosenthal** assumed responsibility for product design at Germany's pre-eminent porcelain manufacturer Rosenthal AG, in 1950, his appointment heralded a new era in postwar German design. His inaugural commission, the Coffee Service 2000, would come to exemplify all that was new and innovative, and was utterly of the moment. The spartan profile of the Coffee Service 2000 (as the series became known) represented a stylistic turn around for a company that had built a brand off the back of its highly decorative tableware and figurines. Coffee Service 2000 was understatement personified. It existed on a slim diet of pure white porcelain, with tall clean lines and thin elongated handles that added a

further degree of poise to this well-mannered design. Free from any further decorative detail, the only thing it had in common with its Rosenthal predecessors was technical expertise, so adept was the group at delivering a flawless finish. Set against the backdrop of 1950s German manufacturing, the service made for a charismatic and optimistic statement of Philip Rosenthal's vision for the company's future. Rosenthal's contemporary ideal was for the main part informed by his acquaintance with some of the best porcelain designers of the period, in particular Richard S Latham and Raymond Loewy, the celebrated American industrial designers. Rosenthal proffered that for the company to survive it had to look neither backwards nor too far forwards

for inspiration, but to strive to provide a contemporary marker that would embrace the spirit of the times. Similar to the artist Friedensreich Hundertwasser's paintings, Latham and Loewy's masterpiece lived up to an ideal. By 1961, seven short years after its introduction, Coffee Service 2000 had clocked up an impressive 20 million sales. The series also rose to critical acclaim, being dubbed by some commentators as the 'classic porcelain design of the twentieth century'. Rosenthal seized on this success by adding more contemporary designers to his stable, and branding the new diffusion line the 'Rosenthal Studio Line' which has been anchored as a brand in its own right since 1961.

**Sofa 1206 (1954)**
**Florence Knoll (1917–)**
**Knoll 1954 to present**

Hans & Florence Knoll

**Florence Knoll** describes her elegant sofas as 'fill-in-pieces that no one else wants to do.' As the design director of Knoll's Planning Unit, Florence Knoll and her husband Hans Knoll commissioned some of the best of modern design. Her contribution to the mix was the background pieces, or as she says, 'meat and potatoes'. When creating an interior, if she found the need for a piece of furniture she would simply design it herself. Many of these pieces found their way into the Knoll catalogue as the company's client list grew. This sofa was created in response to one of those needs. Florence Knoll defined the image of American corporate interiors in the 1950s with a style that used natural light, open spaces and informal groupings of furniture covered in elegant fabrics. The idea of furniture, rather than walls, dividing and defining space was a new concept in the postwar years of the 1940s and 1950s. It was a matter of balancing the formality of the International Style with the openness of the new corporate culture and was the beginning of a more democratic office style that permeates the workplace today, with interiors that flow seamlessly throughout a building. The steel framework of the legs elevates the rectangular forms of the sofa, making it appear to float above the carpet, and the modularity of the chair, settee and sofa, and the tufting is reminiscent of Mies's Barcelona Chair, which again reinforces its relationship with International Style way of thinking. The thin, low arms act as a visual end to the piece rather than as true arms. The sofas were meant as perches, unlike the deep softness of most others then available, and act as a design bridge between crisp Modernism and the older, more traditional forms, and instead create a viewing platform from which to take in the new interiors. Florence Knoll's interiors for the CBS Building and the office of the Seagram and Heinz companies pioneered much of what we consider today to be corporate interior design. The sofas succeed at remaining in the background, letting other more flamboyant designs create a statement and Florence Knoll's pieces are statements of a quiet Modernism.

Vintage (1954)
Giovanni Guzzini (1927–)
Raimondo Guzzini (1928–78)
Fratelli Guzzini 1954 to c.1964,
2002 to present

**Guzzini's Vintage tableware** collection is a unique range of large and small salad bowls with servers, available in dual colours of black and white, yellow and white or cherry-red and white. Each has a highly polished lacquer finish, which lends the range an elegant, Eastern style. It was in 1954 that Giovanni Guzzini created the first Guzzini two-tone products, using double injection moulding, a technique which he later patented. In this technique, initially carried out by hand, two sheets of plastic were moulded together to create a single sheet. It proved to be very successful in producing a striking collection of coffee cups. The cups were so popular with consumers that further designs were quickly introduced to form a complete collection of tableware, which included the very successful square presentation bowls introduced in the late 1950s. Fratelli Guzzini was founded in Italy in 1912 by Enrico Guzzini, and originally made craft-based products from ox horn, including snuffboxes, cutlery, ladles and shoehorns. In 1938 horn was replaced by plexiglass to make everyday household articles. At the time, this new plastic, when hot-moulded, was found to be ductile and lightweight. Further technological innovations continued over the next two decades and the introduction of double injection moulding in the mid-1950s led to the development of the Vintage tableware collection. The Guzzini label is now synonymous with design innovation, combining the best in cutting-edge materials with leading names in international design. The company continues to update its products in line with contemporary trends and the Vintage tableware collection was reissued in 2002. Guzzini now produces an extensive and varied range of common household articles that extends to small accessories and consumer electronics. The products, with their distinctive Guzzini styling, can be found in the collections of many of the world's major museums.

Fender Stratocaster (1954)
Leo Fender (1909–91)
Fender Musical Instruments 1954 to present

## The Fender Stratocaster,

like so many of the musicians who have played it, occupies a legendary status within popular culture. The introduction of this revolutionary solid-body electric guitar coincided with the birth of rock 'n' roll, and arguably no other single instrument has gone on to shape the music of our times more than the Stratocaster. Remarkably, such is the technical virtuosity of its original design that the model has changed very little since its first appearance in 1954. The Stratocaster was designed by Leo Fender, who, interestingly enough, did not come from a background of instrument building or even music in general. Instead, Fender had worked on radios and electrical equipment, with his main priority being a concern for the utility of every item he designed. Fender brought this same philosophy of functionality first and foremost to the design of his first guitar, the Telecaster, a superior, easy-to-assemble Spanish upright solid-body guitar from which the Stratocaster was to evolve.

But in terms of innovation, the Stratocaster was light years ahead of its predecessor or, indeed, the Rickenbacker or Les Paul models that were available at the time. The Stratocaster blazed a trail. It was the first guitar to feature a built-in tremolo, and its seductively beautiful 'comfort contoured' body was also unprecedented, as were the precisely spaced frets, improved and adjustable pick-ups, which ensured tone balance, and easy-to-use surface-mounted plug. And the iconic head, featuring the easy-to-reach straight row of Kluson tuning machines, meant that the strings were now in a straight line to the peg, and tuning could therefore be stabilized. The Stratocaster's band-sawed body, electronic subassembly and screw-on neck meant not only that mass production could be achieved relatively cheaply and efficiently, but also that worn or damaged parts could be easily replaced, which had huge practical implications for the user. The Stratocaster first entered the public consciousness via one of its first fans, Buddy Holly, and stayed there thanks to the likes of Eric Clapton, Jeff Beck, George Harrison and, perhaps most famously, Jimi Hendrix. Its status as a piece of Americana was confirmed when it appeared alongside Elvis Presley, the American flag and the Corvette on the cover of *Rolling Stone* magazine's thirty-fifth anniversary issue in May 2003.

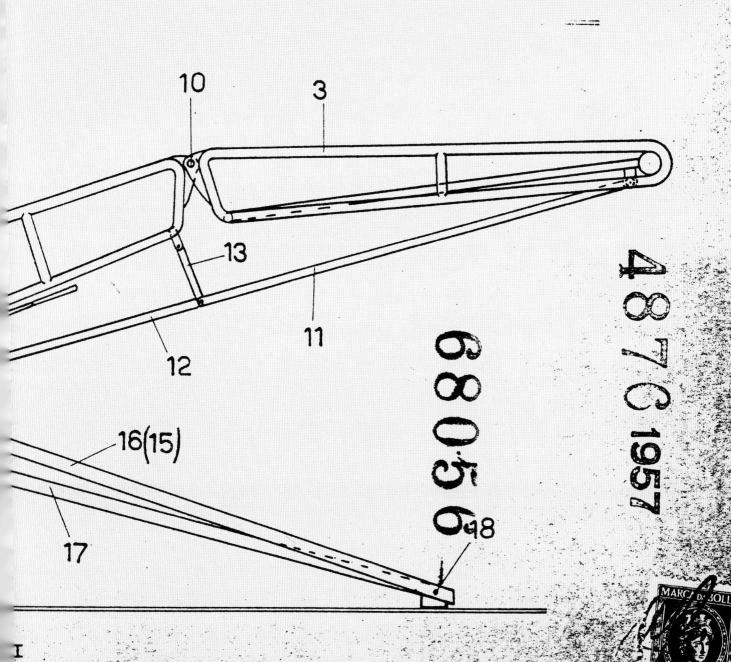

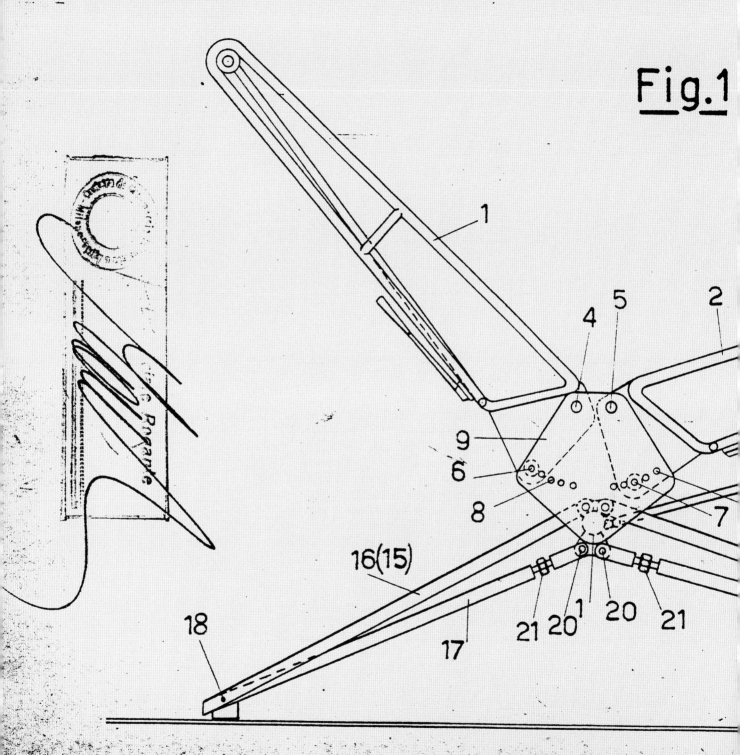

# Fig.1

1

2

4

5

9

6

8

7

16(15)

18

21 20 1 20 21

17

p.p. Signor Osvaldo BOR
p.Ing. Barzanò & Zanar

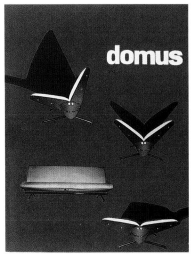

*Domus*, No. 303, February 1955

**Twins Osvaldo and Fulgenzio Borsani** launched their new company, Tecno, at the Milan Triennale in 1954. The early 1950s were heady years in Italian postwar reconstruction and radical advances were made in terms of industrialization and aesthetics. Tecno was introduced the same year as La Rinascente department store created the famous Compasso d'Oro award for design excellence and many products of the time are permeated with a sense of optimism for the future. Industrial production was seen as a panacea for many of the nation's ills. The first Tecno collection of highly engineered upholstered furniture captured this spirit. The D70 is both a product of industrial production and a clear expression of rational design thinking. The streamlined blades that make up the seat and back are at once practical elements and metaphors for a future based on mechanization. Tecno launched the sofa together with model P40, a chair that could be adjusted into 468 different positions. The back of the D70 could be lowered to make it into a sofa-bed, or it could be folded to save space. Housing shortages brought on by the war inspired the design of flexible and multi-functional furniture such as this. Osvaldo Borsani, who remained the chief designer and engineer of Tecno, introduced a variant sofa-bed, model L77, in 1957, with multiple variable positions. All the sofas and chairs in the range are constructed along a beam between the seat and back and reveal, rather than conceal, the mechanisms for tilting the upholstered elements. As the company's name suggests, they are celebrations of technology. In 1966 Osvaldo Borsani co-founded the influential design journal *Ottagano* and steered Tecno towards the leading position in contract and office furniture that it retains today.

1402

C'scape

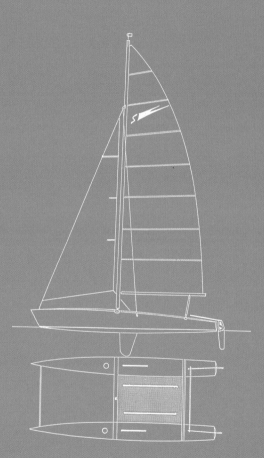

**Olympic competitors,** the Prout brothers, Roland and Francis, who specialized in building dinghies, used their experience as boat builders and their knowledge of kayaks and turned their attention to a new project in the 1930s – building a catamaran. They began developing the Shearwater in 1949, and it was built with a double hull made of two racing kayaks, the rig organized with a small mainsail and the jib of a 4.25 m (14 ft) dinghy. This first boat was fast and successful and generated plenty of interest, and by 1954 the Prout brothers had already moved on to Shearwater III. Winning its first race, from Folkestone to Boulogne in 1956, with an hour to spare, Shearwater III beat the world's best racing dinghy helmsmen. In 1960 Shearwater III became a racing class in Britain and attracted a large number of entrants. Along with the Hobie Cat in California, the Prouts' catamaran revolutionized a sailing world accustomed to mono-hull vessels. The innovations, legacy, and success the of the Shearwater III are clear in the design of later multi-hull boats, which borrow the round-bottomed hull sections, rotating rigs, trampolines, single and twin trapezes, spinnakers and high aspect rigs from the Prouts' design. Apart from a slimmer, symmetrical hull shape in place of the original asymmetrical shape, few modifications have been made to the Shearwater III. Carbon fibre has been introduced to the fibreglass used in construction of the hull to make the boat lighter, with a total weight of 120 kg (264.6 lb), a length of 5.05 m (16.6 ft) and a width of 2.28 m (7.6 ft). The ratio of sail to weight of boat makes it a highly responsive vessel, very fast and easy to tack and, because of its double keel, the Shearwater can also make a close-hauled route.

Compasso d'Oro (1954)
Albe Steiner (1913–74)
Alberto Rosselli (1921–76)
Marco Zanuso (1916–2001)
La Rinascente 1954 to 1957
La Rinascente & ADI 1958 to 1967
ADI 1967 to present

**The Compasso d'Oro** is considered as the Oscar of Italian design, as well as an authoritative barometer of the cultural debates on industrial design itself. More than fifty years since it was established, the Compasso d'Oro award remains the major acknowledgement of Italian design and enjoys this reputation internationally. The award was initially an idea of Gio Ponti and Alberto Rosselli, and was founded in 1954 by the La Rinascente department store in Milan, as a way to promote industrial design in Italy after the end of World War II. To represent this new awareness of Italian design, Albe Steiner, graphic designer and consultant for La Rinascente, chose the compass, invented by Adalbert Goeringer in 1893 to measure the golden section, as a symbol for the award. The logo of the prize was quickly followed by a three-dimensional version realized by the architects Alberto Rosselli and Marco Zanuso. Thus the compass, which in terms of traditional iconography is an emblem of harmony and perfect proportion, has today become an icon in itself, that represents technical and functional innovation. Initially organized by La Rinascente on an annual basis, between 1958 and 1967 the award was managed jointly with ADI, the Association for Industrial Design. Since 1967 the award has been entrusted exclusively to ADI. The prize is currently assigned every three years by an international jury, who make a secondary selection following the initial list of candidates made by the Permanent Design Observatory, a committee of journalists, critics, and specialists, established in 1998. Since 1954, nearly 2,000 products have been given awards or honourable mentions and the range of products taken into consideration has been widely extended: not only consumer goods like furniture and household items, but also work tools and graphic and Web design. This shift is marked by the change in the name of the prize itself, which now rewards 'industrial design', rather than just 'product aesthetics'. Due to the exhibitions promoted by ADI around the world, the prize has acquired an international reputation for excellence, and its logo is now a symbol of the strong international affirmation and recognition of Italian design.

Adriano Olivetti, 1955

Invitation for the 50th Anniversary of the Compasso d'Oro ADI, 2004, graphic design by Bob Noorda

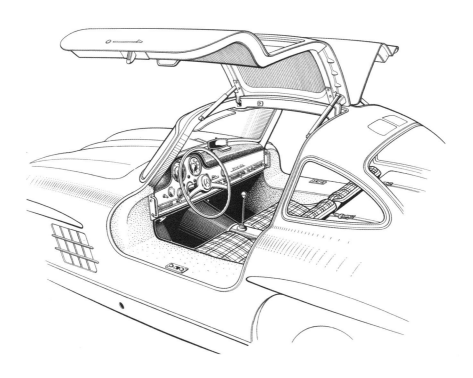

**World War II** hit Daimler-Benz, Mercedes' parent company, very hard. By the end of 1945 both its Untertürkeim factory and its Sindelfingen body shop had been all but destroyed. A year later the company made only 214 vehicles and they were largely vans and pickups. However, the 300 SL was designed to return the company to its racing roots. Starting life as a thoroughbred track car, it more or less invented the supercar genre when it was finally allowed on the public highways in 1954. Elegant, reliable in the best traditions of its manufacturer, the 300 SL was, above all else, extremely fast. The 300 SL could be afforded only by the extremely wealthy, but they got plenty for their cash because it came loaded with technical and aesthetic innovations. All parts of the design are done with purpose – from the anodized aluminium belt and trim mouldings, the slight use of adornments and knobs – either to cover seams in the panel, or permit access to the structure. It had the first fuel-injection system in a series production car with a four-stroke engine, for example, an output of 215 hp from a three-litre unit and a truly remarkable top speed of 250 kph (155 mph). The 300

SL was exceptional because it was a fully synthesized design, and stood ahead of the cars of its time in this respect. Most important, though, was its lightweight space frame that extended up its flanks, preventing the use of conventional doors. Confronted with this problem, Mercedes-Benz struck upon the 'Gullwing' solution, with the doors opening upwards from the roof. Perhaps the company's greatest achievement was making the body and doors seem integrated. The wings look as if they were created at the beginning of the design process to brand the car, rather than slotted in to fit the frame, but by doing so, the gullwings became an instant icon. 300 SL re-established Mercedes-Benz as a formidable power in motor sport after World War II, and the company has kept an SL model in its range ever since – arguably none of them have been able to match the original. Motor critic Andrew Frankel wrote in the *Sunday Times* that 'the Gullwing created the most coveted class of car there has been. What's more it was not simply the first, but half a century later it remains one of the best'.

Photograph for the rally from Liége, Belgium, to Rome, Italy, and back, of which the winners were Willy Mairesse and Willy Genin, 2 August 1956

PHOTO JUNIOR
34 AV. G. CLEMENCEAU
TEL. 23-56 · NICE

# LIÉGE · ROME · LIÉGE 1956

*PAR ZAGREB*

74001

**Elephant Stool (1954)**
**Sori Yanagi (1915–)**
**Kotobuki 1954 to 1977**
**Habitat 2000 to 2003**
**Vitra 2004 to present**

**When fibreglass became** commercially available in Japan after World War II, Sori Yanagi used it for the first ever stool entirely produced in plastic. The stool was initially intended as a seating object that would only be used by the model makers in his atelier, and therefore needed to be light, due to the constraints of space, and stackable. A three-legged stool emerged with a shape that resembled the sturdiness of an elephant's leg, hence its name. Its anonymous appearance is sculptural yet unobtrusive, defining its role as furniture only when called upon as a functional object. Yanagi once said, 'I prefer gentle and rounded forms – they radiate human warmth,' demonstrating his affiliation with human emotions. The stool was initially produced by Kotobuki in 1954 , as its compactness deemed it suitable for the tiny, urban apartments in the larger cities of Japan, as well as for outdoor use. The key idea is represented by the Elephant Stool was that such new materials as fibreglass-reinforced polyester resin were being welcomed into domestic interiors. In the postwar revival period, Japanese industry was embracing the technological production skills being developed in Europe and the United States. Yanagi in particular was intrigued by the malleability of fibreglass, and the stool displays the soft contours that only this material would allow. This material was recently recognized as being environmentally damaging, and so Vitra and Yanagi worked together to recreate a new version, now made with injected-moulded polypropylene, reissued in 2004, and produced in white, black, red or grey. The stool is one of many in his vast body of work (which ranges from tableware to engineering structures), that was meticulously drawn and designed by hand before ever reaching the drafting table.

Fuga Bowls (1954)
Sven Palmqvist (1906–84)
Orrefors 1954 to 1983

Sven Palmqvist

**At a glance** there is very little about the delightfully simple design of the Fuga Bowl series that suggests its arrival on the Swedish glass scene spearheaded a technical revolution in the manufacture of mass-produced glassware. Designed by veteran glassware designer Sven Palmqvist for Orrefors in 1954, Fuga exemplified Scandinavia's democratic design principles. Yet it was Palmqvist's innovative streak that would ultimately mark this design out for praise. During a trip to Czechoslovakia in 1934 Palmqvist observed how cream would climb up the walls of a butter churn as it was rotated and mused as to whether this centrifugal technique could be applied to the manufacture of glass. During the 1940s he invested considerable time and effort in exploring the possibilities of centrifugal force in glass design, much to the chagrin of his conservative colleagues in Sweden. They were suspicious that the introduction of machine manufacturing would cast doubt over the future of a company that had built a reputation solely on handmade glass. However, the benefits of a centrifugal system were obvious to Palmqvist. By spinning molten glass in moulds at high speeds a flawless finish could be produced in a fraction of the time it would take by hand. Palmqvist's perseverance paid off when, in the mid-1940s, he was granted a worldwide patent for centrifugal glass. In commercial terms the centrifugal method opened up exciting opportunities for large-scale manufacturing of designs that were high in quality and yet cheap to produce. Inspired by the commercial implications and the clear marketing opportunity, Stockholm's grand NK department store persuaded Orrefors to put the Fuga design, the first to use the new technique, into production. It was a breakthrough. The reality of low-cost, high-quality glassware meant that Fuga was a huge commercial hit that paved the way for later mass-market glass design. Critically, the design was widely acclaimed too, so when in 1957 it was awarded a Grand Prix at the Milan Triennale, Fuga's impact on the future of glass design was complete.

Solar Panel (1954)
Bell Telephone Laboratories Design Team
Various 1954 to present

**The exploration** of solar energy dates from the seventh century BC when magnifying glasses were first used to start fires and houses were orientated towards the south to capture winter sun and create a warmer domestic environment. In the second half of the eighteenth century Swiss scientist Horace de Saussure invented a hotbox that trapped solar rays and reached temperatures of up to 87.5°C (189.5° F). This box was later used by British astronomer Sir John Herschel to cook food during his expedition to southern Africa in the 1830s. Throughout the nineteenth century important research was done into the conductivity of selenium and thermal solar technology, and in 1891 Baltimore inventor Clarence Kemp patented the first commercial solar water heater. But it was still unclear how to transform thermal energy into electricity and how to store such energy. Just before World War II the installation of a wind turbine in Vermont and some rather limited use of solar water heaters in Florida and California generated interest in renewable sources of energy in the US, but it was the postwar rationing of petrol and an unprecedented demand for energy fuelled by the booming economy that finally brought home the importance of securing adequate energy resources. Recent advances in technology also led the world to believe that with the right allocation of resources and talents to research, anything could be invented. In 1952, three researchers from Bell Telephone Laboratories were trying to understand why dry cell batteries rapidly became degraded in mild climates. Daryl Chapin, a solar enthusiast, started experimenting with selenium as a conductor, but with little initial success, managing to convert only 0.5 per cent of the incoming sunlight into electricity. The breakthrough came when Gerald Pearson and Calvin Fuller started working with silicon. They found a way to transform silicon from an inferior conductor of electricity to a superior one. Combining silicon with gallium (positively charged) and lithium (negatively charged), and shining a lamp onto it, they registered a significant electrical flow, eventually reaching the target of transforming 6 per cent of incoming solar energy into electric energy. In April 1954 Bell held a press conference where a radio transmitting voice and music was powered with its newly invented Bell Solar Battery. Despite great advances in the field of solar panels in the last decades and the widespread commercialization of this technology, efficiency levels in an average commercial solar panel are only between 14 and 20 per cent. A higher efficiency has been achieved but with more expensive production methods, and the viability of this technology is still in doubt.

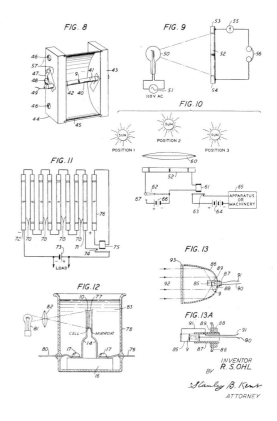

**Something New under the Sun.** It's the Bell Solar Battery, made of thin discs of specially treated silicon, an ingredient of common sand. It converts the sun's rays directly into usable amounts of electricity. Simple and trouble-free. The storage batteries beside the solar battery store up its electricity for night use.

# Bell System Solar Battery Converts Sun's Rays into Electricity!

*Bell Telephone Laboratories invention has great possibilities for telephone service and for all mankind*

Ever since Archimedes, men have been searching for the secret of the sun.

For it is known that the same kindly rays that help the flowers and the grains and the fruits to grow also send us almost limitless power . . . nearly as much every three days as in all known reserves of coal, oil and uranium.

If this energy could be put to use—instead of going to waste—there would be enough to turn every wheel and light every lamp that mankind would ever need.

The dream of ages has been brought closer by the Bell System Solar Battery. It was invented at the Bell Telephone Laboratories after long research and first announced in 1954. Since then its efficiency has been doubled and its usefulness extended.

There's still much to be done before the battery's possibilities in telephony and for other uses are fully developed. But a good and pioneering start has been made.

The progress so far is like the opening of a door through which we can glimpse exciting new things for the future.

Great benefits for telephone users and for all mankind may come from this forward step in putting the energy of the sun to practical use.

**BELL TELEPHONE SYSTEM**

**Florence Knoll's** elegant glass and steel Coffee Table was designed as an unassuming component in a larger context of interior space. Its simple, high-quality construction in polished plate glass, 1.6 cm (0.63 in) thick with a chrome-plated steel base, offered an alternative to the traditional, heavy wood furnishings popular at the time. As sleek, modern steel and glass skyscrapers were changing the exterior landscape of the cityscape, Knoll designed furnishings to complement the interiors of these new architectural spaces, exemplifying her philosophy of the importance of unified design. This table, particularly the glass-topped version, interpreted the play of light and the spatial qualities of these modern buildings. The transparent top and minimal understructure integrated the table directly into the context of its surrounding components. The table was also available with tops in slate, marble and a range of veneered woods. Knoll studied under Eliel Saarinen, and was encouraged by him to study architecture at Cranbrook Academy, then at the Architectural Association in London. Following World War II, Knoll returned to the USA, studying and working with such figures as Mies van der Rohe, Walter Gropius and Marcel Breuer. With this roster of qualifications, in 1943 Hans Knoll hired her as an interior planner for his nascent furniture company. She married Hans in 1946, and became a primary force in the success of Knoll Associates, which grew into Knoll International. After Hans's death in 1955, she assumed the role of president. She became Florence Knoll Bassett in 1958 after marrying Harry Hood Bassett. Florence revolutionized interior design, encouraging a greater understanding of modern design by creating contextual environments in Knoll's showrooms, and convincing a wary public of the potential of these sophisticated and radically new design elements. She reconfigured the functions of office spaces; her interviews with employees about how they worked resulted in a new, humanized design perspective. Her designs introduced domesticated elements to the workplace, incorporating lounge areas and storage credenzas. This table is a quiet yet resolved piece, flexible enough to work in many environments, yet indicative of the strong principles of her design talents. Today, it remains not just popular but also relevant, and is still marketed in a range of sizes and configurations.

Coffee Table (1954 )
Florence Knoll (1917–)
Knoll 1954 to present

**Florence Knoll**

**440**

GA Chair (1954)
Hans Bellmann (1911–1990)
horgenglarus 1954 to present

**The design** of the GA Chair, with its seat split in two, was an effort by Hans Bellmann to minimize, as much as possible, the amount of material used. Bellmann was a designer in the best Swiss tradition of precision engineering and throughout his career he constantly sought to refine furniture to its most spare state. The chair that preceded the design of the GA was a similarly lightweight, plywood piece (albeit a more conventional one) called the One-Point Chair. The seat of this chair was mounted on its frame by a single screw, hence the name. However, the success of this intelligent design was sullied by fellow Swiss designer Max Bill's claims that it was copied from one of his own works. This, perhaps, explains the distinctive, split-seat look of the GA Chair, which to this day has never been imitated. Bellmann and Bill were both tutors at the celebrated Hochschule für Gestaltung in Ulm, an institution that saw Germany continue to lead the way in design education after the demise of the Bauhaus. Bellmann and Bill were not the only champions of the reductionist aesthetic at the Ulm school, as Dieter Rams and Hans Gugelot, both known for their spare designs for Braun, taught there, too. Although Bellmann's legacy is not as passionately upheld as some his contemporaries (perhaps because he ended his career designing sanitation equipment) during the 1950s he was much in demand. Even Knoll, the industry-leading American manufacturer, commissioned designs from Bellmann. It is the GA Chair, though, for which Bellmann is now best known, not only for its unusual split-seat form, but also for the unrivalled quality of its construction.

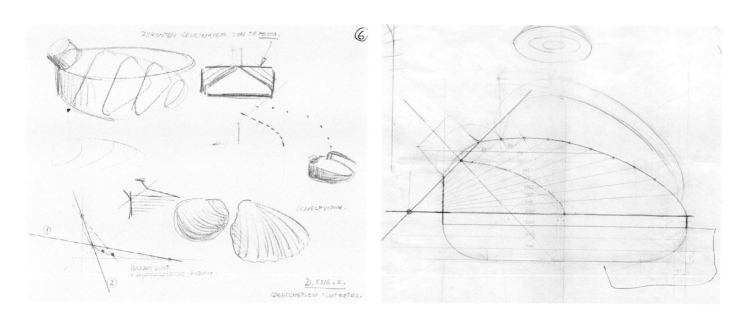

ZIJKANTEN SPULSMODEL ZIJN TE HOOG.

SCHELPVORM.

PARABOLISCHE
D HYPERBOLISCHE BODEM.

D. 5316. 5.

IDEESCHETSEN SLUITKETEL.

⑥

**When Wim Gilles's produced** his kettle for DRU it was, in every respect, an improvement on the company's existing kettle from 1935. It became an emblem of early industrial design in Holland. When developing the design, Gilles referred to research regarding the various diameters of the base of kettles made from aluminium which was undertaken by the Gas Association and the Dutch Household Association. After further research, Gilles arrived at a list of factors essential to creating the perfect marriage between form and function, and between practicality and affordability. The kettle's optimum capacity should be 2.5 L (4.4 pt); the position of the handle in relation to the centre of gravity was crucial for comfortable filling and emptying; and the handgrip should not protrude beyond the sides. In terms of construction, the kettle should consist of an upper and lower half, which can both be pressed in a single action; all welding should be smooth or in a single curved surface; and rounded edges must never be less than 3.5 mm (0.14 in). Of the existing kettle design, Gilles retained the whistle and the retail price. Empirical research had proven that the concave bottom of the old kettle, with a diameter of 17.5 cm (7 in), had a very low output. Further research revealed that a spherical bottom brought water to the boil far more quickly. A prototype made from two welded bottoms of milk boilers proved superior to any existing kettle. However, the prototype was not successful and a shell-shaped model was designed as a replacement. The final shape was determined by a mathematical formula, rather than aesthetics, making the kettle a predecessor to numerous designs which were simplified by computers decades later. Gilles became one of the first Dutch freelance industrial designers and worked for many different companies. For DRU, he designed heaters as well as cooking utensils, but his vocation in the end was teaching and he became a professor at the Academy of Industrial Design in Eindhoven. In the 1970s he left the Netherlands for Canada, where he became an influential professor in industrial design for the rest of his life.

**Alvar Aalto** considered his L-shaped bent leg to be one of his most important contributions to furniture design. As with a number of his original concepts, it was developed and refined over the years, often with contributions from staff such as Maija Heikinheimo who were employed for this very purpose by Aalto's design and distribution company, Artek. The fan-leg Stool X601 was first created for an exhibition of Aalto's furniture held at NK, the Stockholm department store, in 1954. Each individual fan-leg comprises five angled sections cut from a simple L-shaped leg that are then glued together so that the top section splays out in a fan shape. This is then connected to the edge of the stool seat or table top by means of dowels. Since it does not provide any extra strength, its main advantage over the simple L-shaped leg is aesthetic, providing a much smoother and more sophisticated visual transition between leg and top – so much so that they appear to fuse in an almost organic fashion, somewhat reminiscent of Gothic fan vaulting. Aalto, in his best promotional mode, referred to the furniture leg as the 'column's little sister', pointing out that in its simplest form his L-shaped leg gave rise to a range of furniture analogous to the type of architecture originating from the use of the Doric column. Since he had developed several different types of leg – there was an intermediate 'Y-leg' produced in 1946, as well as the fan-leg – his furniture thus consisted of several different orders, each corresponding with a different leg type.

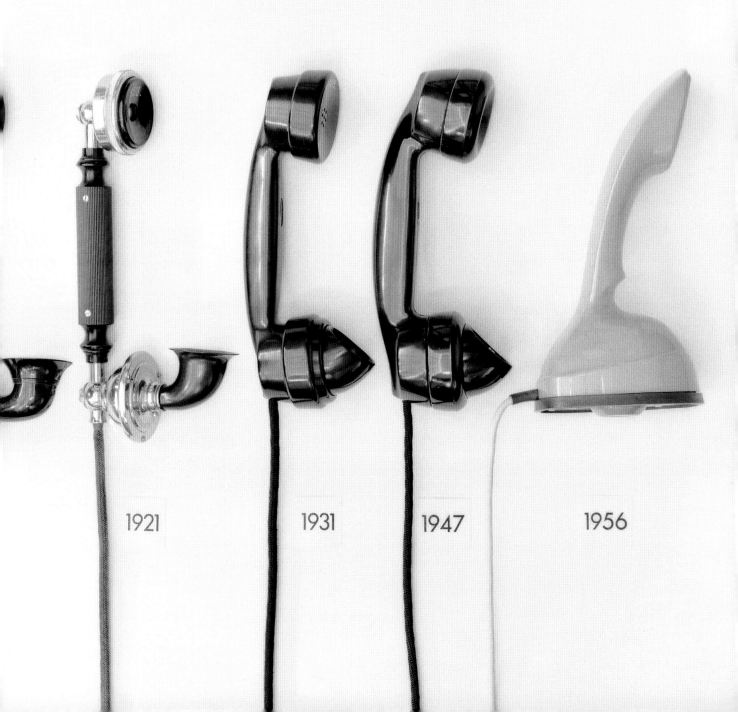

1921           1931           1947           1956

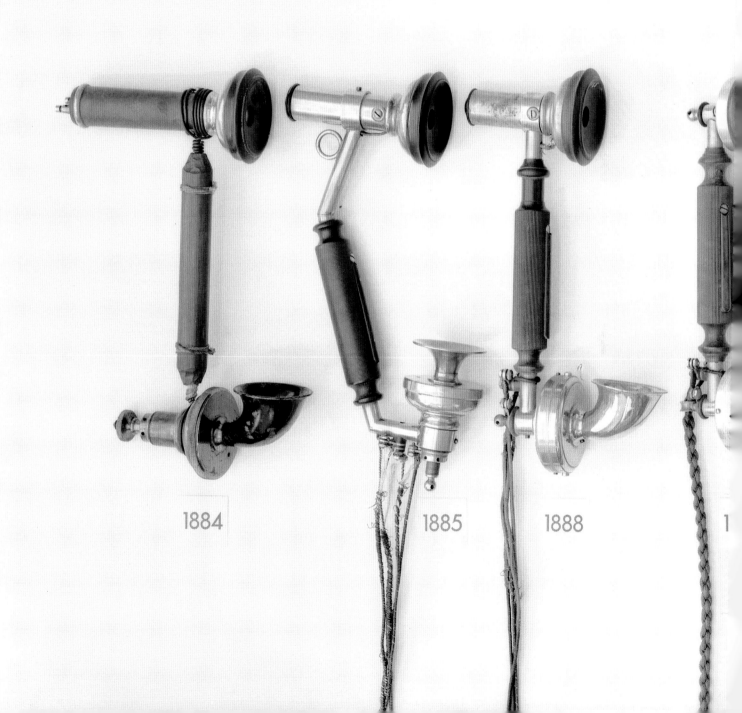

1884       1885   1888   1

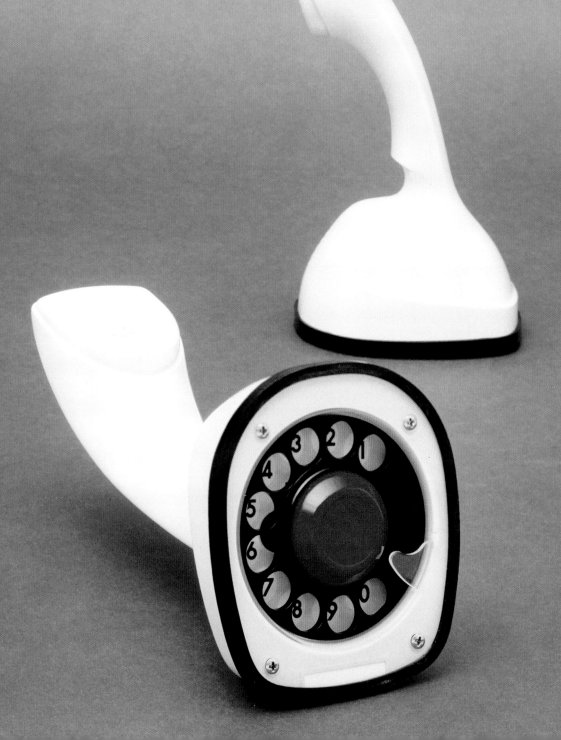

Ericofon (1954)
Hugo Blomberg (1897–1994)
Ralph Lysell (1907–)
Has Gösta Thames (1916–)
LM Ericsson 1956 to 1976
North Electric 1960s to 1972

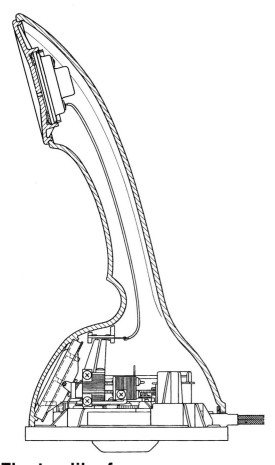

**The toy-like form** and vibrant colours of the 1954 Ericofon telephone have ensured the design's continued presence in lifestyle magazines and position as a coveted collectible today. The telephone is also known as the Cobra because of its zoomorphic, one-piece shape, and since its introduction, the LM Ericsson Company of Sweden has sold approximately 2.5 million devices. In the late 1940s Ericsson put together a design team, headed by Gösta Thames, to come up with a new design for a telephone that would be small, lightweight and easy to use. A prototype by Hugo Blomberg and Ralph Lysell was patented as early as 1941, but it was Thames who created the final design of the Ericofon. An engineer with no formal training in design, Thames believed that 'It's easier to make a designer out of an engineer than the other way round.' One main problem in the early construction of the telephone was that only brittle acrylite and cellulose plastics were available, which were easily scratched. Eventually a solution emerged with the invention of ABS plastic in the mid-1950s. Originally intended for institutional environments, the Ericofon found its most common use in hospitals, with promotional photographs of the period showing patients reclining in bed while dialling the phone. In 1956 it was officially launched in the domestic market and was successfully exported to Italy, Australia, Brazil and Switzerland. For many years the Ericofon was unable to enter the US market because of Bell Telephone's monopoly. When it was eventually introduced in the United States in the 1960s, its sales exceeded capacity by 500 per cent and Ericsson transferred the manufacture for North America to North Electric. Ericsson also modified the phone's design, making it slightly shorter and creating more of an angle at the receiver end. These models are commonly referred to as 'old case' or 'new case' phones. Initially the Ericofon was offered in eighteen colours, but the range was narrowed down to eight during the 1960s. In 1972 North Electric discontinued the Ericofon line and sold the remaining parts and equipment to a telephone refurbishing company named CEAC. To celebrate Ericsson's 100th anniversary in Sweden, Carl-Arne Breger designed a bespoke Ericofon, dubbed the Ericofon 700, but it had limited success.

Johannes Potente

**What makes** a beautiful door handle? Johannes Potente's classic Door Handle No. 1020 for Franz Schneider Brakel just feels good in the hand. But why? The four principles of grip described in the book *Greifen und Griffe* ('Grasps and Grips') by Otl Aicher may provide the explanation. The handle design meets the criteria for all four principles: 1. Thumb stop; 2. Index finger indentation; 3. Roundness; 4. Grip volume. But its classic status is due to more than just following these simple principles. Its purpose is unambiguous; it announces the entrance and urges the user to grab hold, using the handle as an extension of their own hand. It moulds to the hand and guides the user intuitively in opening the door. Its organic curves contrast with the architectonic quality of rectilinear doors, helping to announce its presence. Potente worked for FSB for his entire career, from 1922 to 1972, and continued to produce design work for the company after his retirement until his death in 1987. Trained as a tool-maker and engraver, Potente brought the precision of those professions to the design of door hardware. Potente was surprised at being considered a designer as he thought of himself as someone who built models of door handles that could be manufactured and used easily. He was an 'anonymous' designer, sitting alone in his workshop carefully crafting door handles and concentrating on the substance of the handle, not on its style. No. 1020 was one of the first door handles to be cast in aluminium, a material that was just becoming widely available in 1950. The unique qualities of aluminium, its lustre and light weight, add to the form that Potente developed. Although available in other materials, such as brass, bronze and steel, the aluminium version still seems to best express the form of the No. 1020. It is the designer's devotion to the product that singles out those of enduring beauty, and the door handle meets the criteria of a humble servant with resounding success.

**435**

Antony Chair (1954)

Jean Prouvé (1901–84)

Ateliers Jean Prouvé 1954 to 1956

Galerie Steph Simon 1954 to c.1965

Vitra 2002 to present

**It is always worth looking** at a Prouvé chair from the back as well as the front; from underneath as well as from above. Prouvé himself took great pleasure in the engineering of his furniture and in the details of its construction. His designs were determined not by an attempt to achieve a particular look, but by the qualities and properties of the materials with which he was working. In the Antony Chair the materials used, plywood and steel, appear almost at odds in character and appearance. They have very different tasks to perform: one to provide a light, comfortable seat with just the right amount of 'give', and the other to offer the sturdiest possible support to the seat. The ingenious but honest way in which he treats and combines these materials results in a look that is peculiar to Prouvé and has its own kind of beauty. In contrast to the smooth, chromed finishes so popular at the time, Antony's steel work is painted black with the marks of the welding and manufacturing

processes clearly visible. In order to accommodate the thick crossbar, the flat steel braces supporting the plywood shell have to be wide at the angle of seat and back. At either end they taper towards the points where they attach to the shell. This gives them a sculptural quality reminiscent of the floating shapes in the mobiles of Alexander Calder, of whom Prouvé was a friend and admirer. Made for the Cité Universitaire of Antony, near Paris, in 1954, the Antony Chair was one of the last pieces of furniture Prouvé designed. In 1953 L'Aluminium Français acquired a controlling interest in his rapidly expanding workshop, Ateliers Jean Prouvé. Unhappy with the new system of organization, Prouvé gave up his interest in the enterprise and with it his work as a furniture designer. Without the possibility of hands-on experimentation and the opportunity to engineer these pieces that the workshop provided, furniture design was unthinkable to Prouvé. 'An item of furniture,' he said, 'cannot be constructed on the drawing board.'

**434**

Pride Cutlery (1953)
David Mellor (1930–)
Walker and Hall 1954 to c.1980
David Mellor c.1980 to present

David Mellor

**The beautifully attenuated** and finely balanced forms of David Mellor's Pride Cutlery set the benchmark for postwar cutlery design in the UK. In Pride, Mellor developed a new, simplified language combining the meticulous attention to detail of the silversmithing tradition with the production methods of new industrial manufacturing technology. As a result Pride emerged as a modern 'less is more' challenger to the 'more is more' ornamental Victorian and Regency cutlery that still dominated the high end of the cutlery market at the time. Pride comprises a range of table and dessert knives and forks, and soup, dessert, tea and coffee spoons in silver plate. Originally the knife handles were bone and then xylonite, but are now being produced in a hard nylon resin in order to make them dishwasher-proof. Formally, Mellor has acknowledged the influence of the understated refinement of eighteenth-century Georgian cutlery, but Pride is also unequivocally modernist in its utilitarian approach. It is quite clear that the forms are explicitly designed to embrace the industrial manufacturing process. Indeed, running parallel to Mellor's career as a contemporary metalworker, he was also an influential industrial designer, creating modern street furniture and the traffic signal system for the Ministry of Transport, still in operation today. Remarkably, Mellor designed the Pride range while still a student at the Royal College of Art, London; in fact, he had been preoccupied with the design and manufacture of a knife, fork and spoon while still at college in his native Sheffield. Cutlery manufacturers Walker and Hall of Sheffield eventually picked up on the tooling Mellor created for Pride and before the designer had graduated from the Royal College of Art, it had been proposed that Walker and Hall would manufacture the cutlery range. In 1957 Pride won a Design Centre Award from the Council of Industrial Design for his cutlery. The judges commended its elegant, slim form and its perfect balance in the hand. The range is now being manufactured in David Mellor's factory in the Peak District in the north of England, and remains one of the company's most popular lines.

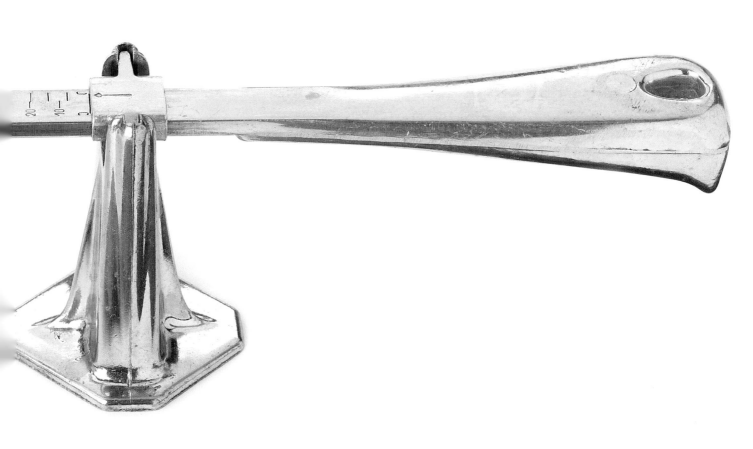

**The Spoon Scale,** a practical implement of anonymous Italian origin, is a succinct testament to the honesty of 1950s domestic worktop design. Current commercial viability is judged against branding potential, but during the 1950s a simple fitness-for-purpose provided a more pragmatic yardstick, and the Spoon Scale exemplifies just that ideal. Measuring approximately 32.5 cm (13 in) long and 8 cm (3.25 in) high, the design allowed for a scale, spoon and ladle to be integrated into one piece of equipment. Made from cast aluminium, the deep ladle end was cantilevered over a fulcrum by a back-weighted handle, so providing a simple form of weighing scale. Along two-thirds of the top of the ladle appeared a scale to measure weight in grams. To gain a reading the user would fill the ladle end, place it on the fulcrum and move it backwards and forwards until it became level. It was quick and easy to use, could remain on the worktop, and was considered by many to be more attractive than the more traditional and cumbersome alternative. Despite its simplicity, however, it was manufactured to exacting standards. Too much aluminium in the counterweight, for instance, or inaccuracy in the markings, would render the tool useless. The ladle was produced in Italy from 1953 up until the late 1970s, and is indicative of the postwar design boom characterized by frugality and providence. At this time, designs made use of limited materials and cast aluminium was popular, catering to the conservative patterns in consumer spending. The key manufacturer, OMG, was acquired by Bialetti (producers of the famous Moka) but production ceased in 2002. The Spoon Scale was exported to the rest of Europe and the USA through HA Macks' Company, a manufacture that continues to specialize in the supply of catering equipment. It has been suggested that the ladle was particularly successful with the diet-conscious, especially those living on a contemporary regime of whole grains and pulses. The Spoon Scale fell prey to the development of both mechanical and electronic scales, and its export to the USA ended in the early 1970s. It received critical accolades throughout its life, the most influential of which was its inclusion in the 1955 'Good Design Series' exhibition and the 1957 'Twentieth-Century Design in Europe and America' exhibition, both curated by New York's Museum of Modern Art.

**Cabinet-making** and
woodwork skills are central to
Danish furniture's reputation for
craftsmanship. The country was
comparatively late to industrialize,
so the traditions of skilled work-
manship in manufacture persisted
long into the twentieth century.
Danish furniture-makers were also
noted for close collaboration with
designers in the pursuit of superior,
hand-crafted goods aimed at
general consumers, not just the
rich. These qualities, of which
Fritz Hansen was perhaps the
most notable standard-bearer,
would bring Danish furniture to
world attention in the immediate
postwar years. Its organic, flowing
lines and its frequent reliance on
wood provided an alternative to
the rigorous straight lines of
Modernism prevalent in Europe.
The Fritz Hansen Stool is out of
character, therefore, both for
designer and manufacturer. Its
tubular steel legs topped with the
simplest of teak seats speak more
of basic mass production. The
stool looks like a slimmed down
version of Alvar Aalto's famous
birch Stool 60 (1932–3), although
the Fritz Hansen Stool became
four-legged in 1970, but both share
the ingenuity of being stackable.
The frame's design allowed for
efficient vertical stacking that
took up very little storage space,
which made it work in a range of
environments, from educational
institutions to bars and cafés.
Catalogues of the time also show
the stool's versatility in different
domestic roles, from dining
seating to replacement side table.
The stool came as the business
moved into another important
phase, combining simplicity with
striking form, and it is possible
to see it as a companion to Arne
Jacobsen's steel-legged Ant Chair,
released by Fritz Hansen the
previous year.

**In the current age** of computer-aided design, photo-realistic visualizations and virtual reality walkthroughs it is hard to understand the impact a small, unassuming technical pen had on the design scene of the early 1950s. The Rotring Rapidograph was a godsend for architects, designers, illustrators and engineers because it freed them from the traditional technical pen, which would often clog or leave unsightly ink blots on the page. The new pen enabled the draftsmen to create precise, consistent ink lines without the daily struggle of clearing clogged ink and battling the often temperamental ink flow from the old-fashioned technical pen. The pen was so successful and popular during the 1950s and 1960s in the design community that Rapidograph became the generic name for the new kind of technical pen. The Rapidograph's simple innovation on the standard technical pen was to replace the old-fashioned, piston filling fountain pen mechanism, which was the source of the clogging, with a modern disposable ink cartridge. The cartridge maintained consistent flow by using the ink's natural surface tension to draw it up a thin delivery tube and onto the page. The system maintained a constant pressure and ensured a steady flow of ink and therefore was a reliable tool for draftsmen. But the pen was popular not only for its convenience and labour-saving qualities but also for its good looks. The gently tapering, dark brown barrel, tipped with a shiny, needlepoint stainless-steel nib was a status symbol of sorts. It marked the user out as a professional and was certainly a notch above the mass-produced, disposable ballpoint pens introduced around the same time. The colour-coded bands around the top of the barrel indicated the thickness of the nib and also added a dash of much needed colour. The Rapidograph is still in production, although the days when a set of well-used Rotring technical pens sat at the side of virtually every drawing board in the world have largely passed with the advent of computer-aided design.

Cocotte Minute (1953)
Frédéric Lescure (nd)
Groupe SEB 1953 to present

**The Cocotte Minute** is, according to its French manufacturer, a direct descendent of a cooker that dates back to the late seventeenth century, when inventor Denis Papin devised a pressurized container that would facilitate the softening of bones and hides. Prior to his invention this laborious task could only be done by hours of boiling, but Papin's contraption essentially trapped steam inside the sealed container, forcing the pressure to build and raising the temperature at which water boils, thereby reducing the cooking time drastically. Three hundred years on, the invention of the domestic pressure-cooker effectively used the same engineering, although, thankfully for its users, in a much safer and more convenient way, early explosions notwithstanding. Postwar America saw eleven manufacturers offering eighty-five different pressure saucepans – as they were then called – to housewives keen to exploit a labour and time-saving, device that preserved vitamins, colour and flavour in their food. In Europe, however, one pressure cooker quickly superseded all others, the Cocotte Minute, developed by Frédéric Lescure and manufactured in 1953 by SEB. The Cocotte was unique in its ability to simmer, brown, roast or braise food, enabling a nation of cooks to quickly whip up traditional recipes like Boeuf Bourguignon or a Pot-au-feu in a fraction of the time and with an intensity of flavour lost in the hours of oven cooking. The French public enthusiastically received the cooker and fifty years later a staggering fifty million Cocottes have been produced. There have been cosmetic restylings and improvements along the way: the pressed aluminium of the original has given way to polished stainless steel, the security on the closing mechanism and pressurization have been improved and the lever, which once had to be screwed into place, has been replaced with a simple mechanism operated by applying pressure with one finger. However, the essential components, including different settings, a recipe book listing hundreds of recipes, a heat diffuser and a range of sizes, engineering and base design of the cooker have remained the same.

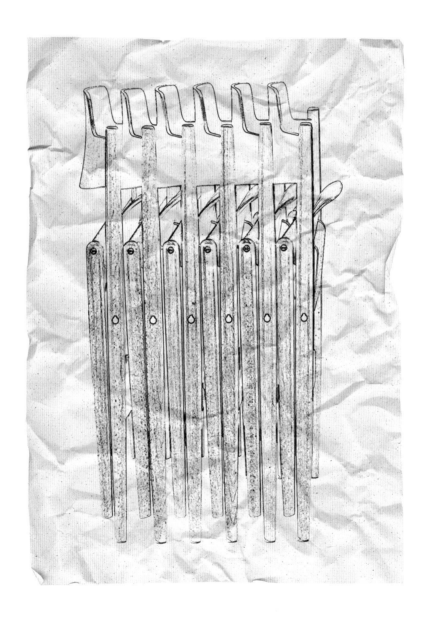

**Germany came late** to the postwar market for inexpensive folding chairs, but this model was an international success whose timeless functionality and versatility ensure that it is still in production. Eiermann, one of Germany's foremost architects, had a long-standing interest in folding furniture and took readily to Wilde & Spieth's commission for a budget concept. He developed the SE 18 Folding Chair design in just three months, rejecting an initial version with arm supports that would have been bulkier, and also costlier to produce. The SE 18's appealingly practical folding mechanism was a key factor in its success. The rear and front leg assemblies were fixed to each other with a triangular metal plate and rod that formed a swivel mechanism. Meanwhile, a strut underneath the seat ran down grooves in the rear legs, pulling them forward when the seat was folded. When it was unfolded, the strut and the upper end of the groove acted as a stop. With all metal parts hidden from view, the chair's smooth beechwood and moulded plywood lines were retained. Launched at a 1953 trade fair in Hanover, the SE 18 was an immediate hit, particularly in the domestic German market, where nothing like it existed. Its robust build, low price (25DM in 1953) and the fact that forty chairs took up just 1.5 m (4.9 ft) of storage space meant it was widely used in environments like canteens, school halls and council chambers. Despite stiffer competition abroad, the SE18 also made inroads internationally. The municipal hall in Bern alone ordered 4,000 units, while its Scandinavian character tapped a ready market in the USA. A 1953 Good Design award from The Museum of Modern Art in New York plus a silver medal at 1954's Milan Triennale confirmed its credentials. Numerous variations on the SE 18 theme appeared, including a 1961 version combining matt black teak with natural finishes. Eiermann and Wilde & Spieth's collaboration yielded thirty models in all until the designer's death in 1970, and the business still produces nine of them.

**No manufacturer embodied** the trail-blazing spirit of industrial product design during the 1950s better than the design dealer's firm of Torben Ørskov. Its aim was to mass-produce items of homeware with exceptional quality, using the most innovative manufacturing processes and the best designers available and, in addition to Herbert Krenchel, employed the likes of Arne Jacobsen and leading silversmith Henning Koppel. The Krenit Bowl is one the most highly regarded pieces Krenchel, originally a civil engineer, developed the design by conducting a series of experiments with extremely thin steel plate, only a millimetre thick. He found that by machine-pressing the steel when cold, it was possible to produce a range of bowls that were acid-resistant, could withstand the heat of a direct flame, and appear extremely elegant as well. The black exterior created a decorative matt finish with an understated aesthetic appeal. The interior was enamelled, allowing the steel plate to be decorated in a variety of colours, as the enamel was composed of powdered glass either painted or pressed onto the surface, then fired at high temperatures, melting the glass. The steel, during the firing of the enamel, became more durable, while the more delicate glass could still be easily damaged. Initially, the edge of the bowl was not thin enough as a result of this process, but the design issue was resolved in 1953, and the bowls were produced by Glud and Marstrand's, in eight colours (such as light green, sky blue, yellow, red, orange or white) and in nine sizes. The bowl was one of several items in the Krenit range, including dishes, jugs and even salad servers. The servers, however, were manufactured in melamine plastic, and Krenchel and Ørskov explored the possibilities of this new plastic material, which quickly replaced enamelled steel. (This process is still being used for industrial chemical vessels and containers.) At the time, steel was unrivalled amongst plastics, and it enabled them to produce highly delicate designs, often incorporating textural effects. These bowls were reasonably priced and popular in both Denmark and the USA, selling approximately 7,000 bowls per week by the end of the fifties, and yet the production ended by 1963. Today, the bowls are highly sought after by collectors, willing to pay a hefty sum for what was once a common item. Given that it was awarded the gold medal in 1954, at the Triennale in Milan, the desire to own these salad bowls continues.

Designed by Ezio Pirali, the managing director of Zerowatt, which was one of Italy's leading electrical appliance manufacturers, the VE 505 table fan is an icon of rationalist postwar Italian design. The fan's highly polished aluminium-encased motor was structurally supported and framed within a chromed metal wire cage, which could be tilted into two positions on rubber feet, and rotated, which allowed the rubber fan blades to be positioned at a variety of levels. Pirali, a trained electromechanical engineer, made no attempt to hide or enclose the mechanical parts, and rejected the prevalent American streamlined approach to styling of the period, for an honest industrial style that emphasized the firm's devotion to precision engineering, purity of form and the rejection of applied decoration. The fan was acknowledged as a triumph of innovation by the Italian design community when it received one of the first Compasso d'Oro awards in 1954. The jury was looking for products that displayed originality and were designed in accordance with functionality, a novel technical and production solution, and a perfectly executed product that fulfilled market demands. The VE 505 was one of only three products deemed to have met these demanding rationalist criteria, which were instrumental in helping to stimulate and promote Italian design and manufacture. Zerowatt continued to produce innovative products under the design stewardship of Ezio Pirali, contributing to Italy's design-driven economic reconstruction and reinvention of the 1950s and 1960s. In 1985 the Italian Electronics conglomerate, Candy, bought the brand and manufacturing plants. The fan has become a highly revered collector's item. It was shown at the seminal 'Design Since 1945' exhibition of 1983 held in Philadelphia, USA and it forms part of The Museum of Modern Art's prestigious permanent design collection in New York.

**By the time** Pierre Guariche originated this, one of his most famous pieces, the use of swooping, organic lines in chair design was in full swing. Pioneered in Scandinavia in the 1930s, this more rounded approach to form came to usurp the angularity of Modernism thanks largely to the pervasive postwar influence of Charles and Ray Eames. Their success in turn owed much to cease-less experimentation with materials including wood, which made increasingly diverse shapes possible. It was this innovative seam that Guariche would employ in developing the Tonneau (literally meaning 'barrel'), which would be the first moulded plywood chair produced in France. Guariche himself was not short of ambition. He had barely graduated from the École Nationale Supérieure des Arts Décoratifs when he formed his own business in 1951. He had come out from under the wing of his first-year tutor, Marcel Gascoin, whose encourage-ment to exhibit at furniture and interiors shows led to early success with Galerie Mai, which showed work by the likes of Max Bill and Alvar Aalto. His collaboration with the manufacturer Steiner, which also began in 1951 and would yield the Tonneau, came amid a period of relent-less activity. It included work on armchairs with Charles Bernard, licensee of the revolutionary 'No Sag' and 'Free Span' springs and the bold Prefacto scheme for the fledgling Airborne business, featuring flexible tubular wood and metal units for use throughout the home. This work shaped an approach towards creating furniture that was practical but comfortable and elegant, and at the same time versatile enough for home and office use. The first Tonneau chair appeared in 1953, with a plastic seat on aluminium legs, but its more innovative and robust plywood and steel tubing successor was a much greater success on its release the following year. A version with wooden legs was also produced.

**425**

Standard Lamp (1953)
Serge Mouille 1922–88)
L'Atelier de Serge Mouille 1953 to 1962
Éditions Serge Mouille 2000 to present

**This prototype lamp** is made from black lacquered metal, with a white lacquered interior and aluminium reflector to maximize the intensity of the light inside. The incredibly light, spindly structure appears at first to be unstable, but the object is carefully balanced so that the light can pivot on its mount without disruption. The breast- or teat-shaped (*tétine*) shade is characteristic of Mouille's work; as well as providing a container for the electrical fitting and a shade to diffuse the light, its form also has organic and erotic connotations. His lamps variously used natural forms and shapes that refer to the human body, in a manner inspired by Surrealism. Mouille trained as a silversmith in Paris before establishing his own studio. He was acquainted with many avant-garde architects and designers, including Jean Prouvé and Louis Sognot, and went on to exhibit and collaborate with them. The architect and designer Jacques Adnet, who was director of the decorative arts company Süe et Mare's Compagnie des Arts Français, commissioned the Standard Lamp, the first in Mouille's series of lamps, in 1953. Using the same spare metal structures and angled shades inspired by natural forms, Mouille's lamps fitted well within the language of organic Modernism. His lighting structures became gradually more complex, incorporating multiple shades and movable arms. The lamps could be hung in space, like an Alexander Calder mobile. Although they were never produced in large quantities, Mouille's lighting fixtures earned him an important place in the history of postwar French design, and he was awarded a number of architectural commissions for lighting. He also played an important role in the encouragement of new design talent, founding the Société de Création de Modèles in 1961. His early lamps, including the 1953 Standard Lamp, were reissued by the artist's widow, who has sole rights and created Éditions Serge Mouille in 2000.

Hang-It-All (1953)
Charles Eames (1907–78)
Ray Eames (1912–88)
Tigrett Enterprises Playhouse Division
1953 to 1961
Herman Miller 1953 to 1961, 1994 to present
Vitra Design Museum 1997 to present

**This hanging device,** made from wooden balls and painted wires, was intended for children to organize anything from coats, scarves and gloves to toys and roller skates. The delightfully coloured balls – red, pink, blue, magenta, ocre, yellow, green, and violet – that appear to float freely in space only enhance the sense of playfulness appropriate for a child's environment. The Hang-It-All also encourages an element of creative involvement and personalization on the part of the owner. The device is incomplete until the child chooses and arranges the objects to hang on it. Like an empty frame or skeletal structure for a mobile, the piece cleverly encourages creativity and involvement. Throughout the couple's remarkably productive careers, two important themes remained essential to much of their designs: a desire to satisfy the consumer's needs and an interest in experimenting with new materials and types of production. This piece meets the need for order in a child's room, while its experimental quality is evident in its structure, which uses the same manufacturing techniques as the low side tables the couple designed a few years earlier. This involved an inexpensive method of mass production that simultaneously, instead of individually, welded metal rods or wires together. The original rack was manufactured by both the Tigrett Enterprises Playhouse Division and Herman Miller from 1953 until 1961. The rack was originally distributed by Tigrett solely through direct mail, and was advertised in various periodicals such as *The New Yorker*, and several thousand were produced and sold, until Tigrett went out of business in 1961. It has recently been reintroduced by Herman Miller and Vitra Design Museum, manufacturers of many pieces of Eames furniture.

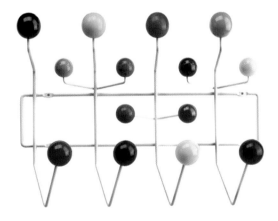

Charles and Ray Eames

**Seen from the front** or the back, the necked profile of the Ant Chair's seat, cut and bent from a single sheet of plywood, is instantly recognizable. Of all Arne Jacobsen's designs for chairs, the Ant is probably his most famous, and is the piece that brought his work to the attention of an international audience. Although Jacobsen had designed several pieces of furniture before he came to the Ant, its form and his use of materials in the design mark both a clear departure from his earlier work and a well-defined formal starting-point for the evolution of his International Style Series Seven chairs and for his Swan and Egg Chairs. The Ant Chair was originally designed in 1952 for the canteen of the pharmaceutical company Novo. Jacobsen's main intentions were to produce a chair that was light in weight and stackable. By using three thin steel rods for the legs and moulded plywood for the seat, Jacobsen was following closely the precedent set by Charles Eames's design for his LCW chair of 1945. But Jacobsen was also building on the technology and experience that had been developed by his manufacturer Fritz Hansen in its production of Peter Hvidt and Orla Mølgård-Nielsen's AX Chair of 1950. The AX Chair was made entirely from bent wooden laminates and its success on the international market had opened the eyes of its manufacturers to the potential sales of well-designed furniture that could be easily packed for shipping. But, characteristically, whatever his sources, Jacobsen managed to leave the work of his predecessors far behind.

35146

Zizi (1952)
Bruno Munari (1907–98)
Pigomma 1952
Clac & Galleria del Design e
dell'Arredamento 2001 to present

**The white-faced** Zizi monkey, made of brown, expanded polyurethane foam around a twisted copper-wire core, could change its body shape and contort into a variety of gestures. It received wide acclaim and led its designer, Bruno Munari, to his first meeting with the prestigious Compasso d'Oro design award in 1954. In 1949 there was a predecessor, a cat with nylon claws, Gatto Meo Romeo, but it is Zizi, in its bendable laminated bag, that is still available since the 1997 Munari-approved edition went into production in 2001. Picasso is said to have had a Zizi hanging around in his atelier and when asked by a visitor what it was he replied, 'It is the work of a philosopher' – a very unexpected result of the Pirelli commission for a design to demonstrate its new 'gommapiuomo' material. Munari started his career in the Rationalist era of the 1920s, interested in the new machine age and creating Futurist-style posters for clients such as Campari, Olivetti and Pirelli. Developing as a Futurist artist, writer, designer, architect, educator and philosopher during the 1930s he broke away from his 'useless machines', declaring interest in lucidity, leanness, exactitude and humour, and no interest in luxury or in placing the trendy before the enduring. He was also a strong protagonist in recognizing the value of the indirect communication between designers and users, declaring, 'Anyone who uses a properly designed object feels the presence of an artist who has worked for him . . . bettering his living conditions and encouraging him to develop his taste and sense of beauty.'

The Zizi monkey was an ingenious application of a technological advancement to a playful form and an unexpected response to the client's brief. Both the character of the toy, reflecting Munari's playfulness, and the way in which the design invites manipulation have made this piece an emblematic design. Involving the user and awakening his or her imagination was Munari's way of inviting all to experience artistic activity.

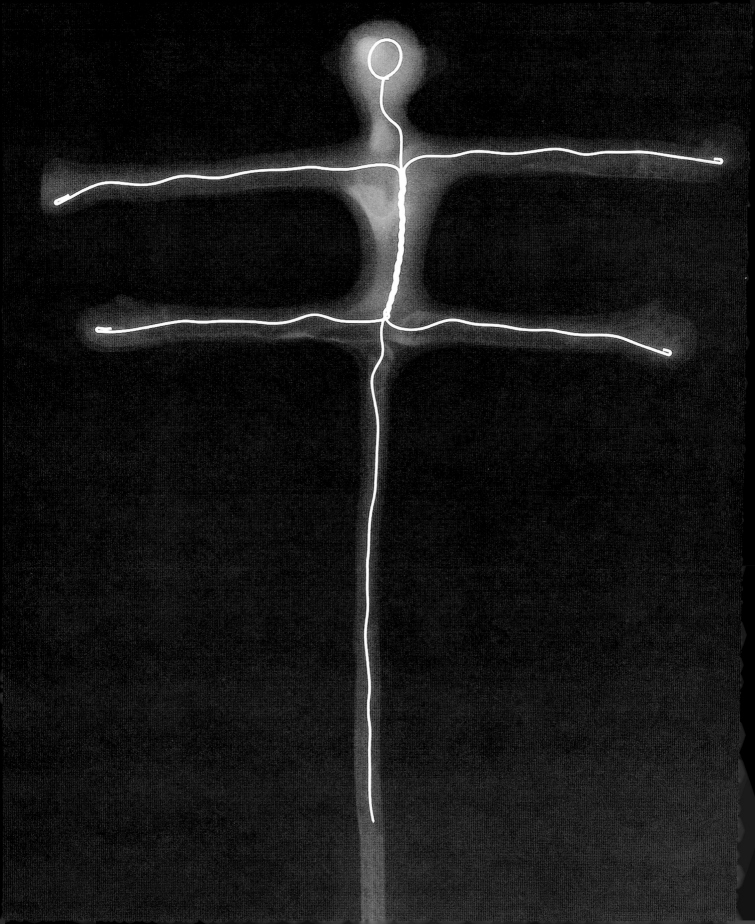

**421**

Sauna Stool (1952)
Antti Nurmesniemi (1927–2003)
Liljamaan Puusepäntehdas 1952
Various 1952 to present

**Antti Nurmesniemi's low stool** was designed for a very specific task, to provide seating before and after visiting the sauna. The shape of the seat is intended to allow water to drain away easily, while providing firm support. The seat is made from layers of plywood bonded together, then carved, with the four teak legs fixed through the seat. In later versions the quality of plywood was changed to exhibit more of the wood's knots and grain. The four slightly splayed legs make the stool steady and well balanced. Nurmesniemi's influence in Finland is immense. As a professor of industrial design, he was renowned in Finland for enforcing positive growth in design, through exhibition design, lectures, and education. As a designer he has produced everything from furniture and telephones to pylons, and many of his designs have become emblematic of contemporary life. This stool was designed at the very beginning of his career, and was originally made for the Palace Hotel in Helsinki. This first-class hotel was constructed for the Olympic Games of 1952, an event that acted as a catalyst for the revival of Finnish design. At this time there was a desire among the young generation of Finnish designers to develop a new, international language of design. Originally mass produced by G Soderstrom, the stool is presently manufactured on a much smaller scale. The design has over the years been refined by Nurmesniemi to make manufacture simpler and more cost effective. Later stools have a rounder seat, rather than the more oval seat of the early stools. A self-assembly flat-pack version has legs that are fixed to the seat by a screw fixing that does not penetrate the plywood. Functional, rugged and rustic, this unpretentious, almost accidental, design is an invitation to sit down. Surprisingly comfortable, it has found many uses outside of its original function as a sauna stool.

Kilta (1952), Teema (1981)
Kaj Franck (1911–89)
Arabia 1952 to 1975, 1981 to 2002
iittala 2002 to present

**When Kaj Franck** started work for the Finnish ceramics manufacturer Arabia in 1945 it was the aim of the company that he should redesign and reorganize its production of utility ware, and he became the artistic director in 1950. Franck believed that the traditional concept of fine tableware, one grand service with a multitude of different pieces, each with a different use, had long outlived its usefulness and had become something of a social straight-jacket. The range that he produced, originally known as Kilta and launched in 1952, was a highly successful and extremely popular attempt to produce a set of ceramics appropriate to the needs of the modern family in the postwar world. Most pieces of the Kilta range, which was made from an inexpensive earthenware, were intended to be multi-functional and adaptable. All pieces were provided in coordinated sizes to help with storage. The underlying geometry was kept simple, and was developed from three basic planar shapes, the circle, the square and the rectangle, providing a stylistic link between individual items. All pieces were in a single colour, originally brown, black, white, yellow or green, and were fired once to help keep the cost down. As Franck saw it, one of the great selling points of Kilta was that the pieces were all available individually, there was no standard or ideal set of pieces, and a group could be assembled from a variety of colours over a period of time. In 1975 Kilta was taken out of production because Arabia decided to stop using the white earthenware from which it was made. This allowed Kaj Franck to make a series of improvements he had long had in mind, and the adapted range was reissued in a more resilient stoneware in 1981, under the new name 'Teema', meaning 'theme'. Teema has been part of the iittala collection since 2002, and in 2005, new colours and sizes were introduced at the Frankfurt Ambiente Fair.

Advertisement, c.1959

**In 1927** an Austrian, Eduard Haas, developed a compressed peppermint candy in an attempt to create a substitute for cigarettes, calling it PEZ, from the first, middle and last letter from the German word for peppermint (PfeffErminZ). In his discovery Haas not only created the world's first interactive candy, but started a collectors' craze that inspired the Burlingame Museum of PEZ Memorabilia and even the founders of eBay. PEZ's early years were not surrounded by the playful character dispensers that would later become iconic. Rather, the first dispenser was a tall container, in the style of cigarette lighter, that neatly and hygienically stored the tiny mints. It was not until Haas introduced the product to the US market in 1952 that the idea of a character dispenser occurred to him. In an attempt to increase sales he began to add extra features to the containers, issuing them in the form of popular characters such as Popeye and Mickey Mouse, where the character's hinged head opened at the neck to release new fruit-flavoured candy. PEZ became a head-popping toy as well as a candy in its own handy case. Add to this the regular intro-duction of new characters and it is easy to see why it became so popular among children and collectors alike. PEZ Candy regularly releases new character dispensers that reflect popular trends, including cartoon characters, animals, heroes, movie and TV personalities. In the 1960s the Psychedelic Eye was released, mirroring the feeling of the period. In the 1980s characters such as the Smurfs and Looney Tunes appeared along with 'feet', which aided collectors in displaying their prized possessions. The 1990s explored such themes as Ninja Turtles and a remake of 'PezPals'- big-headed smiling characters with interchangeable body parts and disguises. To date, over 300 different dispensers have been created, including goblins that glow in the dark, neon characters and scuba divers. The current variety of fruit flavours include orange, grape, lemon and strawberry as well as sugar-free flavours. PEZ Candy does not rely on advertising for its success, yet it reaches annual sales of over 3 billion in the US alone and is found in more than 60 countries. Over the past five decades the playful PEZ dispensers and fruity candy have become a staple in popular culture. From the earliest Full Body Santa to the latest film characters, PEZ remains a favourite amongst adults and children.

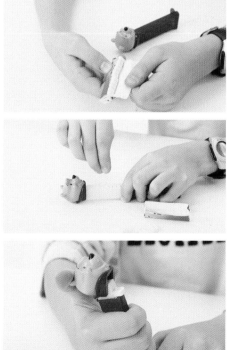

PEZ Candy Dispenser (1952)
PEZ Design Team
PEZ 1952 to present

**Famous Disney cartoon characters: Goofy, Donald Duck, Minnie Mouse, Pluto, Mickey Mouse, and Daisy Duck**

pieces were sold and for the first time, plastic dinnerware in the home became acceptable, due as well to purchasing flexibility and affordable pricing – Americans were persuaded to change their household goods and their style of living. Along with clever marketing, the unprecedented success of Residential is due in part to Wright insisting that the construction was substantial and that the material was saturated with colour, creating a much more durable, solid object than what had been produced previously in plastic. Although promoted in the spirit of Modernism, the dinnerware was not cold and mechanical-looking but was warm and organically shaped. It was coloured to make food look appealing, with names like Lemon Ice, Sea Mist and Black Velvet, and to suit an informal lifestyle. Due to its popularity, Residential was seen as distinctly American, and the result of an ethos to separate European Modernism from new American design.

Residential Melamine Dinnerware (1952)
Russel Wright (1904–1976)
Northern Industrial Chemical Company
1952 to 1960

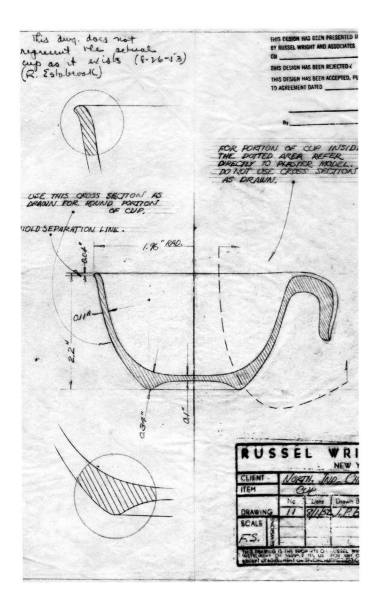

**Despite his modest** Quaker upbringing, Russel Wright became one of America's most visible designers in the 1940s and 1950s, even among such distinguished contemporaries as Raymond Loewy, Henry Dreyfuss and Walter Dorwin Teague. Although he started his career as a stage designer, he considered himself a sculptor and craftsman, turning eventually to industrial design as a way of making a large-scale social impact. Through the quality of his designs for household products and his innovative marketing strategies, Wright was able to make Modernism accessible and attractive to Americans who had previously either resisted it or been unable to afford it. His first great success came in the late Depression era with the introduction of the American Modern line of ceramic dinnerware in 1937, which became the bestselling dinnerware in America and Europe, selling over 80 million units between 1939 and 1959. In 1945,

Wright was engaged by American Cyanamid to explore the possibility of applying the success of his ceramic dinnerware to the plastics industry, using one of the new thermo-set plastics named melamine. After four years of development, American Cyanamid made an agreement with General American Transportation in 1949 to manufacture some of Wright's designs under the names MelMac and Meladur, using the capabilities of compression moulding. Beginning in 1951, MelMac and other collections such as Residential and Flair were produced by Northern Industrial Chemical and as anticipated, within a short time the postwar middle class could not live without them. The stamp at the base of each dish had Wright's signature in raised lettering, but after his contract with Northern expired, Residential was still produced but now read '100% Melamine, made in the USA, by Northern, Boston 27'. Over the next decade, millions of

**Jack Lemmon in** *The Apartment* **(1960), directed by Billy Wilder**

**Arnold Neustadter** was, by all accounts, a fastidious and highly organized man. His numerous inventions from the 1930s on relate to the recording and organization of information of various kinds, but all share the same suffix '-dex.' The first of these was a spill-proof inkwell, dubbed Swivodex, and over the years Neustadter added to this the Clipodex, the Punchodex and the Autodex, but the best-known will always be the Rolodex, a slotted-card filing system based around a rotating cylinder. Development started on this in the 1940s, after evolving out of another innovation, the Wheeldex, but it was not until 1958 that it hit the mass market. This extensive development clearly paid off since the design became an almost instant success. Not only is its system of operation entirely intuitive, but the form of the object is highly expressive of its function. The chrome-plated steel frame has an austere style which is echoed in the simplicity of the double-sided knob. Any desk graced with a Rolodex marks the owner out as an efficient, busy, and well-connected individual. In an era when office management was organized according to F W Taylor's ideas concerning the coordination of workers and the simplification of tasks in order to maximize productivity, this was a potent symbol. This is epitomized in the 1960 film *The Apartment*, starring Jack Lemmon, where a Rolodex is one of the few signifiers of identity that his character has among his 30,000 colleagues. Despite vast changes in the nature of clerical work since the 1950s, the Rolodex remains a fixture of millions of office desks worldwide. It continues to sell several million units every year, and has even entered popular lexicography, along with 'Hoover' and 'Nylon'. In the digital era it is no surprise that the interface has been adapted for computers, as the company (now part of Rubbermaid) continues to develop the theme. Neustadter would doubtless approve of the company's development of the Electrodex in this area.

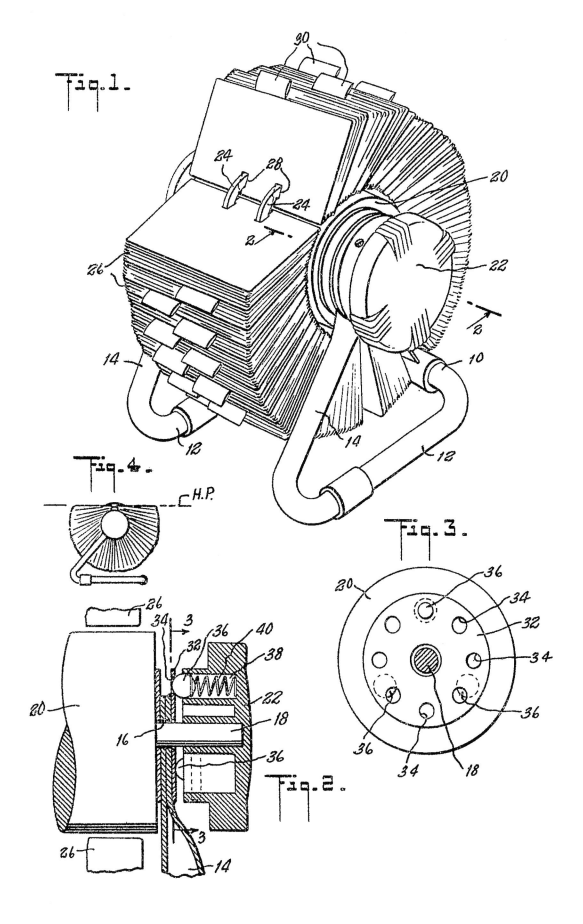

Fig.1.

30

24    28

24

2

26

14

12

20

22

10

14

12

Fig.4.

H.P.

Fig.3.

20    36

34

32

34

36

36

18

34    18

26

34    3

32    36    40

38

22

20

18

16

36

26    3

14

Fig.2.

Mexican Bookshelf (1952)
Charlotte Perriand (1903–99)
Jean Prouvé (1901–84)
Ateliers Jean Prouvé 1953 to 1956
Galerie Steph Simon 1956 to c.1965

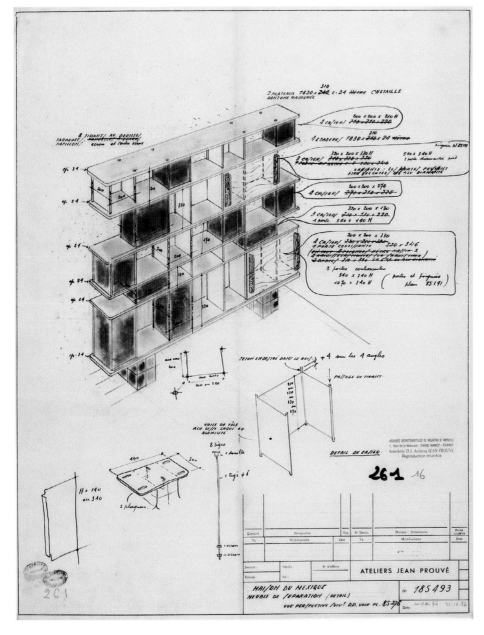

**The Mexican Bookshelf** exemplifies the successful collaboration between Charlotte Perriand and Jean Prouvé, who worked on joint projects for a period of over sixty years, as friends and professionals. Although this bookshelf communicates Perriand's skill in using colour as a device to express scale and volume, it also showcases her abilities to create spaces through ingenious structures. Perriand designed a novel system of metal cubbies that supported the shelves. She conceived the hardware and the method of attachment, an inventive configuration of U-shaped bent steel sheet, constructed from three pieces of steel connected in rolls at the back. This efficient system allowed the back and sides of each U-shaped sheet to create one volume. The rolled front edges echoed the joints of the back, and formed the vertical divider details, adding volume to the front verticals while eliminating the sharp edges of the sheet steel. Perriand engineered this innovative use of sheet steel, and Prouvé refined the results and built the components in his metal workshop. This true collaboration of talents demonstrated a complementary set of design principles and a shared emphasis on beautifully designed, low-cost efficient furnishings. The first conception of the shelf system was in the dormitory shelving for the Maison du Mexique, a seventy-seven-room dormitory in the Cité Universitaire.

The concept was to create a storage system, what Perriand termed 'utilitarian walls' that could divide living/sleeping areas from bathing/dressing areas and provide double-sided access. Originally intended to sit on 'recycled' tiled cement-block legs, a later development replaced the base with wooden legs after Perriand spent time in Japan and sought to bring more of a sense of space into her designs. Prouvé's philosophy emphasized utility, elegant construction methods and exploration of material innovation. Perriand highlighted utility in the context of the total interior, where the proportions of each individual element demanded harmonious consideration to the overall environment. Together, their design used steel for its dimensional strength and efficient production capabilities, wood for its warmth and functionality, diamond point aluminium for its texture and lighter weight, and lacquered polychromed colours, aided by the Russian/French painter Sonia Delaunay (1885–1979), for their composition and graphic depiction of volume. In this shelving unit, Perriand and Prouvé expressed new living patterns by redefining space and use, reflecting Perriand's idealism and Prouvé's pragmatism. The resulting wall system/bookshelf showcases the collaborative force of two design masters working in concert.

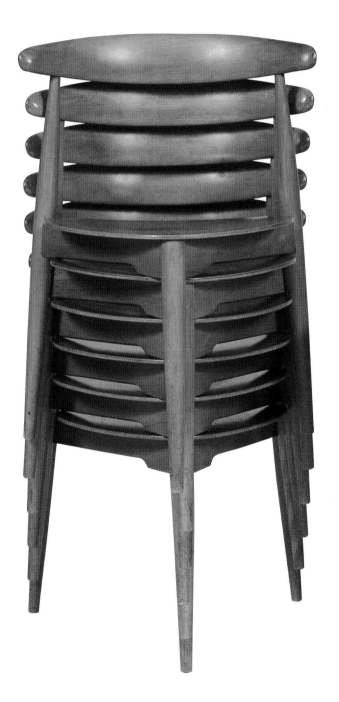

**Known for its technical sophistication** and refinement, Danish design also represents a continuum of tradition. Resolutely humanist, the Scandinavian approach to Modernism demonstrates a respect for materials and the environment that reflects a cultural dialogue between the urban and the rural, and the fact that life outside the cities is remarkably simple and close to nature. Life in the countryside remains familiar and integrated into the psyches of many urban dwellers. Consequently, for designers, references to typologies of products found in rural circumstances are often not esoteric references but part of the fabric of Danish experience. One such example is the three-legged chair that is often noted for its unusually frequent appearance in the Danish design lexicon. Antecedents of the three-legged chair are found on farms where stone and dirt floors create surfaces that make four-legged chairs unsteady. In that environment the milk stool is an extremely practical solution. In 1952, Hans Wegner, getting into his stride as one of the greatest and most prolific chair designers of the twentieth century, focused on form in the Tripod Chair No. 4103, transforming the three-legged stool into a stacking chair that embraces modernist ideas. Designed as part of a set surrounding a round table, No. 4103's thin, birch plywood, guitar-pick-shaped seat allow for the most compact storage of the chair, tapering gracefully into a series of wedges beneath the table surface. Like a milk stool, the No. 4103's teak or beech legs angle outwards, and also taper at their tops and feet, giving an impression of lightness and reaching their greatest dimension at the points where they are intersected by the rectangular chair rails that support the seat. Bowing to the stylistic vanguard of the period, Wegner applied a controlled version of biomorphism to the shaping of No. 4103 elements, particularly the seat and back rest, which becomes more pronounced in its three variations.

a top speed of 72 kph (45 mph) and a 0–30 acceleration of 36 seconds. The car could travel 80 km (49 m) on a single gallon of petrol (3.7 litres), and such low-key performance figures dovetailed with the conservative spending patterns of the day. When the car premiered at the Turin Motor Show in 1954, manufacturing forecasts only extended as far as the Italian and Belgian markets, with little provision for export. But that changed when in 1954

Isetta scooped first, second and third place in the Mille Miglia 1,000 mile race, catching the attention of BMW bosses scouting for a new car to bolster their ailing 502 and 507 brands. BMW took a licence on the design in 1955, replacing the engine with a more reliable BMW four-stroke 247cc motorcycle unit that produced 13 hp. Over the subsequent seven years, the original design was modified to include a three-wheel British version

and several upgraded models for export to Canada, New Zealand and Australia. With Isettas also available in Brazil under licence from BMW, the make was confirmed as an international motoring phenomenon. Production came to an end in 1962 when competition from new small car concepts, began satisfying a more prosperous marketplace. The Isetta nowadays proves highly collectable and enjoys a longevity that further cements its status.

**The Isetta** makes for just as curious a sight today as it did when the design first took to the streets of Europe in 1953. Fifty-two years may have passed since the car was introduced, but they have done nothing to temper the distinctiveness of one of the world's most enigmatic car designs. Measuring just 2.3 m by 1.38 m (7.5 x 4.2 ft), the car is almost insect-like in its proportions. Where the bonnet would usually sit on a conventional car there is instead a single door that opens to allow access to the tiny cabin, big enough for only one person. Gills, located at the side of the rear end, allow exhaust fumes to escape from the rear-mounted engine, and the small button lights at the front and rear only add to its bug-like appearance. The back wheels are fitted a mere 47.5 cm (1.9 in) apart, further emphasizing the car's tapered rear quarters. Renzo Rivolta, the Isetta's Italian designer best known for his ISO refrigerator brand, was already manufacturing scooters and three-wheeled vans when he moved into car design. In postwar Europe, few people could afford to run large vehicles, and scooters were therefore in high demand. These were, however, less suited to longer journeys and so Rivolta designed the Isetta to bridge the gap. Isetta offered cheap, long-distance transport designed around a two-cylinder, two-stroke engine generating

Gibson Les Paul (1952)
Les Paul (1915–)
Ted McCarty (1910–2001)
M H Berlin (1895–1984)
Gibson 1952 to 1964, 1967 to present

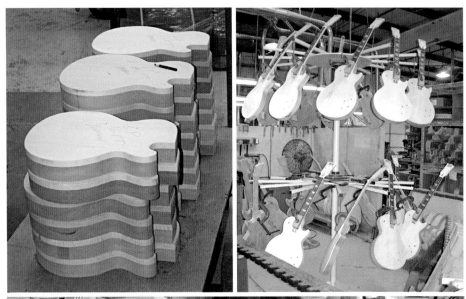

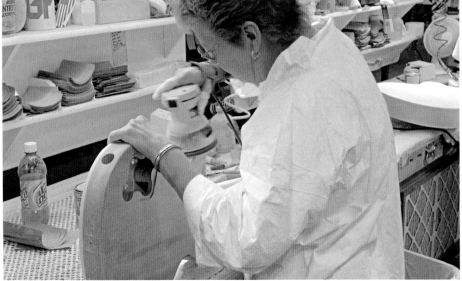

**1951 was the year** that master musician Les Paul made a name for himself by going gold with such hit tunes as 'Mockin' Bird Hill' and 'How High the Moon' and also the year in which engineer and Gibson president Ted McCarty had the idea of attaching a celebrity to a new solid-body guitar that he had in development. Gibson's main competitor, Leo Fender, had designed the first solid-body electric guitars and McCarty was eager to enter this emerging market. In distinction to traditionally crafted guitars, which were composed of a main body that was manually glued together in a labour-intensive process, the solid-body could be industrially produced in factories. The solid-body guitar also delivered the sound of its strings to an amplifier better than electrified hollow-bodied acoustic guitars, which often caused excess feedback and inadequate sustain. Travelling to a mountain top in rural Pennsylvania where Paul and his wife, Mary Ford, were recording, McCarty secured a five-year contract with the musician that mandated Gibson-only public appearances, and the look and sound of rock 'n' roll music changed forever. Although Paul would claim in years to come that he had approached Gibson with ideas for a solid-body design in the 1940s with no success, McCarty and his team were responsible for the revolutionary design, which featured a maple top and mahogany body for greater sustain, a mahogany neck and a shorter length, at 63 cm (25 in), than the Fender Telecaster, which provided a more mellow tonality. The 1952 Les Paul model included a gold nitrocellulose lacquer on top of the maple, which led to it being dubbed the 'Gold Top', and a 'trapeze' tailpiece designed by Paul that had to be replaced in later years by McCarty's trademark 'tune-o-matic' bridge. Although the Les Paul design has received a series of fine tunings over the years, it continues to be Gibson's top-selling electric guitar and has spawned eight versions, including the Les Paul Supreme, Standard, Studio and Special.

Navitimer (1952)
Breitling Design Team
Breitling 1952 to present

**The 1950s** was an exciting period of technical advancement and growth for the aviation industry. The Swiss firm Breitling was there to take advantage of the industry's increasing demand for timepieces, supplying the cockpit clocks and other precision instruments for over twenty-five airlines including Boeing, Lockheed and Douglas. Capitalizing fully on its well-deserved reputation among the industry's key players, the company introduced a product that became something akin to standard issue for all aviation professionals. In 1952, the landmark year that the first civilian jet aircraft, the de Havilland Comet, established a regular chartered flight between London and Johannesburg, Breitling introduced its Navitimer chronograph. As a piece of professional equipment, the Navitimer's aesthetic is inevitably based on clarity and precision; its visual appeal lies in an air of sturdy reliability. The large, predominately monochrome face is held on the wrist with a strong black leather strap, and is easy to read despite providing a wealth of temporal readings, including three timing counters at the 3, 6, and 9 positions. The effectiveness of the original design is borne out by the fact that it has not been significantly altered throughout the fifty-three years of its production. However, what made the Navitimer indispensable for pilots in the 1950s was its in-built 'navigation computer'. The Navitimer (a combination of the words 'navigation' and 'timer') featured a slide rule, a working instrument that enabled the wearer to calculate all basic navigation readings such as climbing and distance rates, fuel consumption, average speed and distance conversions. In the pre-computer era, an instrument of this kind that was also a precision watch was a powerful tool. In recognition of this, in 1952 the Navitimer became the official watch of the Aircraft Owners and Pilots Association (AOPA). Perhaps its most iconic moment came on 24 May 1962 when a specially made version, the Cosmonaute, was blasted into space on the wrist of astronaut Lt Scott Carpenter. The space-going chronograph most significantly featured a 24-hour configuration enabling space travellers to distinguish between midnight and noon, thus allowing them to monitor with less confusion the passing of time in the vacuum of outer space. According to Breitling, the Navitimer is the oldest chronograph still in uninterrupted production and its essentially unchanged form has imbued it with a cult status that connects it to the glory days of aviation history.

## NAVITIMER

Der berühmte Chronograph mit Navigations-Computer. 17 Rubine, drehbarer Glasring, Leuchtzifferblatt, Zählwerk bis 30 Minuten und 12 Stunden, stoßsicher 17 Rubine, robustes Gehäuse

Mod. 806 S Edelstahl DM 385.- *
Mod. 806 P Goldplaqué DM 395.- *
Mod. 806 G Gold 18 Kt. DM 798.- *

Gebrauchsanweisung
auf Anforderung

## SPEZIALCHRONOGRAPH FÜR FLIEGER

Der Breitling-Navitimer ist ein ganz einzigartiger Chronograph. Er allein bietet den Piloten, Funkern usw. nebst allen Annehmlichkeiten eines Armbandchronographen die vollständige Logarithmentafel eines Rechenschiebers für die Luftfahrt. Der Breitling-Navitimer hat sich als zuverlässiger Begleiter für alle Piloten erwiesen. Er gibt die genaue Zeit, zählt die Sekunden und läßt sich mit seinen beiden Drückern beliebig anhalten und wieder in Gang setzen. Die Einteilung auf dem beweglichen Glasreif steht der fixen Skala auf dem Zifferblatt gegenüber. Merkzeichen erleichtern die Umrechnung von Land- und Seemeilen in Kilometer und umgekehrt. Eine weitere Skala innerhalb der fixen gestattet das rasche Bestimmen von Stundengeschwindigkeiten oder des zurückgelegten Weges bei bekannter Geschwindigkeit und gegebener Zeit. Der Navitimer zeigt Halte- und Fehlzeiten an, erleichtert die Aufstellung von Navigationsplänen, die Bestimmung des Zeitpunktes für den nächsten Funkanruf, berechnet den Brennstoffverbrauch und dient der Standort- und Richtungsbestimmung, gibt den Zeitpunkt der Ankunft. Der Navitimer ist ein unentbehrliches Navigationsinstrument. Der Breitling-Navitimer ist einzigartig, ein treuer Begleiter für alle Piloten.

## COSMONAUT-NAVITIMER

Mod. 809 Edelstahl DM 425.- *
Spezialausführung des Navitimers mit 24-Stunden-Zifferblatt

Diese Uhr hat den amerikanischen Raumflug mit Lt. Commander Scott Carpenter im Mai 1962 erfolgreich bestanden.

* Unverbindlicher Richtpreis

2
3

**Scott Carpenter in advertisement for Breitling, who wore the Navitimer on a space flight in May 1962**

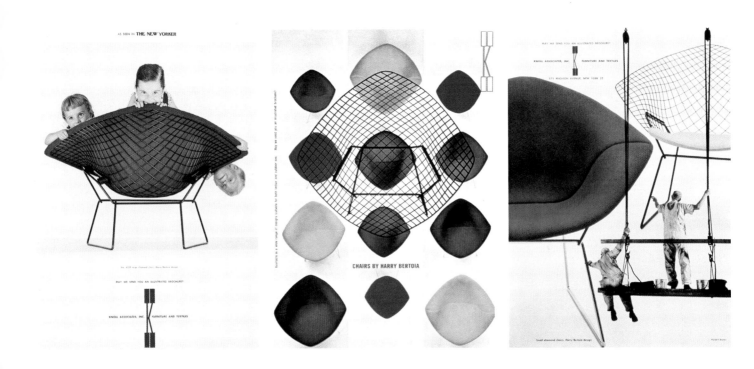

**Advertisements for *The New Yorker*, *Fortune*, and trade magazines, 1950–5, all created by Herbert Matter**

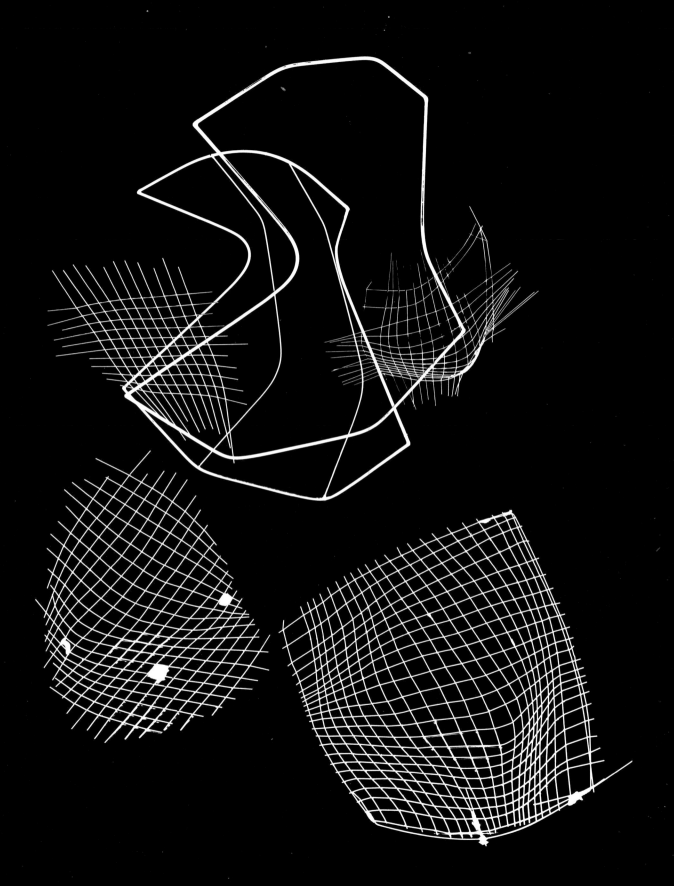

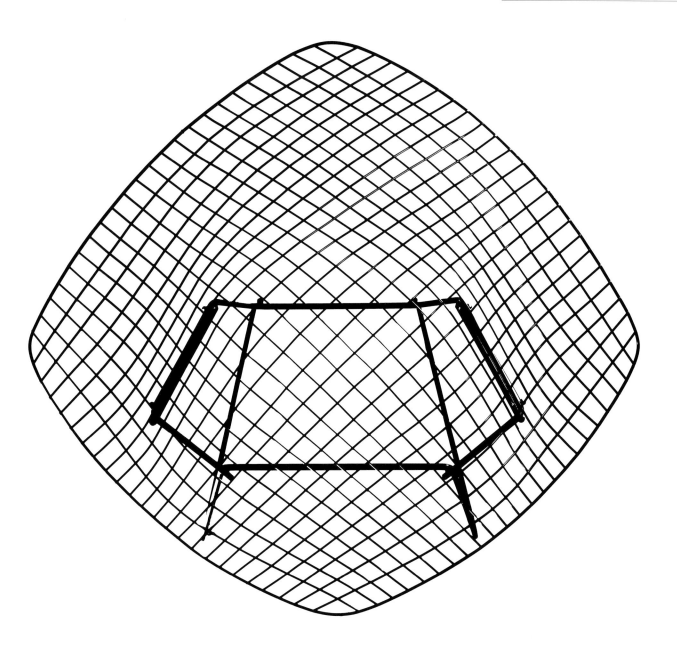

**Harry Bertoia wanted to** create furniture
that allowed the user to sit on air. In his own words: 'If
you look at these chairs, they are mainly made of air,
like sculpture. Space passes through them.' The
Diamond Chair accomplishes this with a seat made
from steel wire floating on thin rod legs. Bertoia
immigrated to the United States in 1930 and began
studying at Cranbrook Academy of Art, Michigan, in
1939 where he met Charles Eames. In 1943 he
accepted a position at Eames's studio and contributed to his furniture designs, particularly the Wire
Chair of the Eames's classic collection. In 1950, after
leaving Eames, Bertoia started to work full time on his
sculpture, but was persuaded by his friends from
Cranbrook, Florence Knoll and her husband Hans, to
create anything that he wished, sculpture or furniture.
The result was the Diamond Chair, one in a series of
chairs and benches that Bertoia created for Knoll,
which was introduced in 1952. The Diamond Chair
could not have been drawn; it had to be sculpted. It is
a most improbable shape for a chair and at first sight
might even seem uninviting. But once seated, the
sitter is transported by Bertoia's dream of sitting on
air. Using resistance-welding technology creating the
manufacturing jigs, which still exist, Bertoia first bent
the wires by hand and then placed them in the jig for
welding. The process is extremely simple and produces
wonderful results. The chair is equally comfortable
without the cushion, and looks even more sculptural.
Richard Schultz, known for his Leisure Collection,
helped Bertoia create the chairs. Bertoia's Diamond
Chair defies its history. It stands as one of the finest
examples of mid-century American design: timeless in
its approach and timeless in its form. It might even
meet most of the criteria for 'green design' or design
for disassembly imposed on many new creations. It is
lightweight, making it easy to transport, its materials
allow it to be easily made and cared for, and its shape
defies logic. Useful both indoors or out, the Diamond
Chair happily resides in any setting.

R-Type Bentley Continental (1952)
Bentley Design Team
Bentley Motors 1952 to 1955

**Some of the most** romantic car designs of the post-World War II era were British, among them Rolls Royce, Jaguar, Daimler and Aston Martin models. But the grandest of all for style, grace and performance was the Bentley. And the best Bentley was the R-type, with coachwork – a wonderful euphemism for the body – by H J Mullliner. The Rolls Royce company owned the Bentley marque and was keen to produce the best sports touring car of the period. Using a wind tunnel, in those days almost unheard of, Rolls engineer Harry Evernden and stylist John Blatchley honed the body shape and came up with the stylish rear wings. Designed to help with longitudinal stability, the swept back body and long fins gave the car an emphatic visual impact and foreshadowed the work of the great American stylist Harley Earl. Unusually in the car industry, Rolls Royce used independent coach-builders to create the bodies of its cars. For the Bentley R-type, Rolls chose H J Mulliner, whose work sets this Bentley apart from all others. A few late model cars were given to other stylists, including Battista 'Pinin' Farina and the traditional Rolls coach-builder, Park Ward. Engineer Harry Evernden worked his magic on the venerable Rolls Royce six-cylinder in-line engine taken from the sedate and regal MkVI Bentley, and Rolls was not shy about proclaiming the R-type's outstanding performance. It could do 161 kph (100 mph) in third gear, and its top speed of almost 188 kph (117 mph) made it easily the fastest production four-seat car in the world. The car was initially produced for the export market only and the first hundred cars went out of Britain. Eventually only 208 cars were produced, including the prototype which is still in existence today, and now belongs to a dedicated enthusiast.

**It may be ubiquitous today,** but the flip-top lid and pedal of the Brabantia Pedal Bin was once an entirely novel idea. In 1952, there was nothing on the market quite like it. Brabantia was formed in Aalst, in the Netherlands, in 1919, and started out making milk sieves and watering cans. In 1930 the small, family-run company, with a staff of fifteen engineers and craftsmen, turned to the production of umbrella stands. In 1947 this led to the first version of its wastepaper bin. By now, Brabantia had found a niche in the market and the company's engineers concentrated their efforts on updating the rubbish bin. The idea of developing a lid to contain odours and a pedal to prevent back strain was one that soon provided the bedrock of Brabantia's business. The company now makes a wide range of products in addition to the rubbish bins, including postboxes, food storage containers, and kitchenware. Using the basic shape of the original wastepaper bin, the company developed a sophisticated set of tools to produce the pedal bin. As the bin incorporated metal in both sheet and wire form, and needed to be corrosion-resistant, it was a far from simple process. Indeed, its difficulty is evidenced by the fact that, from the first model in 1952 right up to the present day, the production process for the Pedal Bin has been continually reworked and refined. The major changes to the design occurred in 1957 with addition of a rim at the bottom of the bin to protect the floor and, a year later, the inclusion of a plastic inner bucket. Although today's model looks remarkably similar to the original version produced over fifty years ago, it is no longer made by craftsmen in Aalst but by numerous factories around the world.

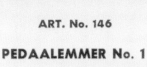

## ART. No. 146
## PEDAALEMMER No. 1

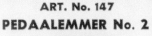

## ART. No. 147
## PEDAALEMMER No. 2

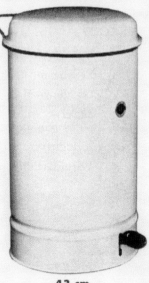

## ART. No. 148
## PEDAALEMMER No. 3

**36 cm**      **43 cm**      **53 cm**

VERKOOP-ARGUMENTEN:

Zwaar gefosfateerde plaat. Extra stevig deksel. Met geluid-dempende rubberrand. Zwaar gegalvaniseerde binnenemmers van resp. 10, 12 en 16 liter inhoud. Diameter 24 cm. Hoogten 36, 43 en 53 cm. Zwaar scharnier, verchroomde greep en drukstang. Een super-kwaliteitsproduct. Een metalen met rubber overtrokken pedaal. Trapt verrassend licht. — Per stuk in doos verpakt.

## ART. No. 163
## POETSDOOS

*....twee handen vrij....*

VERKOOP-ARGUMENTEN:

Zeer ruim model uit één stuk geperst, dus naadloos.
Gemakkelijk hanteerbaar.
Gemakkelijk verplaatsbaar.
Verchroomde neerklapbare beugel.
Hygiënisch, modern, afwasbaar.
Verpakking: 2 stuks in doos
          kleur turquoise.

## ART. No. 113b
## LOS RONDREK

**408**

Antelope Chair (1951)
Ernest Race (1913–64)
Race Furniture 1951 to present

**With the exception** of its seat, the Antelope Chair is made up entirely of thin circular sections of painted steel rod. The rod is bent and welded into shape to form the back, arms and legs of the chair. A moulded and painted plywood panel seat is bolted to this frame. Because of the relative uniformity of the steel section, the chair has the appearance of a line drawing in space. The earlier metal chair frames of the Bauhaus were parallel, rectilinear forms and used a larger diameter tube, while Race's design used thin, solid steel to draw a more generous and organic shape and, through this linear device, produced a chair that appeared both airy and substantial. Its horn-like corners at the top back and on the arms suggest the name 'Antelope'. The Antelope was originally designed for the outdoor terraces of the Royal Festival Hall in London. This building in turn formed part of the Festival of Britain exhibition of 1951. The festival marked an era of postwar regeneration and innovation. The chair was widely publicized throughout this event and came to symbolize forward thinking and optimism for design and manufacturing in Britain. Its dynamic legs ending in ball feet also reflected the popular 'atomic' imagery of what were seen as new and progressive sciences, namely molecular chemistry and nuclear physics. The chair was manufactured by Race himself through Race Furniture, a company he founded in 1946 in collaboration with engineer Noel Jordan. The company was set up to re-employ the largely redundant metal-working facility and scrap metal resource left over from World War II production. It was the Antelope's flamboyant image that captured the essential spirit of the period.

**The Flying Dutchman's story** began in 1951 when the International Yacht Race Union organized a competition to design a high performance, two-person racing dinghy, intended for important races. The winning boat, by Dutch designer Uilke van Essen, quickly showed its high speed performance ability and was named the Flying Dutchman. At 6.05 m (19.75 ft) overall length, and a weight of 130 kg (286 lb), early models of the boat were built of wood. Production soon switched to Kevlar, fibreglass and carbon fibre when these new materials became widely available, improving the rigidity of the boat on the waves but making little difference to performance and maximum speed. In 1971 the boat took part in a record speed week and was sailed at a record speed of 14.5 knots. A week later it achieved 18 knots. The boat has a large wet area, slightly disproportionate to the enormous sail area of 36.1 mq including the spinnaker and jib, making it very fast with a light wind, and even faster, but dangerous for the inexperienced sailor, in a heavy wind. While the boat is not complicated to sail, it offers a wide range of adjustments: the main sail or jib's halyard, the angle and the length of the cross tree and consequently the mast. The helmsman has a choice of two rudders – one for strong wind and one for light. The popularity of the Flying Dutchman took off after trials in 1955 on European lakes. Five years later it was approved for participation in the Olympic Games and made its first appearance at the 1960 Olympics in Naples. It remains as the precursor of and inspiration for larger racing boats, and its water lines are still considered modern. Van Essen went on to design the Flying Junior, a slower and simpler version of the Flying Dutchman that was quickly adopted by sailing schools. The Flying Dutchman remains popular in the US and Europe, and particularly in the Netherlands.

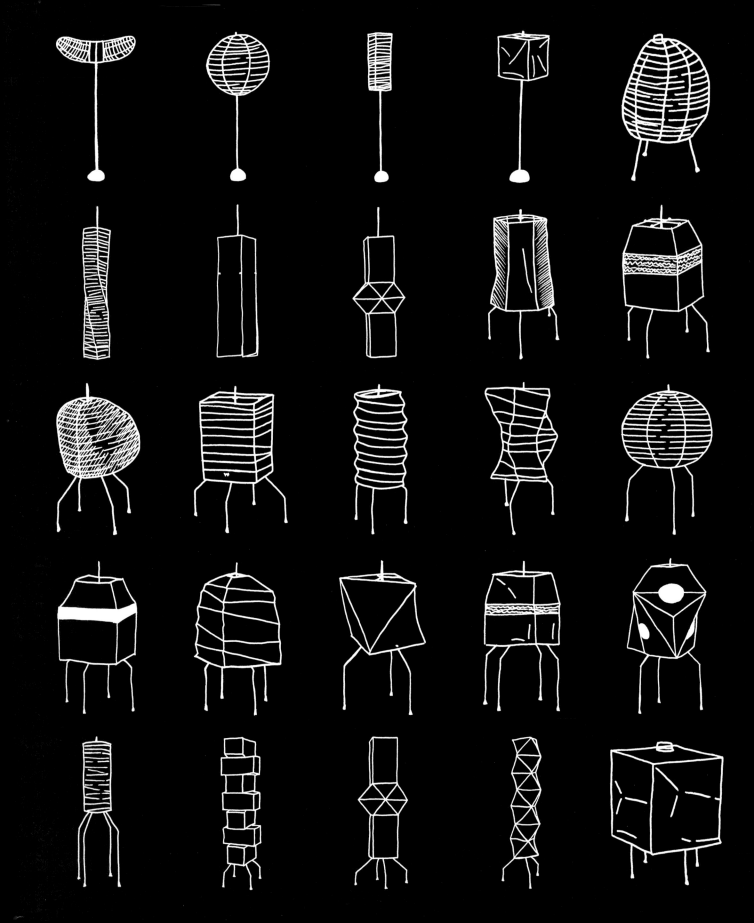

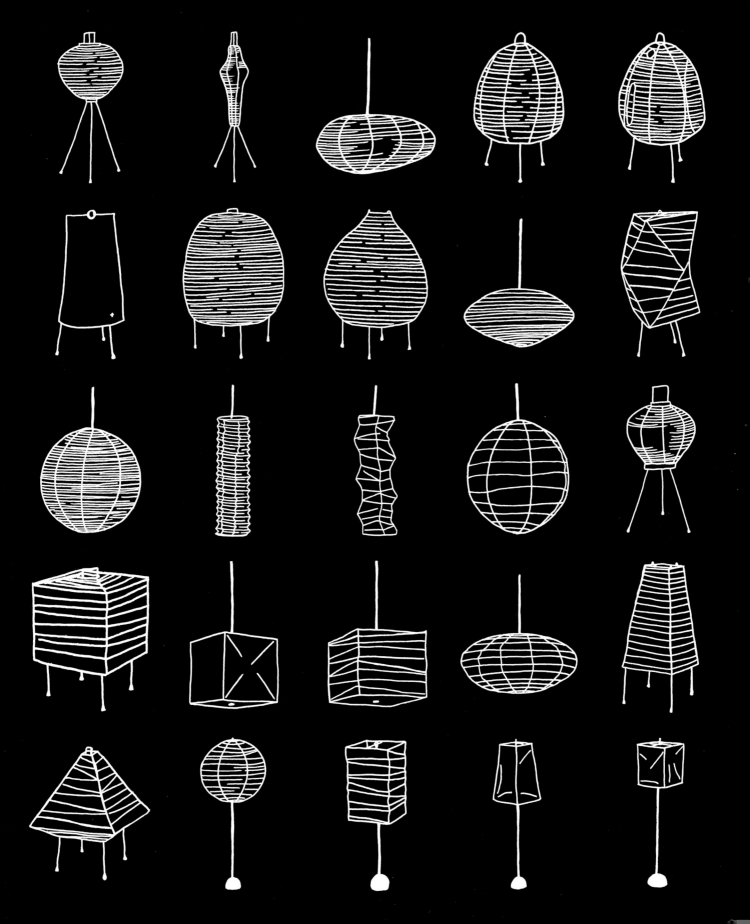

**406**
Akari Pod Lamp and Light Sculptures (1951)
Isamu Noguchi (1904–88)
Ozeki & Co 1952 to present
Vitra Design Museum 2001 to present

**Isamu Noguchi's** radical reinterpretation of the traditional Japanese paper lantern is a symbol of modernist design that has had tremendous impact in the West. Fashioned from paper, which was handmade from the bark of the mulberry tree, with a thin wooden structure, Noguchi's lamp retained the basic principles of traditional lantern manufacture, but without the customary painted decorations. The lamp was entitled 'Akari', which translates variously as 'light', 'sun' or 'moon'. From the first Akari Lamps produced in 1951, Noguchi went on to create a range of organic and later geometric shapes. He designed over 100 variations from the 1950s to the 1980s, as the basis for hanging, standing and floor lamps. Noguchi had first experimented with artificial illumination in the 1930s and incorporated electrical light into his Lunar sculptural works of the 1940s. The surreal Lunar forms, biomorphic shapes with recessed or concealed lights, were often seamlessly integrated into interiors, so that the distinction between fine art and functional design was blurred. His first lighting products for American manufacturers, such as the 1940 Three-Legged Cylinder Lamp for Knoll, furthered his ambition to produce affordable sculptural objects for a wider market. In 1951, while on his way to Hiroshima, Noguchi made a detour to visit Gifu, the manufacturing centre of traditional paper products such as lanterns and umbrellas. He was invited by the city's mayor to design a lamp for export that would help to revitalize the paper-craft industry. Sketching out his first ideas for Akari that same day, Noguchi created a fusion of sculpture with design and a marriage of traditional techniques with modernist principles. The Akari lights were the product of a collaboration with the Gifu paper-lantern producers Ozeki & Co, who produce them to this day. The first lamps were widely published in interiors magazines of the early 1950s, and exhibited in Tokyo in 1952 and in New York in 1954. Priced at only a few dollars (the first at around $7.50), the lamps were an inexpensive and adaptable form of modern design that have spawned many imitators.

Isamu Noguchi

forms. He exploited the dense repetitive lines in the plywood, using these contours to capture a sense of movement and momentary energy running through each object. Wirkkala's work helped to redefine the distinctions between art and design. He continued as a designer of functional glasswork for iittala, while at the same time working on his abstracted sculptural forms. He was in a league of his own in the 1950s, capturing the essence of Scandinavian Modernism by combining abstract forms from nature with traditional precision and craftsmanship.

Leaf Dish (1951)
Tapio Wirkkala (1915–85)

Tapio Wirkkala

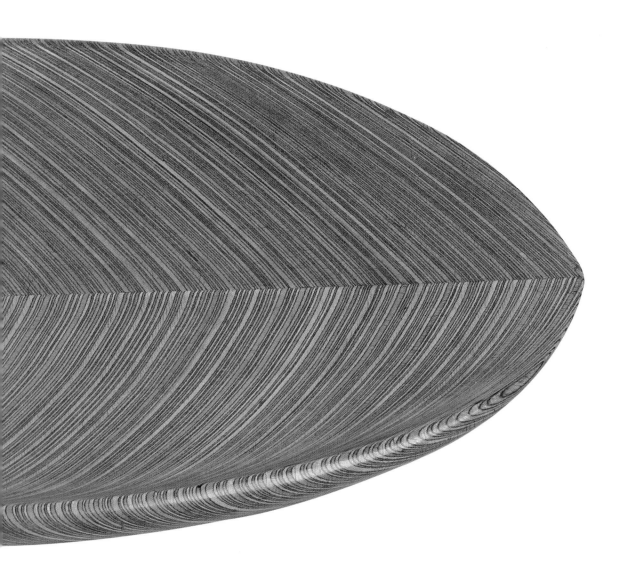

**Tapio Wirkkala** is one of Finland's most influential designers of the twentieth-century, with a staggeringly versatile approach to materials and creative disciplines. His multi-disciplinary talent saw him confidently manipulate glass, ceramic, wood and metal, and apply them to tableware, lighting, furniture, appliances and exhibition design. His advance into plywood experimentation came about in 1948 after an inspiring visit to the factory of the Soinne family in Helsinki, who manufactured plywood for aircraft propellers. Plywood is made from thin sheets of wood (usually birch) that are glued on top of each other at right angles. The characteristic dark lines are created by the adhesive holding the sheets together. Wirkkala experimented with both clear and coloured glues and woods of various tones and thicknesses to allow him to introduce and control new veins and streaks throughout the surface patterning, as seen in this leaf-shaped platter. The Leaf Dish was one of his first plywood objects, made with his assistant Martti Lindqvist and were made as one-off pieces. He used the plywood for larger sculptures as well. As Wirkkala grew more confident with the material and its capabilities, he applied his technique to furniture, while investing a lot of his time carving nature-inspired sculptures of spiral or vortex

'La Conca' Flatware (1951)
Gio Ponti (1891–1979)
Argenteria Krupp/Fraser 1951 to 1960s

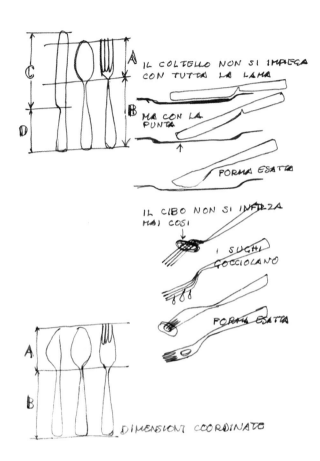

**In his 1951** 'La Conca' Flatware, Gio Ponti applied his intuitive awareness of the possibilities of cutlery design within an Italian functionalist idiom. The tableware consists of basic pared-down forms combined with a beauty in the clarity of line and shape displaying its innovation. For over fifty years Gio Ponti successfully championed modern Italian design, not only through his own work as an architect and designer, but also through the magazines he directed, *Domus* and *Stile*. Ponti, like rationalist Italian designers of the 1920s and 1930s, sought to achieve a synthesis between the strong tradition of Italian classicism and the simple structural logic demanded by the increasingly influential international machine age. This was a middle ground proposed by the Futurists that lay between historicism and the design vocabulary of the industrialists. Ponti's work drew heavily on the legacy of the Wiener Werkstätte and the Vienna Secession, and this flatware is the perfect example of the stripped-down minimal form of Neoclassicism, similar to the work of Josef Hoffmann, and the more organic shapes seen in the bowls of the spoon and fork and the curved line of the knife blade. The linear profile of this flatware reveals Ponti's architectural credentials. Each piece in the set possesses a sophisticated simplicity that is particularly visible in the elongated triangular handles. When Ponti launched the design it marked a key departure in styling from both the stainless steel flatware that was being produced in traditional designs as well as the new avant-garde designs coming from America, Scandinavia and Germany. This flatware cutlery includes Ponti's innovative fork-spoon or *forchetta-cucchiaio*. With shortened tines and a deepened bowl the utensil was designed to catch sauce, such an essential ingredient in Italian cuisine. The wedge-shaped profile of the knife blade is a further example of Ponti's design principles; the shape was born from Ponti's observations that the protracted length of blade on traditional knife forms was suited only to the cutting of meat.

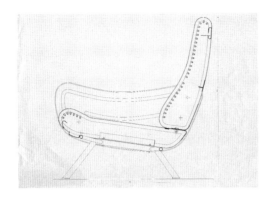

**Marco Zanuso's** Lady Armchair became an instant success when it was introduced in 1951. The chair's organic form, with its kidney-shaped armrest elements and its playful style, became an emblem of much 1950s furniture and graphic design. The Lady Armchair design featured a metal frame combined with injection-moulded polyurethane foam padding and a polyester fibre with an adhesive velveteen and employed a breakthrough method to join the fabric seat to the frame. The chair's reinforced elastic strap is another Zanuso innovation, and an integral part of this legendary design. In 1948 Pirelli opened a new division, Arflex, to design seating with foam-rubber upholstery and commissioned Zanuso to produce its first models. His brief was to investigate the potential of *gommapiuma* (foam latex) as a suitable material for upholstery. His Antropus Chair, first produced by Arflex, came out in 1949, followed by the Lady Armchair, which won first prize at the 1951 Milan Triennale. Zanuso was able to use this new material to sculpt forms, creating visually interesting contours. Zanuso himself lauded the new material, 'One could revolutionize not only the system of upholstery, but also the structural manufacturing and formal potential. Our prototypes acquired visually exciting and new contours with industrial standards that were previously unimaginable.' Zanuso's relationship with Arflex reflects his dedication to analysing materials and techniques to maintain high quality in mass production. The Lady Armchair's embodiment of these ideals means it is still in production by Arflex today.

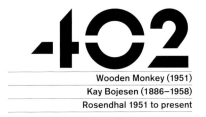

Wooden Monkey (1951)
Kay Bojesen (1886–1958)
Rosendhal 1951 to present

**Designer Kay Bojesen's nickname** in his native Denmark was 'the man who loved to play', so it comes as no surprise that his most enduring design is a toy monkey. An impish chimp made of richly toned teak with a round belly and oblong horizontal face of lighter limba wood, Bojesen's creation was targeted at children who were four and five – the designer's favourite audience, as they were situated between the fantasy of early childhood and the intellectual curiosity of older children. Having grown up in a lively, humour-filled home (his father was a famous publisher and renowned prankster) Bojesen retained a desire to encourage children to stretch their imaginations and remind adults of simple forgotten pleasures. Long of arm, with hands and feet perfectly designed to hang from branches real or imaginary, the Wooden Monkey was created in Bojesen's woodshop by skilled craftsmen who executed his designs carefully. Sturdy and virtually unbreakable in structure, Bojesen's Monkey was never intended to look like a real animal, but to suggest the characteristics of one through a series of exaggerated features that released a child's own imagination. The monkey was the member of a trio that included a bear and elephant which also bore the hallmarks of slightly elongated traits. Bojesen received his first order for 1,000 chimps after showing a prototype to the managing director of the Danish design showroom Den Permanente. Although the chimp went on to become a Danish emblem, the toy was initially rejected by Denmark's official Selection Committee for Better Tourist Articles because monkeys are not an indigenous animal. In a typically humorous response, Bojesen responded that he could, in fact, easily name several Danish monkeys, and that last he checked there were no such thing as real mermaids swimming in Danish waters. Bojesen's chimp, as a result, cleverly swings on today.

**The sweeping S-shape** of André Bloc's Bellevue Chair hints at the fact that Bloc was a sculptor and architect as well as a furniture designer. The elegant tongue of wood is clearly the most important aspect of the chair, with the steel legs merely providing support for the flowing plywood form. Born in Algiers, Bloc settled in Meudon, near Paris, in the 1940s, where he built his own house. It was for this house, known as Bellevue, hence the name, that Bloc designed this chair. Now a highly desirable collectors' piece, the chair only had a very limited production run in 1951. An advertisement for the chair in *L'Architecture d'aujord'hui*, a journal set up by Bloc with Robert Mallet-Stevens and Pierre Chareau, described it as 'very light', 'easily assembled' and available in 'all shades'. Besides this chair, Bloc designed very little other furniture. Indeed, his reputation as a furniture designer was so slight that, in 1953, when George Nelson produced his era-defining *Chairs* book, Bloc's name was nowhere to be seen, despite the Bellevue chair being clearly illustrated. While almost every other illustration was accompanied by a designer's name, Bloc's chair was only listed as 'Produced in France'. The moulded plywood construction of the chair, although not entirely new, was ambitious nonetheless. To have a single piece of wood function as both the seat of the chair and a leg was an audacious approach, but it allowed Bloc to realize his vision of pure form. While the manufacture of the wooden portion of the chair was something of a technical feat (and therefore made the chair relatively expensive), the steel legs were a more basic component. Attached to the underside of the wood beneath the seat and behind the front, leg-forming section, the steel provides a remarkable contrast to the soft, warm appearance of the plywood. Other plywood chairs of the period might be more interesting from a practical viewpoint, but few are as impressive when it comes to their eloquence of expression.

TETRA PAK

**The journey** of Tetra Pak, from patent application to scaled production of a tetrahedron-shaped milk container, spanned nearly a decade and required radical innovations in everything from plastics, paper and printing to machinery, production and distribution. In early 1940s Sweden, milk was still largely sold 'loose' through dedicated shops rather than in the more expensive glass bottles beginning to appear in the first supermarkets. While the search for alternative packaging remained important because of wartime shortages of glass, any meaningful impact on distribution and sales required a solution of greater convenience at no added cost. Tetra Pak delivered this, and as a result triggered a revolution in the delivery of packaged milk that stretched from Sweden to some of the remotest regions of the world. Dr Ruben Rausing, the founder of Tetra Park with Erik Wallenberg, established Tetra Pak AB, in Lund, Sweden in 1951. The first Tetra Pak machine for the tetrahedron-shaped cartons was delivered to Lund in September 1952, and by 1959, one billion cartons per year were being produced. The striking shape was both formed and filled in an innovative single process. Long narrow sheets of coated paper were curled continuously to form an equivalent cylindrical length that was

then stamped shut at perpendicular angles and at regular intervals. The constant flow of milk pouring into this cylindrical length was packaged as intermittent clamps sealed first the base, and then the top at opposing right angles. By sealing each package with pressure from the outside-inward, Tetra Pak created a continuous-fill, automated packaging process that ensured a uniform quantity in each package. The air-free packages removed the possibility for the milk to foam and, most importantly, gave it a longer shelf-life. Risk of contamination was significantly reduced as the packaging machinery was never in direct contact with either the milk or the interior lining. Another challenge in realizing the Tetra Pak vision was finding the right paper. In 1944, when plastics were young and plastic-coated paper unknown, Tetra Pak worked alongside DuPont to create an impermeable, strong packaging material for consumable liquids that was also odourless, tasteless and printable. It is a testament to Tetra Pak's ingenuity and innovation that, to this day, the company remains the world's largest supplier of packaging, and the many subsequent forms of the 'Tetra Pak' remain rooted in some of these earliest innovations.

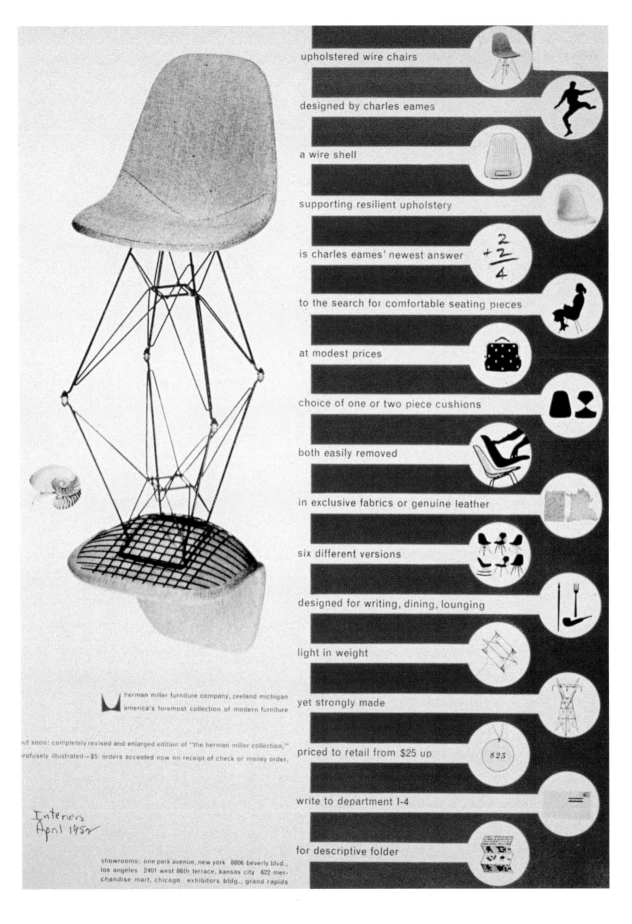

upholstered wire chairs

designed by charles eames

a wire shell

supporting resilient upholstery

is charles eames' newest answer

$$\begin{array}{r} 2 \\ +2 \\ \hline 4 \end{array}$$

to the search for comfortable seating pieces

at modest prices

choice of one or two piece cushions

both easily removed

in exclusive fabrics or genuine leather

six different versions

designed for writing, dining, lounging

light in weight

yet strongly made

priced to retail from $25 up

write to department I-4

for descriptive folder

herman miller furniture company, zeeland michigan
america's foremost collection of modern furniture

out soon: completely revised and enlarged edition of "the herman miller collection,"
profusely illustrated—$5. orders accepted now on receipt of check or money order.

Interiors
April 1952

showrooms: one park avenue, new york  8806 beverly blvd.,
los angeles  2401 west 86th terrace, kansas city  622 merchandise mart, chicago  exhibitors bldg., grand rapids

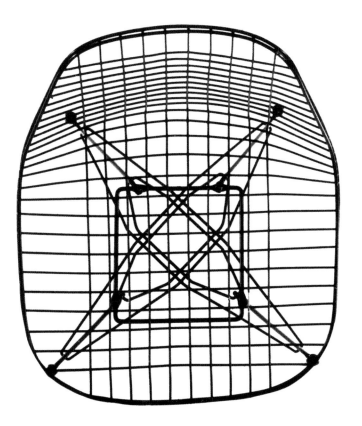

range of bases, to suit a wide variety of applications. The most iconic of these bases is the 'Eiffel Tower' base, which creates a dramatic vision of fine cross-hatching of chrome or black steel. The use of the new technology of resistance-welding in furniture design expressed a futurist vision through lightness and form. Although there is still some debate over whose design came first, the Charles and Ray Eameses' chair or Harry Bertoia's mesh furniture for Knoll, the first American mechanical patent was awarded to the Eames design. Charles and Ray Eames led the international postwar design period with industrially produced furniture designs and systems for seating. Using a manufacturing base that was unaffected by the war, they utilized technology to create rational and sculptural designs, advocating organic Modernism. Their revolutionary designs made Herman Miller a world leader in the production of office and domestic furniture. The couple went on to excel in the creation of film and exhibition design. The Wire Chair proved to be immediately successful and the international market for this now timeless design remains strong.

# 399

Wire Chair (1951)
Charles Eames (1907–78)
Ray Eames (1912–88)
Herman Miller 1951 to 1967
Vitra 1958 to present

**The transparency** of this single-piece seat proposes a sculptural quality rarely seen in postwar furniture design. The influence of fine art is often considered secondary to the industrial processes and ideology of systems favoured by Charles and Ray Eames. However, in this instance, the piece's artistic value combines with its industrial process to achieve its landmark status. The artistic input of Ray Eames is married with the more engineering sensibilities provided by Charles to create a design of balanced values from both disciplines. The Wire Chair falls within a series of wire-based designs and is closely related to earlier fibreglass side-chairs, such as the DAR (1948), and the DSR (1950). Although its outline is almost identical to the shell of the DSR and other models from this range, the Wire Chair is characterized by quite a different technology. The Wire Chair is symbolic of the success of the couple's design philosophy. The organic form offers comfort without the need for upholstery, although the chair readily accepted seat or back pads, which also create a beautiful pattern. It is a design that may be translated via an interchangeable

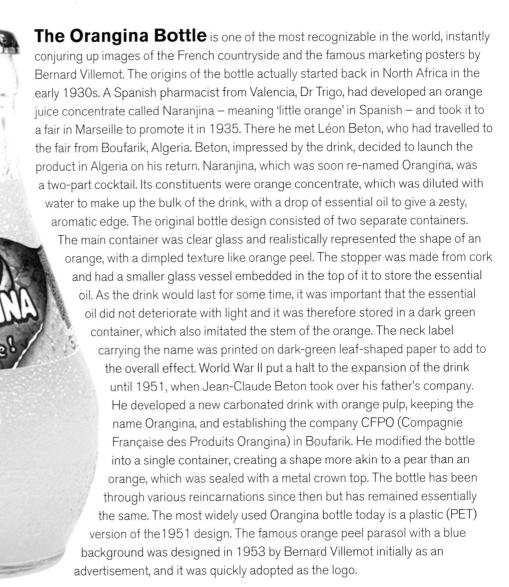

**The Orangina Bottle** is one of the most recognizable in the world, instantly conjuring up images of the French countryside and the famous marketing posters by Bernard Villemot. The origins of the bottle actually started back in North Africa in the early 1930s. A Spanish pharmacist from Valencia, Dr Trigo, had developed an orange juice concentrate called Naranjina – meaning 'little orange' in Spanish – and took it to a fair in Marseille to promote it in 1935. There he met Léon Beton, who had travelled to the fair from Boufarik, Algeria. Beton, impressed by the drink, decided to launch the product in Algeria on his return. Naranjina, which was soon re-named Orangina, was a two-part cocktail. Its constituents were orange concentrate, which was diluted with water to make up the bulk of the drink, with a drop of essential oil to give a zesty, aromatic edge. The original bottle design consisted of two separate containers. The main container was clear glass and realistically represented the shape of an orange, with a dimpled texture like orange peel. The stopper was made from cork and had a smaller glass vessel embedded in the top of it to store the essential oil. As the drink would last for some time, it was important that the essential oil did not deteriorate with light and it was therefore stored in a dark green container, which also imitated the stem of the orange. The neck label carrying the name was printed on dark-green leaf-shaped paper to add to the overall effect. World War II put a halt to the expansion of the drink until 1951, when Jean-Claude Beton took over his father's company. He developed a new carbonated drink with orange pulp, keeping the name Orangina, and establishing the company CFPO (Compagnie Française des Produits Orangina) in Boufarik. He modified the bottle into a single container, creating a shape more akin to a pear than an orange, which was sealed with a metal crown top. The bottle has been through various reincarnations since then but has remained essentially the same. The most widely used Orangina bottle today is a plastic (PET) version of the 1951 design. The famous orange peel parasol with a blue background was designed in 1953 by Bernard Villemot initially as an advertisement, and it was quickly adopted as the logo.

# ORANGINA

Advertisement, 1956, by Bernard Villemot

**One of the primary reasons** for the success of the Bisley Multidrawer Cabinet is the simplicity of its design. An anonymous, almost monolithic block, it blends into any environment, making it ideal for both domestic and office use. Indeed, its seemingly uninspired appearance is the secret of its popularity. Freddy Brown was a sheet-metal worker who started a one-man car repair business in 1931. During World War II, he moved his business to Bisley in Surrey, England, and undertook various defence contracts; among these was the design and manufacture of containers that could be dropped by parachute. After the war, when the company's manufacturing arm was looking dangerously redundant, Bisley used its increased manufacturing capacity to produce office products. The solid and durable construction of its military products was transferred to items like the Multidrawer Cabinet which has remained one of the hallmarks of the brand. The cabinet is made of welded steel and can either stand alone, or be used to support a desktop. It is available in a variety of configurations, with drawers mounted on ball-bearing slides to provide a smooth and efficient action. In 1963, Bisley ceased its car-repair activities and focused exclusively on the manufacture of steel office equipment. Today it is the largest manufacturer of office furniture in the UK, recording sales of £76.7 million in 2001.

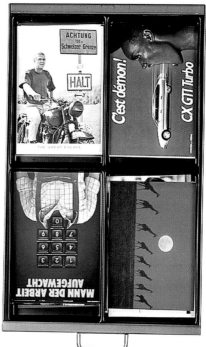

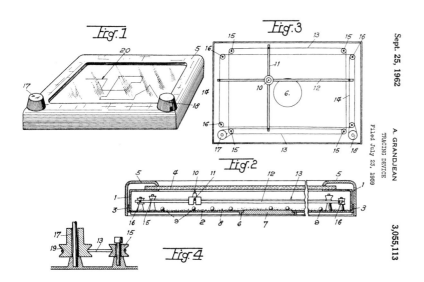

**Invented in the 1950s** by Arthur Granjean, the Etch A Sketch, as it would soon become known, is an unmistakable icon. In fact, it would be as difficult to find someone unfamiliar with its bold red frame as it is to draw a circle on its entrancing grey screen. The simple red frame with its two large white knobs make the Etch A Sketch look like a flat TV set. Yet beneath its minimal exterior the Etch A Sketch hides quite complex engineering. Thousands of tiny plastic beads and aluminum powder exist behind the glass screen. The two white turning knobs individually control vertical and horizontal rods, which meet to move a stylus. The stylus scrapes the screen as it moves through the powder, leaving a bold line behind. When the toy is shaken the powder is remixed, clearing the screen for new work. In 1959 Granjean presented the toy at the International Toy Fair in Nuremburg, under the name 'Magic Screen' ('L'Ecran Magique'). Although it was initially overlooked, the Ohio Art Company eventually agreed to produce the toy and it became a selling sensation when it was launched just in time for the 1960 Christmas season. To enthusiastic children the Etch A Sketch appeared to defy explanation. By turning the knobs on the front of the toy, a line would magically move about the screen. No pencil or crayon was needed and when the toy was shaken the image would magically disappear. The possibilities for creativity were limitless, yet for most users the toy was as much a puzzle as a medium for artistic expression. For, no matter how hard one tried, the joys of curvature seemed unattainable. There are now several different types available, including the angular Zooper, a modern purple version complete with sound effects. There is the smaller Hot Pocket and even tinier versions on key rings, but the original red and white Etch A Sketch still retains its magic after all these years. With patience, apparently, it is even possible to draw a curve: details of how to achieve this are listed on the official Etch A Sketch website.

No. 505 ETCH-A-SKETCH

No. 505 Etch-A-Sketch is an absorbing new toy that's fun, and educational . . . truly a toy for all ages. Manipulate the knobs to form letters, pictures, charts, designs — whatever the imagination dictates. Turn the Etch-A-Sketch upside down, shake it, and the printing disappears.

This original Ohio Art toy made of plastic and glass, is approximately 9½" wide, 7⅝" high and 1¼" thick. Each in a box. One-half dozen to the carton. 7 lbs.

Fascinating
FAMILY FUN!

THE OHIO ART COMPANY, Bryan, Ohio

New York Office
200 Fifth Avenue Building
Suite 852

**The process of aerating red** wine has been well known for centuries. The necessary design requirements for the purpose of any decanter is to enable the maximum amount of air to reach the largest surface area of wine, allowing aromas to be released and flavour improved. The larger the surface of the wine exposed, the more efficient the process. The bulbous form of the hand-blown Carafe Surcouf, with its slender and elongated neck leading to the vast and squat chamber, responds to this requirement. This surprising contrast between straight neck and rounded organic body set the Carafe Surcouf apart from earlier decanters, and yet it was a product of pure mechanical function. Previously, wine decanters had employed a more fluid and sympathetic line between components, much more akin to the form of a traditional bottle. The combined efficiency and modernity of the crystalline Carafe Surcouf made it the favourite decanter among both professional and amateur sommeliers. The widely copied Carafe Surcouf form is now a familiar one, with interpretations of the design found in the catalogues of most glass and crystal manufacturers. The Carafe Surcouf began on St. Vincent's Turning Day, the famous event for wine tasting in Burgundy. The technician glassmakers at La Rochère decided not to create a cork, joking that they carafe was made to be emptied – which is why it lacks a stopper. The curious name for the decanter , which has an impressive capacity of 150 cl (2.6 pt) was borrowed from one of France's most distinguished vessels. At the beginning of World War II, the Surcouf was the world's largest submarine, which belonged to the French navy, and it featured a vast storage chamber. The comparisons of form between the submarine and the decanter make for an interesting parallel, and an anecdotal story. Alongside more contemporary mass production methods, La Rochère still employ the hand-blown method of glass manufacture which dates back to 1475.

# 394

Trapèze Table (1950)
Jean Prouvé (1901–84)
Ateliers Jean Prouvé 1950
Tecta 1990 to 2000
Vitra 2002 to present

**Sculptural simplicity** and mass-production methods are hallmarks of Jean Prouvé's work. Both are well represented in the Trapèze Table, originally designed, like the Antony Chair, for the university campus in Antony, France. The table's name refers to the distinctive shape of its paired legs, constructed from lacquered black sheet steel and reminiscent of aircraft wings. Combined with the thick, obliquely canted edges of the black laminate tabletop, the legs emphasize the apparent massiveness of the construction. It would be difficult to find another table in twentieth-century furniture design that summarizes industrial chic in the same was as the Trapèze. Its large size means it can function as a dining table or in the office as a conference table or in sales areas. When asked in 1970 by Bernard Oudin, author of *Dictionnaire des Architectes*, to describe his profession, Prouvé said, 'I am not an architect, I am not an engineer. I am a factory man.' Yet Le Corbusier stated that Prouvé embodied a combination of architect and builder, since everything he conceived was 'a stylish plastic form with physical problems of resistance and manufacturing brilliantly solved.' Prouvé had a lifelong dedication and belief in creating democratic design via an industrial aesthetic. He was a champion of affordable modern furniture and housing, a pioneer of prefabrication, and worked towards solving France's postwar housing shortage. His furniture pieces reflect his architectural style, using clean, straightforward lines with an attention to techniques like electric welding and folding sheet metal. Although many of Prouvé's designs were created for French universities, their use has been adapted through the years, helping them to become enduring icons. In particular, Vitra's recent reissuing of the Trapèze Table, among other pieces, has meant that Prouvé's furniture has left the realm of the collector to return to one of mass production.

First Diners Card, 1950

# 393

Diners Club Card (1950)
Frank McNamara (1917–1957)
Diners Club Design Team
Diners Club International 1950 to present

First American Express Credit Card, 1958

American Express McQueen Gold Card

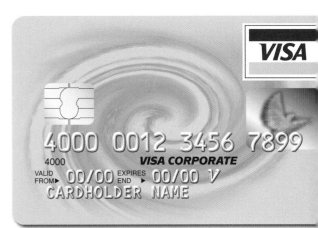

Visa Corporate Silver Card

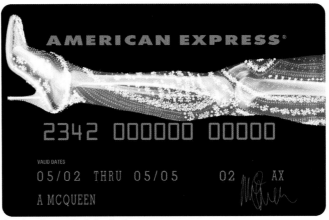

American Express Centurion Card

Film poster of *The Man from the Diner's Club*, 1963, starring Danny Kaye (right), directed by Frank Tashlin

**Credit has existed** as long as money has existed, if not longer. The concept of paying later is, however, based on trust and if the deal-making parties do not know each other, then the vendor is far more likely to want to see cash up front. This was precisely the problem faced by Frank McNamara in 1949 when, receiving the bill for a meal in a New York restaurant, he discovered that he had left his wallet at home. His wife paid for the meal, but the incident prompted McNamara to look for a solution; as a successful businessman, he could afford the meal easily, but he simply did not have the cash on him. And as a businessman, McNamara grasped that he would not be alone in this dilemma and that a big opportunity existed. Thus Diners Club was created, and the first Diners Club Card – literally a card, since it was made of cardboard – was used at the very same restaurant in February 1950. Effectively, the credit card demonstrates that the holder is a member of an organization that will pay a business for goods or services up front, on the understanding that the holder will repay the lending organization, with interest, later. In this way, it reduces the risk to the retailer. The name stems from the card's original purpose, to permit business people to pay for meals in restaurants. The first card was distributed to two hundred of McNamara's friends and colleagues, and was accepted by fourteen New York restaurants. However, it rapidly became clear that the idea had scores of applications and could be used to pay for just about anything and everything. At first Diners Club expanded with the needs of travelling salesmen in mind, and was soon accepted by airlines, hotels, and restaurants across the United States. Although its market dominance has dwindled through the years, it remains the first example of its kind. And thanks to its initial applications, it imbued all credit cards with a psychological link to glamorous activities such as travel and dining out, which was inevitably a factor in their huge success.

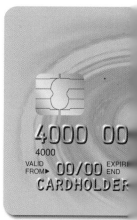

Visa Business Gold Card

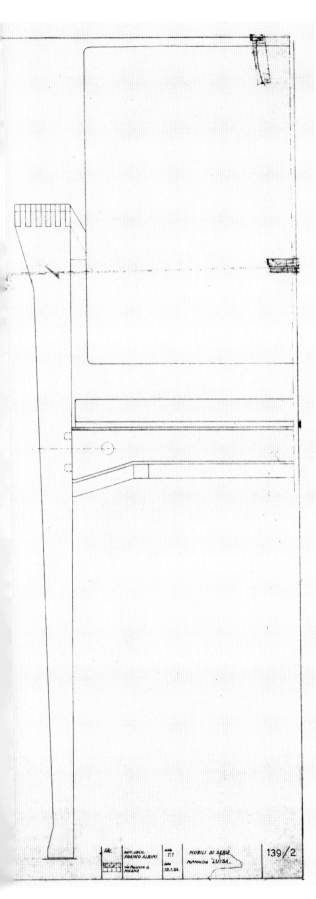

**392**
Luisa Chair (1950)
Franco Albini (1905–77)
Poggi 1950 to present

**The stark** angularity of Franco Albini's Luisa Chair could lead a viewer to think that here was a minimalist designer who liked to imbue his designs with the rigorous austerity of modernist architectural practice. In actual fact such thinking couldn't be further from the truth. Albini did indeed study architecture at the Polytechnic of Milan before setting up an individual practice to become what many consider to be the most important of the Italian neo-rationalist designers, and his work helped to herald in a style of furniture design that combined the new forms of modernism with a more traditional artisanship. But the beauty of his design ideas lay in their diversity and versatility. Here was a man unwilling to adhere to a single stylistic solution and limited materials. Instead Albini chose to design with a range of materials, including steel wires and canvas in a 1943 chair, metal and glass (for the hugely innovative Securit Wireless Set of 1938) and rattan as well as the hardwoods for the Luisa. All these designs were underpinned by a sensitivity to the materials and an understanding of structure, but the key aspect of Albini's design was his enthusiastic and successful marrying of the new (ie, modernism), with the old (the craft traditions and the skills of the artisan). Nowhere is this more evident than in the Luisa, which displays a spartan, rationalist clarity combined with sensitivity to context. An elegant design whose formal, expressive lines are unimpeded by unnecessary decoration, the Luisa's dramatic profile and ergonomic rigorousness demonstrates Albini's commitment to architectonic forms, and his consistently unorthodox approach to, and successful balance, of issues of construction and form. Produced by Poggi, the Luisa Chair won a coveted Compasso d'Oro prize in 1955. It was the first of three such prizes Albini would go on to win.

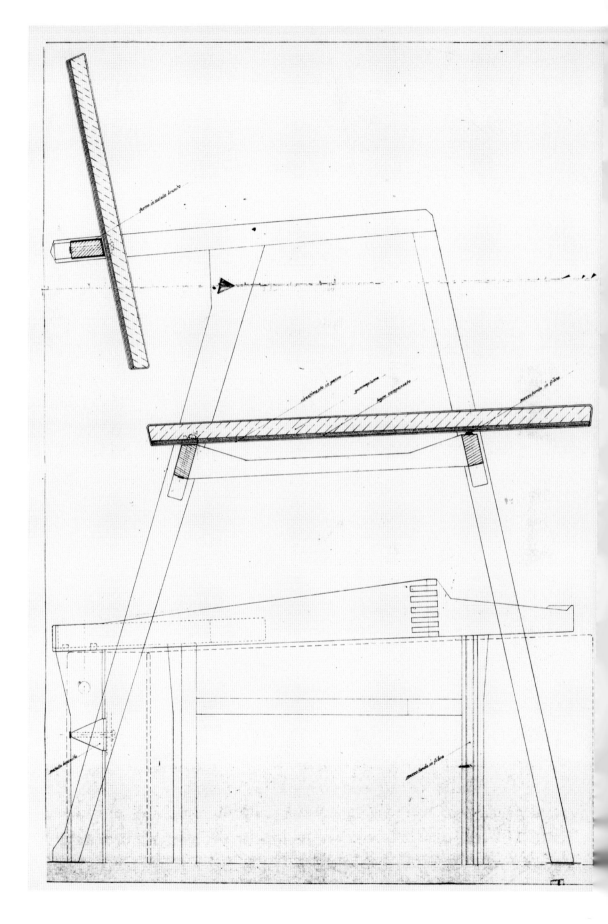

Florence Knoll

# 391

Stool (1950)
Florence Knoll (1917–)
Knoll 1950 to 1970

**This Stool is distinctly** different from other furniture pieces designed by Florence Knoll. The linear metal base supporting a simple geometric top is a common format in her furniture. She consistently incorporated innovative manufacturing techniques, minimal structures, concise geometry and simple forms beautifully proportioned. Her design discipline in all of her work ensured fully resolved details and a sophisticated balance of materials, each utilized for their potential. What is unusual about this piece is the more playful character of the running line formed by the enamelled bent metal tube, playing with negative and positive spaces. The resulting form echoes drum lacings, or suggests the outline of implied solid legs. These allusions are uncommon in Knoll's furniture pieces, which are typically strong articulations of a planned programme. In fact, the running line is very functional, as one continuous line becomes both foot and top support, but the resulting feel of this piece is different from her better-known works. This lightweight, stackable stool also functioned as a side table. Versatility was a common characteristic of her furniture, particularly of her stools, tables and benches. Designed in 1950, while she was married to Hans Knoll, its expressive form anticipates the hairpin furniture of the decade ahead. Today, this association to a particular era situates the stool in the realm of period collectables, particularly since the stool is no longer in production. Known for her extraordinary space planning talents and superb ability to reshape difficult interior spaces, Knoll never considered herself a furniture designer. She explained that she designed furniture in response to the needs generated by a specific plan and particular patterns of use and regarded her furniture as a component within a larger architectural programme. She loved the challenges that spaces presented, preferring the idiosyncrasies of older, less homogenous buildings than the regularity of modular spaces. It is worth noting that Florence Knoll not only redefined the modern office space, including its furnishings, but also the design profession itself.

Magnum Champagne Glass No. 15881 (1950)
Cristalleries de Baccarat Design Team
Cristalleries de Baccarat 1950 to 1960s

**The Cristalleries de Baccarat** was founded in 1764 in Lorraine, France, by the Bishop Montmorency-Laval of Metz under the patronage of Louis XV, and established a tradition in manufacturing the highest quality luxury opaline glassware. It started producing crystal in 1816 and became famous for producing opalines and pressed bowls. In comparison with normal glass, crystal is preferred for its radiance, its particular sound when tapped and its light-reflecting qualities. King Louis XVIII commissioned the first complete crystal glass service in 1823. From 1949 Baccarat added a range of contemporary pieces to its catalogue of traditional products, and began a programme of working with some of the world's most respected and innovative designers, such as Roberto Sambonet, Ettore Sottsass and Philippe Starck. The Magnum Champagne Glass No. 15881 was designed and first produced in 1950 and perfectly illustrates the Baccarat approach to quality crystal glassware. The glass is a classic form and shape. With a simple foot, stem and bowl, the Magnum Champagnne Glass easily fits into any typology of traditional glassware. It uses the highest quality crystal glass and stands at a conventional 11 cm (4.5 in) high, but, in keeping with its name, the stem supports a colossal bowl with a 15 cm (6 in) diameter. The visual effect is stunning, but the design is also practical as it allows the bubbles to rise and the scent to be enjoyed while the flavour is savoured. Champagne goblets are believed to have been invented when Marie Antoinette took a mould of her breast, and the Magnum Champagne Glass could well be seen as a direct descendant of this original shape.

**Good industrial design** is characterized by suitability to purpose, material, process of manufacture and aesthetics. Industrial objects in the home can be conceived as units of architectural equipment, which make up a whole domestic living space. Following the principles of early twentieth-century modern architecture, household objects had a machine-like quality, smooth surfaces and an absence of adornment. Based on utility, the modern view was that industrial design was functionally motivated and followed the same principle of simplicity as architecture. Useful designs had to be available to all, and therefore easy to manufacture and inexpensive. The Whisk, as an example of good industrial design for home use, combines purity of form with economic efficiency. Whisks are used to blend ingredients into a smooth liquid or frothy consistency by whipping air into the mixture. Varying in length and shape, there are whisks for use in different mixtures, such as gravies, creams, sauces and eggs. The Whisk consists of a narrow handle, usually made from stainless steel, bamboo or copper, with a series of stiff wire loops joined at the handle. The wires were originally metal but today, plastic is used for non-stick cookware. The looping of the wires, so they cross and overlap at the base, forms a cage that maximizes the aeration of the liquid mixture, and makes the Whisk flexible enough so that it can be pressed against the bowl sides, enabling the mixture to be thinned and separated easily. The thin cylindrical wires of the loops decrease the metal surface area and cause the liquid to flow and divide freely over the Whisk, allowing it to become quickly and evenly mixed. The equal weight distribution of the wires also facilitates easy stirring. The light stainless steel material makes whipping less tiring than if a nineteenth-century iron egg-beater or a less efficient fork was used. Additionally, Whisks are handcrafted using tensile strength stainless steel wire. Each wire is soldered and sealed into the handle, making the Whisk durable and preventing the mixture and water from entering the handle. A combination of good performance with timeless design and cost-efficiency has ensured that the Whisk remains an unchanged and much used industrial household object, even today.

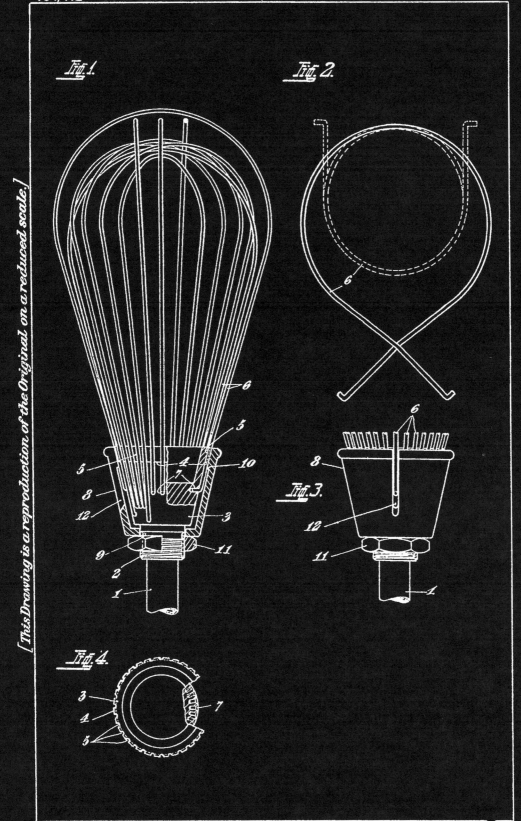

*Fig. 1.*

*Fig. 2.*

*Fig. 3.*

*Fig. 4.*

**Today's mass-produced** self-assembly furniture owes much to the systematic design approach of architect and designer Hans Gugelot. His M125 'knock-down' system of modular units, which customers could mix and match in a wide array of combinations, was first designed in 1950. Gugelot found in Rudolf Graber, owner of the Zurich-based Wohnbedarf Company, a patron for his early designs. But it was not until 1956 that German firm Wilhelm Bofinger took an improved version into large-scale production. Fundamental to Gugelot's idea was the principle of multiples of 125 mm (4.9 in) as the basis of efficient storage. For instance, 250 mm (9.8 in) was the ideal depth for bookshelves, while 1250 mm (49 in) was the optimum width for a cabinet or shelves. The concept promised users functional and endlessly flexible furniture at a reasonable price, while the producer would benefit from simpler, machine-based manufacturing processes and far lower transport and storage costs because they were making only flat elements that customers would assemble themselves to suit their own requirements. But such thinking was a culture shock to Bofinger, a traditional joinery and carpentry operation with no mass-production experience and a plant lacking both ground-floor facilities and lifts. Nevertheless, manufacturer and designer worked through lengthy trial and error to turn the initial, rather complicated iteration, with its glued plywood parts and prefabricated doorframes, into a viable product. When the system was eventually premiered at a 1957 '8. Deutsche Industrieausstellung' Berlin trade show, it was still so untried that the display model was held together with a precautionary nail. M125's development paralleled a significant new movement in German design. From 1953, a scientific, rational approach emerged from the Hochschule für Gestaltung in Ulm, where Gugelot lectured from 1954. The simple forms, muted colours and systematic thinking the school advocated are embodied in M125, whose stark, PVC-clad lines, while not an instant hit, began to find favour from 1960 onwards. Gugelot continued to collaborate with Bofinger until his untimely death in 1965.

757,372  COMPLETE SPECIFICATION
2 SHEETS  This drawing is a reproduction of
the Original on a reduced scale.
SHEETS 1 & 2

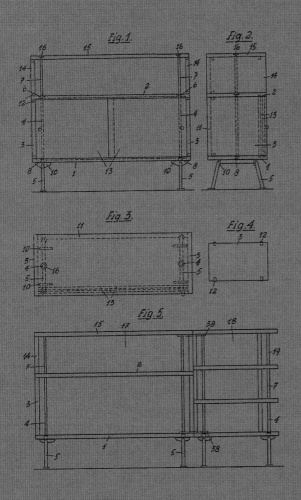

Fig.1. Fig.2. Fig.3. Fig.4. Fig.5.

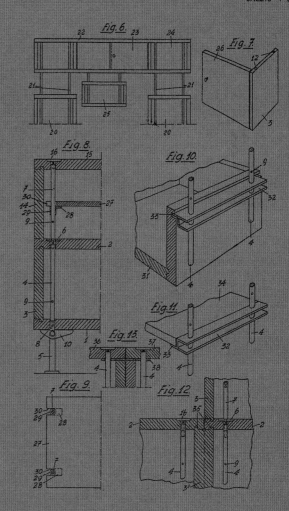

Fig.6. Fig.7. Fig.8. Fig.9. Fig.10. Fig.11. Fig.12. Fig.13.

**388**

M125 Modular System (1950)
Hans Gugelot (1920–65)
Wilhelm Bofinger 1956 to 1973
Habit Ulrich Lodholz 1974 to 1988

# 387

Ice Cube Tray (1950)
Arthur J Frei (1900–71)
Inland Manufacturing (General Motors)
1950 to 1960s
Various 1960s to present

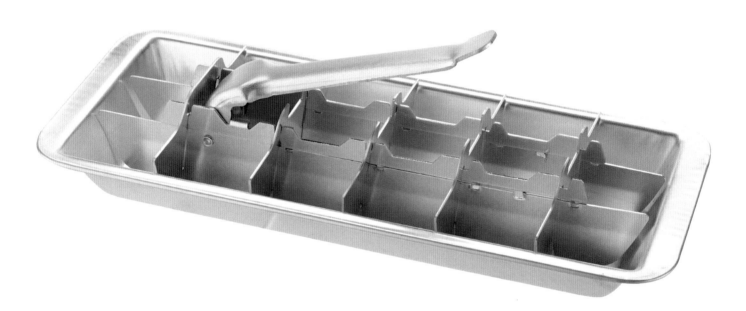

in 1914 featured an ice cube tray. It is then that ice for domestic use must have changed its shape, from big ice bars whose vital purpose was to preserve food inside the ice box, to the more mundane little cubes used to keep drinks chilled. The glamour of Ingrid Bergman drinking champagne with Humphrey Bogart in *Casablanca* is, to some extent, enhanced by the ice cubes chilling their sultry night. Frei worked at Inland well into the 1960s and by the end of a career that saw him rise to the position of chief engineer, he was the proud inventor of twenty-three patents for a variety of Ice Cube Trays. The city of Dayton, Iowa, where Inland Manufacturing was based, is renowned as the innovation capital of the world, and has immortalized the Ice Cube Tray by building a monument to it on its Inventors River Walk, next to the Wright Flyer, the Pop Top Cans and the Cash Register.

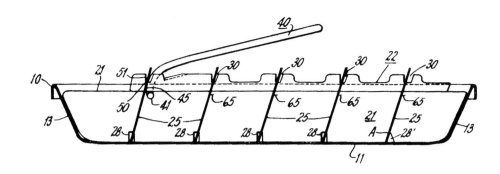

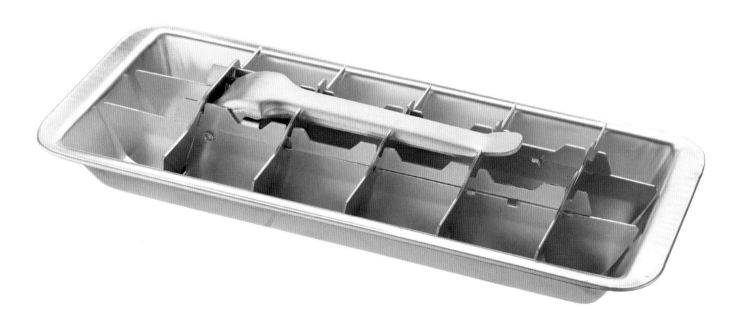

**During World War II,** as manufacturing became difficult due to the shortage of essential materials used for defence purposes, Inland Manufacturing Division of General Motors helped the US war effort by producing one of the most famous carbines of the war. When the war finished, Inland resumed its original appliance accessories production and Arthur J Frei, an engineer at Inland since 1931, returned to his position. By 1950, Frei patented a freezing tray that was destined to become an indispensable fixture in most modern households. The Ice Cube Tray consists of a container pan and a partitioning grid that is activated by a hand lever, thus mechanically dislodging the ice cubes. The simplicity of his design has endured technical and material innovation and is still produced today. Although Frei's design became famous, ice cube trays were invented earlier than 1950; the first household refrigerator invented

# 386

Ulmer Hocker (1950)
Max Bill (1908–94)
Hans Gugelot (1920–65)
Zanotta 1975 to present
Wohnbedarf Zurich 1993 to 2003
Vitra 2003 to present

**As a piece of postwar furniture,** Max Bill's Ulmer Hocker stool of 1950 perhaps stands on its own as a design committed to the inherent values of prewar modernist Functionalism, having little affinity with its more organically conceived, 1950s avant-garde contemporaries. Constructed of ebonized wood in a simple triplanar form and detailed only with one cylindrical, off-set footrest, the stool, one of Bill's best-known products, is an articulation of geometric, architectural clarity. The design context in which the stool was conceived underlines the tension of German design development during this period. An important centre for design debate was the Hochschule für Gestaltung, the design school at Ulm (then, West Germany), of which the Swiss-born Bill was one of its founders in 1951, and also its first rector. Bill's own studies and training before the war were fundamental to the ethos of the school. After studying at the Bauhaus, Bill adopted the concept of 'concrete art'. This firm belief that structural and visual clarity moved form towards universal appreciation shaped both Bill's teaching and his design work throughout the 1950s. At Ulm, Bill and his colleagues initially promoted a curriculum predicated upon a new Bauhaus model. However, by the end of the decade, Bill's philosophy of design and education increasingly were at odds with a younger generation of students and teachers, now committed to a curriculum with greater emphasis on theoretical ideologies. The result of Bill's didactic approach was an extreme geometry in his own work; indeed, the severity of his designs attracted criticism that they lacked humanizing qualities. The Ulmer Hocker was a product of his tenure at the school. The stool continues to be produced by the Milan furniture manu-facturer Zanotta, and it is now offered in varnished, layered birch or black lacquered MDF, and marketed under the name Sgabillo.

Students at Hochschule für Gestaltung, Ulm

Sugar Dispenser (1950s)
Designer Unknown
Various 1950s to present

**The success** of the sugar dispenser design is evident in both its continuing popularity today and its ubiquitous presence. As postwar rationing was finally lifted in 1954, there was a widespread desire to celebrate the end of austerity and the arrival of a new age. Café culture gained popularity on both sides of the Atlantic, and the sugar dispenser owed much of its design to the style of the diner. With its chrome lid and roughened glass, the dispenser matches the diner's widespread use of steel and glass in its walls and kitchen splashbacks. Sitting on a counter top or on individual tables, the sugar dispenser would have as a faithful companion a napkin holder, salt and pepper and a squeezable bottle of ketchup. Replacing the conventional bowl of sugar lumps, the free flowing sugar of the dispenser represented a new opulence. While the 1950s age of design allowed for the extravagance of stylish non-essential objects, the dispenser did however have practical aspects: the toughened glass container was sturdy, easy to clean and hygienic, while the chrome-plated shaker directed the flow of sugar. It was a desirable, designed and utilitarian object. A quintessential item of its time, its enduring appeal makes it now a retro kitchenalia mainstay, a design with international status, widely reproduced and copied, and as common in an American diner as in a traditional English café.

large main compartment in which heavy-duty rubber bands hold in place the case's contents, the Topas Briefcase further secures its contents. Compliant with IATA hand luggage standards, its size, leather carrying handles and feet on two sides facilitate transporting it on long flights. Guaranteed for five years, the Topas Briefcase continues to sell well among globetrotters. Having built its place in the attaché case market over half a century, Rimowa has now issued a challenge to its lightness, durability, beauty and ease of transport in a polycarbonate version. Nevertheless, the distinctiveness of Rimowa's ribbed aluminium shell continues to separate the Topas Briefcase from the crowd.

Advertisement, 1950s

**In the middle** of the last century the defining characteristics of a businessman with style and taste occupied a very narrow spectrum of choices, among them blue to brown to grey fabric, brown or black leather, a white or pale-coloured shirt, or subtle changes in the cut of the ever-present suit. Materials frequently defined status and accessories confirmed position. It was in this environment, among a sea of black or brown leather boxes, that Rimowa's Topas business case made its appearance in 1950. Rimowa had begun to introduce aluminium into the structure of luggage in 1937, a year after *Aluminum Newsletter* announced that, 'aluminium has become the speed metal of a new and faster age'. The Rimowa Briefcase and the rest of its family of suitcases declared themselves as symbols of the elite, standing as silvery beacons in the darkness, as emblematic and cutting-edge as a new jet on the runway. Developed in Cologne by Richard Morszeck, the son of Rimowa's founder, the Topas Briefcase, with its trademark ridges that serve to strengthen the ultra-light structure of its aluminium-magnesium shell, combines its machine-age beauty with features that continue to distinguish its design. Conceived to withstand extreme humidity, tropical heat and Arctic cold, this briefcase also includes a removable interior consisting of pockets for pens and business cards and staged compartments for files. With two combination locks and a

**383**

Margrethe Bowl (1950)
Sigvard Bernadotte (1907–2002)
Acton Bjørn (1910–1992)
Rosti Housewares 1950 to present

**Bernadotte and Bjørn,** founded in 1950 by Sigvard Bernadotte (at one time second in line to the Swedish throne) and the architect Acton Bjørn, was the first industrial design consultancy in Scandinavia. Sigvard Bernadotte had the idea for forming such a company and had visited North America to see how the offices of such designer as Walter Dorwin Teague and Raymond Loewy, among others, operated. The set of Margrethe Bowls was one of the company's first major success stories. The name 'Margrethe' poetically referred to the Danish princess, who at that time, had just been crowned. The bowls were at least partly designed by Jacob Jensen (well known for his later work with Bang & Olufsen) who had his first job with Bernadotte and Bjørn after leaving the School of Arts, Crafts and Design in Copenhagen, where he had studied furniture design. The commission to design the Margrethe range came from a plastics manufacturing firm then in its infancy called Rosti. Jensen was given the job by Bernadotte and Bjørn, but told that he should not spend too much time on it because the fee was small. A design was produced making use of studies of function, hence the thin pouring lip on one side, and the fuller side for the hand grip. The resistant thermoset melamine – a material which can confront high temperatures – was used to create the famous weight of the bowl. A demonstration model was made up to show Rosti, which they approved immediately. They then asked Jensen for his advice on the choice of colour and he chose a red close to that used for Japanese lacquers. It was finally offered to the public in 1954, in three sizes, and in the colours of white, pastel green, yellow, and blue. In 1968, the 'Tivoli colours' (olive, orange, red, and mauve), a version with a rubber ring on the base, and five bowl sizes, were brought onto the market. Attempts at improving the design have failed abysmally. At one point Rosti commissioned a study to produce a version that was easier to hold and that offered more stability when mixing. This version was rejected by the public, despite having been demonstrated to be more practical. Over fifty years later, the Margrethe Bowls are still in production, and found in most kitchens in all corners of the world.

**Both the form and material of Fjord Cutlery** by the Danish designer Jens Quistgaard epitomize modern Scandinavian design. First designed as an artisan collection around 1950 its clean lines, flowing forms, pared-down decoration and the use of natural materials are all typical characteristics of Scandinavian design of the mid-twentieth century. Created in stainless steel with teakwood handles, the Fjord pattern demonstrates Quistgaard's expertise in different materials. With a vast range of skills allowing him to design objects in wood, glass and metal, Quistgaard served his apprenticeship at Georg Jensen, the silversmith. Like that of many Danish designers, Quistgaard's work is steeped in the craft traditions of Scandinavia. Strongly sculptural though economical in form, Quistgaard's designs exploit the inherent nature of the materials employed, whether they be natural wood, unglazed stoneware or cast metal, and present a post-industrial craft approach to design. Specializing in metalware, Quistgaard had a passion for Japanese ceramics and a love of wood, in particular teak. He achieved his major recognition in 1954, winning both gold and silver medals at the Milan Triennale and was awarded the Lunning Prize in Copenhagen for the hand-forged knife, fork and spoon of this cutlery. Fjord was simple yet elegant. Despite its seeming simplicity, Quistgaard was told by manufacturers that Fjord was too difficult to produce. However, during a visit to Denmark, New York entrepreneur Ted Nierenberg saw the design and persuaded Quistgaard to allow him to see sources for manufacture. The result was both the successful production of the Fjord Cutlery pattern and the establishment of the company Dansk International Designs, co-founded by Quistgaard and Nierenberg. The Dansk range of products has been synonymous with modern Scandinavian style worldwide for more than three decades, and Quistgaard was one of the principal designers. Extremely successful, Fjord was subsequently manufactured for thirty years, being finally discontinued in 1984. The 1950s saw a revolution in flatware design, mainly with the use of stainless steel to produce elegant and precise forms. With his Fjord design Quistgaard proved that stainless-steel flatware could be beautiful as well as useful.

# 381

LTR (1950)
Charles Eames (1907–78)
Ray Eames (1912–88)
Herman Miller 1950 to present
Vitra Design Museum 2002 to present

**The use of metal rod bases** featured in much of the furniture designed by the Eameses throughout the 1940s and collectively evolved into a signature style for the couple. They never met a material that they did not like, and their inquisitive nature invariably resulted in almost obsessive experimentation. Ease of manufacture was top of the list of priorities when designing any new products and the LTR proved no exception. The Eameses had previously developed a mass-production technique for welding wire rods in the late 1940s. The small occasional table was conceived to suit this manufacturing process, while employing materials already used in furniture production at the time. The reasonable cost for manufacture was typically their primary concern. The supporting structure for the plastic-laminated plywood tabletop reveals its construction with striking visual honesty, an engaging characteristic of much of the Eameses' work. Two U-shaped metal rods are screwed to the underside of the tabletop to provide basic support. Thinner resistance-welded metal cross-bracing provides all necessary stability. The edges of the table are bevelled at a twenty-degree angle to expose the top's layers of plywood, a detail in keeping with the Eameses' love of honest materials. 'The details are not details,' said Charles, 'They make the product.' The designers experimented with various table-top surfaces such as gold and silver leaf, and patterned papers sealed with a protective coating. However, these ideas were discarded on the grounds that they were impractical for mass production. Today, these lightweight yet strong and durable tables are still in production with either an ash veneer or high-pressure laminate in black or white.

# 8 Basic Parts:

**Ball**
Perfect sphere of tungsten carbide

**Brass Point**
Solid, precision machined

**Support**
Acetal plastic

**Ink Reservoir**
Polypropylene plastic tube allows for complete write-out

**Ink**
Free-flowing and fast drying

**Barrel**
Clear polystyrene plastic

**Button**
Polystyrene plastic

**Assembly**

**Cap**
Polypropylene plastic

## 380

Bic ® Cristal (1950)
Lázló Bíró (1899–1985)
Décolletage Plastique Design Team
© Société Bic 1950 to present

Margaret Thatcher, 1993

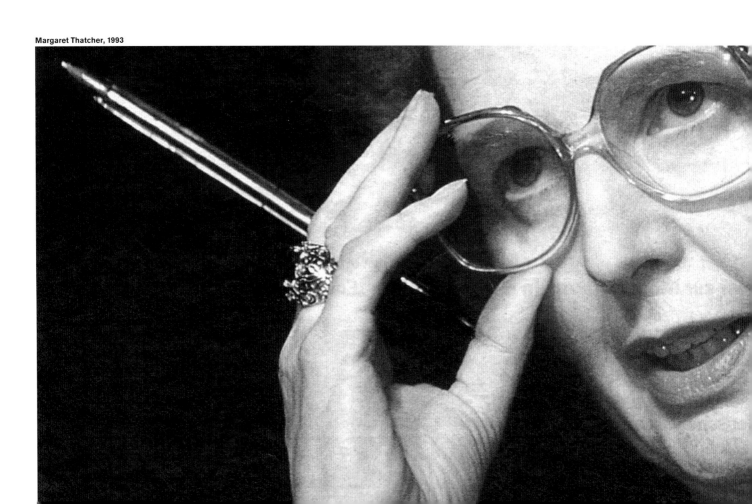

Marcel Bich

**The Bic Cristal** is iconic as an invention, due to the genius of the ballpoint mechanism, but it is the inexpensive commodification of the pen by Bic that has made this little scribbler one of the most indispensable and enduring products ever. The rib-edged cylinder of brittle transparent plastic, the curved pen top (always the same colour as the ink) with the clip that adorns shirt pockets and clipboards, the little curved plastic stopper on the end of the pen that inevitably succumbs to the ravages of biting and chewing: these traits are recognized worldwide. Although the inventor, László Bíró patented the pen in 1943, he had worked on the invention for the previous twenty years. As a young journalist, he was frequently annoyed by the difficulties involved in using a fountain pen and wanted to find an alternative. He realized that a technique used in printing, by which a rotary cylinder ensures continuous and uniform application of ink, could be adapted for use in a pen by using a tube filled with ink with a small ball bearing that applied the ink continuously to paper. The design depended on precision ball bearings and special ink with the viscosity to allow smooth application without drying up the ball. A Swedish company created a tungsten ball that provided the writing tip. Bíró also worked with his chemist brother Georg on the quick-drying ink. On completion, Bíró sold the patent rights to several manufacturers and governments who wanted the pen for use in pressurized cabins of military aircraft. It was French manufacturer Marcel Bich who developed an industrial process for the pens that lowered the unit cost dramatically. In 1950, Bich introduced his pens into Europe, called 'Bic', a shortened, easy-to-remember version of his name. The Bic became the commodity version of Bíró's innovation as we know it today. In recent years the pen cap has been redesigned to allow airflow through it, as a safety measure against choking if accidentally swallowed.

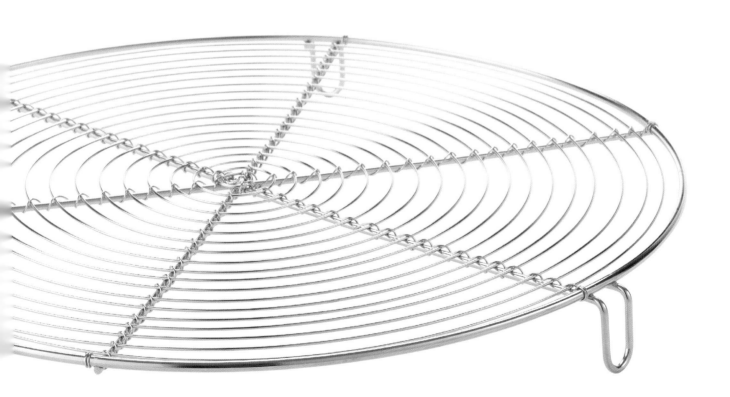

**Cake Coolers** can be found listed in early Victorian trade catalogues, particularly for those companies that specialize in wirework. They were intricately woven trellis-like coolers that accompanied the gridiron in the kitchen as a cooking essential. Its appearance in the home can be traced to the early nineteenth century when bread and cakes were mainly produced in domestic kitchens as opposed to bakeries. This led to the modification of the design for home use in the 1950s, and the longevity and unchanging nature of this mass produced version make it a significant marker for good industrial design. As an object of machine and industrial art, the tray can be viewed according to both criteria. High importance was attributed to the research stage of the design process and the resulting minimal aesthetic of this type of cooler resulted in the production of basic geometric forms. Repetition of form was often balanced against a surface of aluminium or steel, emphasizing geometry and utility. The stark and elegant nature of the cake cooling tray is perfectly demonstrated in this design model. As a flat grid of closely spaced metal wires resting on three small wire feet, the geometrical alignment of the surface wire attests to the principles of machine art. Functionally, the efficiency of the design considers the needs of the user. The thin wires and slightly raised surface maximize airflow around the cake, and allows cooling, while preventing condensation. Unlike flat sheet metal, the thin wires are evenly spaced so that the cake does not sink while still hot, and its smooth surface reduces the possibility of the food sticking to the rack. With these characteristics, the tray performs its use efficiently, and is more effective than the alternative method of flipping baked goods upside down. The Cake Cooler is a durable, simple product that has lasted into the twenty-first century as a domestic utensil with little change to its original form.

**The unlikely and surprising** combination of rope, painted and chrome-plated steel, sheepskin and a linen-covered cushion, as used in the construction of Hans Wegner's Flag Halyard Chair, are unprecedented in furniture manufacture. Wegner's motivation in using such contrasting materials was not to exploit their textural interplay but more simply to demonstrate the breadth of his skills, particularly his ability to design innovative, practical and comfortable furniture in any material, not just wood. The Flag Halyard Chair breaks to some extent with the general rationale of Danish furniture design as a process of a thoughtful modification of timeless 'types'. At the time Wegner created this design, he had been experimenting with the idea of developing chairs made from plywood shells supported on metal frames. It is not clear where the curious idea came from for replacing a plywood shell seat with a metal frame strung with rope, but there is an apocryphal story that Wegner conceived this design whilst on the beach near Aarhus: he is supposed to have modelled the grid-like seat in a sand dune, presumably with some old rope that lay close to hand. Interestingly, a 'halyard', a nautical term, is a line which hoists or covers a sail. Since the chair stands, in a sense, as a *tour de force*, and often used as an advertisement for Wegner's work, one assumes that it has always been produced on a large scale. Initially it was made by the firm of Getama in limited numbers, but was never a runaway commercial success and was then unavailable for a number of years. More recently it has been put back into production by PP Møbler and at the time of production it may have seemed a little eccentric.

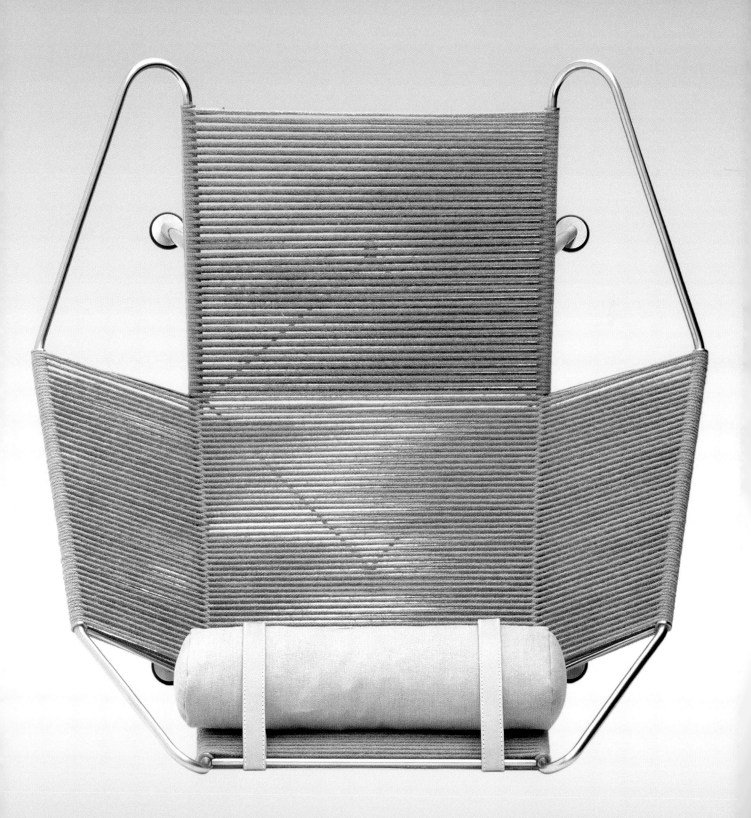

Lettera 22 Typewriter (1950)
Marcello Nizzoli (1887–1969)
Olivetti 1950 to 1963

**When Adriano Olivetti** took over his father Camillo's typewriter business in 1932, he put design at the heart of a drive to establish a consistent corporate identity across everything the business did. The policy to raise the firm's profile through a coordinated approach to a growing range of office equipment products, advertising, graphics, exhibitions and even architecture would be echoed some two decades later in Germany by Braun, with the founder's sons again taking the initiative. Marcello Nizzoli, a key figure in developing the Olivetti style, was a truly multifaceted designer. By the time Olivetti took him on to design a shop in Venice in 1938, he was already experienced in graphic, textile and retail design. He really hit his stride in the postwar period, when his employer began feeling the benefits of an economy buoyed by American investment. The Lexicon 80 Typewriter of 1948, Nizzoli's first, began a run of products with distinctively sleek, organically sculpted body shells. The Lettera 22 Typewriter added portability to the mix, and this, added to the machine's straightforward robustness, won over journalists and students. The Lettera 22 was a key product in evolving a house style expressing the characteristics of Olivetti's wares as clearly and honestly as possible. The style was a pragmatic design response to the manufacturing restrictions of the day; it was far more economic to manipulate sheet metal into shallow curves than the sharp angles that would later mark the Lettera 22's sassy descendent, Ettore Sottsass's bright red Valentine of 1969. Nevertheless, the look would persist well into the 1960s, when the Lettera DL, an update of the Lettera 22, showed its enduring popularity. The Lettera 22 received the Compasso d'Oro design prize in 1954. Both it and the Lexicon 80 are part of the permanent collection in New York's Museum of Modern Art.

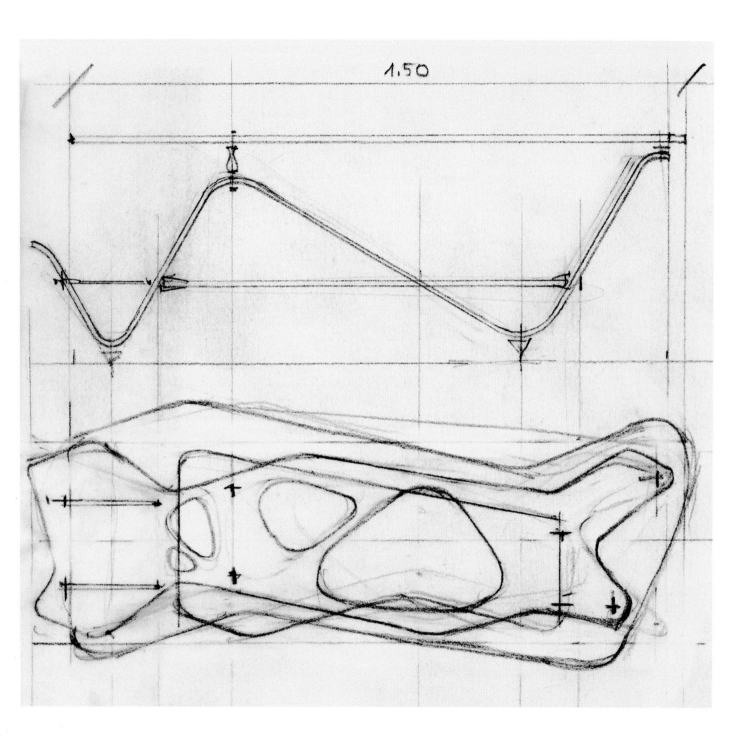

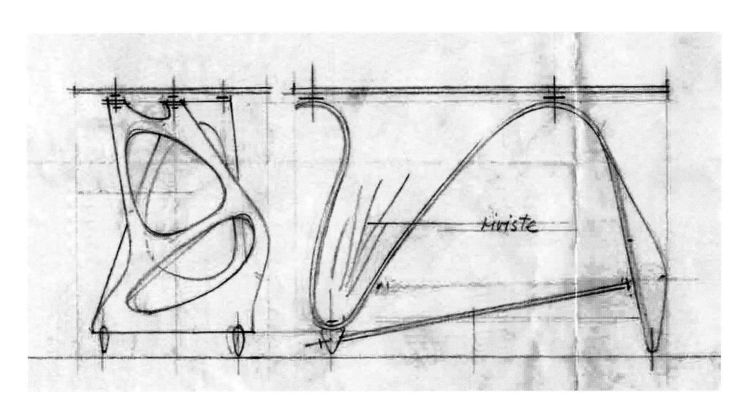

**Turin-born designer and** architect Carlo Mollino, had a love for sensuous shapes which is reflected in his Arabesque Table. The table has an undulating form with an upper and lower glass surface supported by a cascading frame of moulded plywood, which is bent to form a magazine rack. The first Arabesque Table was designed for the living room of one of Mollino's commissioned interiors, Casa Oregno, in Turin. It was also used for the interior of the Singer store in Turin. The table has been described as a 'cocoon of lovers perched on four insect legs'. The shape of the glass top is believed to be taken from a Surrealist drawing of a woman's back by Leonor Fini, while the wooden frame makes reference to the sculpture of Jean Arp. One of Mollino's most popular designs, the table epitomizes his talent for crafting intricate constructions out of glass and plywood, produced thanks to evolving technology of working with wood. Mollino, the son of a wealthy engineer and architect, represents the more flamboyant side of the 1950s Modernist movement of Italian furniture design. Mollino embraced decoration and sensuality, producing pieces that were more sculptural than functional. Indeed, very few of his pieces ever made it into production or gained a wide audience. His work is often inspired by the ornamental motifs of Art Nouveau and the work of Antoni Gaudí, as well as by natural and human shapes. Sweeping curved lines of wood, emulating the female torso, are combined with elements of glass or upholstery to create his trademark biomorphic designs. There is always a decadent element to his ideas: his 1937 Milo Mirror's silhouette recalls the Venus de Milo, his interiors often feature draped curtains and mirrors, and a mirrored bedhead is sculpted into flames and would not look out of place in a boudoir. Many of Mollino's furniture pieces were one-off designs or part of interior projects and bespoke commissions. The Arabesque is one of the few Mollino pieces by Zanotta available today.

# 376

Arabesque Table (1950)
Carlo Mollino (1905–73)
Apelli & Varesio c.1950s to 1960
Zanotta 1998 to present

Carlo Mollino

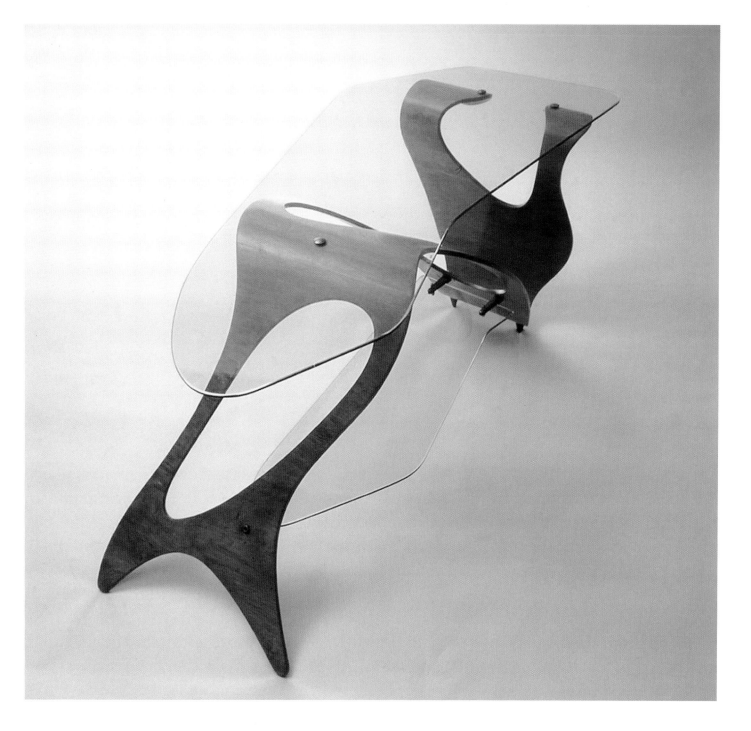

**This tough tumbler,** available in three sizes, is the quintessential everyday glass. It is used for coffee, juice, wine – indeed everything, everywhere, in every social milieu. It is a product that has been made in its millions and is cheap, strong, safe and durable. The key to the tumbler's success is its manufacture from Duralex, a tempered glass invented by Saint-Gobain in 1939, which is also used in car windscreens and security glass. Tempering is a process very similar to that of manufacturing stainless steel. It subjects glass to thermal shock by heating it to 600 degrees centigrade followed by quick cooling. This is repeated several times to build up layers within the glass and is visible under examination by polarized light. This creates a glass that is heat-proof and can withstand stress up to five times greater than conventional glass or china. It has the additional advantage that when it shatters it does so in chunks rather than the usual shards. The design of the tumbler reflects this rugged quality; rather than trying to make it more refined and 'glass'-like, it is distinctly utilitarian in its sturdiness. Its stackable quality is an added advantage. The tumbler quickly became a café staple, ubiquitously found, offering a sense of the familiar. Then in the 1960s its practicality combined with its aura of being symbolic of another, more relaxed way of life, took it into the homes of the thinking classes – from there it went global. It has been much copied and was in production until 2004.

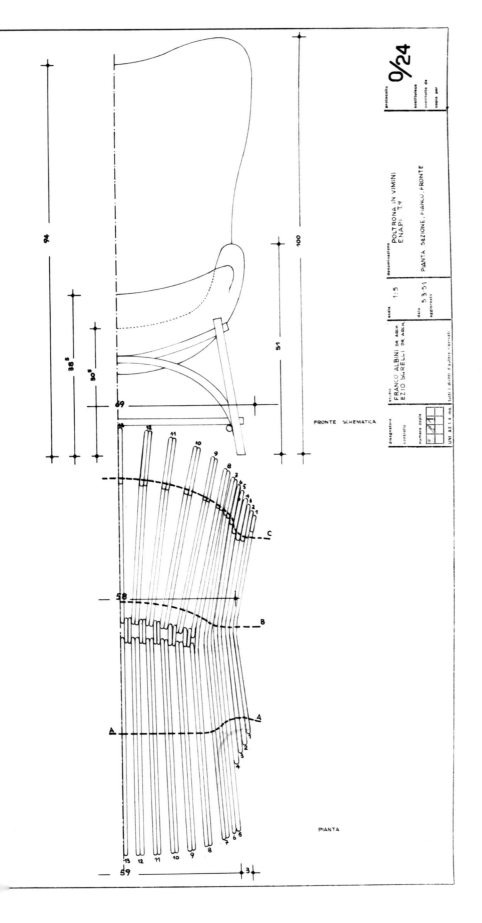

FRONTE SCHEMATICA

PIANTA

disegnatore
controllo
numero copie

studio
FRANCO ALBINI DR.ARCH.
EZIO SGRELLI DR.ARCH.

scala          1:5

data          5.3.51
aggiornato

denominazione   POLTRONA IN VIMINI
                ENAPI: T.4

PIANTA SEZIONE, FIANCO, FRONTE

prototipo        0/24

sostituisce
sostituito da
copia per

tutti i diritti d'autore riservati
UNI A2 14 mm

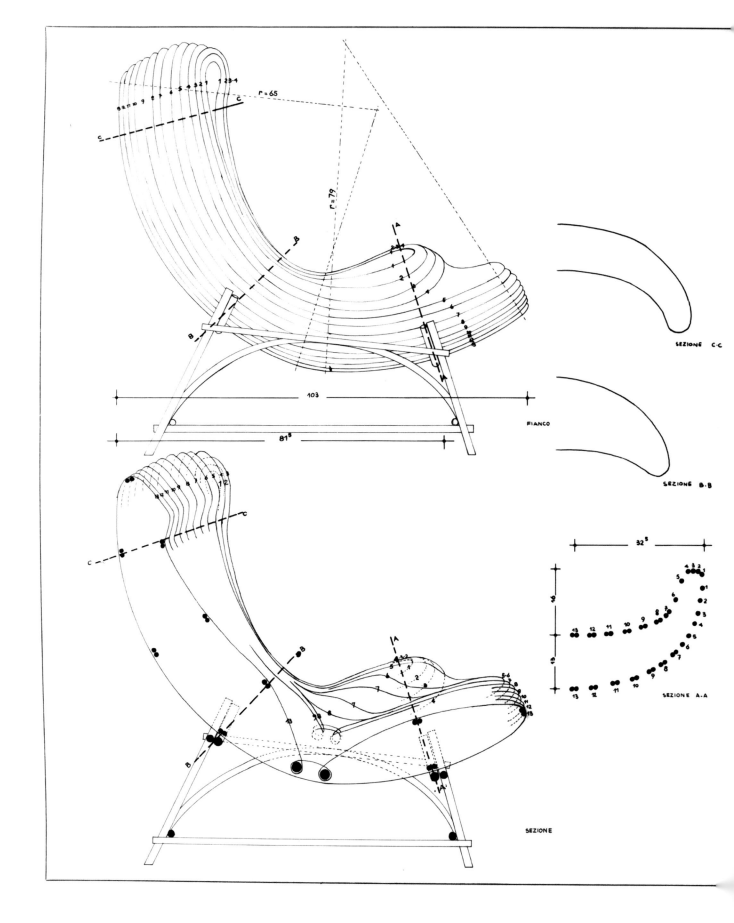

r = 65

r = 79

SEZIONE C-C

SEZIONE B.B

103

FIANCO

81⁵

32⁵

SEZIONE A.A

SEZIONE

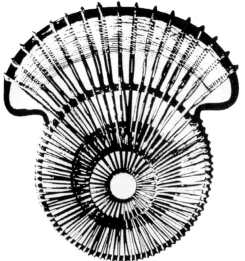

**The Margherita chair** is part of a group of designs by Albini from the early 1950s that combine traditional techniques with modern beauty. The chair's form is resolutely of its period and relates to contemporary experiments by Saarinen, the Eameses and others. It is essentially a bucket form resting on a pedestal base. Whereas his peers may have experimented with plastics, fibreglass and advanced plywood mouldings to produce these forms, Albini chose rattan and Indian cane. These are easily worked and readily available materials. In the years immediately after World War II traditional craft skills like basket-making were more available to designers than technological processes like moulding plastics, which took longer to re-establish. This was one reason why Albini chose cane for his designs of this period. The economic reconstruction of Italy after the war may have been spearheaded by new technologies, but it was underpinned by the reinvention of traditional materials such as these. The cane structure of the Margherita chair is comparable with another, mostly American, innovation of the period, namely the wire furniture epitomized by chairs by Harry Bertoia's chair designers. In both examples the chair is dematerialized, in so much as the volume of the chair appears to be reduced by its transparency. It is almost as if Albini has only designed the frame, without the upholstery. Like many other Italian designers of his generation, Albini had studied architecture at the Polytechnic in Milan, graduating in 1929. After a brief spell with Gio Ponti he set up his own studio in 1930. Albini's architecture and furniture designs are regarded as fine examples of Rationalism, a particular strand of logical Modernism to be found in mid-century Italy. They often demonstrate a sensitive use of materials and a carefully thought-through approach to manufacture.

**In 1924,** Caran d'Ache was a small, newly acquired pencil factory based in Geneva, Switzerland. Today, the name is a byword for fine quality drawing and art materials, a reputation built on the back of product innovation, of which the Fixpencil design has proved the most influential. The Fixpencil 2, designed in 1950, is an updated version of the original of 1929 and although technically similar, it benefits from subtle changes in appearance, such as the slim, hexagonal, all-metal black shaft housing the lead, and the push-button mechanism mounted on the top end of the pencil. A clip has been added to the shaft just below the push-button and the words 'Swiss Made Fixpencil Caran d'Ache' further distinguishes the patented Fixpencil from competitive designs. When Caran d'Ache bought the patent for a spring-loaded mechanical clutch pencil from the Geneva-based designer Carlo Schmid in 1929, it established a benchmark against which all other clutch pencils would be measured. Schmid's main innovation was the push-button spring clutch which, although known by earlier draughtsmen of the nineteenth century, had never before been rendered with such precision. Earlier attempts failed at holding the lead as firmly as a professional draughts-man required. Fixpencil's twist-lock clutch system allowed for the clamping pressure to be adjusted in accordance with the draughtsmen's demands and the precisely engineered jaws increased their hold as pressure was applied. When the updated Fixpencil 2 was introduced in 1950 it allowed for even greater control, due to its new lightweight shaft. The Fixpencil 2 model brought what had previously been a specialist drawing and writing tool aimed at the professional into the mass-market domain. Caran d'Ache has further developed the pencil to include lead diameters ranging from 0.5 to 3 mm (0.12 to 1.2 in), as well as launching an inexpensive plastic model. It remains a common sight in most offices and homes, and is exported in large quantities around the world.

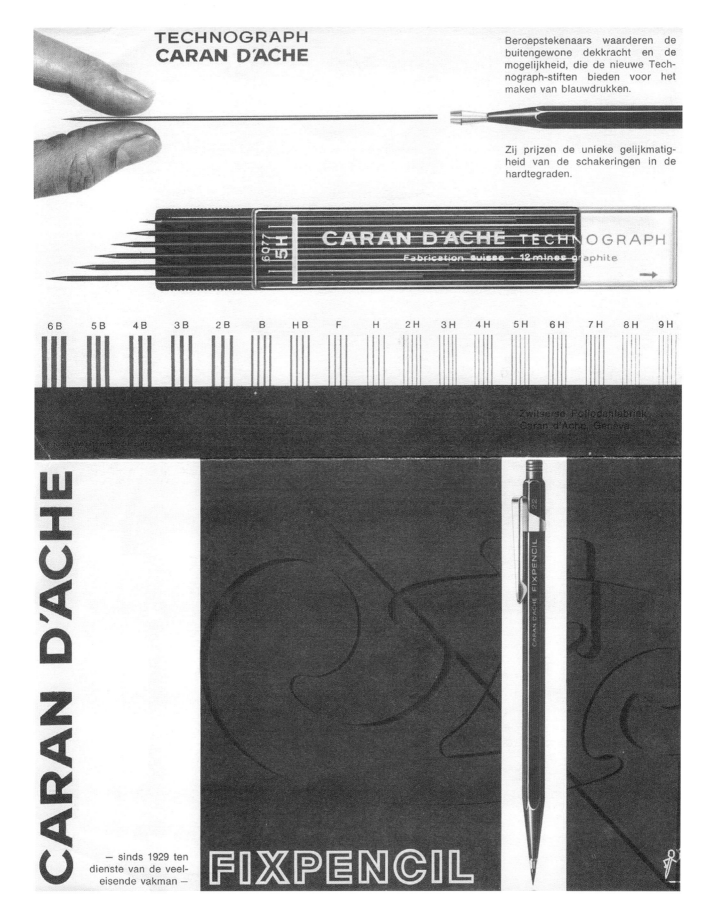

# TECHNOGRAPH
## CARAN D'ACHE

Beroepstekenaars waarderen de buitengewone dekkracht en de mogelijkheid, die de nieuwe Technograph-stiften bieden voor het maken van blauwdrukken.

Zij prijzen de unieke gelijkmatigheid van de schakeringen in de hardtegraden.

CARAN D'ACHE TECHNOGRAPH
Fabrication suisse · 12 mines graphite

6B  5B  4B  3B  2B  B  HB  F  H  2H  3H  4H  5H  6H  7H  8H  9H

Zwitserse Potlodenfabriek
Caran d'Ache, Genève.

# CARAN D'ACHE

— sinds 1929 ten dienste van de veeleisende vakman —

FIXPENCIL

## The Eames Storage

Units were conceived as a kit of parts. These parts broke down into three subgroups. First the upright supports, made from L-section steel bars painted black, and supplied in five different lengths. Next horizontal shelves in lacquered plywood. Finally vertical panels forming backs and sliding doors in several materials including embossed plywood, perforated metal and Masonite. These came in a range of finishes and colours. There were also sliding doors, open-back wire X-frame braces and sections containing three drawers. A huge variety of arrangements, in both formal layout and visual appearance, could be assembled from this collection of elements. By making discrete components interchangeable the Eameses were able to provide the potential for bespoke cabinets from mass-produced parts. This level of sophistication was a *tour de force* in flexibility and potential. It followed, on a more intimate scale, the principles of 'Case Study House No. 8', the Eameses' own home built in 1949. ESU was produced by Herman Miller in 1950 but withdrawn in 1955, and then re-introduced in 1998. In its rhetorically visual richness and display of textural potential it was way ahead of its time in terms of buyer response. It was difficult to assemble, and even when supplied in pre-assembled form it was hard to sell. The promise of flexible variety in functional and constructional terms turned out to be more philosophically alluring to designer and manufacturer than to the customer of the time. As with most of the Eameses' chair output, this storage unit has been significant in its pioneering and predictive character. Its extensive exploration of modularity has spawned many subsequent, though less richly idiosyncratic, storage facilities for both the office and the domestic market. Chairs most often represent classic status in the furniture genre, presenting the greatest structural, formal and cultural challenge.

**Like most of Achille Castiglioni's** work, the Leonardo table resonates on multiple frequencies. The first impression is of the simplest of tables, but shortly afterwards the layers of its complexity immediately begin to suggest themselves. The base of the table is comprised of two plain trestles made out of steamed beech, held together by four rubber washers, which stabilize the whole form. The top is either comprised of 22 mm (0.9 in) thick sheet of white plastic laminate or 12 mm (0.5 in) tempered glass. The trestles, commonly used by craftsmen are adjustable in height to five positions, allowing the table to be used for dining or work. This flexibility is a consideration of practicality while being a cultural commentary on the part of the designer. Before the seventeenth century in Europe, when furniture became more stationary and specialized, it was common to set up a large table only when it was needed and one table sufficed for various activities like dining and working. This is no longer so necessary or common but the vestiges of it provided the young Castiglioni with an opportunity to develop a way of working for which he would become famous, demonstrating his fascination with the history of material culture and his rejection of formalism. In its later life as a successful product marketed by Zanotta since 1969, the design of this table also created a perceived need and then satisfied it. Although it is listed as a work table in the Zanotta catalogue, the table reminds us of the ways that furniture is an expression of the interdependent relationships between style, technology and culture. Castiglioni had designed a similar table for the manufacturer, Dino Gavina, in 1964, but the Leonardo table is the archetypal model, reinventing the work table by uniting tradition and use. The table's name recalls an icon of earlier glory but in the spirit of minimalism and rationalism it has been cleansed of ornamentation. Achille Castiglioni designed the Leonardo Table in 1950, when he worked with his brothers Livio and Pier Giacomo, and it is one of the first designs attributed to him as a sole author. His interest was in reinterpreting the everyday object as cultural commentary and as an expression of methodology. The Leonardo table is one of the earliest examples of his long-term interest in the re-designed object, which can also be seen in numerous later designs.

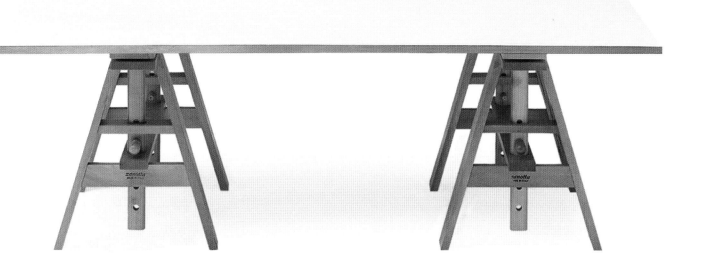

**First mass-produced** in the late nineteenth century for blue-collar workers, the lunchbox was as emblematic of the American schoolchild as the Yellow School Bus, by the mid-twentieth century. Children in the 1880s had begun creating their own personal lunchboxes by reusing tins that originally held biscuits or tobacco. It was in 1902 that the first real child's lunchbox emerged, resembling a picnic basket. While the Mickey Mouse lunchbox of 1935 set a precedent, the latter half of the twentieth century saw the development of the lunchbox that reads much like a flickbook of American popular culture. Synonymous with TV and film merchandising, the lunchbox will call to mind different fantasy heroes depending on one's generation. In 1950 the Aladdin Company of Nashville, Tennessee, released a lunchbox that was also a piece of TV merchandising. Available in red or blue, the metal box with matching thermos featured a decal (a decorative sticker) of Hopalong Cassidy, the hero of a popular series of Westerns in the 1930s and 1940s and a subsequent TV series in the by the 1950s. The decal was the work of industrial designer and commercial artist Robert O Burton, who deserves a certain notoriety for going on to design the Kentucky Fried Chicken logo. Trading on the TV series' popularity, Aladdin sold 600,000 of the 'Hoppy' lunchboxes in the first year alone. Competition brought inevitable evolution to the trend for licensed designs: first, rival American Thermos Company released a Roy Rogers lunchbox in 1953 with colour lithography on every side, then, in 1962, Aladdin came back with a range of embossed designs. But Burton's original watercolour painting of Hopalong Cassidy set in motion a cycle of faddish replacement that saw Superman and Spiderman replaced by Star Wars and the Muppet Show and countless successors to the present day. Heavy competition arose between Aladdin, American Thermos Company, ADCO Liberty and Universal, and Ohio Art, but Aladdin set itself apart with its embossed designs, which became its trademark. Over 120 million boxes sold between 1950 and 1970, but metal lunchboxes began to be phased out because of concerns by a group of mothers in Florida who eventually had the lunchboxes banned in 1972, over their violent potential in the playground. Now universally plastic, the last lunchbox to be manufactured in metal was a Rambo model in 1985, a suitably die-hard end note.

# HEY KIDS!

### TELL MOM YOU WANT TO CARRY A FRESH HOME MADE LUNCH IN YOUR OWN...

## *Aladdin*

# HOPALONG CASSIDY

### CHUCK WAGON SCHOOL LUNCH KIT AND VACUUM BOTTLE·

BRAND YOUR HOPPY KIT AS YOUR VERY OWN — WITH A FREE NAME PLATE DECAL

TELL MOM THE BOTTLE HAS THE SWELL NEW ALADDIN SWEET SEAL RUBBER STOPPER — KEEPS CONTENTS SWEET AND FRESH. EASY FOR YOU TO GET IN AND OUT OF THE BOTTLE.

TELL HER IT HAS BOTH THE SEALS OF APPROVAL

and best of all — tell Mom the Half-Pint Bottle is only $1.69 — the Kit and Bottle together only $2.89 . . . For fresh lunches every day!

## ALADDIN INDUSTRIES, INCORPORATED
### NASHVILLE, TENNESSEE

Y Chair CH 24 (1949)

Hans Wegner (1914–)

Carl Hansen & Søn 1950 to present

## Throughout the

history of Modernism, artists and designers have engaged in interpretations of non-Western traditions for reasons that have been particular to their times and contexts. In the middle of the twentieth century, inspired by portraits of merchants seated in Chinese chairs, Danish furniture designer Hans Wegner made a series of articulate contributions to the dialogue between East and West. After working as an assistant to Arne Jacobsen and Erik Møller, Wegner opened his own office in 1943. That year Wegner designed the Chinese Chair, which used as its points of departure chairs of the Ming dynasty, the modernist quest for structural simplification and Scandinavian reverence for material integrity. The 'Chinese

Chair' became the basis for many of Wegner's future pieces, at least nine of which were designed for Fritz Hansen. Both chairs, in Wegner's words 'cut [the structure] down to the simplest elements of four legs, a seat and a combined top rail and an arm rest', and, while inspired by Ming furniture, did not seek to achieve the same structural goals. The Y Chair, designed in 1949, differed significantly from the earlier pieces and built the strength of their structures into substantial rectangular compo-nents that functioned both as rail and seat structure. In the Y Chair round front and back rails, as well as rectangular side rails that impede racking, were used between round legs and a seat structure of round rails and woven papercord. Back legs that begin at the floor as tapering rounded

oak elements angle inwards toward the seat corners, gracefully making double curves outward to join the shaped arc of the back's top rail. Distinguishing this chair and providing its name is the distinctive Y-shaped, flat back splat, which gently curves outward from the rear seat rail. The total effect is a lightweight, elegant, durable and a refined piece of furniture, rooted in Eastern and Western tradition but conceived for contemporary manufacturing techniques.

**Jean Prouvé** opened a workshop in Nancy in 1923, having studied as a metal-worker under Emile Robert in the 1910s, and collaborated with architects such as Robert Mallet-Stevens, Le Corbusier, and Albert Laprade. After building wrought-iron gateways and railings, Prouvé created his first pieces of furniture using aluminium as corrugated sheet-steel and applied electric-welding techniques. Using fine steel less than 1 mm (0.4 in) thick allowed the creation of hollow-bodied objects, and the production of structures with strict outlines, and exceptional uniform strength and resistance. Prouvé viewed furniture as similar to the seating of heavy-duty machinery, and designed his products applying the same materials and standards of production. The lightweight nature of Prouvé's industrial prefabricated components was a key feature to the popularity and practicality of his creations, making them easy to transport and assemble. As an industrial innovator, Prouvé designed products using a unique approach based in mechanical engineering, rather than the industrial aesthetic of the 1920s and 1930s. Rather than working to an ideal, Prouvé's designs reflected the mechanical principles and discipline of the aircraft industry. In 1930, Prouvé became a founding member of the Union des Artistes Modernes, along with contemporaries Le Corbusier, Robert Mallet-Stevens, Charlotte Perriand and Pierre Chareau. The association promoted a closer relationship between art and industry, and the search for methods of producing applied art. At the time, a large proportion of architects were unfamiliar with the metal industry and its useful application for art and design. Prouvé's final creations developed from a concern for the nature of industrial and non-industrial materials, and a desire to build new and unconventional forms of furniture, like his panelled doors with portholes. Prouvé used sheet-steel to construct a necessarily strong and lightweight door for human use, whilst creating porthole windows resembling the very industrial nature of the boat-building industry. Prouvé displaced and reinvented the standard door, by replacing the traditional wood panelled ideal with a new industrially crafted and inspired alternative.

Jean Prouvé

VENINI

Fulvio Bianconi's Fazzoletto (Handkerchief) vase is a variation of an earlier vase by Piero Chiesa, the Cartoccio vase, designed for Fontana Arte in 1935. The Cartoccio vase was made of industrial glass that was pressed into a mould, with a biased top. Bianconi's vase differed in its asymmetrical tips, created by spinning molten glass in a circle and leaving gravity to form random peaks. What started on the blowing pipe as a globe changed during production into a fluttering freeform in space, as if a lace handkerchief were taken up by the wind. There were countless variations in the colour combinations, but Venini began producing a single coloured vase from 1960. In 1987, the vase was made by overlaying one colour with another, and was known as the Fazzoletto Opalino. The Fazzoletto vase is produced in three variations: *Lattimo*, *A Canne* and *Zanfirico*. The most common *Lattimo* model is a milky-coloured white glass, which has an opacity created by micro-crystals that separate when the molten glass cools, and reflect incoming light. *Lattimo* glass was popular in the sixteenth century and was used for multicoloured enamels, but was then abandoned until the twentieth century, when it was reintroduced by the Murano glass factories. The *A Canne* model derives its name from a thin, heated rod used in glass making that allows the molten glass to be drawn out to a particular temperature, in extremely long pipes of glass. The numerous colour variations for the Fazzoletto vase are done through this process, as the coloured glass is laid over an opaque base. *Zanfirico* refers to the process whereby a glass rod is heated to melting point, while two metal rods are attached to the ends of the molten mass. Two glass makers draw the molten glass out, rotate it and twist it to create a spiral shape. The vase quickly became one of the most popular of Venini's products, and was sold internationally in two sizes, the larger being 35 cm (14 in) and the smaller 27.5 cm (11 in). Its popularity grew further after it was seen in the exhibition 'Italy at Work', which toured the United States from 1951 to 1953. The Fazzoletto has been in production for decades and has become an icon of 1950s Italian glass making. Originals are identified by the acid stamp on each and every one, proving their authenticity.

pending investigation. Extensive tests were conducted to ascertain what exactly had gone wrong and after thousands of test cycles, the cause was identified. It appeared that the distinctive cabin windows, with their square edges, were susceptible to hairline cracks, which over time would reach a critical size and result in a catastrophic failure, causing the aircraft to de-pressurize and then disintegrate in flight. All Comets in commercial service or under construction were scrapped or modified with rounded-corner cabin windows to correct the fatigue problem. It took over four years of redesigning and testing for the aircraft to be recertified for commercial service. The Comet 4C had excellent performance, and was the first jet aircraft to cross the Atlantic with paying passengers on board in 1958. Despite this, the four-year hiatus had driven most prospective customers to its American rivals, the Boeing 707 and the Douglas DC-8. Consequently Britain lost its initial domination of the civil aviation industry. The last commercial Comet was withdrawn from service in 1980, although the basic design lives on in the form of the Royal Air Force's military reconnaissance plane, the Nimrod.

**The DH 106 Comet** bears the distinction of being the very first jet-powered passenger airliner. First flown in 1949, the British-built aircraft, with its 772 kph (480 mph) cruising speed, was an immediate success and made rival manufacturers look archaic due to its superior technology and performance. Building on Frank Whittle's revolutionary jet engine development, de Havilland created a striking airliner that used four de Havilland Ghost turbojet engines mounted in the wings' leading edges. This represented an enormous technological advance in commercial aviation. The Comet was put through over three years of extensive test flights and certifications. Having completed over 500 hours of rigorous air flight development with no apparent difficulties, the Comet was granted permission to be flown commercially by the launch customer BOAC in 1952. However, just as it seemed that de Havilland had sewn up the burgeoning commercial air-transport market, disaster struck. The first hint of trouble came in 1953 when a Comet mysteriously crashed shortly after take-off. Two similar crashes in early 1954 forced the British aviation authorities to ground the entire fleet

DH 106 Comet (1949)
Geoffrey de Havilland (1882–1965)
De Havilland Aircraft Company 1951 to 1964

Prototype of the DH 106 Comet which first flew 27 July 1949

**365**

PP 501 The Chair (1949)
Hans Wegner (1914–)
Johannes Hansen 1949 to 1991
PP Møbler 1991 to present

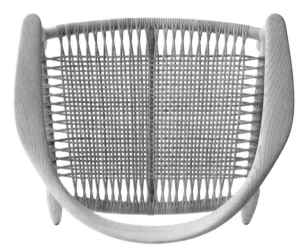

**This work** by Danish designer Hans Wegner, who has designed more than 500 chairs. Originally named the Round Chair, it first came to worldwide attention in 1950, when it was featured on the front cover of Interiors magazine in the United States. The publication described it as 'the world's most beautiful chair' and soon it was known simply as 'The Chair'. The Chair's fame was further established when in 1960 it was used for the televised presidential debates between John F Kennedy and Richard Nixon. Wegner has said that design is 'a continuous process of purification, and simplification'. The Chair is the result of gradual refinement, rather than from innovation. It can be seen as a distillation of his Y Chair (1949), which in turn was inspired by chairs of the Ming dynasty. Wegner expressed a desire to cut chair design 'down to the simplest possible elements of four legs, a seat and combined top rail and armrest.' In early versions, the top rail (back) of the chair was covered with cane. This was not only a response to the woven cane seat, but also was to hide the joints between the arms and the back. Wegner later used a W-shaped finger joint to join the parts, which requires great skill to produce. Because of this he decided to show off the joint and the cane coverings were removed. This idea of displaying the joint was a turning point for Wegner, and he designed many chairs based on this idea, with the beautiful joint becoming a signature of Wegner's chairs. The Chair has been produced in a number of versions, including one with a woven cane seat and a leather upholstered seat. Now produced by the Danish company PP Møbler, it remains a favourite of contemporary designers and architects.

John F Kennedy

Kay Bojesen trained as a silversmith with Georg Jensen's firm in Copenhagen from 1907 to 1910. After a period of further training in Germany and some time spent working in Paris, he returned to Copenhagen where he set up his own workshop producing silver and work in wood. By 1928 he had developed a style of humble forms, akin to the Danish 'skønvirke' (or fairwork) style, which were easily adapted to mechanized production. There was a revival in applied arts amongst the Danish, in reaction to the importation of mass-produced objects, which saw the production of highly crafted pieces in ceramics, tapestry and weaving. The style was functional and, although there was no intention that function should become a style unto itself, it did. Among the professional community Bojesen was widely recognized for the design of domestic utensils, winning prestigious awards at the Milan Triennale for his 'Grand Prix' cutlery in 1951 and a gold medal in 1954 for this impressive teak Salad Bowl. It was a little surprising to find that someone following in the opulent tradition of Georg Jensen should produce such an unpretentious piece of work as a wooden, lathe-turned salad bowl. However, fairly early on in his career Bojesen rejected the more dramatic excesses of his training in favour of a direct Functionalism, coupled with a determination to avoid all stylistic eccentricities. This manifested itself in his treatment of material which, except for his famous wooden painted toys, was usually left unadorned in any way, and in his treatment of form, which was always simple, sensible and straightforward. Above all, Bojesen was concerned with producing sincere objects of optimum utility, using materials of the highest quality, to the highest standards of craftsmanship, all without any appearance of superabundance or indulgence. A variety of his charming designs continue to be produced through his workshop established in 1932, now run by his son.

**Hans Wegner** was instrumental in shaping and defining twentieth-century Danish design with his exquisitely refined furniture, of which the low slung PP 512 Folding Chair is a prime example. The son of a master cobbler and himself a qualified cabinet-maker, Wegner was steeped in the handicraft traditions of his native Denmark. As a result the furniture he designed from the mid-1930s onwards was characterized by high-quality craftsmanship and balance, and by his instinctual and sensual response to the tactile properties of his chosen materials - principally wood. Wegner's PP 512 Folding Chair, beautifully articulated in oak with a woven cane back and seat, is lower and wider than most other folding chairs. Yet despite being low slung and having no arm rails, the chair is particularly noted for its comfort and how easy it is to get in and out of. Among its features are the two little handles on the seat front and a strengthening frame under the seat that moves inwards when the chair is folded. The PP 512 comes with a bespoke wooden wall-hanging hook, a unique feature according to current manufacturer PP Møbler. When the chair is folded with its legs turned upwards, the two small waves on the frame's lower rail can be used to secure the chair to the hook. Almost Shaker-like in its simplicity, the PP 512 was designed in 1949 for Johannes Hansen's Møbelsnedkeri, or cabinet-maker's workshop, and was exhibited in the same year at the annual Copenhagen Cabinet-Makers' Guild Exhibition. The enduring popularity of the PP 512 Chair has ensured its uninterrupted production since 1949, both in its original oak form and in ash.

**Charlotte Perriand** had a fascination with materials and technique that informed her work, development and experimental approach throughout her life, and her three-legged Stool (confusingly first designed in 1949 but referred to as the Stool from 1960) is an excellent example of this. With its minimalist lines and pure wooden construction, it clearly referenced elements of 1920s Modernism, but was also the result of two other experiences in Perriand's life: a period spent working in rural France, particularly in the mountains, and a trip to Japan in 1940 (which resulted in enforced exile in Vietnam from 1942 until 1946), where she studied local techniques of woodwork and weaving. These two experiences combined to produce an elegant, simple piece that not only referenced the rustic wooden milking stools used by farmers but also used the techniques and materials – including bamboo, rattan and tree branches – discovered in the Far East and used for many years later in her work. The stools were originally designed under Charlotte Perriand's own name, developed and refined in Le Corbusier's atelier in the 1940s and finally produced in 1960 by the gallery owner and editor Steph Simon. Perriand, who worked with Le Corbusier for ten years and is responsible for most of his tubular steel designs, established an architectural practice for the design of prefabricated aluminium buildings and designed a number of interiors, buildings and furniture. While she is best known for these works, her interest in craft and natural materials was perpetually alive in her work alongside the modernist designs.

Polo Mint (1948)
Rowntree Development Team
Rowntree (Nestlé) 1948 to present

# POLO

The Polo, known universally as 'the mint with the hole' (apart from in Italy, where it is known as 'the hole with a mint around it') is surely a worthy contender for the title of Britain's best-loved sweet. Born in the grim days of postwar rationing, it has remained an ever-present bestseller in the nation's sweetshops, corner shops, newsagents and, latterly, supermarkets. Intriguingly, though, it seems Polos are emphatically female sweets – according to the BBC, two-thirds are sold to women – and their continued success appears also to owe much to those who can remember when they made their market debut. A quarter of the 38 million Polos produced daily are bought by pensioners. But the Polo was not the first mint with a hole. The American Life Saver mint was created in 1912 by Cleveland chocolate maker Clarence Crane, who wanted confectionary that would not melt in hot weather. But a strong marketing campaign by Polo manufacturer Rowntree ensured the newcomer's success in Britain and Europe. Polos are highly compressed rings of sugar and glucose shaped under pressure equivalent to the weight of two elephants. But, unlike Life Savers, so named for their resemblance to mini lifebelts, the distinctive shape did not prompt the name. Instead, that came from the icy cool, or 'polar', sensation imparted by the high-quality peppermint oil used to flavour them. The Polo's success has insulated it against changes wrought by corporate ebb and flow, notably Rowntree's merger with Mackintosh in 1969 and the 1988 takeover by Nestlé. In fact, there have been numerous variations on the theme as the makers have sought to keep the brand fresh for successive generations. First came Fruit Polos in 1953 and later spin-offs included spearmint, sugar-free and mini versions, as well as Polo Smoothies, launched in 2003, which are around 30 per cent larger than the original with various creamy fruit flavours. There was even a tongue-in-cheek attempt to market Polo 'Holes', which purported to be the discarded material from the middle of the mint, but the experiment was short-lived.

**One of the contemporary claims** for the Vélo Solex was that its speed was limited to 30 kph (17 mph), virtually guaranteeing the safety of the rider. Actually, 30 kph was an optimistic claim. The Vélo Solex is little more than a motorized bicycle, and its tiny engine was a scant 45cc in size, producing less than 1 hp. So a top speed of 30 kph was barely possible without some assistance from the rider. You end up pedalling with comical effort, like something out of the cartoon *Triplets of Belleville*, when facing headwind. In spite of such an anaemic performance, or maybe even because of it, the Vélo Solex was a huge hit in postwar France. And there is something undeniably appealing about its shape and its concept. It was also helped, over the years, by very good marketing, to the extent that its image is indelibly etched on the modern European design sensibility. Marcel Goudard's and Marcel Mennesson's design concept was gloriously simple and hearkened back to the very rubrics of motorcycle design, which were solidly founded in France. After all, the very first motorcycle, the Michaux Perreaux, was designed and patented in Paris in 1868, and it comprised no more than a velocipede with an engine attached.  But Goudard and Mennesson did something even bolder. Instead of the usual arrangement of gears and a chain to get the engine's drive to the wheel, they bypassed all of that and simply bolted an engine onto the front forks. The rider built up speed by pedalling the bike, then, at the critical moment, he or she (it was most often a she) leaned forward and, using a lever, dropped the engine into contact with the front wheel. When the tiny friction wheel on the engine hit the speeding tyre, the engine burst into life, rushing along with aplomb and *vitesse* somewhere around 20 kph (12.5 mph), at a maximum. It was charming and successful, resulting in the production of many millions of these bikes, which are still made under licence in Hungary.

## 359

Tubino (1948)
Achille Castiglioni (1918–2002)
Pier Giacomo Castiglioni (1913–68)
Arredoluce 1949 to 1974
Flos 1974 to 1999
Habitat 1999 to present

**Achille and Pier Giacomo Castiglioni's** Tubino lamp, or 'little tube', is that rare piece of design: a product that exploits technological breakthrough to create something that not only has aesthetic appeal but was in tune with its time, capturing the spirit of an era. Postwar Italy, just like the United States and Britain, was in need not only of consumer goods but also of a forward-thinking approach to them. In the United States, General Electric had just developed a small, 6-watt fluorescent tube that offered consumers much-needed savings. On its arrival in Italy the Castiglionis went to work creating a metaphor for this cost-effective utilitarian product. The result was a minimalist design that would embody the new technology and spirit of the modern age, stripping away unnecessary decoration and material to illustrate simply the workings of illuminated light in a bold, flexible form that evoked a strong but delicate geometric line drawing. Using industrial materials such as metal tubing, enamelled metal and aluminium, the Milanese brothers simply took one of the new bulbs and set it next to the switch, which sat next to the reactor, which was joined to the starter on its way to the plug. An aluminium plate behind the lamp reduced glare and reflected the light, and that was it: an exposed linear design that echoed the technology and, as the Castiglionis said at the time, 'subordinated the fixture itself to the effects of light it produces'. Manufactured by Arredoluce, then Flos, and now Habitat, the Tubino remains innovative, and a great example of the Castiglionis' belief that design must restructure an object's form and production process.

**At a time** when UFOs were beginning to occupy the popular imagination and wartime innovations in plastics technology made moulding new shapes easier than ever before, the Frisbee flew onto the scene, bringing with it the promise of a cult pastime and the invention of a brand new sport. The brainchild of two World War II veterans – Warren Franscioni and Walter Morrison – the famous flying disc was the result of repeated attempts to render the perfect aerodynamic plastic platter that could fly easily through the air and be caught without hurting the hands. Working out of Franscioni's garage, the partners managed to conceive a rounded lip that would assure maximum lift during flight and was easily snatched out of the air. Franscioni and Morrison dubbed their 1948 creation the Flyin' Saucer after going through names with less consumer appeal such as the Arcuate Vane Model, the Rotary Fingernail Clipper and the Pipco Crash. The two founded their own company to market their design, Partners in Plastic (Pipco). The disc that would one day become the Frisbee became the source of contention at this point in history. A string of financial hardships saw the disbanding of Pipco, and while Franscioni rejoined the air force, Morrison continued marketing the disc as a separate product of his own devising called the Pluto Platter in 1951. When Morrison was seen by Wham-O owners Richard Knerr and Arthur Melin at an outdoors demonstration, they knew they had found something new and exciting. Morrison signed a contract with Wham-O in 1955, which put its money and marketing savvy behind the Pluto Platter and in 1958 released it as Frisbee, after a game New England college students were fond of playing with tin pie plates from the Frisbie Bakery in Bridgeport, Connecticut. Although the Frisbee went on to become a cult design object, Franscioni was excised from any official Wham-O histories in favour of promoting Morrison; a bitter if all-too-common phenomenon in the annals of invention.

**FLIES STRAIGHT, BOOMERANGS, CURVES.**
**PLAY CATCH AT 10 OR 200 FEET!**
Soft-safe-unbreakable,
in three bright colors.

SPECIFICATIONS:

| Stock No. 1322 | Stock No. 1326 |
|---|---|
| Packed for rack or dump display 24 per carton | Packed 6 doz. per dump display carton |
| Weight: 8 lbs. | Weight: 26 lbs. |
| Carton size: 19½"x14¾"x11¼" | Carton size: 27½"x11½"x30" |

**Notice:** This product is covered by U.S. letters Patent No. 3,359,678 which will be vigorously enforced.

# REGULAR FRISBEE ®

**Charles and Ray Eames** designed La Chaise in 1948 for a competition at New York's Museum of Modern Art for low-cost furniture design. Its cloud-like shape was inspired by *Floating Figure,* a sculpture by Gaston Lachaise and its title was a reference to the a pun on the sculptor's name. La Chaise's concept had evolved out of a similar shell developed in the Saarinen studio in the 1940s. Its design was also strongly influenced by the main group of moulded plastic chairs (the DAR) presented during the 1941 MoMA 'Organic Design in Home Furnishings' competition. The exhibition allowed Charles and Ray to explore their belief in affordable, yet high-quality furniture for the average consumer. Functionalism informed all their designs, an ethos backed by Ray's famous quote that, 'What works is better than what looks good. The "looks good" can change, but what works, works.' After the MoMA competition, La Chaise was separated from the more serious chairs submitted, which were manufactured with Herman Miller, UCLA and Zenith Plastics. True to their quest for affordable designs, the Eameses had to shelve plans to manufacture La Chaise, since its composition, two fibreglass shells fixed together and painted white with a chrome-plated tubular steel frame and solid oak cross-shaped base, proved too expensive and impractical to manufacture. Only one prototype was made at the time. It is only since 1990 that Vitra has manufactured small quantities of the design in serial production. In the mid 1990s, La Chaise enjoyed belated popularity, thanks to a revival of interest in the Eameses' work and the chair's own photogenic features, which turned it into a staple prop for fashion and lifestyle magazines and music videos. Suitable for both sitting and lounging on, it has become a status symbol for those aspiring to cool, urban living.

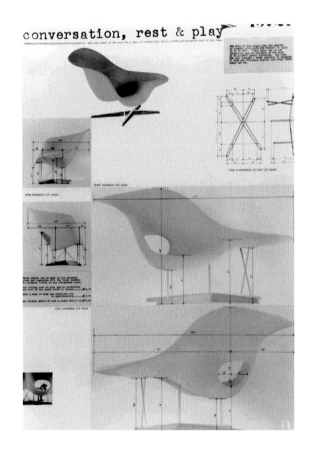

conversation, rest & play

**Few inventions can be credited** to one individual, but Edwin Land's invention of instant photography is one such example. Land's Polaroid Model 95 Camera was developed specifically to take the Polaroid Land picture roll, which produced a positive print in one minute. The camera was a typical upright folding-bellows design, albeit somewhat oversized to accommodate the film pack. The important part of the camera was the back, which incorporated rollers designed to burst a special pod of viscous processing reagent evenly on to the print. The reagent combined a developer and fixer. Once the processing was complete a flap in the back of the camera was opened and the finished print peeled away from the negative strip. Land was a successful inventor and businessman and formed the Polaroid Corporation in 1937 to manufacture and market his filters and objects utilizing them. Land was inspired to develop an instant photography process in 1944 when, on a family holiday, his daughter Jennifer asked why she could not see the photographs immediately. He at once started to work on the problem and later claimed that within an hour the camera, the film and the physical chemistry were clear to him. Polaroid instant photography was demonstrated to the Optical Society of America in February 1947 and offered for sale on 26 November 1948 (at the retail price of $89.75). A range of similar cameras and improved instant materials followed and in 1963 Polacolor instant colour film was announced. The Polaroid process remained dominant despite attempts from Eastman Kodak, Fuji and Agfa to enter the market. From the mid-1990s, with the advent of affordable digital photography, the market for Polaroids declined rapidly and the company fortunes went into a dramatic decline.

Polaroid Model 95 (1948)
Edwin Herbert Land (1909–91)
Polaroid 1948 to 1953

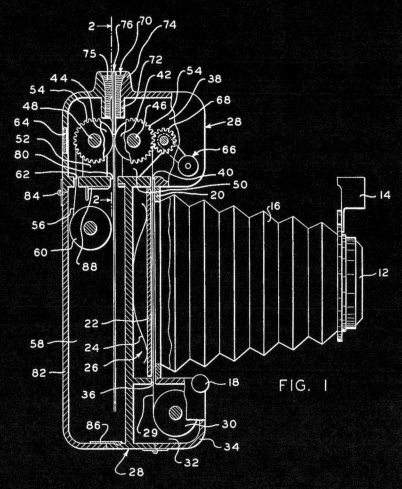

FIG. I

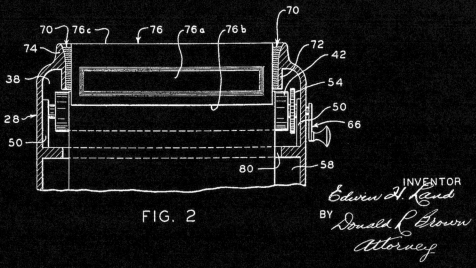

FIG. 2

INVENTOR

Edwin H. Land

BY Donald L Brown

Attorney

**SCRABBLE,** NOW A WORLDWIDE PHENOMENON, AND THE SUBJECT OF FIERCELY FOUGHT TOURNAMENTS ACROSS THE WORLD, STARTED OUT AS AN UNPUBLISHED GAME CALLED LEXICO. LEXICO WAS INVENTED IN AMERICA IN 1931 DURING THE DEPRESSION BY ALFRED MOSHER BUTTS, AN OUT-OF-WORK ARCHITECT, WHO WANTED TO INVENT A GAME THAT WAS NOT TOO HIGHBROW FOR THE GENERAL PUBLIC AND WAS NOT RELIANT ON LUCK OR THE THROW OF DICE. THE ORIGINAL GAME CONSISTED OF TILES OF LETTERS BUT NO BOARD, AND PLAYERS SCORED ACCORDING TO THE LENGTH OF THE WORDS. HE THEN HONED THE GAME BY GIVING VALUES TO EACH LETTER FOR SCORING. BUTTS CALCULATED THE LETTER FREQUENCY AND VALUE OF EACH LETTER OF THE ALPHABET BY METICULOUSLY ANALYSING THE FRONT PAGE OF *THE NEW YORK TIMES*. HE REALIZED THAT TOO MANY OF THE LETTER 'S' MADE THE GAME TOO EASY, AND REDUCED THE NUMBER TO FOUR. BUTTS MANUFACTURED THE GAMES HIMSELF FOR THE FIRST FEW YEARS, WHILE SUBMITTING APPLICATIONS TO TWO GAMES MANUFACTURERS, PARKER BROTHERS AND MILTON BRADLEY. BOTH MET WITH REFUSALS. IT WAS IN 1938 THAT HE MADE THE BREAK-THROUGH OF COMBINING THE LETTERS WITH A PLAYING BOARD ON WHICH THE LETTERS COULD BE ARRANGED LIKE A CROSSWORD. FROM THIS POINT THE GAME REMAINED FUNDAMENTALLY UNCHANGED, WITH THE FIFTEEN-BY-FIFTEEN-SQUARE BOARD, THE SEVEN-TILE RACK AND THE DISTRIBUTION AND VALUE OF THE LETTERS REMAINING THE SAME TO THIS DAY. IN 1948, JAMES BRUNOT, OWNER OF ONE OF THE ORIGINAL CRISS-CROSSWORDS SETS, THOUGHT THE GAME SHOULD BE MARKETED. BUTTS AUTHORIZED BRUNOT TO MANUFACTURE THE GAME AFTER THEY MADE SOME SMALL CHANGES TO THE RULES AND, MOST IMPORTANTLY, CHANGED THE NAME TO SCRABBLE. A COPYRIGHT APPLICATION WAS GRANTED ON 1 DECEMBER 1948. INITIALLY SALES WERE DISAPPOINTING, BUT IN 1952 MACY'S DEPARTMENT STORE BEGAN STOCKING THE GAME AND IT TOOK OFF. WITHIN TWO YEARS SCRABBLE HAD SOLD OVER FOUR MILLION SETS. BRUNOT SOLD THE RIGHTS TO SELCHOW AND RIGHTER IN THE UNITED STATES AND JW SPEAR & SONS IN THE UNITED KINGDOM AND AUSTRALIA. THE BEAUTIFULLY LAID OUT BOARD IS NOW AN EMBLEMATIC PIECE OF GRAPHIC DESIGN AND INCLUDES CLEVER FEATURES SUCH AS THE ZIGZAG EDGES AROUND THE MULTIPLE LETTER SCORE SQUARES, WHICH ALLOW PLAYERS TO SEE THE VALUE WITHOUT REMOVING THE TILES. THE ORIGINAL TILES WERE MADE FROM CHERRYWOOD AND STAMPED WITH THE LETTERS IN BLACK. THEY ARE NOW MOSTLY MADE FROM PLASTIC WITH SCREEN-PRINTED LETTERS, WHICH IS APPARENTLY BETTER FOR TOURNAMENTS AS IT IS NOT POSSIBLE TO FEEL WHICH LETTER YOU ARE CHOOSING. THE BEAUTY OF THE GAME IS IN ITS SIMPLICITY AND THE FACT THAT ENTHUSIASTS OF ALL AGES CAN MAKE THE GAME AS COMPLEX OR SIMPLE AS DESIRED. THE GAME HAS BEEN ADAPTED TO SUIT THE TIMES, AND IS NOW ALSO AVAILABLE IN A TRAVEL VERSION AND AS A COMPUTER GAME. TODAY, IT IS ONE OF THE BESTSELLING BOARD GAMES IN THE WORLD, ESTIMATED TO SELL 2 MILLION SETS A YEAR.

# 355

Scrabble ® (1948)
Alfred Mosher Butts (1900–93)
Brunots' Production and Marketing 1948 to 1952
Selchow & Righter 1953 to 1986
Coleco Industries 1986 to 1987
Milton Bradley 1987 to present
J W Spear & Sons 1953 to 1994
Mattel 1994 to present

S₁ C₃ R₁ A₁ B₃ B₃ L₁ E₁

'**Interest in the 1948 truck** is greater than that shown in any previous truck models we have ever announced,' said J D Ball, Ford's director of the truck and fleet sales department, at the launch of the F series. And there were a couple of very good reasons why. The F series was Ford's first postwar product and as such represented a new era. Its F-1 carried a number of new features: advertised as 'Bonus-Built', the F-1 was unusually light, weighing half a ton compared to the 3 tons of its sister vehicle, the F-8. All the vehicles in the series featured a one-piece windshield, side vent windows and, unusually for trucks of that era, a surprisingly roomy cab. At the original launch Ford boasted about the F series's coach-type seats (that even came with cushions), its new three-way air control system, the large ashtray and the sun visor. Interestingly, the company was aware of the importance of style, claiming in its original press release that 'the new trucks are attractively styled without losing ruggedness necessary for good performance and long life'. The F-1's radiator grille and headlights were recessed into the body of the truck, giving the front a sense of permanence and lingering power, while the spare tyre was moved from the side and mounted under the load floor, as it is today. For the first time the truck became more than an afterthought; it became a lifestyle option rather than merely a working vehicle. Predictably the F-1 was an instant hit, rapidly becoming a symbol of the new optimistic United States. Although the original F-1 was produced only until 1952, it remained in production in one guise or another (later being re-badged as the F-100) until 1974, when it was merged with the F-150 to simplify the choice for consumers.

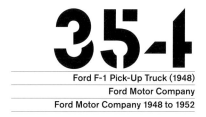

Brand NEW for '48

*Listen to the Ford Theater over NBC stations .
Sunday afternoons, 5:00 to 6:00 p.m., E.S.T.*

# FORD *Bonus* Built TRUCKS

## BUILT STRONGER TO LAST LONGER

### Star-spangled NEW! . . . Excitingly MODERN! . . . Strikingly DIFFERENT!

You'll find Ford Bonus Built Trucks for '48 brand-spanking new! New engines! New cabs! New axles! New brakes! New steering! New clear through!

With this newness comes the world's best truck know-how. We've built more trucks than anyone else! There are more Ford Trucks on the road today than any other make! That's proof we've got the know-how. We've packed it into the new Ford Bonus Built Trucks for '48! Every Ford Truck is built. extra

strong in every vital part. We call this Bonus Built construction. It pays off in two big ways. First, it takes our trucks out of the rut of extreme specialization. It makes them good all-around workers on a wide range of jobs. Second, it makes our trucks last longer. Life insurance experts certify proof that Ford Trucks last up to 19.6% longer.

See the new Fords for '48! They're at your Ford Dealers' now!

*BONUS: "Something given in addition to what is usual or strictly due." — Webster's Dictionary*

### SIX YEARS OF NEWNESS PACKED INTO ONE

**2 NEW BIG JOBS!** Biggest Ford Trucks ever built! Up to 21,500 lbs. G.V.W.! 145 H.P. engine! Up to 10.00-20 tires!

**NEW MILLION DOLLAR TRUCK CAB** with living room comfort! Biggest contribution to driver comfort in 20 years! New 3-way air control. New coach-type seats. New picture-window visibility! New Level Action cab suspension!

**3 NEW ENGINES!** A new Six, two new V-8's! Most modern engine line in the truck field! Up to 145 H.P.! High turbulence combustion chambers! New Loadomatic ignition! 4-ring pistons!

**OVER 139 CHASSIS-BODY COMBINATIONS!** Widest job coverage in Ford Truck history! Cab-Over-Engine and conventional chassis! Panel, Pickup, Express, Stake and Platform bodies! G.V.W. ratings 4,700 lbs. up to 21,500 lbs.

**LIFE INSURANCE EXPERTS PROVE . . . FORD TRUCKS LAST UP TO 19.6% LONGER!**

T-54 7" Television (1948)
Richard Latham (1920–91)
Raymond Loewy (1893–1986)
Hallicrafters 1948

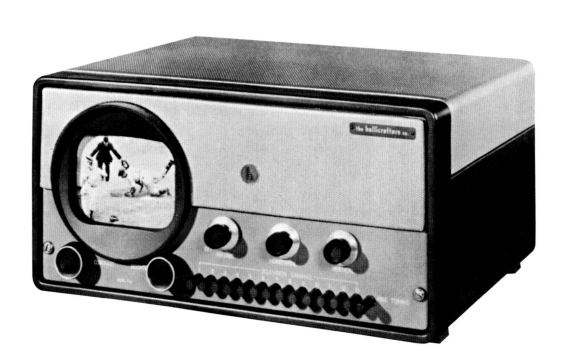

**The late 1940s** was a time of opportunity for American consumer product manufacturers, with postwar optimism accompanied by signs of growing affluence. Since the early 1930s, Hallicrafters had produced high quality 'ham' radio sets for enthusiasts, switching to military contracts during the war years. But, with electronic innovation gathering pace alongside the economy, the business knew it now had to broaden its appeal both in radio and the still fledgling field of television. The Chicago-based company aimed high by calling in the city office of the successful Raymond Loewy Associates to look at its existing radios but also to plot the best way to make an impression in television. By 1946, the US had adopted a single television broadcasting standard, television networks were starting up and the refinement of tube technology was making affordable television sets possible. As a result the number of televisions in the US had grown from a few hundred in the early 1940s to around 45,000 by 1947. The design team, led by Richard Latham, chose not to redesign from scratch but to update the 'ham' look to achieve a sleeker, more precise appearance for the radios. With Hallicrafters' engineers, the designers looked at every element of earlier products and then simplified the interface by creating a clearer hierarchy of controls: black-and-white on-off dials, they emphasized the tuning and volume, while the less important controls were reduced in size and organized into groups. The quality and ability of the technological advances were presented in a clear, direct manner; the radio was encased in metal instead of gaudy walnut. A very similar approach was used for the T-54 7" Television, which came in the same metal cabinet as the SX-42 Radio. The 7-inch screen replaced the radio dial, while the scale and position of the pre-tuned push-button controls again suggested their relative importance. In general, while clearer and more organized than previous Hallicrafters products, the design suggested enough of the company's reputation for solidity to instil confidence in buyers making their first television purchase. The Hallicrafters television was commercially successful, demonstrating that consumers were growing to appreciate this simple design. Japanese companies built upon the Hallicrafters aesthetic, using it since the 1960s and creating an international style and trend for this type of design.

A variety of moulded fibreglass chairs, plywood tables and plywood chairs, photograped on the terrace of the Eameses' house, 1952

Armshell with chrome legs and plastic glides, 1950

DAR (1948)
Charles Eames (1907–78)
Ray Eames (1912–88)
Herman Miller 1948 to present

## Charles and Ray Eames's

prophetic dining chair, DAR or Dining Armchair Rod, was a revolutionary piece of design that altered, in form and in construction, ideas about furniture in the second half of the twentieth century and, most immediately, in the 1950s. Built entirely with industrial materials and through industrial processes, the moulded, reinforced polyester seat is supported by a metal-rod base; the unique splayed 'Eiffel Tower' configuration is given flexibility and strength with rubber mounts positioned at the joints. The success of the chair's construction, which allowed for full mass production, was the result of Charles's previous developmental research, first with Eero Saarinen on the prize-winning moulded plywood chair of 1940, and then with the US Navy, to experiment with new materials for equipment such as leg splints. In 1946 Eames mounted a one-man show at The Museum of Modern Art, New York, where he exhibited a number of prototypes that he had conceived with Ray. The early steel-rod based chair was among them. By 1948, Eames's designs had received acclaim throughout the international design community; he entered The Museum of Modern Art's 'International Competition for Low-Cost Furniture Design', and won second prize. The entry was a proposal for a series of the steel-rod chairs, now in conjunction with a seat manufactured in fibreglass – the promising new synthetic material set to replace moulded plywood in larger-scale furniture production. The Herman Miller furniture company, headed by George Nelson, was already a supporter and patron of Eames's work; after the success of the 1948 competition, the company produced a number of his designs. The DAR, as one of the initial production pieces, symbolically anticipated the innovative, collaborative partnership the Eameses were to have with Herman Miller over the next two decades. As an industrially designed object, the chair embodied Modernism's mass-production intent: the universal seat shell, interchangeable with a range of bases, allowed for a number of variations. It was a clear articulation of the couple's intention, 'to get the most of the best to the greatest number of people for the least.'

**The Long Playing Record** is one of those extraordinary products, which have helped transform twentieth-century popular culture. Columbia Records launched its new LP in 1948, but the idea of a larger record that could hold more music had been around since the beginning of the century. As early as 1904 a London firm called Neophone had tried to introduce a long player, but was unsuccessful, while Thomas Edison in the US launched a long-playing record in the 1920s that failed to catch on due to poor sound quality. RCA-Victor's long player of 1931 was similar in design to the successful Columbia model, but the product fell foul of the Depression when record sales plummeted from 104 million records in 1927 to just 6 million in 1932. Columbia launched the LP at exactly the right time. The product capitalized on the consumer boom of the postwar period and was also able to exploit recent advances in plastics and recording technology, notably the recent introduction of the plastic vinyl. The LP has an iconic shape and is a product born out of techno-logical necessity as well as conscious design. Columbia sold 1.25 million discs in just the first year of the LP's release. It was popular because it could hold twenty-three minutes of music per side, compared to just four or five minutes a side for the chunkier 78 records. This meant entire symphonies and operas could be released on a single disc for the first time. The convenience and relative cheapness of the LP meant it was the most popular medium for music during the 1950s, 1960s and 1970s. Its popularity was eroded by the launch of the audio cassette in the 1970s, while the introduction of the compact disc in the 1980s instigated the final demise of the format – but the LP still lives on. Gold discs are still presented to bestselling artists regardless of whether the record was released on vinyl. The LP has also been kept alive by music DJs in clubs, who prefer vinyl LPs because they are easier to control and manipulate for mixing dance music. And those with vast music collections will most likely retain their records, instead of trading them in for digital formats, as most die-hard fans love their LPs, even as the needles collect dust, crackling nostalgically through the speakers.

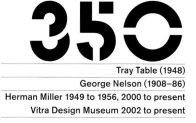

**350**

Tray Table (1948)
George Nelson (1908–86)
Herman Miller 1949 to 1956, 2000 to present
Vitra Design Museum 2002 to present

**George Nelson's Tray Table** looks more like a product from the Bauhaus than an American product of the 1940s. However, in the early 1930s Nelson had spurned what he saw as the shallow hypocrisy of American stylists such as Raymond Loewy and instead travelled to Europe to immerse himself in the deeper philosophies espoused there by the Modernist movement. With such a background, the Tray Table's lineage can clearly be traced to the tubular steel furniture of the likes of Marcel Breuer and Eileen Gray. A tray table in name alone as its square, moulded plywood surface is not removable, the piece adjusts in height via a metal collet that holds the two yokes of the steel frame together. This adjustability, along with the offset stem, gives the piece considerable versatility as a bedside or sofa side-table, enabling the surface to be positioned over the user's lap. In the year of its design the table formed part of Nelson's room set for 'An Exhibition for Modern Living' held at the Detroit Institute of Arts and curated by Herman Miller colleague and fellow designer Alexander Girard. Nelson decided to pursue the notion of a room where the furniture was virtually invisible, a brave stance as the design director of a major furniture company. The minimal frames of the tray tables made their tops appear to float above the lounge chairs and sofas accompanying them. The piece remained in production with Herman Miller for only seven years from 1949, but in 2002 Vitra Design Museum re-released the table using models and drawings supplied by Nelson's archive in New York. Herman Miller also resumed the production of the Tray Table in 2000 and is still producing it today.

Truly new, the "Tra-table"!    Brainchild of George Nelson, it adjusts in height

from 17½", to 29", is just right    for holding smoking accessories, a book,

or for serving buffet supper    Any living room can use two or three.

Can serve as bedside table, too    Ample 14" walnut or primavera plywood top

on sturdy chrome-plated metal base.    Retails for only $12.50.

Professional discounts    of course

Showrooms • one park ave., new york    622 merchandise mart, chicago

exhibitors' bldg., grand rapids    8810 beverly blvd., los angeles.

herman miller  zeeland, mich.

18

**Introduced in 1948** as an instrument of accuracy, durability and legibility, the Mark XI is the most iconic of military wristwatches, famous for its precision and understated design. Collectors scramble to acquire one, and those who have the Mark XI can be assured of their investment because of the high demand for pilot's watches at auction. What is so incredible about the Mark XI is its hand-wound movement based on absolute precision (the inner case is made of a soft iron which protects the movement of the watch against any magnetic fields) and the renowned 89-calibre manual-wind movement. The Mark XI introduced a black face with white lettering, designed to increase visibility in the cockpit and now standard for military watches, and differently shaped hour, minute and second hands to avoid confusion in the heat of the moment. The style of the watch were reincarnated most recently in the Mark XII model introduced in 1993, which now has automatic movement, replacing the hand-wound movement after forty-five years. The International Watch Company (IWC) in Schaffhausen created the watch specifically according to the specification of the Royal Air Force (RAF). In the 1930s IWC began to throw its expertise into devising accurate time-keeping in an aircraft cockpit. Problems encountered included extreme temperatures, varying light conditions, high levels of vibration and strong magnetic fields. The first of the series, the Mark IX (1936), was one of the first wristwatches to be tested in extreme temperatures – the temperature in the cockpit of early aircraft would drop below freezing level. This is one of the most collected of the IWC pilot watches. It was not until 1948 that IWC produced what it described as the ultimate synthesis of design and execution, the Mark XI – the official pilot's watch. Each watch supplied to the RAF had been subjected to a rigorous forty-four-day testing period. The stark, clear legibility of the Mark XI was a design triumph and enjoyed a nearly forty-year production run. Technological updates included automatic movement, a date function and improved water resistance. The original Mark XI remains the collectors' favourite, however, not least for the talismanic significance of its being worn in battle.

# High Fashion

This picture by JAMES ABBE, Jr., is one of many he has made with the HASSELBLAD Camera. Best known for his fashion photography, Mr. Abbe exhibits rare artistic command of subject and technique that make up an effective illustration. In the HASSELBLAD he finds an instrument to match his own exacting talent.

*Prices:* The camera, with 80mm Kodak Ektar f/2.8 Lens and 2¼ × 2¼ roll-film magazine, $535. Accessory 135mm Kodak Ektar f/3.5 Lens, $250, and 250mm Zeiss Opton Sonnar f/4 Lens, $421. Prices include Federal Tax.

# High PERFORMANCE

This camera by HASSELBLAD sets a new high in photographic performance. Interchangeable roll-film magazines, for example, permit the photographer to switch at any time from one type of film to another . . . color or black-and-white. Interchangeable lenses, automatic controls, speeds to $^1/_{1600}$ second, built-in flash — these and other features will bring a new range, a new sureness, to *your* picture taking. Precision-crafted in Sweden with an eye to the photographic perfectionist, the 2¼ × 2¼ HASSELBLAD Camera well merits your personal inspection . . . at your camera dealer's.

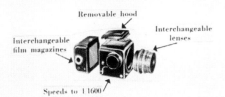

Removable hood

Interchangeable lenses

Interchangeable film magazines

Speeds to 1 1600

# ≡Ⓥ HASSELBLAD
## THE NEW SWEDISH CAMERA

Write for the descriptive HASSELBLAD booklet to

*Willoughbys*

Dept.   110 West 32nd Street · New York 1, N. Y.

**3-48**

Hasselblad 1600F (1948)
Sixten Sason (1912–67)
Victor Hasselblad 1948 to 1952

**The Hasselblad camera** has a reputation as the ultimate professional tool, reflecting the quality of its design, its lenses and a certain cachet that the camera has acquired since its introduction in 1948. The camera has been used by many well-known professionals and artists, as well as in specialized commercial applications, most notably on NASA space missions. F W Hasselblad was established in 1841 as a trading company. A photographic division, Hasselblad's Fotografiska, was established in 1908, acting as a photographic distributor for the Eastman Kodak Company. In 1940 the firm was approached by the Swedish government to produce a surveillance camera, and the HK7 became Hasselblad's first camera. After the war Victor Hasselblad set about designing a quality medium-format camera. The camera was similar to prewar models such as the German Primarflex, but was innovative in having fully interchangeable film backs, which permitted different types of film to be used quickly and without waste. Although Hasselblad was responsible for the mechanical design, Sixten Sason, a

respected industrial designer, was brought in to style the look of the camera. Sason produced a streamlined camera with no sharp corners that was comfortable to use whether the camera was on a tripod or hand-held. The Hasselblad 1600F was well received on its launch in 1948. The first model had an unreliable shutter mechanism and a new model, the Hasselblad 1000F, with a slightly slower top shutter speed, was introduced in 1952. The new camera included other technical refinements and a greater range of lenses, and 10,396 were made. Hasselblad continued to develop new models, each improving on its predecessors, and sales rose rapidly. A range of film backs, viewing accessories and specially designed lenses from respected German lens-makers such as Carl Zeiss and Schneider superseded the original Eastman Kodak Ektar lenses. The Hasselblad remains the leading professional medium-format camera, with new ranges of camera in different formats, with built-in exposure metering systems, auto-focus lenses and digital backs.

Victor Hasselblad

# 3-17

Compas Desk (1948)
Jean Prouvé (1901–84)
Ateliers Jean Prouvé 1948 to 1956
Galerie Steph Simon 1956 to 1965
Vitra 2003 to present

or scale his solution intended. He used materials appropriated from the automotive and aviation industries to create pieces that were affordable and easily mass-produced and that continue to be influential. The Compas Desk, with its namesake base, is an elegant illustration of the very essence of Prouvé's work. Built during a productive period from 1947 to 1953 at his Maxéville factory, the structure is exposed, self-evident and in constant tension. From his earliest

work, Prouvé had rejected reliance on more common, popular materials such as tubular steel. The laminated-wood desk sits atop welded sheet-metal components made using a folder-press, and initially finished with car body paint. The desk appeared in various versions over the years and occasionally came with a set of plastic drawers designed by Charlotte Perriand. Each step in the desk's production was rooted in heavy industry, and each step brought a unique visual vocabulary that

had never before existed: elegantly bent metal assemblies more reminiscent of industry and architecture than of furniture. The structure of the Compas Desk also draws attention to a defining character of Prouvé's work: the separation of scale from solution. The compass imagery surfaces in different forms and on different scales in Prouvé's work, whether for the veranda of the Sécurité Sociale building in Le Mans, the planned interior of the École de Villejuif, Paris, or the refreshment bar in

Évian. The ease and versatility of solution implied by such diverse applications illustrates a vision of construction that needed only material, structure and assembly to create beauty independent of scale.

**Jean Prouvé** was not an
architect, nor did he consider
himself a designer or artist,
but rather insisted on referring
to himself as a *constructeur* –
a reference capturing his
training as a blacksmith, his
inspiration as a self-taught
engineer and his inseparable
participation in the process of
creation. He did not separate
design from production, nor
architecture from furniture.
The economy of materials,
the means of assembly and
the visibility of structure
appear no matter what form

**Aarne Glassware,** with its pure, minimalist lines, designed by, Göran Hongell –  primarily a decorative glass artist, trained in the glass-works of Karhula – has become barely known for anything else, despite his key place in the history of Finnish glassware. He began working with Finnish glass manufacturer iittala after World War II. Today he is considered one of the pioneers of Finnish glassmaking. The glassware set consists of ten pieces, including eight different glasses, pitcher and ice bucket, in various sizes, from the 5 cl shot glass to the 150 cl pitcher. The range has tremendous visual coherence, and all the variations use the same basic profile: a thick, circular glass base, with a receptacle with straight glass sides that diverge from bottom to top. The glasses made their film debut in Alfred Hitchcock's *The Birds* (1963), in a scene in which Tippi Hedren elegantly drank a martini. Hitchcock had seen the glasses at the Ritz Bar in London, and immediately purchased a dozen. The two martini glasses used in the film were actually Hitchcock's own, and were used to emphasize the blond actress's sophisticated image. The range of glasses include a pilsner, double old-fashioned, martini, cordial, old-fashioned universal, and a champagne glass, and each are hand-turned and moulded blown glass. Aarne was designed in 1948 and, although it comes out of the tradition of the time and was intended for daily use, the elegance of its manufacture lends a certain luxury to the pieces. This glassware set a trend for minimal design during the 1950s. The set was an instant success for Hongell and for iittala, winning the gold medal at the Milan Triennale in 1954 and going on to become a classic of Finnish glass design, collected in museums all over the world, including the permanent collection of New York's Museum of Modern Art. In 1981 Aarne was chosen as iittala's symbol to mark the company's centenary, as it remains the company's best-selling glassware.

*Kumbh Mela, Allahabad, Uttar Pradesh, 1977, by Raghubir Singh*

**Hindusthan Motors was** the first Indian car company to start production in its homeland in 1942. The production of the Ambassador began in 1948, using the tooling from the defunct Series 2 Morris Oxford, manufactured by the Nuffield Group, later part of the British Motor Corporation in England. The Amby, as it is affectionately known, has retained its distinctive rounded contours, large bonnet and prominent headlights while successfully evolving under the skin, through a series of mechanical upgrades over the last five decades. It has consistently responded to new generations of consumers' needs and aspirations. The Ambassador's enduring appeal and success are due to its famed dependability, inherent mechanical simplicity, ease of service and outstanding ability to handle punishment on India's tough roads. This rugged reliability has made the Amby the nation's taxi, with its upright matronly stance resulting in excellent passenger and luggage capacity. To date, Hindusthan Motors has built more than 4 million Ambassadors at its plant in Uttarpur, West Bengal, and the car is a ubiquitous sight across India and the subcontinent. Its enduring popularity is such that the Ambassador has arguably become a national symbol of India's industrial development and statehood, with the Indian prime minister's official state transport being a white Ambassador. It is the official Indian governmental car, with a fifth of all production bought by the state. Limited competition from rival manufacturers meant that the Ambassador's success in the marketplace was unchallenged until the 1970s. In recent years the Ambassador has struggled to maintain its once dominant market share in the face of new models on the market. In the light of this, Hindusthan Motors has concentrated on niche markets, continuing to sell to the Indian government, hotels and, increasingly, to retro-obsessed consumers in the UK and Japan, who covet the 'grand old lady's' period looks and cultural iconography.

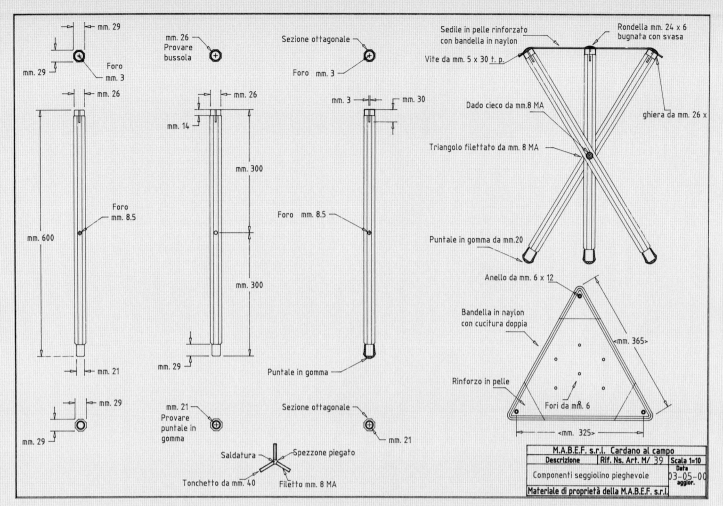

mm. 29

Foro
mm. 3

mm. 29

mm. 26

Foro
mm. 8.5

mm. 600

mm. 21

mm. 29

mm. 29

mm. 29

mm. 26
Provare
bussola

mm. 26

mm. 14

mm. 300

Foro
mm. 8.5

mm. 300

mm. 29

mm. 21
Provare
puntale in
gomma

Saldatura — Spezzone piegato

Tonchetto da mm. 40    Filetto mm. 8 MA

Sezione ottagonale

Foro    mm. 3

mm. 3    mm. 30

Foro    mm. 8.5

Puntale in gomma

Sezione ottagonale

mm. 21

Sedile in pelle rinforzato
con bandella in naylon

Rondella mm. 24 x 6
bugnata con svasa

Vite da mm. 5 x 30 t. p.

ghiera da mm. 26 x

Dado cieco da mm.8 MA

Triangolo filettato da mm. 8 MA

Puntale in gomma da mm.20

Anello da mm. 6 x 12

Bandella in naylon
con cucitura doppia

<mm. 365>

Rinforzo in pelle

Fori da mm. 6

<mm. 325>

| M.A.B.E.F. s.r.l. Cardano al campo | | |
|---|---|---|
| Descrizione | Rif. Ns. Art. M/ 39 | Scala 1=10 |
| Componenti seggiolino pieghevole | | Data 03-05-00 aggior. |
| Materiale di proprietà della M.A.B.E.F. s.r.l. | | |

**For outdoor pursuits** that involve long periods of sitting – angling, for instance, or landscape painting – the ideal seat has a variety of important design considerations. It should be highly portable for a start – compact and light, and stable – so that it can be used on uneven ground. Unfortunately, comfort is often sacrificed to satisfy these more pressing demands. Such a stool, a three-legged portable stool, has existed since the fifteenth century, and since 1948 a version has been manufactured in Italy by Mabef, a leading producer of wooden articles for painters. The stool, designed by Albino Bruno Mariotto, the founder of Mabef, is one of its most successful pieces with an annual production run rising from a mere 300 in the 1950s to 2000 pieces today. Composed of three oiled, stain-resistant beech wood rods joined in the centre, the folded stool expands to create a tripod. Mabef originally made the legs and leather strips for the seat by hand. In the 1980s, Albino's son, Luciano, updated the design replacing the strips with a one-piece leather triangle and started the industrial production of the stool. The collapsible three-legged stool easily meets all the functional criteria. While the notion of a collapsible seat may not be entirely reassuring, because the artist's stool is anchored by the weight of the occupant, it feels naturally stable. The beautiful simplicity of the central mechanism – the joint connecting the three legs – is curiously reassuring in itself. Needing no instructions and having no secrets, the stool is instantly understandable. In design terms, it is an example of an elegant idea that needs no improvement, and today's version is very similar to its fifteenth-century prototype. The fact that it can be built in a variety of materials just adds to its broad appeal, with a basic utility variation available in lightweight aluminium and artificial fabric. The hardwood legs and leather seat of the Three Legs Stool, however, cannot be beaten for style and looks.

# ON GREAT SKIS

## A DISSERTATION

A ski is less innocent than it looks. A rascal, an enigma—an uncommon complex of shape, camber, flexibility, weight, tip, running surface, groove, edge—expressed in materials of more or less beauty and durability.

Ah, you say, you know the devious nature of a ski. You know the way it drags or floats, overturns or stubbornly refuses to turn at all, grabs now or lets go just when you need its bite. Then you've been using an ordinary ski—not a great one.

An ordinary ski may hide its knavish character from a casual glance, so examine carefully before taking a ski to your heart. Are its edges flush and square with the running surface? Are they single strips of tempered steel with no sections, screws, or rivets to drag and loosen? When flexed, does the ski form a flowing curve from tip to tail, or does its awkward angular bend foretell gawky action on the snow? Does the tip turn up elegantly just right, neither gaping open prematurely nor breaking tardily with snubnosed abruptness? When you press the bottoms together does the entire length close at once with a lovely whispered snap?

A great ski combines precisely the right form and fusion of all these elements, and thus becomes a thing of beauty. Use it, and discover its magical ability to turn with a breath or equally follow without question your bidding to track. Buy it, and years from now rejoice in the final attribute of a great ski—that it lasts as long as your devotion.

**and who makes great skis?**

HEAD of course.

## HEAD

HEAD SKI CO., INC.
Timonium, Maryland

HEAD STANDARD—$94.50
HEAD VECTOR—$117.50
HEAD SKI POLE—$24.50

# THE NEW HEAD 360 SKI

Skiers: Why not start this season off on the right ski—the new 360 by Head Ski Company, Inc., 15 W. Aylesbury Rd., Timonium, Md. 21093.

Expert? Intermediate? Good beginner? Whatever your class, you'll find the 360 an extremely lively and satisfying all-around ski that'll perform reliably on anything from soft snow to hard pack and ice.

Need extra confidence for those tight turns and breath-taking jumps? The 360's sandwich construction of missile-grade Alcoa aluminum sheet on top and bottom, plastic and wood in the middle, gives you all you need.

A tough running surface of high-molecular-weight polyethylene lets the ski run smoothly without drag or icing, while a neoprene-aluminum laminated topskin cuts vibration and dampens noise.

The 360 combines the monocoque structural principles of other Head skis with a new bottom-groove shape and a built-in, shock-resistant Alcoa aluminum tailguard.

Head guarantees that the aluminum skis won't warp, deteriorate or twist from action. Neither will they lose their resilience, camber, strength or weatherability.

The 360 comes in eleven sizes and is backed by a manufacturer's warranty. It has been thoroughly race-tested for speed, quiet, sure control, and it's engineered for superlative skiability.

# HEAD
# INTERNATIONAL

**When Howard Head** pioneered the design of the aluminium ski in 1947, his technology-driven design laid the foundations for the modern-day ski industry. Up until that point, wooden skis were omnipresent and had been for centuries, but wood had proven heavy, difficult to manoeuvre, prone to water damage, and tested the patience of skiers of all abilities. In contrast, Head's aluminium ski was vastly more user-friendly as well as being a technical innovation. It swapped the parallel lines of the wooden design with a one-piece construction that introduced a subtle waistline, a gently flared tail and a curved nose, all of which lent the ski an aerodynamic advantage and a shape that was decidedly futuristic. When in 1947 as a fledgling skier Head descended the piste for the first time, he was left frustrated that he could not master the technique first off and, like many beginners before him, he stated that the unwieldy hickory-wood skis were to blame. At that point, Head was working as an aeronautical engineer at the Glenn L Martin Aircraft Company and he mused that if 'wood was the best material, then we would still be making aircrafts out of wood.' Indeed, much of the technical improvements he employed in the aluminium ski originated in aeronautical design, such as the metal sandwich construction that was used in fuselages. Head used a sandwich of plastic, wood and aluminium to produce a ski that was stiffer in torsion, allowing it to turn and track more easily. The metal ski resisted twisting approximately three times better than a wooden one. Whereas the tips and the tail of a wooden ski would bend away from the curve of a turn, causing the skier to lose control, the Head ski maintained a straight edge that kept in contact with the snow. The resulting skis were faster in all kinds of snow, more durable than the wooden alternative, and softer in flex, opening up opportunities to skiers of only modest ability. So fast were these new skis that they were quickly nicknamed 'cheaters' by those unwilling to trade in their wooden counterparts – just yet, that is. Head named his ski the 'Standard' and as word of the aluminium design's advantages spread around resorts the skis soon caught on. By 1963, after riding a year-on-year manufacturing growth rate of 15 per cent, Head was a global sporting brand that was behind legendary sporting achievements such as the 1963 win by Joos Minsch of the pre-Olympic downhill at Innsbruck.

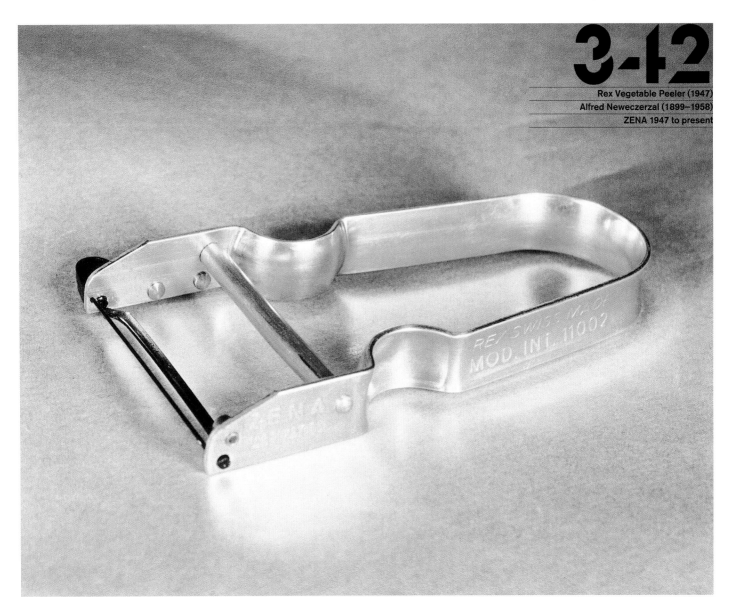

**For such a simple and** unassuming object the Rex Vegetable Peeler is a masterpiece of innovation, reduction and quality. It embodies all the properties that are needed for the perfect mass-produced product and duly sells 3 million pieces a year. The peeler is made from only six parts. An aluminium strip, 13 mm (0.5 in) wide and 1 mm (0.04 in) thick, is bent into a horseshoe shape, which has generous indents in the sides for thumb and forefinger, to prevent slipping as the peeler is drawn across the potato. The innovative swivel blade is punched from sheet steel, but the exact process is a well-kept company secret. The crossbar holds the utensil together and the potato-eye remover is riveted to the side of the horseshoe. Originally, to keep costs down, the potato-eye remover was made from scrap metal left after the blades had been punched. The remaining two parts are fixings. The Rex is not just good for peeling vegetables. It also slices Parmesan cheese, and fishermen praise the peeler for its ability to scale fish when used in reverse, using the blunt side. According to Peter Newec, who now runs the company and is the designer's grandson, Alfred Neweczerzal

'was a practical man with business skills who invented to make money and did not think in terms of design.' Neweczerzal worked in partnership with a businessman named Engros Zweifel and in 1931, in the basement of Neweczerzal's house in Zürich, they began  manufacturing the peeler with a mechanical die-cutting machine. In 1947 a patent was registered for the Rex and in the following year the company became know as ZENA-produkte (an acronym of the inventors' names). The Rex is still produced by the company, now known as ZENA. Since 1984 the peeler has been available in plastic as well as in a stainless-steel version that reduces the components from six to three. The steel is stronger and eliminates the necessity for extra parts, but the increased weight means the stainless-steel version is not exported. The peeler has been known to last thirty years in some households, although many meet their demise much earlier by accidentally ending up on the compost heap.

July 21, 1953      A. M. FERRIN      2,645,851

ADJUSTABLE IMPLEMENT FOR PARING VEGETABLES

Filed April 23, 1951

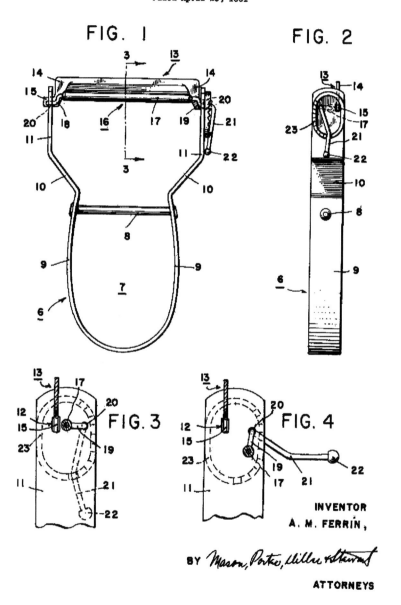

FIG. 1

FIG. 2

FIG. 3

FIG. 4

INVENTOR

A. M. FERRIN,

BY *Mason, Porter, Miller & Stewart*

ATTORNEYS

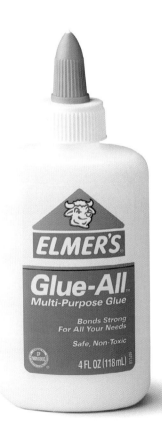

**Elmer's Glue-All** has been a household and schoolroom staple since its inception in 1947, when the American company Borden introduced the world's first white consumer glue. Marketed under the trade name Cascorez Glue, Borden's product took the form of a just-add-water substance that came in a glass bottle with an applicator reminiscent of a popsicle stick attached to a screw-top lid. Although it made reference to the glue's main ingredient, casein (a milk by-product) the name Cascorez had less than stellar recognition in the marketplace. Borden responded to lacklustre sales by completely redesigning the graphics and bottle in the early 1950s, and in so doing made Elmer's the country's most ubiquitous adhesive. Borden, largely a dairy company at the time, had been branding itself aggressively since 1936 with an anthropomorphized cow named Elsie, who appeared prominently in print ads and packaging. In an effort to connect with its new adhesive consumers in a similar way, in 1951 the company conceived Elmer, Elsie's bull 'husband', whose physically stronger appearance denoted the strength of its trademarked substance. One year later, the company replaced its glass bottle with a plastic squeeze bottle that offered not only more surface on which to splash Elmer's bullish visage and the company's crisp orange-and-blue colour scheme, but also a neater, more efficient means of delivery. Borden touted the fact its product could be washed out of clothes easily – a clear indication that the glue was being used by schoolchildren – and added to that a ribbed missile-shaped screw top in brilliant orange that could be shut tight by little hands.

**The Optimist Dinghy** is the first boat of any budding sailor, with its easy rig and simple handling, and its famous, uncanny resemblance to a bathtub. It was designed by Clark Mills in 1947, for the charity the Optimist Club of America, and the original brief was to build a boat that would cost less than $50. Mills gave a drawing to this association, hoping it would bring the little sailboat some attention. The Optimist is a single-handed dinghy, with a squared bow, and a cat arm, that has just one simple sail, one control line and one centre board. Being only 2.3 m (7.5 ft) in length, it is ideal for children between the ages of eight and fifteen who are just learning to sail. The further success of the boat can be attributed to its low price and low weight of 35 kg (77 lb), meaning it could be easily transported on the roof of a car. More than 500,000 boats have been built since 1960, and in almost every country in the world, from China to Kurdistan, there is a Class Association for the Optimist. While Mills can be recognized as the key designer, its popularity is due to Axel Daamgaard, a Danish skipper of three tall-masted ships, who brought the boat from the United States to Scandinavia. In 1954, Daamgaard saw the Optimist around Clearwater and St Petersburg, Florida, and decided to bring the boat to Europe, under the official name International Optimist Dinghy, where it became very popular in a short period. The Optimist was the humble winner of a world championship in 1962, and the International Optimist Dinghy Association was soon established in 1965. Today, over one hundred and fifty children can be found on their dinghies at any given international race.

**Como Door Handle (1947)**
**Angelo Mangiarotti (1921–)**
**Olivari 1947 to 1992**

## Architect, designer, sculptor

and town planner Angelo Mangiarotti's beautifully crafted mass-market Como Door Handle could be seen as a triumphant and groundbreaking piece of architectonic sculpture. Within four years of graduating as an architect from the Polytechnic of Milan, Mangiarotti was already winning prizes for his architectural work and immersing himself in the Modern Movement, associating and working with luminaries such Walter Gropius, Ludwig Mies van der Rohe and Konrad Wachsmann. Fascinated from the outset with materials and structural and construction techniques, he experimented widely with the possibilities offered by the techniques of prefabrication and industrial production. The beauty of Mangiarotti's approach was that he applied it to all his work, irrespective of different scales, so the Como Door Handle is as well-crafted and suited to its function as are his Milan railway stations, the station clocks for Le Porte-Echappement Universal and the Elmag Factory at Monza. Designed for Olivari in 1947, the Como was first seen at the VIII Triennale in Milan as a brass model that had been rigorously researched to achieve an 'ergonomic' usability. The Como was the first handle Mangiarotti designed, but it its contours and organic shape illustrate a key theme in his design work, namely designing mass-produced naturalistic, organic objects. The Como's machine-tooled curves and smooth rounded form are reminiscent of the work of Art Nouveau architects Antoni Gaudí and Hector Guimard, but above all the Como adheres to the natural functionalism of ergonomics. The handle sits comfortably in the hand, requiring only the lightest of grasps to turn it, and is as such typical of Mangiarotti's work, in which the use of an object is never subordinated to formal design considerations.

# 338

Peacock Chair (1947)
Hans Wegner (1914–)
Johannes Hansen 1947 to 1991
PP Møbler 1991 to present

**The Peacock Chair** was first shown as part of the 'Living room for a Young Family' at the 1947 Cabinet-makers' Exhibition in Copenhagen. It featured on the stand of Danish furniture manufacturer, Johannes Hansen, whose collaboration with Hans Wegner had begun in 1940. The chair is based on the English Windsor chair, one of the standard designs in the history of wooden furniture. It is a spindle-back chair with curved wooden struts and a solid wooden seat. The Windsor chair has been made in England since the eighteenth century and features a number of different components: turned legs, a solid seat, turned bars for the back and wooden struts for the back- and armrests. Wegner launched a number of different spindle-back chairs inspired by the Windsor design and, characteristically, gave them a simpler and clearer form, often with a unique feature. For example, the Peacock Chair features distinctive back slats, which give the designs its name. Wegner believed that sitting was a concept invented by man and alien to nature and so his concern was to make this position both dignified and stable. He intended his chairs to be continuations of the body, saying that 'a chair is not finished until someone sits in it.' His ability to draw on

historical reference is evident in the Peacock Chair, which represents, like all of Wegner's work, the Danish modernist tradition of fusing time-honoured craft techniques with the use of natural materials. Wegner's designs utilize a brilliant meeting between the art of the craftsman, applying methods of turning and joining wood, and the dictates of industrial production. Wegner was trained in the traditional techniques of joinery, and in 1938 first participated in the Cabinet-makers' Guild Exhibition, producing a dining-room suite in natural oak. In the same year he moved to Arhus where he became involved in designing furniture for the new Arhus Town Hall. It was at this time that Wegner developed his philosophy of 'stripping the old chairs of their outer style and letting them appear in their pure construction of four legs, a seat and combined top rail and armrest.' In 1943 he opened his own design office and since then designed more than 500 pieces of furniture. The Peacock Chair was originally produced by Johannes Hansen and has been produced since 1991 by PP Møbler, now the largest manufacturer of Wegner's furniture. It is available in solid ash with a laminated hoop and a choice of teak or ash arms.

Hans Wegner

**The Pogo Stick's** familiar frame and rewarding spring jump have inspired generations to bounce since it was first launched over eighty years ago. A popular account of the Pogo's history tells the story of an anonymous German who, while travelling through Burma just before World War I, encountered a shoeless young girl using a stick to 'hop' the rocky path on her daily trips to the temple. The girl's name was Pogo, and upon returning home the observant traveller created a similar jumping stick but attached a spring to the base for extra bounce. In 1919 Gimble Brothers Department Store in the US ordered a shipment of these wooden 'pogo' sticks. However, on delivery, the sticks had been warped by the humid conditions on the journey and were unusable. Gimble Brothers then asked American baby furniture and toy designer, George B Hansburg, to create a better design for the wooden stick. That same year Hansburg created a metal version, featuring an enclosed spring, and patented the soon-to-be popular Pogo Stick from his own company, SBI Enterprises (now part of the larger group JM Originals). The 1920s saw a surge in Pogo Stick sales and it was not long before the Pogo was brought to the stage during a Ziegfeld Follies performance featuring a marriage on Pogos. Chorus girls at the New York Hippodrome used the sticks for an entire performance and Pogo Stick stunts and publicity tricks were devised in order to boost sales. Pogo bouncing records were set, only to be broken regularly throughout the twentieth century, and are frequently attempted today. In 1947 Hansburg designed an improved steel model with a longer-lasting spring. This Master Pogo would become the classic Pogo Stick and a global seller, manufactured by Hansburg's own factory in Elmhurst, New York. Hansburg eventually sold his factory in the 1970s, but the Master Pogo would continue to dominate sales. Many companies have attempted to redesign the stick, adding accessories such as bounce-o-meters and even creating sticks with superhero torsos for handlebars. Custom models, such as the double-barrelled pogo, have been built to aid enthusiasts in breaking world records. And there are even smaller versions for toddlers as well as the 'Bowgo', a motorized Pogo Stick for extreme bouncing. Today the Pogo Stick, still based on Hansburg's original design, remains the archetypal model. The art of staying aboard for any length of time remains the real test.

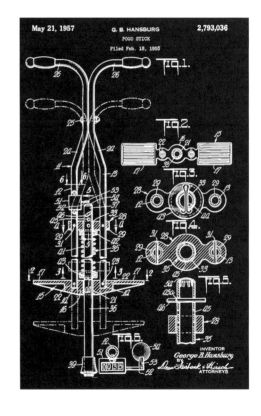

**1918**                    **1947**                    **2000**

**During the 1940s and 1950s,** designers were able to explore a new range of industrial materials and applied processes initially made available for the defence industry during World War II. Aside from improving the performance of traditional media such as glass and wood, designers experimented with the flexibility and fluidity of plastics to produce innovative and functional forms. Resins and polymers were advantageous as plastics because they could be shaped when soft and heated, and then hardened when cooled. These plastics were especially valuable for the development of the modern surfboard, because they could produce smooth and curved board surfaces. During the 1940s, surfboard design went through an important period of change in material, weight and shape. Surfer Bob Simmons initially introduced fibreglass, resin and polystyrene to surfboard construction. Contemporaries Joe Quigg, Matt Kivlin, Tommy Zahn and Dave Rochlen, who would eventually develop Simmons's board design to create the Malibu Surfboard, began riding Simmons's boards constructed from balsa-wood encased in fibreglass and resin. This was the first time balsa boards had been sealed to prevent water damage. Joe Quigg was the primary force in creating the modern Malibu Surfboard. In 1947 he created the Darrylin Board for Zahn's girlfriend, Darrylin Zanuck. Initially designed to be short, light and easy to carry, the Darrylin was designed for women. Using light wood, the Darrylin was a varnished balsa board, 305 cm (120 in) long, with a curved rail throughout, a flat bottom, and a fin. Because of its light weight and sleek shape, it allowed surfers to make turns and ride waves like no other board and because of this, it made a massive contribution to the evolution of the modern surfboard. During the summer of 1947, Quigg shaped three additional revolutionary surfboards. One had the first fibreglass fin, while another had the first modern pintail gun shape. The pintail featured a flat bottom with low rails sloping down to a sharp-edged rear, designed for speed and manoeuvrability. The third board was an all-foam design built to further reduce weight. While most boards averaged 3.6 m (12 ft) long and weighed 14–45 kg (35–100 lbs), Quigg's shorter and lighter boards measured 2.1–2.7 m (7–9 ft) in length and weighed around 9 kg (20 lbs). Their elliptical, rounded tail shape gave rise to the name 'egg board.' By 1948, Quigg's boards were making waves in Malibu surf culture and by 1949 the use of foam was a key issue in surfboard design. Joe Quigg was one of the first great surfboard shapers because he combined his knowledge of hydrodynamics and surfing practice with an innovative use of materials.

HM Queen Elizabeth & HRH Duke of Edinburgh, 1959

**325**

Land Rover (1947)
Maurice Wilks (1904–63)
Rover 1947 to 1957

HMS ALBION

18
RN
65

Winston Churchill with Land Rover Series 1

**The Land Rover,** undisputedly the emblem of off-road cars for more than fifty years, has earned its status because of its versatility and ruggedness. Land Rovers have been used as farm workhorses, military trucks, ambulances, fire engines and, more extravagantly, as work platforms, rail rovers and mobile cinemas. Born almost by accident as a 'stop gap' for the underused Rover plants, the Land Rover became an instant success when it was first introduced at the Amsterdam motor show in 1948. Shortly after World War II the British government could not assure the supply of steel; Rover's managing director Spencer Wilks and his chief designer and brother Maurice realized that, without steel, their hope to restart the full production of the company's prewar luxury cars would be impossible. Rover plants had been fully functioning throughout the war, producing aircrafts and tanks, and afterwards still had a highly skilled workforce and some raw materials from wartime production. The war had also left behind a great number of Willys Jeeps, battered, and with little possibility of repair, as the supply of spare parts was still erratic. The Willys Jeep immediately became the model for a countryside vehicle, at ease both in the farmland and on normal roads. Such a product, thought the Wilks brothers, would also be easy to export, bringing in much-needed foreign currency. With its body made from Brimabright, an aluminium and magnesium alloy used for the construction of aircrafts during the war, steel became superfluous. Using the Jeep's existing P3 engine, gearbox and back axle meant that the car was ready for the Amsterdam show in less than a year. Over the years, developments have been made on the overall performance of the Land Rover but, even when the Discovery series was introduced at the end of the 1980s as a mid-size luxury SUV (Sports Utility Vehicle), in order to accommodate an urban public, Land Rover has always remained true to its tough, outdoor spirit. Today, unofficial figures claim that 75 per cent of the Land Rovers from 1955 are still on the road.

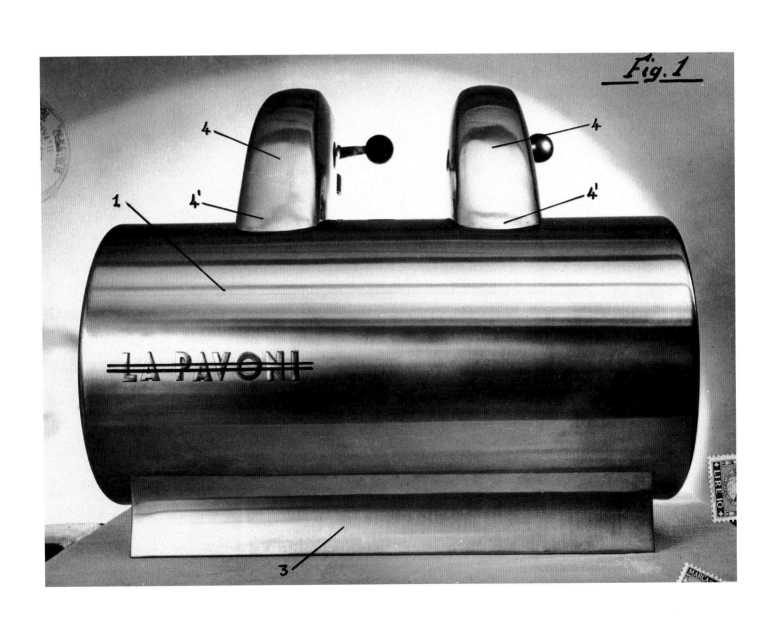

Fig.1

PAVONI
COFFEE MACHINE

**Before the Milanese** company La Pavoni introduced La Cornuta Model 47, patented in 1947 but produced in 1948, the shape of a coffee machine was dictated by its boiler, conventionally an upright urn with a host of awkward protuberances. Gio Ponti, working for La Pavoni alongside Antonio Fornaroli and Alberto Rosselli, turned the boiler on its side to form a horizontal cylinder from which the arms of the dispensers curve gracefully upwards and inwards. Dynamic, elegant and proud, La Cornuta ('the horn') demanded to be placed on the most prominent part of the bar where it could be admired from all angles. Quickly overtaken by rapid advances in technology, La Cornuta was in production only briefly. Today only one or two examples remain in existence. So how has La Pavoni's machine achieved its status as one of the most commonly illustrated icons of Italian design? Before La Cornuta, often coffee produced by a machine had a sour or burnt taste that was created by the process of brewing, in which steam was let through the coffee. The new machine by La Pavoni instead only took water from the boiler under pressure, and then it was filtered through the coffee by a piston, pushed by a spring at ten bars pressure. The coffee no longer had the burnt taste due to the machine having a horizontal boiler. The gleaming seductiveness of its lines, the timing of its production, the purpose for which it was designed and, above all, the identity of its designer have combined to make La Cornuta an eloquent symbol of the huge contribution that Italian designers made to the remarkable recovery of their country's economy after World War II. In 1948, while working for La Pavoni, Ponti was also busy at the helm of his hugely influential magazine Domus and was central to the organization of the important VIII Milan Triennale. Just as the quintessentially Italian habit of drinking coffee at the bar was becoming fashionable across Europe and beyond, Ponti created the perfect machine from which to serve it.

The 999 design classics included in this book have been chosen in consultation with a wide range of international design-world insiders. Academics, critics, historians, curators, journalists, designers and architects were asked to select industrially-manufactured objects that conform to our definition of a Phaidon Design Classic, as specified on the cover. Every object selected meets at least one of the criteria within our overall definition and many of them meet more than one.

The final choice of objects illustrated in this three-volume set is the result of a rigorous selection process and meticulous research. The collection includes a huge variety of consumer products, ranging from chairs to aeroplanes, which date from the Industrial Revolution to the present day. Garments, fashion accessories and objects that have been designed for highly specialist use, are not included.

Most of the objects are still in production and the majority of them are available to buy. When something is no longer manufactured, it is not usually because the design itself has become obsolete, but rather because the technology it was designed for has since become outdated.

To make the book as contemporary as possible we have also included objects created more recently. It is, of course, more difficult to judge which of the products created in more recent decades will eventually be regarded as classics, but we have included those we consider to be the 'classics of tomorrow' according, once again, to our definition.

**PHAIDON DESIGN CLASSICS VOLUME TWO**

Φ